Kinesics
and Context

University of Pennsylvania Publications in

Conduct and Communication
Edited by ERVING GOFFMAN *and* DELL HYMES

Erving Goffman, *Strategic Interaction*
Ray L. Birdwhistell, *Kinesics and Context:*
  Essays on Body Motion Communication

Kinesics
and Context

Essays on Body Motion Communication

RAY L. BIRDWHISTELL

UNIVERSITY OF PENNSYLVANIA PRESS
PHILADELPHIA

Editor's Note

THIS book contains a selection of Ray L. Birdwhistell's essays on body movement and human communication, some published here for the first time, others published before in widely scattered places.

Birdwhistell views communication as a process to which all participants in an interaction constantly contribute by messages of various, overlapping lengths along one or more channels (such as language, movement, and smell), whose elements are culturally patterned. With the aid of movie cameras and slow-motion projectors, he has analyzed many motions in detail—especially those which Americans make while talking, and their relation to American English. He has also devised two transcription systems for recording body movement.

Part I includes the less technical essays, especially those dealing with children's learning of kinesic systems and with communication in families. Part II contains some theoretical observations, Part III general principles and some specific findings on the American movement system. Part IV will hold interest especially for other researchers. Part V includes some of his latest thinking and a detailed analysis of an interview.

The author's theoretical viewpoint is summarized in essay 2 and developed more fully in essay 11; essays 26 and 27 apply it specifically to movement and speech. Some of his most central discussions concern communicational redundancy (pp. 85–91, 107–108), relevant time (pp. 158–166), the relations of communication to society and culture (pp. 50–56, 95–98, 250–251), and pathological miscommunication (pp. 15–25).

Birdwhistell has approved the selections and did much of the arranging. Bracketed footnotes to the text are mine.

BARTON JONES

For Jill and Nancy

Contents

PART IV. Collecting Data: Observing, Filming, and Interviewing

PART V. Research on An Interview

APPENDIXES

Introduction

THESE essays are based on the conviction that body motion is a learned form of communication, which is patterned within a culture and which can be broken down into an ordered system of isolable elements. This book is not a journal of completed research. Nor is it designed as a textbook in kinesics. Neither is it a manual of instruction for those who would memorize annotational conventions and, without other training, buy a tape recorder or a motion analyst projector and turn movies into scientific documents. It is a book about the study of body motion, communication, and the need for the location of natural contexts of occurrence in the study of human behavior. These essays, an edited assemblage of published and unpublished writings, are not intended to be a finally integrated or comprehensive statement of kinesics and communication. It is my hope, however, that they will introduce the reader not already committed to particular lines of research or reasoning to the conception that the investigation of human communication by means of linguistic and kinesic techniques is desirable and relevant.

By 1959 systematic review of filmed material had provided evidence which supported the emergent assessment of kinesic morphology. The intense sessions at the Center for Advanced Study in the Behavioral Sciences in which linguists (Norman McQuown and Charles Hockett), anthropologists (Gregory Bateson and Ray Birdwhistell), and psychiatrists (Henry Brosin and Frieda Fromm-Reichmann) participated had produced a mass of data which demonstrated the interdependence of visible and audible behavior in the flow of conversation. Equally intense analysis and review sessions at the University of Buffalo, with the wise and talented assistance of H. L. Smith, Jr., and G. L. Trager, confirmed the conviction that it was not only possible but desirable to study interactional behavior by the exhaustive techniques of linguistics and kinesics. The advantages of working with naturalistic settings seemed to be demonstrated, too, by this devoted and concerted effort.

During the course of investigation, techniques were developed that reduced recording and analysis time (when working with conversants speaking American English) from about 100 hours per second to less than one hour per second. Because of the richness of a 10-second stretch (isolated for study, but always returned to context for comparative analysis), these methods, which gave us data at the rate of one hour of investigation per second of behavior, seemed efficient enough to use in larger research. The linguistic-kinesic method, however, was recognized to be a crude and nascent instrument. All of the co-workers agreed that it needed refinement and, more importantly, it needed testing. The method could be tested only by scientists trained to control it and the data it was designed to investigate.

The work of the author, of Albert Scheflen and Jacques Van Vlack has been supported in studies at Eastern Pennsylvania Psychiatric Institute. Work plans originally evolved by the Interdisciplinary Committee on Culture and Communication at the University of Louisville and given shape at the University of Buffalo seemed to need only a more adequate and reliable audio-visual hardware to be brought to fruition. Henry Brosin has been successful in recruiting a unit at Western Pennsylvania Psychiatric Institute and Clinic. Norman A. McQuown and his students have been engaged in the demanding and tedious tasks of rechecking and refining the records collected earlier (1956) at the Center for Advanced Study in the Behavioral Sciences.

Determinative influences came from the investigations of Eliot Chapple, Edward T. Hall, and Roger Barker. The logic of the structure of interactional style, as demonstrated by Chapple's interaction chronograph, while directed to data very different from our own, supported our conviction that whatever "meaning" is, it is not merely conventional understandings boxed in words. Edward T. Hall's penetrating observations of variant conceptions about space and of human dyadal space arrangements have provided a persistent stimulus to our attempt to comprehend multiperson social space arrangements in behavioral terms. In proxemics, Hall has pioneered directions in research which have stimulated a number of perceptive students and, along with the work of Robert Sommers and Roger Barker, he has laid the groundwork for observations of social interaction which are strongly influencing young workers to recognize the incompleteness of studies of word exchange as measures of social intercourse.

A sustaining influence has come from Erving Goffman, whose contributions to the sociological analysis of interactional activity, from his *The Presentation of Self in Everyday Life,* through *Asylum* to *Encounters,* have pointed up the structures of the context within which, or by means of which, men interact with meaningful regularity. Of at least equal importance has been Goffman's challenge to linguistic-kinesic investigators to recognize the hiatus which exists between linguistic-kinesic units and those necessary to investigate the social situations he has isolated.

Still another aspect of the research climate was provided by a series of scholars who sought to examine selected and manageable slices of the interactional stream. R. E. Pittenger and J. J. Danehy had with Hockett provided an intense and extended analysis of a stream of a speech sliced from a psychiatric encounter. G. F. Mahl and A. T. Dittmann, with differing procedures, selected bits of body motion and of paralinguistic behavior and treated them as heuristic units. Their results were heartening to us, for their data supported, in negative fashion, our contention that communication was multi-channel and that communicational shapes are not to be found in microuniverses of paralanguage or gesture any more than they are to be discovered in words alone. While the work of Paul Ekman was to develop somewhat later than these, it too confirmed our decision to search for units based upon linguistic and kinesic analysis.

As will be shown throughout this volume, the theory and research of the structural linguist has provided the prime outside determinant of kinesic research techniques. However, the student who described kinesics as "pseudolinguistics" was misled by the nomenclatural conventions of kinesics which adapted linguistic forms for kinesic research in an attempt to facilitate and implement interdisciplinary research. From its inception as a discipline, kinesics has accepted structural and descriptive linguistic research techniques (particularly as these have been employed by anthropological linguists) as models which encourage the discipline required for the analysis of infracommunicational units and structure. My goal was to develop a methodology which would exhaustively analyze the communicative behavior of the body, and the linguist's insistence upon testing his data alternatively as unit and as structural component seemed a necessary and *minimal* rule of research procedure. Finally, linguistic methodologists, it seemed to me, had demonstrated better than any other behavioral scientists a technique which permitted description and structural analysis, while avoiding premature psychological and sociological explanations (*a priori* or *a posteriori*) of events whose manipulable reality was in linguistic structure.

This is an academic and probably unnecessarily pedantic way of saying that the course of kinesic research has been strongly influenced by the sensitive, tough, disciplined, and seemingly tireless linguistic scientists with whom I have been associated. I learned from John Broderius, who first forced me to face the artifacts of premature interpretation of signal behavior. Henry Lee Smith, Jr., and George L. Trager nurtured the writing of the *Introduction to Kinesics* and were later to teach me enough linguistics to help me forego further quasi-linguistic analysis. Norman A. McQuown, whose sensitive analytic mind and capacity for painstaking and creative work has consistently guided the attempt to correlate linguistic and kinesic material, and William Austin, who worked patiently with Sheflen and myself for a year, helped de-reify many linguistic concepts which we had come to overaccept. I must include Kenneth Pike, who, as I write, is gently but firmly forcing me to attend to phonetic pitch—a matter which I'd like to avoid, but which, as he points out, may contain some of the secrets of linguistic-kinesic interdependence—at least for American English. And finally, Fred Eggan and Margaret Mead, in very different ways, helped me leave the formal world of social structure to explore behavior without the sense that I was leaving anthropology, without the fear that I would lose the fellowship of my discipline.

All of these, among many others, shaped the original ideas which led to these writings. Yet the book would not have appeared if it had not been envisaged by Erving Goffman and brought into order by Barton Jones. Jones, a linguistics graduate student, dredged my writings and gleaned what he felt to be significant. He is another student from whom I have learned.

The material in this book is derived from a variety of researches done under the respective sponsorships of the University of Louisville, The University of Buffalo, the Center for Advanced Study in the Behavioral Sciences with assistance from a Research Fellowship Award from the National Institute of Mental Health, and the Commonwealth of Pennsylvania's Eastern Pennsylvania Psychiatric Institute.

August 1969   RAY L. BIRDWHISTELL

PART 1

Learning To Be a Human Body

1. *"There Was a Child Went Forth . . ."* *

A HUMAN BEING is not a black box with one orifice for emitting a chunk of stuff called *communication* and another for receiving it. And, at the same time, communication is not simply the sum of the bits of information which pass between two people in a given period of time.

Let us suppose that some wealthy and benevolent foundation was impressed with the fact that the human organism is a fantastically sensitive system capable of receiving literally hundreds of thousands of bits of information and became so concerned with the implications of this that they were willing to support extended research into the nature of the interconnections between this organism and the remainder of the universe. Let us further imagine that we decided to make up an experimental *universe à deux* and put two human beings in an elaborate box, and then decided to record all the informational signal units that flowed into the box and were potentially receivable by its occupants. Theoretically, the various machines would feed to a master tape some 2,500–5,000 bits (and up to about 10,000) of information per second. These recorded bits are notations of minimally discernible changes in the sound, light, and odor stream. Obviously their identity as units is dependent on the refinements of the recording devices. However we refine it, we are already swamped by the flood of data. And if we were to play this game of astronomical numbers to its awe-full end, probably the lifetime efforts of roughly half the adult population of the United States would be required to sort the units deposited on one tape

---

* Adapted from "Contribution of Linguistic—Kinesic Studies to the Understanding of Schizophrenia." From *Schizophrenia—An Integrated Approach,* edited by Alfred Auerback. Copyright © 1959 The Ronald Press Company, New York. [The first excerpt points out how much information passes between two interacting people. The amount is so enormous that no human being could use or comprehend it unless it was culturally patterned; the second excerpt discusses how children become adapted to the communicational systems of their society.—B. J.]

record in the course of an hour's interaction between the two subjects! Nor is there any comfort in the thought of Univac's speedy digestive system. Univac could deliver stacks of counted units and further stacks of correlations, but at this level that is all we would have—stacks of figures. This kind of practical infinity play is all the more depressing if we are tough enough scientists to know that we deal with an interdependent universe which cannot include accidental, isolated, or finally meaningless units. Something is always happening, but if we just count signals, it has no more value than if nothing were happening. If we had to stop our studies at this point we might just as well go back to an atomistic and mentalistic model of a human being as a thing in itself. With such a model we are condemned to do our research on little balloons full of words which are somehow framed or filled out by gesticulation which we could dignify although not clarify by calling them *nonverbal communications*.

Fortunately, however, we do not have to engage in such elaborate census-taking in order systematically to analyze human interaction any more than we have to isolate and tag every molecule of water in order to do hydrography. All we need to do to make communication research efficient, manageable, and meaningful is to construct a methodology which will enable us to order our record so that we can isolate from it the testably significant classes of events.

*   *   *

The discussion here is centered around the introduction of the child into the communication system of the society. If the discussion is overgeneral or too programmatic, this very inadequacy will perhaps make manifest the need for research in this area.

The work of the ethologists and comparative psychologists in the last few years has forced us to re-evaluate our previous conceptions of the relationship between human and animal behavior. Many of us marveled at the intricacies of the associations (which we termed *genetically determined* and let it go at that) which are present in insect societies. We looked at apes and studied them somatically as carrying clues which might give us insight into the evolution of man. But, because of the nature of our theory and the tremendously difficult task of making sustained and verifiable observations, we were largely concerned with watching the behavior of individual animals. We described them as operating in groups, or herds, or prides, or flocks and in anthropomorphic amazement projected upon them certain human characteristics, most of which were individually psychological in nature. Recently, however, we have been forced to review if not completely to revamp these conceptions. With the work of Tinbergen, Hess, Lorenz, Blauvelt, and others, it has become increasingly evident that social living is an adaptational imperative for the membership of many nonhuman species. As we became willing to forego simplistic arguments concerning heredity and, or rather versus, environment and turned to the behavioral description of critical developmental moments in the individual's life, atomistic theoretics began to give way before more dynamic system models.

These insights, plus the theoretical and technical achievements of the linguist and the kinesicist, in a new experimental world made possible by the sound camera, the slow-motion analyzer, and the tape recorder, have forced us to a re-evaluation of evolution. Such a re-evaluation has carried with it a new perspective on what we mean by *human behavior*—and by extension what is significant about the patterned interdependence of human beings. If we are willing to concede that the evolutionary ladder runs from the inorganic to the organic to the social and, finally, through many animal species to the human, we shall probably also be willing to re-evaluate our primary postulates as to the nature of man himself. Certainly we may find ourselves in a position which makes less conscionable any isolation of disease and particularly mental disease within man's epidermatic frontiers. We are ready to look with new eyes at the life history of an individual and to ask new questions about the violence we commit when we act as though we are dealing with a preformed and plastic personality shaped by isolated traumatic events.

Who knows how any human internalizes the conventional understandings of his social group to the extent that his social behavior becomes by and large predictable to other members of his group? Even the sketchiest survey of human societies reveals that he does this. There is little solace in a so-called "learning theory," although one is impressed with the brilliance of the learning experimentalist who can create a training situation in which human beings can be persuaded to deal with new information in a manner analogous to that apparently employed by white rats or Grey Walter's machines. The fact remains that infants from every society in the world can and *do* internalize the communicational system of that society in approximately the same amount of time, so that the "normal" 6-year-old is able to move smoothly within the communication system of his society. There is no need to become involved in arguments for gestalt versus associational or any other model of learning. Years of carefully ordered observation and analysis of children in the learning situation are necessary before the mechanisms of this incorporation can be known, and the traditional learning experiment apparatus does seem inapplicable for this study. But one thing is clear. We cannot study the social behavior of a fish by taking him out of water. The child is a child in his world—the pieces he displays in a laboratory represent a very small and, perhaps, unrepresentative sample of his repertoire.

The child is born into a society already keyed for his coming. A system exists into which he must be assimilated if the society is to sustain itself. If his behavior cannot, after a period of time, become predictable to a degree expected in that society, he must be specially treated. In some societies the nonassimilator will be allowed to die; in others he may be given special institutional treatment. This special treatment can range from deification to incarceration. But ultimately the goal is the same: to make *that child's* behavior sufficiently predictable that the society can go about the rest of its business.

From a different point of view, depending upon the society's expectancy structure, the child must in a given period of time learn how to learn what the society expects of him, how to use this as a source of new learning, and he must learn how not to learn and to use that skill in not being diverted. Perhaps even more fundamental than this, his very survival depends upon his receiving and sending certain orders of message from and to those about him. The Spitz babies, like the Blauvelt kids and lambs, provide us with all too clear insights into the fact that the organism must receive certain kinds of stimulating experiences or it dies. We can combine the results of these suggestive experiments with the data provided by the sensory-deprivation studies and evaluate this insight in the light of our increasing knowledge about the complexity of the perceptive process. This outline of the problem of bringing a new member into society reveals a process so critical and complex that even the least impressionable student is inclined to wonder how we make it at all. This process is commonplace for every society. Yet the fact that we must, in every psychiatric setting, discuss this matter is testament to the fact that the process is not always successful.

We know so little about the dimensions of biological or social time that we cannot say whether the infant and the society have a long or short time in which to accomplish the basic task of incorporation. We know only that it must be done and that some societies act as though there were very little time for this task while others do not even conceive of it as a problem. We may, however, make this generalization: in every society, before attaining membership in that society, the child must gain control of the pattern of, and be incorporated into, the communication system of the society. And, to repeat, in every society we know anything about, at least insofar as language is concerned, this occurs by the time a child is six years old. Now to state explicitly what was implied before: gaining control of language is not the simple accumulation of an aggregate of words; it is not the possession of a certain-sized vocabulary. Nor is the control of that infracommunicational system, body motion, made up of memorizing a list of facial expressions or gestures. Communication control is not achieved through a simple additive process which involves the accumulation of parcels of sounds or body motion which carry encapsulated chunks of meaning. Nor is it the slightly more complex matter of hooking together these pieces called *words* and *gestures* into little meaning trains called *sentences*. I use the word *simple* here in derision, for if this were the way we had to incorporate our communicational system, the human life span would not be long enough to permit us ever to achieve such control. Human culture is possible because we do not have to do it this way—because we learn in a patterned way.

Look for a moment at the pitifully little that is known about the rate and sequence of human language and motion incorporation. When I say "pitifully little," however, I imply no apology. Recent developments in linguistics and paralinguistics, in kinesics and parakinesics, at least make possible the systematic descriptive analysis of this developmental process. Even these few and very tentative descriptions, gathered from all too little observation, make it possible for us to envision a day when we can objectively analyze the communication behavior of a particular child and forecast his ability to adapt to his communicational milieu. For the linguistic material I rely on the observations of Smith and Trager, modified by discussion with Hockett and McQuown, and strained through my own conceptions which are, at least in part, the result of kinesic observation.

The number of sounds distinguishable from each other that the so-called vocal apparatus can make may run into the thousands, depending upon the instruments used for delineating them. The possible combinations of these is beyond the number of atoms postulated for the universe. Yet we need not trouble ourselves with these possibility figures. The fact of the matter is that while societies choose different segments and sections of the range, phoneticians have found no society whose significant phonologic sounds could not be described from a set of 42 basic positional symbols each modifiable by from five to ten marks which indicate special placement or release. And to do phonemic analysis, which deals with the least meaningful classes of sounds used by any language, even fewer symbols may be required. Trager has said that no society that he knows anything about has less than fifteen of such basic units or many more than fifty. The number of phonemes in the repertoire of any given society does not seem to mean very much about the complexity of that society. In our own we utilize 45, which includes nine vowels, three semivowels, twenty-one consonants, four stresses, four pitches, and four junctures.

Comparably, while the human face alone is capable of making some 250,000 different expressions, I have fifteen placement symbols plus eleven special markers sufficient to record the significant positions of all the faces I have seen. Less than one hundred symbols are all that are required to deal with any kinesic subject which I have yet studied—and this recording covers the activity of the whole body in its through-time activity.

The human infant is an amoral mass of wrigglings and vocalizing; it lives in a milieu of moral speakers and movers. By the age of six it will be a moral vocalizer, that is, it will have reduced its range of noises to that narrow list employed by the members of his milieu. I am not sure *when* he becomes a moral wriggler, although there is every indication that adolescence (and here generalization is restricted to North American culture) marks a period in which the wriggling becomes restrained into moral limits. The difference between the kinesic and linguistic system is probably related to the fact that although body-motion communicational behavior is just as much learned behavior as is language behavior, we simply have not, heretofore, known enough about it to teach it. That is, parents and peers have the range and structure of the phonemic system sufficiently in awareness to direct and more or less explicitly rectify the behavior of the young speaker. Yet this teaching aspect should not be overstressed. It is said that the apparently incoherent babbling of a 6-month-old is already sufficiently structured that a French baby will have a predominance of French phonemes and an American baby a predominance of those characteristic of American English. I have not watched enough babies from enough different societies to make a similar generalization about their respective kinesic repertoires.

All this discussion has been about very old babies, because by the time a baby is a year old he has already gained some acquaintance and, I am tempted to say, control of large portions of the cross-referencing phenomena which will make his language a patterned system and the incorporation of which will make him a patterned learner of the details to follow. By the age of 6 weeks he begins to respond fairly systematically to the vocal qualifiers used by the children and adults who verbalize around him. These include particular variations in intensity and pitch height and in extent variation, which would include drawl and clipping. Again, research in kinesic phenomena is too limited to permit our determining what is systematically reacted to by the child. Although I do not have the experimental data to support it, I am inclined to believe that the child comes to comprehend his kinesic qualifier behavior and his vocalization behavior, which includes the vocal qualifiers and the vocal characterizers, in a full package. The vocal characterizers, incidentally, include that patterned behavior which encases language, such as giggling, snickering, whimpering, sobbing, yelling, whispering, moaning, groaning, whining, breaking, belching, and yawning. There is need to demonstrate that these are structured by each society in its paralinguistic and parakinesic system. However, these phenomena are patterned and are learned. It requires very little observation to see that at least by the age of two the child has considerable comprehension of what the mother is doing when he cannot hear her and what she feels about what she is saying when he can only see her.

We are getting too far ahead of the developmental picture. There is reason to believe that by the age of four months a child is responding to the intonation patterns of the language and that by the age of nine months, if not already talking in partial sentences, he is usually babbling in his language's intonation pattern and engaging in some kinemorphs at least characteristic of the children of his group. The range of using meaningful lexemes, words, is considerable. We have reports of children as young as five months saying "mamma" or other clumps of phonemes which the parents respond to as meaningful symbolizations. On the other hand, even extremely bright children may not begin to talk until well into the third or fourth year, sometimes breaking their self-imposed silence with appallingly sophisticated statements. A similar story seems to prevail for the quiet child. If we use eye focus as a marker for the presence of complex kinemorphic constructions, we see some children who maintain "overwide focus" well into kindergarten—and some females look as though even marriage will not make them forego it! On the other hand, I have seen children who began this kind of communicative focus behavior as early as the tenth month. By "overwide focus" is meant the open-eyed contemplation of others that infants have which gives them the appearance of looking out from behind their eyes.

Even with our present limited knowledge about the process, which admittedly has been gathered by a dual process of limited observation and questionable extrapolation backward from the behavior of older children, we can generalize that the child learns his communication behavior through the incorporation of a series of modifying and interlocking patterns. Intimately associated with his enculturation and socialization, his language and his motion system provide him with contact with the problems of his environment and often with their solutions. Through this system he finds out who he is in relation to others and what his expectancies and responsibilities are. In short, it is through the various modalities of his communication system that he structures, anticipates, and is rewarded or failed by his environment. Through out-of-awareness, but clearly discrete, signals he learns the directives, the prohibitions, the encouragements, and the warnings which govern his consistent association with other members of his society. His language and his body motion system are flexible and malleable, yet, at the same time, they are adaptive and functional only because they are so systematically organized. Not only do they carry instructions and descriptions and responses—reaffirmation of old understandings and directions which result in the acceptance of new ones—but also these messages are cross-referenced by statements about the messages themselves. For this insight I am particularly grateful to Gregory Bateson. The messages are cross-referenced by explicit and analyzable behavior which instructs as to whether the message is to be taken literally or metaphorically, as a joke, or as an unavoidable prescription. These systems contain explicit instructions as to the relationship between the speaker and the auditor and are even so styled that a series of apparently contradictory messages can be put under a rubric which assembles them as noncontradictory.

A recording sheet for the communicational behavior of human beings requires at least one hundred separate lines for each actor. No item is nonfunctional; such a recording represents the course of an interaction of two or more human beings playing out their adjustments and adaptations to each other, to themselves, and to the larger universe. Its success as a system depends upon the child's having been assimilated in a manner which permits a growing and positive participation in the society.

2. The Age of a Baby*

T RADITIONALLY, we have regarded communication as that process by which one individual imparted knowledge to another. Many scholars have felt that an exhaustive measurement of communication could be accomplished through so-called black box research. By this procedure one subject is given a set of clearly limited pieces of information which he is instructed to impart to another. It is recognized that there are certain external interferences in this process. These interferences, called "noise," are kept in mind when the receiver subject is tested to determine the proportion of the original message which he has received. The data derived from this kind of research are not what I am talking about when I discuss communication. The universe to be measured by such a methodology, however brilliantly conceived and executed, properly belongs to the informational theorist or researcher. The anthropological linguist or kinesicist utilizes a different method to deal with phenomena he feels are too complex to be reduced to such a formula.

Few serious students of information theory lay claim to their

---

* Presented to the American Society of Clinical Hypnosis at their Annual Scientific Assembly, October 10, 1959, under the title "The Frames in the Communication Process."

methodology as a technique for unraveling the intricacies of social interaction. All too often, however, the dilettante finds in the exquisite clarity of the information model a familiar and attractive construction which permits a simple and mechanical "explanation" of human interaction. The term "interaction" is the significant concept here. The order of phenomena we are tracing, analyzing, and describing cannot be reduced to the familiar action-reaction formula.

When we talk about communication we are not talking about a situation in which John acts and Mary reacts to John's action and in turn John reacts to Mary's action in some simple, ongoing, one-after-another sequence. Essentially, we discuss communication as a complex and sustaining system through which various members of the society interrelate with more or less efficiency and facility. According to communication theory, John does not communicate to Mary, and Mary does not communicate to John; Mary and John engage in communication.

Now there is a good reason, or rather, there are a plethora of reasons, why the action-reaction formula feels so familiar. Most of us who engage in extended cogitation about such an abstract conception as communication are literate, even educated, men. Our special conception of interaction, modeled on the relationship between the teacher and the taught, the physician and the patient, the demogogue or the plutogogue and his followers, serves to reinforce our earliest learning. Our memories of our earliest interactions are full of situations in which our parents told us what to do. And, for many of us, infancy and childhood was a period in which we acted and they, the parents, reacted.

The introspective view of the natural course of experience was further shaped by our experience as readers. In the novel, and even more clearly, in the drama, we find individuals who speak politely in turn. And, if we really accept the literary model of social interaction, we would be convinced that most people speak in complete sentences, and more important, that they listen with awareness to what the other person says—most of the time. One day in the average home or office reveals how poetic is such a conception. Parenthetically, many avid and otherwise sophisticated readers become so impressed with literary reproductions of social interaction that they give these a special historical significance and grieve loudly and evangelically that "the art of conversation is lost." It seems doubtful that, except in highly stylized imitations of the written language, there ever were conversations of the kind we grieve for. Certainly, we have no records on tape or in sound movie form which would indicate that in this, or in any of the societies which we have studied, such conversations ever take place except in ritualized circumstances.

Gregory Bateson, in a brilliant article on what he describes as "deutero-learning," points out that human learning is patterned, that we learn to learn, that we learn to learn to learn, and that we also learn to learn not to learn. We perceive in pattern, and we remember in pattern. Only in this way are we able to incorporate our society's way of viewing and testing the universe.

This problem of patterned remembering constitutes one of the most difficult barriers to communication research. When we take a tape recording and turn it over to a secretary for typing, her patterned memory, her belief that human beings speak in turn and her belief that most human beings, on paper at least, speak in complete sentences, leads to a situation in which she hears this kind of material on the tape. By actual count, even skilled secretaries working from unstructured interviews make about one mistake every five words. Thus, her typescript may contain a good record of what the discussion or the interaction was about, but it is very inaccurate as a record of the actual behavior in the interaction. Lest we get some ideas that this is a disease which is peculiarly secretarial, let me add that our experience, utilizing the ears of some of the best linguists in America, has shown that even these experts, when working with shapes of material larger than a word or simple syntactic sentence, give us records with errors every ten to fifteen words. By careful cross checking, with independent recording, and, finally, with group assessment, we have been able to reduce the error to one in every twenty-five to thirty words.

One last remark about theoretical or practical impediments to communication research: until very recently, most of us, if we accepted the theory of evolution at all, saw evolution as a process which could be schematized as development from the inorganic to the organic to the higher organisms to man and finally to society. The work of the last quarter century of the ethologist, the comparative psychologist, the information theorist, and the anthropologist has led the student of communication to the overwhelming conviction that such a reconstruction is faulty and misleading. It has long been clear that a complex organism is not merely an assemblage of cells each of which independently becomes a part of the complex system. The cell components of a complex system are, rather, by the very dynamic of their genetic selection and development absolutely *dependent* for life upon the activities of the other cells within the organism which have other kinds of specialized jobs to do. Comparably, the more research we have done into animal, fish, and bird behavior (and I stress the word "behavior"), the more we have become convinced that society is absolutely necessary for the maturation of the given animal individual. Most students of animal or human behavior are now prepared to agree that social life, or society, to put the statement in a different form, is absolutely an adaptive necessity for human existence. Communication, in this sense, is that system of coadaptation by which society is sustained, and, which in turn, makes human life possible.

Viewed from this perspective, communication is that system through which human beings establish a predictable continuity in life. Far from being a process centrally devoted to change, most of social interaction is concerned with maintaining an ongoing equilibrium. We are aware of the change points, but this awareness should not delude us into limiting communication to these points of stress in the system. We must remember that the system, as an essentially steady-state organization, operates to inhibit as well as to permit parameters of change in interpersonal activity. While the study of change is rewarding, research on communication if it is aimed at understanding its processes cannot be limited to parametric aspects of interaction.

In order for us to deal with other human beings in any systematic and comfortable way they must behave in a predictable manner. In turn *we* must behave predictably if we are to comprehend ourselves, much less be predictable to them. Being in some measure predictable constitutes the *sine qua non* of sanity and humanity. However, it must be kept in mind that, while communication is necessary for life, all people who do not communicate precisely as we do do not immediately die. As we grow up, we learn that other people may speak different languages, and we can learn that it is possible, if not necessary, to learn how to translate these differences.

As we grow up we may become so sophisticated as to realize that the other man's language is just as natural as ours. If we are to live in a complex society, we must learn that even within a given language, within a given communication system, people from different regions of the country and with subcultural backgrounds different from ours do not communicate exactly like us. To successfully operate we must internalize the fact that there are systematic variations in the way in which a child, or an adolescent, or an aged person engages in communication. A few even become so sophisticated as to realize that the male and the female subcultures are sufficiently different that there can be imperfect understanding between male and female. As we mature, we become socialized. This is just another way of saying that we learn that many of the differences in the way in which people communicate or respond to our communication reveal the differences between their roles, their social position and activity, and ours.

If the communicational behavior of an individual is sufficiently unexpected and idiosyncratic as to be beyond the range of our previous experience, we may be unable to relate to him successfully. We can bear inappropriate behavior only if we can anticipate its inappropriateness. Undiagnosed unpredictability in others leaves us with doubts about ourselves. So, the definition of others as insane permits us to deal with them. There is nothing novel about the recognition that insanity is a state which evidences itself in distortions of the communication process. It is possibly somewhat less commonplace to recognize that many of those whom we call insane are not as chaotic or disordered in their communication behavior as we, the observers, would like to believe.

Our preliminary but intensive investigations into schizophrenia have convinced us that the schizophrenic is not chaotic or disordered in his communication; rather, he has a different pattern, a different system of communication. It is probably the systematic distortion of what still appears familiar to us that makes us feel so distressed. We are forced to describe as chaotic or fragmented that which under analysis can be seen as a perfectly understandable but still distorted system. As a systematic disturbance schizophrenia becomes a comprehensible phenomenon. We are now engaged in trying to find out how the pathological system differs from that employed by those we characterize as "normal." We must know much more about both to make efficient comparison possible.

If we recognize that our communication system is not something we invent but rather something which we internalized in the process of becoming human, we must study the socialization process if we are to isolate those factors which contribute to mislearning or misusing this system.

Although the line of approach which I, as an anthropologist and as a student of communication theory and research, must follow is concerned with the communication process, I do not believe that *the* cause of mental illness is so simple as "bad communication." I think that as research proceeds we will continue to discover genetic, chemical, and organic factors in mental illness. It is already clear from preliminary research that even the most severe social environmental influences do not necessarily create serious mental illness. However, what I am concerned with is the delineation of those factors in the early incorporation of the communication system which lead the child to be inadequately prepared to deal with life as a maturing human. If his system is different from that of the group in which he grows up, he will consistently feed his parents and peers distorted information about himself and his state of mind. He will receive from the outside world information that cannot help but lead him into further distress or privacy.

The child, in order to communicate, must learn to comprehend and enunciate a complex hierarchy of systems which makes up the language.

Out of the thousands of possible sounds that can be made with the so-called vocal apparatus, which can be heard by that intricate organization, the human ear, only certain of these provide the significant particles of his vocalic system. Each society chooses certain classes of sound, some fifteen hundredths of a second in duration, and assembles them in its own special way. Through these assemblages special orders of experience that stand for experience can be transmitted to others. It is not difficult for us to comprehend that the sound *d o g* is not a four-legged canine. It is somewhat more difficult for us to comprehend that these pieces of assembled sound, regardless of how intricately combined, do not have meaning in and of themselves. It is not easy to appreciate the fact that each piece of experience (of whatever duration) exists in a larger context which structures its function in the communication system. That is, while we can hear that the *p* in *pit* differs from the *b* in *bit,* it is somewhat more difficult to comprehend that, without context, *pit* does not have a meaning in itself other than that it is different from *bit.* A little thought will tell us that we must look at a larger context to find out whether a *pit* is a hole in the ground or the hard core of a peach. *Bit* can be a tiny particle, a piece of iron in the horse's mouth, or a part of a drill. Even such a limited exercise makes us recognize that these words are not absolute carriers of meaning. They can be comprehended only by reference to their context.

As we move to the analysis of the sentence, a special assemblage of these things called words, we discover that there are communication signals designed to cover larger and larger, meaningful stretches of material. To steal one of Professor Henry Lee Smith's favorite examples, any normal child of six will recognize that, though they are made up of the same words, he has no difficulty in distinguishing between "She is a nice girl" and "She is a nice girl." Or to put it differently, although he cannot tell you exactly how it is done, any normal American informant will tell you that you have given quite a different message when you say "She is a nice girl?"# and "She is a nice girl."‖ The difference between those two sentences takes place in about 3 to 5 milliseconds. The way in which the terminal pitch of the two sentences is handled makes the first what we might call a declarative statement and the second an interrogatory or doubt statement. The more acute observers will note that when one speaks, he is not simply presenting data which linguists term phonetics or phonemics or morphology or simple syntax. When these linguistic particles are put together in a communicational frame, in actual speech one does a series of things with one's body. In speaking these sentences, I do not have very much choice about which movements I make. Each of these sentences, within its context, requires a very special set of movements. To review, "She is a nice girl" is marked by a set of head movements which take place over the *She,* the *nice,* and the *girl.* In this example I mark the sentence by lowering my head. I can just as easily do this with my eyelids, with my hand, or even with my entire body. These kinesic markers, as we have termed them, can be seen, too, in the contrast sentence "She's a nice girl#" in which I cross-reference with the markers just as I can with drawl in my voice over the "she's," the "nice," and the "girl." I could vary this but, essentially, the "sweep" marker over the "nice" indicates that I am not totally enthusiastic about the young lady. Comparably, the example, "She is a nice girl"‖ contains a series in which I may knit my brows over "nice" and make a slight lateral and upward movement over "girl." Obviously, this does not exhaust the possibilities. In actual practice, I can vary this in a number of ways—the meaning varying in a consistent manner with each significant vocalic or kinesic shift.

I am trying to demonstrate the necessary interdependence of the kinesic and linguistic; without going into an extensive course in kinesics, we can see that in communication we handle an extensive number of signals which all of us have learned, but only after such signals are abstracted can they be taught. The duration and velocity—that is, the timing—of each of these is significant and important.

There is clearly a difference between the order of statement which I make about myself when I close my lids with no perceptible duration of holding at the point of closure, and when I close the lids at the same rate of speed, allowing about a quarter of a second duration of the closure. Or again, contrast these with the situation in which I close my eyelids much more slowly, leave them closed for a duration, or close them slowly and leave them closed for a hardly perceptible duration.

Practiced observers will recognize that the remainder of my face cannot remain immobile in an actual speech situation. Necessary shifts take place in the remainder of my physiognomy and my head as well as in the positioning of my body and hands. A series of movements in any part of my body could have changed the nature of the communication in a manner analogic to the shifts which occur if I change the quality of my voice, the words, or the phonemes in the verbalized material. These are only a few of the communicational particles which must be understood if we are to comprehend the complex phenomenon of communication. Only extended research can reveal the full structure, traces of which we can now detect.

In kinesics we engage in experimentation in the British sense. That is, we look at phenomena to trace what is happening, rather than attempt to control the variables and make something happen in an artificial situation. This is the natural history approach. For years a group of linguists, Norman A. McQuown, Charles Hockett, Henry Lee Smith, Jr., and George Trager, the ethnologist Gregory Bateson, the psychiatrists Henry Brosin, and, for an unfortunately limited period of time, Frieda Fromm-Reichmann, and myself as the anthropological kinesicist studied a series of family films taken by Mr. Bateson at Stanford in research on schizophrenogenic families. We continually asked ourselves the question: What is it about the communication between these disturbed families that is somehow different, either in quality or in intensity or quantity, from that which we have seen in other families of comparable social station in which there is no mental disturbance? What we are seeking at present are hypotheses, propositions, and working models upon which further research in normal and pathological family situations can be based.

The family in this study is made up of a middle-class father and mother and three children. We originally studied the mother as an ideal type for what we were calling self-containment—that is, she had a minimal response to the messages being sent to her by others within her family. This unhappy woman has three children. The first,

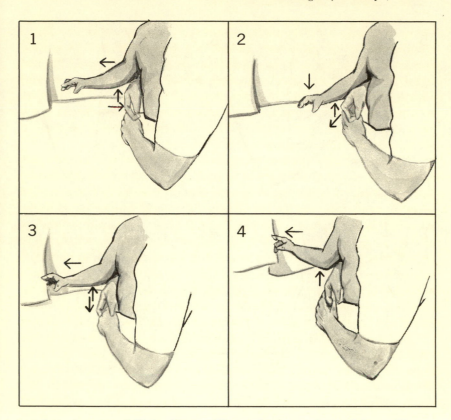

Mother changing baby's diaper. Illustrations are derived from film sequences 0–42. Frames 0, 3, 6, 9 of film sequence.

already in school, has shown serious disturbance. The diagnosis of the child's behavior by skilled child psychiatrists ranges from a statement of "schizophrenic-like" to "seriously disturbed." The second child, whom we see at four and a half, seems, at first glance, to be hopefully healthy. Sustained consideration of this complex family situation makes us wonder whether this child's adaptation to *this* family will equip him for adaptation to families whose messages are somewhat less contradictory. For present purposes, however, we shall largely ignore these older children and pay special attention to the relationship between the mother and the third child, an infant, who is at the time of the filming about seven months old.

Running through the film we made of the family would make it possible to see the adjustment pattern of these families. Following

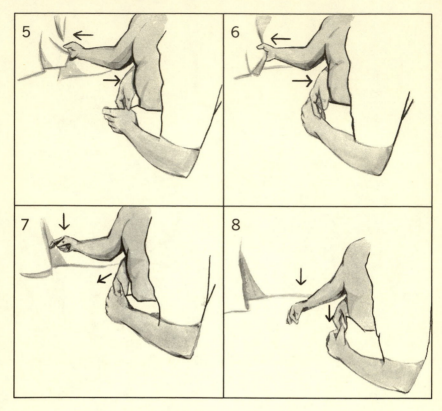

Frames 12, 15, 18, 21 of film sequence.

this exercise we can examine the relationship between the mother and the baby, a little girl.

Any sustained interaction between mother and baby may be used to assess the structure of the social relationship. What we have chosen to look at is that situation in which the mother changes the baby's diaper—a task which she will perform several times a day for 18 to 30 months. The structure imposed by the task seems to eliminate some of the intrusions occasioned by the presence of the researchers. That is, a familiar task (with regularized component behavior) resists observer intrusion.

The onset of the film shows the mother with her left arm supporting and balancing the baby's weight. The mother's left hand assists her right in the removal of the diaper. It is to be noted that the mother's right hand, at the wrist, is pressed against the extended

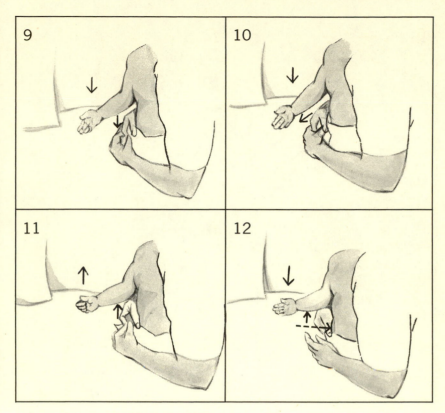

Frames 24, 25, 27, 28 of film sequence.

right arm of the baby. Simultaneously, the lateral aspects of the thumb side of the mother's right hand press against the baby's body in the lateral abdominal region.

In the next pictograph we see that the baby's hand has started to move down. Mother continues her pressure on the baby's upper arm, but she moves the thumb aspect of her right hand away from the baby's body and directs it in the removal of the diaper.

The third pictograph is a continued movement on the part of both which extends into the next picture.

In the fifth pictograph, as the infant's hand makes contact with the curtain, mother presses against the body of the infant with her right wrist, an action which she continues in the sixth picture.

In the seventh pictograph the baby relinquishes its hold on the curtain and begins to move its hand down. At the same time, the

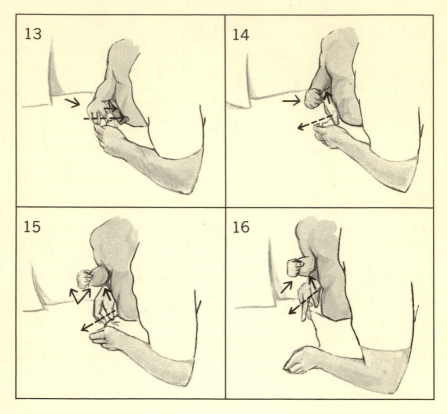

Frames 32, 35, 38, 42 of film sequence.

mother moves her hand away from the child's body and turns her attention completely to the task of removing the diaper.

In the eighth, ninth, and tenth pictographs we see the continued progress of the infant's hand down while mother continues to busy herself with the diaper.

In the eleventh pictograph, mother presses against the upper arm of the infant and reverses the movement of the infant's arm.

By the twelfth pictograph we see something entirely different. Now, she pushes not only up but toward the baby's body.

To review, in the first series, she pushed upward to extend the baby's arm, she pushed against the body to push it down. In the second instance the pressure against the baby's body indicated that the hand should come down and toward the body either of the mother or the child. Pictures twelve and thirteen are critical. She now sends both messages at once, seemingly emphasizing one of the messages somewhat more strongly than the other. This time she uses not only the wrist but she curls her thumb against the baby's body. At the same time, she thrusts her wrist against the child's upper arm. Thus, the child is in what Gregory Bateson has called the double-bind—neither of the messages can be obeyed without disobeying the other. In picture fourteen mother presses upward again against the arm, relieves the pressure against the body and pushes the baby's hand and arm toward a lateral position. By the sixteenth picture we see that the baby's hand is moving again toward an outstretched position. Following this sequence the baby waves its arm up and down in the air.

It would be easy to dismiss this scene as, on the one hand, a way in which a mother protects the baby from being stuck with a pin while she removes the diaper. On the other hand, it is all too easy to be horror-struck by the inevitable confusion which the baby feels, or at least we feel, in such a situation. It is clear that only extended further research will let us know the significance of small portions of times like this. However, if we place this scene in the larger context of the family, this scene gains new significance as an item in the complicated situation of communication within this family. Thus, this small scene, $1\frac{3}{4}$ seconds in duration, becomes exceedingly important. The exact nature of its significance must wait for future research.

When one thinks how many $1\frac{3}{4}$ seconds of interaction there are in the socialization process of this or any other infant, it is clear that by the time babies become children they are very old indeed. If, as we suspect from the observation of extended contact between this mother and this infant, this $1\frac{3}{4}$ seconds contains within it a micropattern which is duplicated many times in a scope of minutes, hours, and weeks, we have come close to the problem, or at least near certain problems, of the relationship between human learning and human health.

3. *Becoming Predictable**

I HAVE SPENT almost two decades exploring the social potentiality of the human body. During this period we have studied hundreds of thousands of feet of film. Thousands of hours have been spent on minutes of recorded human interaction. I have talked with artists, anatomists, and athletes. With my colleagues from psychiatry, I have observed the strange distortions of the bodies of the mentally ill and have listened to their even stranger reflections on these bodies. It was my hope that I could be forced by these caricatured performances to recognize characteristics of pathology, and, by contrast, of "normality." This has been only a partially realized hope. What I have learned is that the emotionally disturbed do *not* express gestures or facial expressions and do *not* assume postural positions that are *not part of the repertoire of the remainder of the community*. Rather, they display their behavior for durations, at intensities, or in situations that are inappropriate for such behavior. The emotionally disturbed seem to have less capacity for comprehending the behavior of others—or, rather, they seem to have a greater capacity for misinterpretation of the behavior of others. And, when ill, they do not seem to have the same ability to modify their behavior when it is offensive or misunderstood by others. But—there appears to be nothing in the *particular* pieces of behavior they exhibit which is "normal" or pathological. I recall several years ago at the University of Buffalo, Gregory Bateson was asked by a member of his audience whether there was any difference between schizophrenia and art. He thought for a moment, and then in his best Cambridge drawl, replied, "The difference, you know, is probably a matter of discipline. The artist can do purposefully that over which the schizophrenic has but partial control." My work with the emotionally disturbed has taught me that I need to know more about normal communicative practices and the way these are learned. It is my faith that if I could understand the way children learn the structure of the communi-

*From "The Artist, the Scientist, and a Smile," presented at the Maryland Institute of Art on December 4, 1964.

cative process by which as men they will coordinate their activities, I might, someday, have greater understanding of the way this structure can be misused by man in his self-isolation. I have not traveled very far along the road toward this discovery; I am getting some idea about where I am on the road map.

---

4. Backgrounds*

A̲s̲ ̲w̲i̲l̲l̲ ̲b̲e̲ evident in the essays in this volume, the paramount and sustaining influence upon my work has been that of anthropological linguistics. This dependency was not occasioned by a preoccupation with linguistics *per se*. Rather, it was only in linguistic analysis that I could find either data or models which could penetrate my preconceptions. A short but productive stay among the Kutenai, aimed at the study of Kutenai kinship, had raised problems about words and behavior in my mind. These were magnified rather than solved by an extended study of kinship practices in two Kentucky communities.

My earliest field work made me aware that societies made very different use of verbal material (including kinship terminology) in their particular social adaptations. The relationship between words and talk, and, words and social behavior, intrigued me. Societies which had a very low rate of vocalization seemed quite as capable of producing persons to manage their affairs as those which vocalized at a great rate. Laconic families seemed to instill the values of the community at least as effectively as those which were loquacious. I became aware that I had accepted without serious thought a simplistic formula which described human learning as being derived either from verbalized precept, warning, punishment, or reward, or, *by imitation*. As a concept, "imitation" seemed to be a catchall category in which social theorists put everything that was not stored and transmitted in words. In its technical definition and as used by careful researchers, the term had more content but, by and large,

---

*[These remarks on the development of the author's ideas on the learning patterns of body movement within a culture were prepared for this volume.—B. J.]

"monkey see, monkey do" exhausted the contribution of the theory.

The recognition that much learning and social interaction had been effectively removed from scrutiny because it was accepted that they were learned by imitation (particularly when imitation is seen as a process of observation shaped and channeled by reinforcement or punishment) unfortunately did not immediately open the behavioral universe for observation and comprehension. Every piece of data to which I had access led me to believe that the differences to be seen between Hopis and Navajos, Eskimos and Quakiutls, proper Philadelphians and equally proper Virginians, or even between Kentuckians from different communities, could not be assigned either to genetic differences, on the one hand, or to language or exclusively verbal training, on the other. What was it that the children in each of these groups learned which made them different from those in the other communities? More importantly, if the continuities so evident in each of the societies were maintained by social inheritance, how was information passed along, if that information was not encapsulated in the dicta and interdicta of vocalized words? Obviously, reading contributes to the shape of human value systems. However, nonliterate communities sustain themselves quite as effectively as do literate ones. There is no easy answer in assigning to telecommunicative writing and reading that which is not contained in spoken words and sentences. Man is dependent upon spoken language but as a social being cannot be explained exhaustively in terms of that dependency.

My training in linguistics at the University of Chicago had been sufficient to make me realize that social meaning is signaled by multiple processes of language and is not merely a property of the words or the glossaries of words of a language. For a number of years this remained an unproductive truism for me, for further insight was precluded by the unquestioned preconception that *what* a speaker said was carried in words and in the logic imposed by sentence structure upon these words, while *how* he *felt about* what he said was carried by style, tone of voice, degrees of vehemence, and the like. Moreover, while it was evident that formal circumstances demanded formal speech accompaniment, the failure to recognize the orderly, if not coercive, nature of interactional processes prevented students from seeing that all social interaction inevitably reflects and is, itself, immanent in the speech behavior of the participants—because speech behavior is an *aspect* of interactional behavior as social behavior. At least this seems a tenable position if "speech behavior" is seen not merely as the transmission of words and sentences, but as containing in its sounds and silences the real substance of socially organized interpersonal behavior.

In retrospect, this traditional and myopic view of communication which saw words and sentences as denotative, and the behavioral context of these words as connotative, was probably owing to the fact that without being aware of it, students had developed a conception of social structure and social interaction which was dominated by a simplistic role theory: they saw society as a structure of formalized institutions, with these institutions made up of formalized social roles and human beings as having a repertoire of active and potential formalized roles. With such a mechanical and discontinuous conception, it seemed evident that individuals in stylized roles engaged in the exchange of prestructured vocalic and gestural messages. Perhaps the most insidious aspect of this position was that students somehow felt that when they were not in a formal situation, people, except when malfunctioning, became more "natural" and then merely talked to one another—the accompanying body behavior being "spontaneous" and unformalized—i.e., natural rather than traditional.

Perhaps even more serious was the fact that the language employed to discuss human social speech behavior was basically normative in nature. Terms such as "artificial," "sincere," "honest," "affected," and even "natural" have had definitive value for many. Within the larger conceptual framework I had erected, it was impossible to see that such terms, however normative their conventional usage, are susceptible to behavioral analysis and, as such, can be made descriptive of communicative relationships. Such terms, without analysis, are still more than simple statements of the personality characteristics of the individuals who perform particular actions in special ways in an interactional sequence.

The implicit separation of the behavior of humans and, thus, the humans themselves, as *artificial* in nonintimate, impersonal association, and *natural* in familiar situations was introspectively substantiated by the companion conception that the content in a social interchange is intellectual (and a product of mental activity) while variations in performance are emotional (and a product of physiological or "psychological" activity). These conceptions, taken together, for a number of years effectively prevented my recognizing that social personality is in large part a structure composed of interdependent social relationships and that social relations (their expectancies, permissions, and controls) are a necessary and perhaps predominant constituent of the content exchanged between vocalizing humans. As such, social relationships and the shared feelings about these relationships could not be haphazard, emotionally based additives, but must be patterned, learned, and integral aspects of communication behavior. Not until my work in kinesic structure revealed the structured nature of relational body motion (parakinesic) material was I prepared to accept the implications of those aspects of speech behavior which are so easily ignored as idiosyncratic or merely emotive. Some of this material is discussed on pages 108ff. on paralanguage.

My study of Kutenai kinship contributed little that was noteworthy about circum-Plains kinship systems, but out of the Kutenai experience came insights which continue to shape the direction of my research. Perhaps the most important was that perception is shaped by culture—that men do not take common perceptions and *then* shape them into differential conceptions. I was immediately impressed by the eyesight of the Kutenai, who could tell an Indian from a white man far beyond the point where features were at all distinguishable. That I was able to do the same thing within weeks did not reduce my pastoralist certainty about native visual acuity. To my mind, I had "learned" to do what they did "naturally." It was only after I made a mistake and misjudged two men at a distance as white men when one was Indian that I again became curious about appearance and identification, a matter which I am still studying and only beginning to get into perspective.

During the latter days of my stay in British Columbia I realized that Kutenai speakers moved differently when speaking Kutenai and when speaking English. Was the Kutenai when speaking English being an imitation white man? My premature judgment that the Indian was "acting like" a white man inhibited the discovery that there was a systematic relationship between audible and visible communicative behavior, that these are coercive and interdependent language systems. That recognition was not to come until I began to isolate kinesic morphology and, with the aid of linguists, to study the relationship between speech and body motion. I returned from the field in 1946 knowing that the Kutenai looked different from Canadian whites. And I was aware that both Indians and whites looked and moved differently in differing situations. However, these insights had insufficient strength to erase my commitment to the traditional conception that body motion was *from time to time* stereotyped and conventionalized in matters such as stance and gesture, and thus, in formal interaction, was an artificial appendage to speech. Inherent in this position was the belief that more customarily body motion was "natural," that is, a "primitive" response to underlying and universal physiological and emotional states. The hypotheses based upon these beliefs were challenged by the data and I came to question the beliefs, as the following selections show, and eventually discarded both of them, but with reluctance.

5. *There Are Smiles* . . .

L AUGHING and crying seem to be such universally recognized human expressions that from the beginning of my interest in human body motion communication I was tempted to see these as basic physiologically derived expressions, the study of which could provide us with a starting point for measuring special individual conventionalized behavior. When I began to film real children in real contexts, the temptation remained but the confidence in the method rapidly faded.

As long as we studied the laughing or crying situations as identified by the participants, it was easy to code (linguistically and kinesically) the laughter as laughter, the crying as such. It was not nearly so easy to code the constituents of these contrastive social acts exhibited by an isolated individual whose context was unknown. Since I found the sounds made by persons laughing or crying confusing, I decided to turn to smiling and "sad-faced." The latter category proved impossible to handle, but over the years the question of smiling, of when it is appropriate, and of how the child learns its appropriate employment have remained as concerns—particularly when we are trying to understand the children we see who are, socially and emotionally, seriously distressed and distressing.

Early in my research on human body motion, influenced by Darwin's *Expression of the Emotions in Man and Animals,* and by my own preoccupation with human universals, I attempted to study the human "smile." * Without recognizing my own preconceptions, I had been attracted to a simplistic theory which saw "verbal" communication as subject to (and responsible for) human diversification while "nonverbal" communication provided a primitive and underlying base for (and was the resultant of) human unity. Smiling, it seemed to me, provided the perfect example of a behavior bit which in every culture expressed pleasure (in the jargon which I was using then, "positive response") on the part of the actor. Almost as soon as I started to study "smiling" I found myself in a mass of contradictions. From the outset, the *signal* value of the smile proved debatable. Even the most preliminary procedures provided data which were difficult to rationalize. For example, not only did I find that a number of my subjects "smiled" when they were subjected to what seemed to be a positive environment, but some "smiled" in an aversive one. My psychiatric friends provided me with a variety of psychological explanations for this apparent contradiction, but I was determined to develop social data without recourse to such explanations. Yet, inevitably, these ideas shaped my early research.

As I enlarged my observational survey, it became evident that there was little constancy to the phenomenon. It was almost immediately clear that the frequency of smiling varied from one part of the United States to another. Middle-class individuals from Ohio, Indiana, and Illinois, as counted on the street, smiled more often than did New Englanders with a comparable background from Massachusetts, New Hampshire, and Maine. Moreover, these latter subjects smiled with a higher frequency than did western New Yorkers. At the other extreme, the highest incidence of smiling was observed in Atlanta, Louisville, Memphis, and Nashville. Closer study indicated that even within Georgia, Kentucky, and Tennessee there were systematic differences in the frequency of smiling; subjects from tidewater Georgia, the Bluegrass of Kentucky and western Tennessee were much more likely to be observed smiling than were their compatriots from the Appalachian sections of their states. If I could have maintained my faith in the smile as a "natural" gesture of expression, an automatic neuromuscular reaction to an underlying and "pleasurable" endocrine or neural state, I would have had a sure measure to establish isoglosses of pleasure with which to map the United States. Unfortunately, data continued to come in.

*The pages which follow are adapted from "Kinesics, Inter- and Intra-Channel Research," in *Studies in Semiotics,* Thomas A. Sebeok, ed. Social Science Information, International Social Science Council (Paris, Mouton, 1968), Vol. VII-6, pp. 9–26.

Almost as soon as I attempted to isolate contexts of propriety for smiling, data emerged which made it clear that while it was perfectly appropriate (as measured by social response) for a young female to smile among strangers on Peachtree Street in Atlanta, Georgia, such behavior would be highly inappropriate on Main Street in Buffalo, New York. In one part of the country, an unsmiling individual might be queried as to whether he was "angry about something," while in another, the smiling individual might be asked, "What's funny?" In one area, an apology required an accompanying smile; in another, the smile elicited the response that the apology was not "serious." That is to say, the presence of a smile in particular contexts indicated "pleasure," in another "humor," in others "ridicule," and, in still others, "friendliness" or "good manners." Smiles have been seen to indicate "doubt" and "acceptance," "equality" and "superordination" or "subordination." They occur in situations where insult is intended and in others as a denial of insult. Except with the most elastic conception of "pleasure," charts of smile frequency clearly were not going to be very reliable as maps for the location of happy Americans.

But what about the "natural" smile of the "happy" infant? (Twenty-five years ago, we believed that babies were not only more "natural" than grownups but also more like grown animals and more "primitive." By the time we were ready to forego the term primitive as applicable to non-Western people, we were not ready to give it up as descriptive of Western and non-Western children.) Friends who were studying child development said that as the infant matured past the point where his smiles were grimaces from gas pains he had a natural smile which some felt provided a naturally seductive stance with which to involve adults in care and protection. Others insisted that this infantile smile was a natural expression of pleasure and that, until the adult and peer world converted or suppressed it, the child would continue to smile "naturally" in response to his own euphoria or to situations of social euphoria. Others insisted that while there was a "natural tendency" to smile, this tendency was constrained as the child was conditioned to use the smile as a symbolic cue. That is, the infantile smile, as an organic or physiological and automatic reflex of pleasure, with maturation comes under voluntary control and becomes utilizable as a unit of the communication system. At the other extreme were those who, believing that the fetus resists birth and is born angry, see the infantile smile as descendent from the teeth-baring of an animal ancestry and thus signifying threat. The threat is mediated and the child subjugated by the social insistence upon converting the meaning of the smile from malevolent intent to benevolent intent. Finally, this apparent divergence of opinion is bridged by others who solve such problems by blending the dichotomy and who see man as basically ambivalent. For these persons the smile is a naturally ambivalent gesture which can be and is used to express the gamut of human feelings.

This is not the occasion to review some of the attempts to test these and other dependent hypotheses using caricatures, photos, and smiling models with infants in laboratory conditions. As I have read them I find them indeterminate although interesting. We do not have very reliable information about infant smiling in cultures other than those of the Western world. At the time of this writing I do not know whether infants in all societies smile prior to *any* socialization nor do I know what happens to infants in any particular society who do not smile at all or who smile all the time. On the other hand, there is considerable clinical and anecdotal material to indicate that at least in Western cultures children must learn to smile in appropriate situations. That is, they must learn how and when to smile; if they do not they are somehow isolated for special attention.

It is this latter point which is relevant to our communicational studies. Smiles do not override context. That is, insofar as we can ascertain, whatever smiles are and whatever their genesis, they are not visible transforms of underlying physiological states which are emitted as direct and unmitigated signal forms of that state. And, the fact that subjects are not always aware that they are or are not smiling or are not always skilled enough to emit convincing smiles upon demand does not relegate such smiles into the realm of the psychologist or the physiologist. Linguistic or kinesic structure is no less orderly because performers are not conscious of their utilization of it.

At this stage of the study of smiling (I am fictionalizing the order of investigation and discovery somewhat for purposes of discussion) it had become clear that not only could I not support any proposition that smiles were universal symbols in the sense of having a universal social stimulus value but, insofar as the study of communication went, my work was only complicated by assumptions about communication as an elaboration of a panhuman core *code* emergent from the limited possibilities of physiological response. However, I could not rid myself of the nagging question occasioned by negative evidence from quite another level. I had talked with a great many anthropologists who had studied in the most widely diversified cultures and *none* reported the *absence of any* smiling from their field work. And, in fact, *none* reported societies in which smiling *never* appeared in situations which could be interpreted as pleasurable, friendly, benevolent, positive, and so on. The question was: Even if smiling does not have the same meaning in every society and is not traceably a direct response to a primitive affective state, doesn't its universal distribution as a facial phenomenon give us the right to call it a universal gesture? Obviously it does if we are speaking at the *articulatory level* of description. That is, if a smile is the bilateral extension of the lateral aspects of the lip region from a position of rest, all members of the species *Homo sapiens* smile.

There then emerges the second question: Does not the fact that smiling in every culture can be *in certain of its contexts* related to positive response indicate that man, as he gained spoken language in a prelanguage situation, utilized this expression as a device for interpersonal constraint (in the Durkheimian sense) and that smiling is a kind of urkinesic form which has been absorbed into human communicational systems as they developed? The only answer that I can give to this is that I don't know. Important as it might be to answer this question, at this stage of research I am not particularly interested in origins or in the ethnography of atavistic or "vestigial" forms. However, I am interested in determining, in a descriptive sense, what it is that we mean when we say that someone "smiled." I am interested in being able to examine the structure of events relevant to "smiling" in order to deal with the social situations of which it is a part.

Over the past decade I have been engaged in intrachannel structural kinesic research. I have become aware that, similar to other "gestures," "smiling" is not a thing in itself. The term "smiling" as used by American informants covers an extensive range of complex kinemorphic constructions which are reducible to their structural components. The positioning of the head, variation in the circumorbital region, the forms of the face, and even general body position can be and usually are involved in the performance and reception of what the informant reports as "smiling." I have learned that "he smiled," as a statement on the part of an American informant is as nonspecific and uninformative as the statement on the part of the same informant that "he raised his voice."

Only by intrachannel analysis have I been able to free myself from an ethnocentric preconception that I know what a smile is. We have not done the semiotic or communication research necessary to establish the range of appropriate social contexts within which to measure the range of consequences (meanings) of the possible range of shapes of "smiles." I think that we know *how* to study "smiling" as a *social* act. However, I don't think we will know what a smile means until we understand, from society to society, its intrachannel role and its contextual variability.

Insofar as I have been able to determine, just as there are no universal words, no sound complexes, which carry the same meaning the world over, there are no body motions, facial expressions, or gestures which provoke *identical* responses the world over.* A body can be bowed in grief, in humility, in laughter, or in readiness for aggression. A "smile" in one society portrays friendliness, in another embarrassment, and, in still another may contain a warning that, unless tension is reduced, hostility and attack will follow.

Perhaps it would be useful to discuss the "smile" as a deceptively familiar facial expression. It may be possible through its analysis to make a series of points about so-called gestures and facial expressions. First, what kinds of behavior do we abstract when we say that a man or a woman has a smile on (note the preposition) his or her face? We could, if we wished, make a list of the musculature of the lips and around the mouth. Such a listing might be of interest to an anatomist or to the plastic surgeon attempting to restore expression to a mutilated face or to a neurologist searching for a way to repair the damage of a neural accident. But this is not what we are seeking. Even our most preliminary investigation reveals that the lateral extension of the corners of the mouth or the upward pull on the upper lips, or any combinations of these do not make a recognizable smile. These same activities occur with a snarl or a grimace of pain. The response of an infant to a gas pain seems to involve the same circummouth musculature as the response to its mother.

A detail from a painting which is limited to the behavior immediately associated with the oral cavity is ambiguous. It takes little observation to realize that this ambiguity arises from the fact that our abstraction is partial, that we have inappropriately sliced nature. It is true that a child can be taught to make a large oval, put a

---

*The following section on smiles is part of a paper "The Artist, The Scientist, and a Smile" presented at the Maryland Institute of Art on December 4, 1964.

small circle in its center, two small parallel circles just above the central circle and an upwardly curving line below the central circle and the completed figure can be recognized as representing a face. When the abstraction is presented as a whole, the curved line in this drawing can *stand for* a smile. Yet, this figure is more of a statement about the conventional shorthand of cartoons or of Western European childish representation than it is proof that the smile occurs in the mouth. If one belongs to a culture that sustains this abstractional convention, the curved line *stands for* a smile. In other cultures which do not use this total figure for a face or recognize the curved line symbol for a mouth as a mouth, this abstraction is confusing if not downright nonsensical. The particular organization of sounds which are heard as "smile" stands for a particular facial expression only for members of those cultures which have made this arbitrary and conventionalized association between the complex of sounds "Smile" and a particular range of facial expression. Comparably, the curved line is a symbol, carrying meaning only in those societies which have this convention. However, it is very easy to be deceived into believing that because an abstraction can stand for an activity, the abstraction itself is a universal representation of this expression—that a smile, so abstracted, *is* an activity engaged in by the mouth.

Because artistic representation is always, if meaningful, in some sense conventionalized, we must look at faces and not at pictures of faces if we are to abstract and comprehend either "what" a smile is, how it is made up, or what it "means." That is, "smiles" must be studied in their social setting if we are to understand the ranges of meaning humans of a given society convey to each other when they display facial activity.

If a "smile" is not limited to the mouth, what are the physical involvements characteristic of its performance? If we limit our discussion to an American communicating by body motion, we can study this problem along two different but mutually contributive pathways. One of these is to take the mouth behavior which repeatedly appears in that activity which we, as members of an American, diakinesic system recognize as a smile and which our informants identify as a smile, and see where else it appears. By a few comparative operations we can quickly discover that the lips are pulled back, or up and back, in a variety of other facial expressions. That is, even though some degree of movement is required by the lips in order to smile, this same movement is utilized in expressions that could not by the farthest stretch of the imagination be called "smiling." By this operation we recognize that the mouth movement is a segment of a structure that can be used as part of a code and that it is not specifically meaningful in and of itself.

Analogically, we could compare the movement of the lips which is at times used to compose the expression "smile" as a conventionalized body activity, with the long vowel /uw/, which in my dialect stands between the consonantal clusters in the forms "school" and "fool." There is nothing about the /uw/ sound which signifies that these two words have an underlying common identity. By some other operations we might discover that the /uw/ sound is to "school" and "fool" as the /i/ sound is to "skill" and "fill." That is, these are significant pieces of linguistic structure but are not in themselves meaningful.

The lip movements we are discussing are also pieces of structure. They must be combined with other pieces of comparably derived structure to form a meaningful unit of American communicative body movement. By examining the neighborhood of the curved lips, we can discover that this behavior often, *but not always,* occurs with a shifting tonus in the cheek area. It may *or may not* be accompanied by certain changes in the circumorbital region. It may *or may not* be accompanied by a shift in the positioning in the upper and lower lids. There may *or may not* be involvement of the eyebrows, and/or the forehead. Careful observation may reveal that this behavior may be accompanied by a movement of the scalp. The head may *or may not* be tilted. Continuing this same investigation, we can, using our descriptive and abstractive method of search, discover that the shoulders and the arms may *or may not* be involved. The trunk, too, while often not shifting as the lips curve or assume an original "at rest" position, may at times be seen to move. The hips may *or may not* be involved. And, if we are careful enough observers, we may come to recognize that in many of the situations in which we observe mouths curving, the legs and feet can be seen to move in regular and characteristic ways.

By other operations of isolation and contrast we may discover that each of the variables which we have just discussed also may occur without the appearance of a curving mouth. If each of these taken separately or together in a variety of combinations influence the way that people characteristically respond to a particular complex of behavior, we know that we are dealing with pieces of structure. We can surmise that we have begun to isolate some of the building blocks for the system through which Americans communicate with each other. In other words, we have discovered, on the one hand, that the word "smile" is a lexical (verbal) abstraction of very complex behavior and, on the other, that there are, in the American body movement system, events like words, sentences, and paragraphs. We have demonstrated that some order of lip movement seems required in the activity perceived by Americans as a smile. By extensive operations of search, in fact, we will discover that if other pieces of facial behavior are correctly presented there is no need for an actor to either curl or part his lips—a slight softening is sufficient. The observer will report that the actor has "smiled."

While many of the techniques used in the abstraction and analysis of communication systems are relatively new, the insights on which the approach is based have been around for some time.* A popular beginning point for those concerned with the history of modern communication theory is Darwin's *Expression of the Emotions in Man and Animals.* In this work, the great biologist attempted to organize an extensive body of observations into some kind of ordered theory about the audible and visible behavior of mammals and the emotional states which induce such behavior. A rigorous observer, Darwin set a model for behavioral description which can be read with profit today. However, his concern with certain kinds of psychological problems, many of which remain unsolved, vitiated his attempt to regulate his data. In his role as synthesist he was hampered by preconceptions which even the sternest materialists of his day could not avoid.

Inheritance, as Darwin used it, seems at times a genetic, and at other times a social phenomenon. Perhaps it makes little difference to his major thesis which aspects of human behavior are biologically inherited as long as he demonstrates the continuity of the species and the society. However, for certain problems with which the human sciences are concerned today, it makes a great deal of difference whether or not vocal and body motion systems ultimately derive their order from the biological base or are exclusively a product of social experience. Careful reading of Darwin leads one to believe that if he had had some knowledge about social systems or even

---

*This selection is adapted from "Paralanguage: Twenty-five Years after Sapir," in *Lectures* on *Experimental Psychology,* Henry W. Brosin ed. (Pittsburgh: University of Pittsburgh Press, 1961). [Note: References indicated by date in this paper and those following can be found in the Bibliography.]

about the systematic quality of language and its cultural inheritance, he might have unraveled or at least loosened some of these knots himself. Clearly, his work does set the stage for many of the problems with which some anthropologists, the modern ethnologists, and the comparative psychologists are now concerned:

> Are certain kinds of social behavior, particularly gestures, facial expression, and certain sounds, somehow closer to the biological base than others?

> Are such behaviors biologically inherited and thus specially revealing as descriptions of the emotional life of certain groups or members within the group?

> Are there particular sounds and expressions and gestures which can be studied *in isolation* and which are evidence of particular, predisposing psychological states regardless of the cultural context of their appearance?

Cross-cultural research suggests that the answer to all of these questions is negative. How can we, then, comprehend and rephrase the evident regularities which we observe within particular social groups? And how can we assess the variations within these regularities? Scholars for over a hundred years have been concerned with analyzing the relationship between language and body motion and the personalities which express them. Insightful and even brilliantly intuitive though many of them are, most are directed toward a different order of data than we are developing here. They were largely concerned primarily with isolated examples of vocalic variation or gesture and posture as expressional behavior; their patent ethnocentrism, atomism, or biologism has precluded rather than encouraged cross-cultural study. With few exceptions, most of the work is not of direct concern to this presentation.

The development of microcultural analysis owes much to the work of Boas,* Efron (1942), Bateson,† Devereux,‡ LaBarre (1949) and Margaret Mead, among others. Mead's work especially has been stimulating to the development of kinesic analysis. Her reappraisal of the Gesellian position on development (1956), her work with Bateson which dramatized the usefulness of the camera as a research tool (1952), and her consistent stress on careful problem arrangement

---

* The influence of Franz Boas is expressed in the work of his students, particularly Mead, Sapir, and Efron. Professor Boas was among the first scholars to utilize the movie camera as a field research instrument.

in the analysis of culture and personality data were important contributions to the analytic procedures of kinesics. Several psychologists have also provided hypotheses, the analyses of which have led to the clarification of the linguistic-kinesic approach. Among these are K. Dunlap (1927), M. H. Krout (1933), Otto Klineberg (1927), Gardiner Murphy (1947), John Carroll (1953), and, especially, C. E. Osgood (1954). This is by no means an exhaustive review of the influences contributing to the development of the linguistic-kinesic approach to microcultural analysis. From every discipline making up the behavioral sciences have come insights which lead to the perspective best put by Bateson: "Our new recognition of the complexity and patterning of human behavior has forced us to go back and go through the natural history phase of the study of man which earlier scholars skipped in their haste to get to laboratory experimentation."§

6. *Masculinity and Femininity as Display**

ZOOLOGISTS and biologists have over the years accumulated archives of data which attest to the complex ordering of animal gender display, courtship, and mating behavior. Until recently, the

† Gregory Bateson has been a consistent pioneer in both theoretical and methodological approaches to communication analysis. See particularly G. Bateson and Margaret Mead, *Balinese Character,* Special Publications of the New York Academy of Sciences, Vol. II (New York, 1942); Reusch and Bateson, *Communication: The Social Matrix of Psychiatry* (New York, Norton, 1951). His films, made with the assistance of the Josiah Macy, Jr. Foundation, laid the groundwork for the study of family interaction by microcultural techniques.

‡ George Devereux has shown a consistent interest in the analysis of communication, particularly in the clinical context. For his interest in cross-culturally measured paralanguage, see "Mohave Speech and Speech Mannerisms," *Word,* Vol. 6 (Dec. 1949), pp. 268–272.

§Personal communication in research seminar, CASBS, Palo Alto, 1956.

*Presented to the American Association for the Advancement of Science, in December 1964 under the title "The Tertiary Sexual Characteristics of Man: A Fundamental in Human Communication."

implications of much of this data have been obscured by the governing assumption that this behavior was, while intricate and obviously patterned, essentially a mechanical and instinctual response to a genetically based program. There has been, however, an increasing realization that intragender and intergender behavior throughout the animal kingdom is not simply a response to instinctual mechanisms but is shaped, structured, and released both by the ontogenetic experiences of the participating organisms and by the patterned circumstances of the relevant environment. Behavioral scientists focusing upon human behavior have been forced to relinquish the ethnocentric assumption that human gender and sexual behavior is qualitatively different from that of other animals. Many have conceded that culture, a human invention, is not interpreted profitably as a device for curbing and ordering "animalistic," "brutal," "bestial," or instinctual appetites. The elaborate regulation of fish, bird, and mammalian courtship and mating behavior has been of particular interest to sociologists and anthropologists. That this interest has not been more productive seems to me to be occasioned by confusion in the ordering of gender-centered behavior. In the discussion to follow, which utilizes certain insights derived from analysis of communication, I wish to focus upon one aspect of gender-related interactional behavior—that of gender identification and response.

Biologists have long been aware that the clear demarcation between the production of ova and spermatazoa in organisms of a bisexual species is not necessarily accompanied by any comparable bifurcation in the distribution of secondary sexual characteristics. In some species there is such extreme gender-linked dimorphism that only the specialist in the particular species can recognize that males and females are conspecial. At the other extreme, some species are so unimorphic that near-surgical techniques are required to determine the gender of isolated individuals. By and large, researchers concerned with human behavior have assumed that in relatively unimorphic species there were subtle differences in the perceptible taxonomy of males and females which were easily recognizable by conspecifics even if they were difficult to detect by humans. However, it would be difficult for any reader conversant with Konrad Lorenz' (1957) description of the difficulties involved in the mating of graylag geese to maintain the fiction that gender differences are always apparent to the membership of a unimorphic species. There is humor and a certain pathos in the situation when two graylag males meet and each acts as though the other were a member of the opposite sex. Only the reproductive rate of graylags gives us confidence that even a goose can solve such a problem.

The social biologist Peter Klopfer has pointed out that even with the incomplete evidence now at hand, it would be possible to establish a spectrum of species rated by the extent of their sexual dimorphism.* Insofar as I have been able to determine, no such list has been prepared. However, by establishing an ideal typical gamut with an unimorphic species at one end and an extreme of dimorphy at the other, it has been possible to tentatively locate *Homo sapiens* on this scale. Obviously, the position of any particular species on this scale is a function of both the number of species chosen and the special characteristics of the selected species. When, however, the secondary sexual characteristics themselves are stressed (whether visibly, audibly or, olfactorily perceptible), man seems far closer to the unimorphic end of the spectrum than he might like to believe.

Physical anthropologists have long pointed out that if such anatomical markers as differential bone structure or the distribution of body hair are used, the measurement of human population reveals no bimodal curve in the distribution of secondary sexual characteristics. Most authorities agree that instead of a single curve shaped ⌒, we find two overlapping bell curves: ⌒⌒. Masculine and feminine traits in aural sound production seem to be distributed in a similar manner following puberty. There is as yet no definitive evidence that there is a significant difference in the odor-producing chemicals released by human males and females. This may be due to the crudity of our available measuring instruments, but at the present, odor does not seem to function as a constant gender marker for humans.

The case for the relative unimorphy or the weak dimorphy of man should not be overstressed for the purposes of this argument. The upright position of humans obviously makes for clear visibility of differential mammary development and for the easy display of the genitalia. These may provide sufficient signals in themselves. However, certain pieces of data permit us to discount these as definitive of gender in and of themselves. First, we have long been aware that children do not, even in societies as preoccupied with these organs as ours, immediately note the gender-defining qualities

*Personal communication.

of either the external genitalia or the differential mammary development. I doubt seriously that this represents some psychological denial function in the child's perception of his universe. The near universality of the G-string or other clothing protecting, obscuring, or hiding the genital region, even in societies with minimal shame or embarrassment about genital display, does not seem sufficient evidence for the final importance of genitalia display for gender identification. Furthermore, the fact that the more prominent breasts of females or the less prominent breasts of males do not seem to have universal sexual stimulus value would seem to support our de-emphasis upon mammary dimorphism as gender identifiers. Needless to say, however, until we have more systematic knowledge about clothing and other cosmetological devices, we are not going to be able to settle this particular question. There is no reason to make the *a priori* assumption that uncovered breasts are more or less obvious than covered ones (except of course, to those trained to make these distinctions). It seems permissible to proceed in our discussion while holding this aspect of human dimorphy open for future investigation.

My work in kinesics leads me to postulate that man and probably a number of other weakly dimorphic species necessarily organize much of gender display and recognition at the level of position, movement, and expression. It seems methodologically useful to me to distinguish between *primary* sexual characteristics which relate to the physiology of the production of fertile ova or spermatazoa, the *secondary* sexual characteristics which are anatomical in nature, and the *tertiary* sexual characteristics which are patterned social-behavioral in form. These latter are learned and are situationally produced.

Let me hasten to add that the terms "primary," "secondary," and "tertiary" imply no functional priorities. There seems plenty of reason to believe that these levels are mutually interinfluential. Patterned social behavior seems to be required to permit the necessary physiological functioning requisite for successful and fertile mating. And, we have at least anecdotal evidence and clinical reports that certain of the secondary sexual characteristics respond to both the physiological substratum and the particular social-behavioral context. I hope that premature "explanation" which accounts for this behavior in simplistic psychological or cultural terms does not preclude investigation on other levels.

I have worked with informants from seven different societies.

It has been clear from their responses that not only could native informants distinguish male movement from female movement (and the items of what was regarded as "masculine" and "feminine" varied from society to society) but they easily detected different degrees of accentuation or diminution of such movement, depending upon the situation. In all of these societies (Chinese, middle- and upper-class London British, Kutenai, Shushwap, Hopi, Parisian French, and American) both male and female informants distinguished not only typically male communicational behavior from typically female communicational behavior but, when the opportunity presented itself, distinguished "feminine" males and "masculine" females. This does not imply that any informant could make a complete and explicit list of "masculine" or "feminine" behavior. However, each culture did have stereotypes which could be acted out or roughly described. That the behavior described by the informants did not always coincide with the general range of scientifically abstractable gender-identifying behavior should not come as a surprise to any field worker who has tried to elicit microcultural behavior from native informants. One comment should be included here before we turn for examples to the body motion communicational system most intensively studied, the American. Informants from all of these societies either volunteered or without hesitation responded that young children matured into these behaviors and that as people got older they gave up or matured out of them. As might be expected, both the propedeutic period and the duration of the active gender display varied from society to society. Furthermore, while most informants agreed that in their particular society some individuals learned how to accentuate or obscure these signals, informants from all of these societies interpreted the differences as instinctually and biologically based.

I have no data which would permit me to assess the relative emphasis American culture places upon gender display and recognition as compared to other societies. However, it is quite clear that within American society, class and regional variations occur—not so much in the signals themselves as in the age at which such messages are learned, the length of time and situations in which they are used, and the emphasis placed on them in contrast to other identification signals.

As an illustration, I will describe a few of the most easily recognizable American gender identification signals. Two are derived from the analysis of posture, one from "facial expression." The male-female differences in intrafemoral angle and arm body angle are subject to exact measurement. American females, when sending gender signals and/or as a reciprocal to male gender signals, bring the legs together, at times to the point that the upper legs cross, either in a full leg cross *with feet still together,* the lateral aspects of the two feet parallel to each other, or in standing knee over knee. In contrast, the American male position is one in which the intrafemoral index ranges up to a 10- or 15-degree angle. Comparably, the American female gender presentation arm position involves the proximation of the upper arms to the trunk while the male in gender presentation moves the arms some 5 to 10 degrees away from the body. In movement, the female may present the entire body from neck to ankles as a moving whole, whereas the male moves the arms independent of the trunk. The male may subtly wag his hips with a slight right and left presentation with a movement which involves a twist at the base of the thoracic cage and at the ankles.

Another body position involved in gender presentation is made possible by the flexibility of the pelvic spinal complex. In gender identification the American male tends to carry his pelvis rolled slightly back as contrasted with the female anterior roll. If the range of pelvic positioning is depicted as $\smile$, the female position can be depicted as $\diagdown\smile$, the male as $\smile\diagup$. As males and females grow older or, because of pathology, over- or underemphasize gender messages, the male and female position can become almost indistinguishable, or become bizarrely inappropriate.

One more example may be sufficient for our point. Informants often describe particular lid and eye behavior as masculine or feminine. However, only careful observation and measurement reveal that the structural components of circumorbital behavior are related, in closure of the lid in males, to prohibiting movement of the eyeballs while the lids are closed. Comparably, the communicative convention prescribes that unless accompanying signals indicate sleepiness or distress, males should close and open their lids in a relatively continuous movement. Let me stress again that these positions, movements, and expressions are culturally coded—that what is viewed as masculine in one culture may be regarded as feminine in another.

I have presented these examples with a hesitation occasioned by past experience. Inevitably, such examples have been interpreted as the messages males and females send to each other when they wish consciously or unconsciously to invite coitus. However, I must emphasize that *no position, expression, or movement ever carries meaning in and of itself.* It is true that in certain contexts gender display, appropriately responded to, is an essential element in the complex interchange between humans preliminary to courtship, to coitus, and, even, to mating. However, the identical behavior inappropriately presented may have the opposite function; it may prevent the development of the interaction that might culminate in a more intimate interpersonal exchange. For example, a prematurely presenting male may define a situation in such a manner that the female cannot respond without considerable role sacrifice. Thus, the male can prevent coitus and even courtship from occurring by presenting in a manner which defines his action as insufficiently directed to the receiving female. The so-called "sexy" female can by inappropriate gender display effectively protect herself against intimate heterosexual involvement. The male who sends "feminine" or pubescent and awkward "masculine" display signals may in one context be signaling to a male; in another he degenderizes his female respondent by returning a message more appropriate to a female-female interaction than a male-female interaction. Furthermore, while it is not at all difficult to detect in context the message sent by either a male or a female which reads, "I wish to be considered a homosexual," we have been able to isolate no message, masculine or feminine, which is in itself an indicant of homosexuality or heterosexuality when such sexuality is measured by active genital participation.

For the sociologist and the anthropologist, a more important aspect of the possibility of decoding a given society's gender display and recognition system is that such a code provides him with a tool for more adequately studying the division of labor in the day-to-day life of a community. Social role and status theory have been very useful at one level of social investigation. However, when the researcher seeks to relate such theory to problems of social learning, to personality and character development, or to the solution of individual and social problems, he all too often is prevented from testing high-level generalizations in the crucible of behavior. Gender identity and relationship is only one of several nodal points coded into a society's communicational system. Kinesic and linguistic research has demonstrated, at least for American society, that such nodal behavior never stands alone—it is always modified by other identification signals and by the structure of the context in which the behavior occurs. In these complex but decodable behaviors lies the proof that gender behavior is not limited to a sexual response and that sexual behavior is not always *either* genital or uncompleted genital behavior.

In the discussion so far an attempt has been made to demonstrate the methodological correctness and convenience of ordering gender-related phenomena into primary, secondary, and tertiary characteristics. Tertiary sexual behavior has been described as learned and patterned communicative behavior which in the American body motion communication system acts to identify both the gender of a person and the social expectancies of that gender. It has been presented with the fiat that gender display or response is not necessarily sexually provocative or responsive and is probably never exclusively genital in nature.

The paper was introduced with a discussion of the relatively weak dimorphy in the structure of human secondary sexual characteristics. Until more animal societies are studied as societies and until the nature and range of the possibilities for the division of labor have been investigated in these animal societies, we cannot make any final appraisal of unimorphy or dimorphy as base lines for social interaction. However, we are in a position to postulate that for human society at least, weak dimorphy creates an opportunity for the development of intricate and flexible tertiary sexual characteristics which can be variably exploited in the division of labor.

Finally, in a society like ours, with its complex division of labor and with the rapid change in social role as related to gender, we should not be surprised to find that the young have considerable difficulty in learning appropriate intra- and intergender messages. Nor should we be surprised to find that in such a society messages about sex and gender can become a preoccupation. Children who become confused about the meaning of gender messages can become adults who have difficulty comprehending the relationship between male and female roles in a changing society. Only the fact that children can learn in spite of parental teaching protects us from a situation in which accumulating discrepancy could destroy the necessary conditions for appropriate mating. There is no evidence for the popular statement that men in western European society are becoming "weaker" or that women are becoming "stronger"—there is considerable evidence that both are confused in their communication with each other about such matters.

7. Kinesic Analysis of Filmed Behavior of Children*

IN ORDER to develop better techniques for description and analysis of the communicational aspects of human body motion, the University of Louisville Interdisciplinary Committee on Culture and Communication sponsored my filming of a series of scenes of group behavior in children from a particular neighborhood. Since the project was exploratory only, no attempt was made to set up a control situation for filming, other than that which naturally exists in well-known social situations; that is, the neighborhood was well known to the researchers and it was possible to anticipate play group composition and activities. The children ranged in age from 14 months to 11 years; the central focus was upon children between ten and eleven. We were primarily interested in them in order to find out what they really do, since we felt certain that we did not yet know how to look at the action patterns of children between the ages of eight and eleven. We have a tentative hypothesis that adults may have some amnesia for this particular period in their own lives. We lack or don't know what questions to ask children so that they will tell us what they are doing; because we don't ask them, they don't tell us.

The group studied included my own children, and this no doubt had some influence on the filming situation. The children knew that the pictures were being taken; however, since they were accustomed to my frequent use of a camera in their presence, in the opinion of the Committee this did not make the situation too unusual or artificial.

From these scenes, which in all total about 40 projection minutes, 15 minutes have been chosen and assembled for this presentation. Pedagogical rather than experimental considerations governed my

*Adapted from an article in *Group Processes: Transactions of the Second Conference*, Bertram Schaffner, ed. (New York: Josiah Macy, Jr. Foundation, 1956), pp. 141–144.

selection. No scene has been "edited," in the sense of making any partial deletions. Each scene is presented in its entirety as it was filmed. I used these particular scenes in order to demonstrate developmental sequences in gender and age-grading recognitions.

The methodology for the original analysis of these films was derived from that used in analyzing cross-cultural films. Each strip was viewed and a simple summary of impressions taken. Then each strip was seen from nine to thirteen times over, without comment. Finally, without reference to the initial summary of impressions, each strip was redescribed in subjective terms. This method has been tested on other films and is the best so far developed for pattern analysis in moving pictures. This permits an individual pattern and the pattern of the total scene to imprint themselves firmly on the viewer. In the first viewing of such a film by someone who has not been trained in looking at body positions and interaction in moving pictures, many parts of the film seem far too short, too fast, full of shorthand, and too far away. It is like the experience one has when a linguist turns a tape recorder on and off, demanding that one hear what the linguist's study and skilled ear have equipped him to hear, or when a bacteriologist flashes on a screen a series of slides to which one is not accustomed. The brevity of many of the scenes is very frustrating. Except in a very few scenes, the children often appear to the viewer to be doing "nothing." Actually, they look so much like children that what they are doing is really difficult to see differentially. If we were watching children from another culture, whose behavior is very bizarre in our terms, it would be very much easier to see.

After the multiple viewings of the film at the usual speed, the film is then projected from a slow-motion analyzer.

When these scenes were viewed at 24 frames per second, much of the material was lost to the participant viewer, except for those portions of the film which had been filmed at 32 frames per second. However, from previous analysis at various speeds, the films serve to demonstrate the series of tentative generalizations summarized below:

All kinesic research rests upon the assumption that, without the participant's being necessarily aware of it, *human beings are constantly engaged in adjustments to the presence and activities of other human beings.* As sensitive organisms, they utilize their full sensory equipment in this adjustment. Any particular sensory modality may have paramount definitional power in a particular communication situation, but these modalities may only be heuristically abstracted for study and analysis. That is, although at any punctiform moment a person may be seen to be moving or vocalizing, the study of communicational scenes reveals that *all* the abstractable modalities are necessary to understanding the communicational situation.

Further, it is the working assumption of the kinesicist that, until otherwise demonstrated, all body motion systems contain dominant learned aspects which are of special interest to the behavioral scientist concerned with problems of communication theory. Five years of intensive preliminary recording and analysis have led me to the conviction that kinesic behavior is learned, systematic, and analyzable. This, of course, does not deny the biological base in the behavior, but places the emphasis on the *interpersonal* rather than the *expressional* aspects of kinesic activity. Thus far theory and methodology developed by linguists have dominated much of kinesic research and analysis. This may be the product of a determined attempt to avoid overeasy and premature generalizations about the meaning of particular kinesic particles or systems. It has been the object of all kinesic research to develop techniques whereby body motion behavior, whether in the area of facial expression, gesture, stance, or any other apparent shift of the kinesthesiological system, can be recorded for objective analysis and checking. Until a considerable body of such material is available, any suggestions such as these must remain suggestive rather than definitive.

Our film demonstrates the early differentiation of the sex roles among children. It can be seen that one female infant, for example, by the age of 15 months had learned portions of the diakinesic system (parallel to a dialectic system) of the Southern upper-middle-class female. She had already incorporated the anterior roll of the pelvis and the intrafemoral contact stance which contrasts sharply with the spread-legged and posteriorly rolled pelvis of the 22-month-old boy filmed with her.

A second scene demonstrates a teaching situation in which the infant is seen in emulative and identificational body positioning with an older sister (10 years) whose five-fingeredness and wrist action were sharply distinct from the finger positioning and wrist activity of all but two of the boys in her age group. Of interest is the fact that these "retarded" boys were known from other observations and interviews to be very close to their mothers. "Close," that is, in terms of that neighborhood; of importance, too, is the fact that these two males were *regarded* as "babyish" by the neighborhood children.

Analysis of their behavior showed no particular difference between their play behavior and that of the other boys of the play group except in the area of the socially defined masculine aspects of their kinesic activity.

Another scene demonstrates the differential development of heterosexual consciousness in males and females. This scene shows a group of males, ages 10 to 12, playing "soldier." They capture a series of girls of the same age range who quite skillfully separate the boys from each other. One scene demonstrates the inadequacy of the male in the face of subtle female aggression, before which he can only stamp his foot.

In summary, the movie camera, when used together with the slow-motion analyzer, makes possible observation and analysis of human social behavior which has hitherto been hidden from comparative analysis. Reciprocal behavior, involving two or more participants and observed throughout a period of time, has hitherto resisted all but the most mechanical of observations. Recent improvements in motion picture photography, speed films, and projection techniques together with a developing body of communication theory should bring about a phenomenological revolution in the study of human behavior. Motion picture recording is expensive but preliminary surveys demonstrate conclusively that the expense is justified. No mechanical contrivance, however elaborate and precise, can be more than a supplement to the trained observer; the camera cannot substitute for the trained eye.

8. The Family and Its Open Secrets*

T O FOCUS exclusively upon the *words* humans interchange is to eliminate much of the communicational process from view and, thus, from purposive control. Obviously, in such a situation the

*Adapted from "Certain Considerations in the Concepts of Culture and Communication," in *Perspectives on Communication,* Carl E. Larson and Frank E. X. Dance, eds. (Milwaukee, University of Wisconsin-Milwaukee, 1968), pp. 144–165.

conditions of context, which give special emphasis to lexical exchange, become critical. If we do not understand the communicative process, our only recourse is to legislate the control of its shorthand operation as it exists in words. The following anecdote may illustrate the point behind this discussion:

A FAMILY INCIDENT

When we were both much younger, my brother wrote to say that he had finally decided to be brave and take a young lady home to visit my parents. She was blonde, attractive ("cuddly" was the word then), and had grown up in one of Cleveland's more attractive suburbs. I had never seen her but my brother's description made me suspect that her late adolescent poise and Ohio State sorority-type sophistication would put her in my mother's category of "frisky." "Frisky" was a designation about a third of the way along my mother's scale for evaluating young females, a scale which ran from the almost acceptable "forward" to the totally uncompromising "hussy." I was at that time about twenty-five but still close enough to family ways to be impressed by my 20-year-old brother's courage. At the same time, I was a little suspicious that he had become more involved with his friend than he had intended to become and that the young lady was being transported to Fostoria, Ohio, for the *coup de grâce*.

As I thought about the visit I remembered from my boyhood the stern look that would come over my mother's face when a horn tooted out in front of the house. Somewhat ambiguously she would say that "a lady doesn't blow her horn in front of boys' houses—If she wants something, let her come to the door. Besides, a lady lets the boy come to her." She had had the phone taken out when I reached adolescence (perhaps one of the reasons that I have never been very interested in telecommunication) in spite of my father's murmur (to himself) that he never heard of a girl getting in the family way over the telephone. My parents had come out of farming communities at the edge of the Kentucky Bluegrass and had brought with them the courtesy and hospitality of the region. They had gone to school but that schooling had not disturbed the central values of the home community. My mother had become a power in the local Women's Christian Temperance Union and my father had given up cigars shortly after I got sick from sampling them. TVA had brought electricity to our part of Kentucky and with electricity had come pumps and inside plumbing. But even with inside plumbing, the older people remembered how they carried water and did not waste it. Although my father's job took us from urban area to urban area and we always had running water, my parents' attitudes regarding water conservation did not differ from those of their still-rural brothers and sisters. I recall my father's pronouncement that urine was sterile and that all you had to do was close the lid. Feces were not sterile and should be flushed. My father felt that if everyone in the family was regular (and in our family "regularity" was a prime signal of health) the four of us should use a total of about 2 gallons of water per day for such functions.

But back to the visit. I waited several weeks for some report in either my mother's or my brother's letters. My brother didn't write and my mother's gave the customary census of the health of the neighborhood, lists of what she and my father had eaten at various functions, and what these "suppers" had cost, but no reference to my brother's young lady. Finally, unable to bear the suspense, I wrote and asked directly about the visit. The reply came from my mother. Buried in the usual letter was the three-sentence paragraph: "You ask about the visit of Miss Withers. I think some people would think she is very pretty. . . . She spent the entire time blowing smoke in your father's face and flushing the toilet." Enough said.

WORDS AND COMMUNICATION

Our studies are persuasive that in communicating humans utilize the sensorium in a complex but ordered way and that, depending upon the situation, the central messages may or may not be shared by the participants in audible fashion. And my mother was an expert in untalk—she could emit a silence so loud as to drown out the scuffle of feet, the whish of corduroy trousers, and even the grind of my father's power machinery to which he retreated when, as he said, "Your mother's getting uneasy." My mother took great pride in her role of gracious hostess. She would say firmly, "No matter how much I disagree with a guest I never allow an unchristian word to cross my lips. I just smile." Well, my mother's thin-lipped smile, which could be confined to her mouth, when accompanied by an audible input of air through her tightened nostrils required no words— Christian or otherwise—to reveal her attitude. My mother was a sniffer, a great sniffer. She could be heard for three rooms across the house. And, to paraphrase Mark Twain, her sniff had power; she could sniff a fly off the wall at 30 feet. I might even say, she was an irresponsible sniffer, for she always denied her sniffing. When we'd say, "Well, you don't have to sniff about it," she'd respond firmly, "I have something in my passages—and a lady doesn't blow her nose." "Mark my words," she'd say and then sniff again.

The fact that my mother felt that her smile was friendly and forgiving and the fact she didn't realize that her sniffs were as reliable a detector as radar to the males around her and the fact that she never admitted that she sniffed are all quite trivial to the family communication system. These cues were as reliable aspects of the code as were my father's signals that he was developing gas, my brother's silently thrust lower lip, or my own talk-talk-talk. My parents and my brother were unaware of the pervading force of *their* messages: It was to be 20 years before I was to learn that I had had the technique of telling a story which formed an audible camouflage under which to escape—timing it to end as I went out the door. Uninterruptible, the story could preclude the intrusion of prohibitions to go out that night or to use the car. And such stories avoided discussion of torn pants or of inadequate report cards—They used words to drown out relevant information or as a place to store messages full of trivial information.

I have often thought of the test of the young lady from Shaker Heights. Her background and her familial system were sufficiently similar to ours that she must have known very soon that this had not been a successful visit. But, in a larger sense, perhaps it was successful. She and my brother may have each been steered by the incident to more appropriate mating later, the incident a temporary setback in the courting procedure. A failure at one level of communication is often a success at another. The reverse can be equally true. Regardless of the sentimental or legal definition of the roles, the young lady's appointment as my brother's wife, my parents' daughter-in-law, or my sister-in-law would not have made her privy to the information code which governed our family. Such information was not hoarded or withheld—no member of the family held it for dispensation—the message system was in the family, not in the individual member of the family. We might, from our perspective, say she was interviewed and did not get or take the position. Or, we could say that the familial context could not adapt to her addition. It would be unfortunate if we limited our perspective to the point that we see her or the family as failing because she did not become a family member.

However reliably this young woman may have comprehended items in the code, without further information about the larger contexts of experience she was powerless to modify her behavior to gain admission to the easy but measured camaraderie of the family. For example, she could not know, from knowing my brother or from noting my mother's heavily polite inattention to her smoking, that my mother and her circle were devoted to the principle that "a young girl who smokes cigarettes in public will do anything in private." Nor could she possibly know that the gentle swirl of water in the commode was a cascade in my parents' ears, a Niagara of information about wastefulness, carelessness, and general moral laxity.

9. Talk and Motion in the Theater and at Family Meals*

STUDENTS of the theater have long been aware that there are significant cross-societal differences in acting, direction, and stage-craft. The French, the Germans, the English, and the Americans seem each to put a national stamp upon their productions. The same script produced in each of these countries, according to *afficionados* of the stage, is so flavored by the conventions of production and direction as almost to become different plays. These differences are not simply matters of schools of acting, although these do vary. Nor are these only matters of styles of timing, stage construction, or wardrobe which vary from country to country. Such styles are important but are insufficient to explain certain perceptible differences between the performances. I am not sufficiently conversant with cross-cultural dramatic traditions to discuss these national variations with authority; however I would like to spend a moment with one aspect of the difference between French and American stagecraft patterning.

If one contrasts a French production with an American per-

* Adapted from "Communication: Group Structure and Process," *Pennsylvania Psychiatric Quarterly* (Spring 1965), pp. 37–45.

formance, it is possible to see that an important distinction between the two lies in the difference in stress on the minor or secondary actors. A French audience attending an American play complains of the poor acting ability of the minor characters. The French say that the minor actors perform so poorly that the audience is distracted from the play. Americans, at a French play, on the other hand, while at times pleased with the acting of the secondary characters, more often complain that the French secondary actors are so "busy" that it is impossible to concentrate on the performance as carried by the principal characters. Comparative observation of the two kinds of plays leads me to sympathize with French critics who complain that the American play stresses the dialogue, the speakers, and the words spoken, rather than the "spirit" of the play. Although there are notable exceptions, American actors when speaking do tend to project more than when they do not have lines. When not speaking, American actors tend to drop into a background role. At times, they almost seem to stop acting while they await their turn to speak. The French actors, on the other hand, seem to "stay in character" and French audiences are not diverted from the central theme of the drama by such activity.

Obviously, the differences to be seen between the two traditions of stagecraft and between the perceptual patterning of French and American audiences are insufficient data upon which to base theories of difference in national character. For those who are interested in French national character and wish to pursue these leads on their own, I recommend Dr. Rhoda Metraux's *Themes in French Culture* as a starting place. For our purposes here, I wish to stress the American emphasis on dialogue, on the words, as carrying the central meaning of an interaction. I think that we would have no difficulty in agreeing that this emphasis is not restricted to the stage. Radio, television, and movie performances seem to utilize the same convention. It is tempting to extrapolate from this to generalize about other aspects of American life. Perhaps we can get a different perspective if we add another piece of data.

The reader may recall Margaret Mead's delightful discussion of the difference between the British and American breakfast table. At the British breakfast table, the father does the talking and the mother and children listen. It is mother's job to keep the children quiet and to insist they "listen" to father. In contrast, at the American breakfast table, the mother acts as stage manager. It is her task to keep the father quiet while the children express themselves in turn.

If we assume that the dramatic performance in any medium is somehow representative of the culture in which it appears, we should be able to say that American culture is a highly verbal one, that the audio-aural channel is the preferred channel for the passage of important information from one participant to the other. Yet, this is a dangerous leap in logic. It is just as arguable that in his rituals man makes an abstraction of *preferred* self themes, that the ritual is not directly iconic of primary cultural patterning but is, rather, for certain cultures a conventionalization of the way it should like to experience the world, not the way it does experience it. As Mead has pointed out, when the Englishman makes a speech, he stands erect, presents his material with authority, and makes no apology for his appearance before a group. He is there to instruct them and feels none of the American speaker's need to tell a joke to the audience to cool them out or warm them up before he starts. He is certainly unlikely to terminate his discussion with either a joke or an apology. It may very well be that the experiences men have at the family table are somehow mirrored in public speaking performances. However, it would be careless to assume that English and American stylizations in the public speech situation or that the differential emphasis upon the carriers of dialogue in French and American plays are diagnostic of the everyday usage of the communicational modalities. In our choice of examples I may, as an American, be hiding in the vocalic aspect of the interactional scene.

Children in both American and British society escape from the family table with delight. While there are exceptions in both societies, interviews with children and with adults are revealing as to the extent of resentment and emotional tension engendered by the experience. Many American families have great difficulty in getting everyone to the table at once. Others systematically avoid the situation, tandem meals being the answer to the threatening crisis of the family conclave. However, one thing is evident from the observation of families at mealtime or interviews in depth about the family table: much more goes on than is evident from reading a script of the vocalizations at the table.

If we take a tape recording of a family at the table, depending upon the class and ethnic background of the family, we may get a tape that is full of overlapping cross-discussion or one in which the only sounds are those of the dishware, chewing, sighing, and the like. In either case one is impressed with the stereotypy of family dinner table behavior. A series of tapes of vocal families reveals little variation from meal to meal. In a highly organized manner the vocalists play their roles, exchange statements and even break into quarrels with such regularity that the observer can only conclude that this is a ritual. It sounds almost as though each member of the family has learned his lines, knows his cues, and synchronizes in the family drama. The fact that the participants are unaware that they are in such a standardized ritual is unimportant here. The regularity is the fact. That the membership of the family do not call what they are doing a ritual or do not recognize the orderly nature of the verbal interaction as regulated, not by their own private impulses, but by the rules of the ritual does not negate the regularity.

Those who have worked in family therapy know the difficulty of interrupting such conventionalized behavior as this. Not only do the family members deny that their vocal performances are so regularized but organize against any attempt on the part of the therapist to attempt to get the family into motion by making these rituals manifest. Incidentally, I don't know how different so-called healthy families are in this. Those that I have studied, with few exceptions, seem equally stylized. One possible explanation of this regularity is that the audio-verbal channel may carry the "official" behavior of the family. It can serve as a screen behind which the family members can covertly go about the remainder of their communication. What I am stressing here in this exaggerated profile of family interaction is that while a theatrical performance may use the vocalic channel for carrying the central theme of a drama, vocalizations in the everyday interchange between family members may have precisely the opposite function. These vocalic interchanges may function as a public performance which in its very stereotypy serves to instruct the membership to look elsewhere in the communicative system for significant information.

I do not wish for a moment to imply that the other communicational channels possessed by this family throb with individually structured new information. The kinesic, the tactile, the olfactory channels are just as subject to regulation as is the audio-aural. In fact, a movie taken of a series of family table scenes is convincing as to the stereotypy of the kinesic behavior, too. Yet, as we watch and listen to a sound movie of a table scene we can become aware that many of these dialogues are consistently modified by behavior at another level, that we cannot abstract the meaning even of the verbal behavior by only attending to that behavior captured on a tape recorder. One of the first things that impresses the systematic observer is that the membership of the family drama is not restricted to the vocalizers. In many families the "noisiest" contributor to the communicational situation may be the most silent. The quantifiable amount of activity, vocalic or kinesic, has never proved to be a reliable measure of the *significance* of the contribution of a particular member of the family group. The highly verbal or highly active individual may under study prove to influence few parameters in family activity. On the other hand, while the content of his messages may be exceedingly limited, he may have the very important function of representing the family to itself. He supplies the quota of talk necessary to reassure the family that it has some kind of cohesion. He may even provide an acceptable image, a preferred version of the family for the family to live with.

10. *Tactile Communication in a Family**

As I HAVE lectured before a variety of audiences over the past 15 years about the complex multisensory system I conceive communication to be, I have been repeatedly asked how I "stood" on extrasensory perception. My answer to this question has always been and still is that much research on the various sensory modalities needs to be done before we conclude that the *unexplained is unexplainable* in terms of the known sensory modalities. Occam's razor dictates that I utilize a simpler hypothesis of sensory explanation before I employ the more complex one which would divide all of communication into sensory and extrasensory.

About a year ago Drs. John Bok, Stanley Leonberg, and James Harris of the Institute of the Pennsylvania Hospital called to tell me of an unusual case which they were treating.† A young man of twenty-two had been admitted to their care. He did not vocalize

* From "Research in Exceptional Phenomena," presented to the American Society of Clinical Hypnosis on October 10, 1965.

† Drs. Bok and Leonberg are preparing an extensive case history of this patient and his family for further publication.

intelligibly and the case history alleged that he had not done so since he was about 2 years of age. He had been examined many times during the intervening 20 years; his parents were in an economic position to investigate both the neurological and the psychiatric medical possibilities for their son. What made the case interesting to us originally was the fact that this boy (whom some suggested exhibited many of the symptoms of the schizophrenic) and his mother carried on detailed conversations with the use of a tablet upon which the alphabet was written. He apparently pointed to letters and made up sentences which she recognized and responded to. To record these events, Jacques D. Van Vlack, the research technologist for our project, decided to employ a filming technique which he had developed for research purposes. In this technique a camera crew goes into the home and films a house tour. The patient and the family conduct the tour and the researcher is supplied both with data about the family's living conditions and about family interaction. (We have a sound film record of this tour.)

During this filming, Drs. Harris, Bok, and Leonberg told us that the boy seemed to be extraordinarily perceptive and had, in fact, in a way unusual even for certain kinds of mental patients, made up messages for his doctor about events in the doctor's life which the boy had had no evident opportunity to know about. Furthermore, these conversations brought out the fact that this boy and his mother seemed to have an extraordinary awareness of what the other was thinking. The mother could, for example, out of the boy's range of vision (in another room) be shown a word selected at random out of the dictionary. Upon the mother's return to the room where the son waited, the boy could pick out the letters to form the word which the mother had been given in the other room.

We asked if we could film this phenomenon and suggested that we should also like to see what happened if, after the mother returned, his therapist rather than the mother held the tablet. (We have several thousand feet of film of these events.)

I have now viewed the entire film several times, either by myself or with Dr. Albert Scheflen in the company of visiting scientists specially interested in such phenomena. I have viewed some 10 minutes of each of the two filming sessions more than ten times. I have not attempted to record any of the events shown in the film by detailed microkinesic techniques. However, I have attempted to isolate and verify my impressions of certain events which I or one of the other viewing scientists suggested as occurring in the film. These are listed in part below.

First, the overall impression is that while (a) the alphabet is recorded on the tablet, (b) the boy at times looks at the tablet, and (c) the mother watches his finger and the tablet, the phenomenon is insufficiently explained by reference to visible body motion behavior. It would be overeasy to interpret the visible (to each other) behavior as *the* compensation for the boy's refusal to lexicate (to speak intelligible words). However, only extended context analysis will reveal when it is that the boy suddenly stops and appears to stare at his mother or when she appears to look at him. This could be pseudolooking.

Second, the overall impression is that tactile communication is very important between the mother and the son. She maintains contact with him at all times during the alphabet work. The film records perceptible shifts in parts of her trunk and shoulder in contact with him, which occur before, after, and during perceptible shifts in his body parts. These parallel or complementary shifts occur before, during, and after the situation of particular letter choice. During the period that she is grasping him with her hand she and the boy shift both in intensity and extent of contact.

Third, she does not hold the tablet in one position but moves it before, after, and during the letter choice. In several instances, her extent of movement has been measured to be as much as $2\frac{1}{2}$ inches. This leads to an immediate impression that she, not he, at times dictates the choice of letter and word or words. Further viewing leads to the unsubstantiated impression that this is a coalitional choice situation. Both or either suggest or monitor a joint message which is purported (in the interviews) as always originating with him.

Fourth, this cannot be studied solely as a dyadic relationship. The role of the father is demonstrably of importance here. In one case the mother turns to him and asks him to state lexically what the boy has just said and he makes a clear restatement of the "boy's" words. In general impression, it might be said that the father behaves in a manner consistent with other such family constellations which we have viewed. One investigator (Scheflen) suggests that it is the father's task to reinforce the public myth that the mother and son communicate independently.

Fifth, the success of the mother and son in locating the proper word (even words unknown to either insofar as we can ascertain) is indisputable. In the longer stretches of film, we have recorded mistakes, but these are rare and usually in the form of missed prefixes, suffixes, and so forth.

Sixth, in the piece of film which we are discussing here neither the therapist nor the boy is able to point out the word read by the mother. It is reported by the therapist that he is able to take the mother's place in the demonstration but does not have the same rate of success. The failure seen in this film *may* be a matter of filming interference or of particular positioning during the text.

Seventh, at least one clinical observer expressed a strong conviction that the therapist and the boy cooperate to censor the boy's response from "Y-O-U Q-U-I-T" to "Y-O-U Q-U-I-T-E T-O-U-G-H T-O-D-A-Y." There has been a general impression that both mother and therapist cooperate with the boy in the communicative exercise. (Whether or not this is an extension of the mother-father-son system is subject to a variety of interpretations.)

Eighth, there are data in the longer stretches of film which a number of clinicians feel is evidence that mother, father, and boy cooperate to *reduce independent* lexication.

This case is of genuine interest to me. The methods to which I am wedded by training emphasize observation, description, and comparison. This methodology demands systematic rather than random observation, explicit rather than impressionistic description, and is dependent upon relevant comparative data. The controlling elements of systematic observation, the conditions and conventions of description, and the cogent orders of relevancy cannot be predefined. They are functions of the theoretical position from which is drawn the hypotheses which would be tested in further investigation. It is my *impression* that tactility is of special importance to the comprehension of this communicative situation. However, we have only the most preliminary notion of the structuring of human interbody contact. Thus, we have only a theoretical preconception to guide our thinking about this case as an exceptional example of tactile involvement. That is, its unusualness or its novelty may be a function of its dramatic presentation in this kind of family. Without more knowledge about customary interpersonal contact, we cannot be sure that this family has an unusual dependency upon tactile contact. That is, the tactile involvement seen here may only be unusual in its effect upon us, the observers.

For perspective upon this particular case, the investigator may look at the parlor game "Find It." In this game, which has been popular from time to time among adolescents, one player is led from the room while an object is hidden. When the "Searcher" returns (usually blindfolded) he takes the hand of the "Hider." Very often the "Hider" then, unaware, leads the Searcher by minimal muscular movements to the object that has been hidden. I have observed this game a number of times and have been impressed by the wide variation in Searcher response.

There is a considerable body of anecdotal material about the use of "muscle-reading" (either consciously or nonconsciously employed) by fortunetellers and mind readers. In mind-reading acts and in the fortunetelling situation one member of the interaction is literally led to certain insights by not easily perceptible movements on the part of the other. In every society there seems to be a portion of the population unusually sensitive to such stimuli. There is some temptation to close the argument at this point by saying that the boy in the case discussed is probably a sensorily sensitive individual. However, to do so would be to substitute one noninvestigated explanation, "sensorily sensitive" for another, "extrasensory perception."

Depending upon how we understand "communication," we may judge this instance an *exceptional* case of coalitional information sharing or we may see it only as a particularly public case of the customary coalition required of any ongoing associative group. The truth of the matter is that I have still not discovered where to start to begin to answer these preliminary questions. The data as they stand, contain, I am convinced, attractive suggestions to explain "phenomena" such as these. However, so far as I am concerned, I must know more about communication, in general, and tactility, in particular, before I can spend time and energy investigating this or comparable cases. There is something special about this particular case. Whether or not this case represents an example of exceptional phenomena remains to be ascertained, but this case provides an unusual research opportunity. The film, which is ready for viewing (at Eastern Pennsylvania Psychiatric Institute), is protected in its original in film vaults. When and if we or others do develop techniques for studying the phenomenology of such cases there is a clear and unalterable record for examination.

Furthermore, this is a well-studied case in terms of systematic clinical investigation. Excellent case records still being gathered by the psychiatric research team at the Institute of the Pennsylvania Hospital stand ready to be put into perspective by future scholars. No one has yet been entirely successful in combining sound film data with material from clinical records, but there is evidence that we are learning how to make use of the two kinds of data.

PART 2

Isolating Behavior

11. *It Depends on the Point of View**

THERE IS a large, though scarcely comprehensive, literature dealing with the rules, the etiquette, the conventions of formal, interpersonal exchanges. In a sense, such studies might be regarded as describing interpersonal exchanges from above. We are concerned here with studying them from below. That is, by studying that systematic and patterned behavior by means of which men engage in communication with each other, we may be able to understand how these processes order, set limits upon, or, at times, determine the interactive process.

Concern with communication is probably as old as man himself, but the history of the scientific investigation of communicative activity begins relatively recently. Only within the past quarter of a century has there been an effort to describe communication as a systematic process. Up until that time most of the discussion centered upon the talents of men as "good" or "bad" communicators. And, as long as the communicational universe is divided into "good" speakers or listeners and "bad" speakers or listeners or, by extension, into "good" or "bad" writers or readers, the nature of communication can be neither conceptualized nor investigated. Further, if communication is seen as only the expression of the abilities or the personalities of individual men, its nature will remain hidden behind more primary misconceptions about the nature of man.

The intellectual history of Western society could be written in terms of philosophies which describe man as basically good but influenced by evil, or basically bad but influenced by good. A variation on the same theme is provided by those who see man as neutral but torn by the tug-of-war between the imp who rides the left shoulder and the angel on the right. There are those too, who, more

---

*From "Communicating on Purpose," the keynote address at a conference of the Virginia Personnel and Guidance Association, March 21, 1963. [Only a brief introduction and conclusion addressed to that specialized audience are omitted.—B.J.]

discriminating than their fellows who generalize upon all men, distribute good and evil along racial or geographical lines. But the theme remains the same. Western man is psycholinguistically dichotomous. That is, he finds it comfortable, logical, and reasonable to divide the universe into paired categories like tall and short, good and bad, black and white, and simple and complex. We should not be surprised to discover that when man began to investigate man, he should find dichotomous categories such as rational and irrational and intellectual and emotional both familiar and natural.

It has not been sufficient to describe man's *behavior* as either rational or emotional. Western man has always believed that any behavior which the observer sees has to have been the result of a behaver, a causal agent. So, he located emotion in the glandular complex somewhere below the rib case, rationality in the head. By association, "bad" became located with the emotions, "good" with mentality. To be good it was necessary to keep any of the evil from leaking out of the lower aspects of the body (the nether regions) into the upper. Parenthetically, while maintaining the same devotion to the original dichotomy, "experts" have recently advised us not to be *too* mental. They tell us that we should learn to control our emotions properly. And, while I listen respectfully to my fellows who advocate temperance in emotions, I am old enough to remember when temperance meant total abstention.

But what has this to do with communication? By and large those who have discussed communication have been concerned with the production of words and their *proper* usage. Communication has been seen as the result of mental activity which is distorted by emotional activity. Thus, the conception has been that the brain, by definition a naturally good producer of logical thoughts composed of words with precise meanings, emits these under proper stimulation. That is, good, clean, logical, rational, denotative, semantically correct utterances are emitted out of the head if the membrane between mind and body efficiently separates this area of the body from that which produces the bad, dirty, illogical, irrational, connotative, and semantically confusing adulterants. Good communication thus takes place if the unadulterated message enters the ear of the receiver and goes through a clean pipe into an aseptic brain. Of course, it is recognized that the brain may be either imperfect or out of repair. The focus upon communication and its measurement from this perspective is dominated by such an atomistic and loaded conception of man and his behavior that research or theory about communication becomes prescriptive rather than descriptive.

Communication, furthermore, in logical extension of these pre-conceptions, is seen as a process remarkably like that portrayed in the cartoon strips. Man A sends words, assembled grammatically by certain rules, through the air in little balloons into the ear of Man B, who runs them through his mental machinery and sends response sentences in little balloons into the ear of A and so on. It is presumed that if both A and B have properly learned their grammar, have good enough dictionaries which they studied adequately, spoke loud enough and were neither of them deaf, and did not become too emotional, communication has taken place. It is further assumed that by the study of these words, utilizing the same grammars and dictionaries, an outsider will be able to ascertain what it is that was communicated.

With such philosophies as these, scholars were hardly encouraged to look at the actual behavior of communication. The records which we are able to review about early conceptions of communication are records left by literate men. Not only were these men literate but they were devoted to the perfection of literacy. It is scarcely surprising that they placed such a high evaluation upon reading and writing that they unconsciously conceived the spoken language to be a clumsy and imperfect derivation of the written. Such a position cannot possibly reveal that the written language is rather a special shorthand of the spoken. A majority of all discussions of communication have thus been phrased in terms of the passage of words from writer to reader, from speaker to auditor. The accompanying behavior, even when recognized as coterminous with the words, has been by and large relegated to a position of being, at best, a modifier of the messages carried by the words. More commonly, the accompanying behavior is seen to interfere with the transmission of meaning, and "good" communication depends upon the elimination or reduction of the extraneous circumlexical behavior.

Let us pause for a moment to consider this more fully. By such definitions as these preconceptions invoke, communication is that process whereby A, having information not possessed by B, passes that information or some portion of it on to B. B then, in response, informs A what he has received. Hopefully, B responds in a way that makes it possible for A to repeat or amend the message to make the original information more completely accessible to B. It requires little thought to recognize that communication is thus restricted to those situations in which we have a teacher (A) and a learner (B); A possessing and sending the knowledge, B receiving it. If we examine as communicative *only* situations like the relationships between a priest and the parishioner, a sergeant and a private, a doctor and a patient, an omnipotent parent and a totally dependent child, we are going to have a very special conception of communication. And we are likely to think of these situations in a very narrow and limited way. We shall return to this point later in our discussion.

It has been this conception which has occasioned much of the prevalent misuse of that highly useful tool, information theory. As a theory or as a model, information theory is not to be denigrated because borrowers have misused it. However, at its simplest—and, unfortunately, it has been the simplest conception of the work of the information theorists which has been borrowed by specialists from other fields—information theory sets out the following model:

In Figure 1, a black box, A, has only three pieces of information in it. These are □ ⬜ and △. A has a transmission orifice (a) through which the information passes on its way to B, a black box with a reception orifice (b). All of the difficulties of encoding or decoding which intervene between A and B are described as "noise." By this theory, the information to be found in B following transmission as compared with the information emitted by A—if the noise is taken into account—can be regarded as a measure of the communication. Now, so far as I know, no information theorist is so naive as to fail to see that the situation is much more complicated than this and that this is hardly a model for the exhaustive examination of human behavior.

Customarily, a second diagram is designed to come closer to, although not to be taken as more than a model of, certain very limited real situations:

Figure 2 indicates that A and B have orifices (a) and (b) which are both senders and receivers. Thus, (1) is a stimulus message, which is followed by a response (2) from B. This message (2) is a corrective to A who sends (3). B responds to (3) by correcting the originally

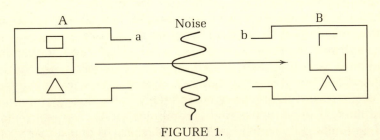

FIGURE 1.

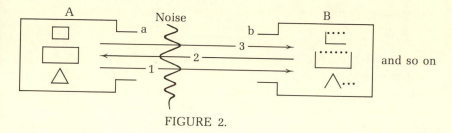

FIGURE 2.

received message. He then transmits the shape of the correction back to A who then sends another message, and so on. This model represents a theoretical position which is elegant and attractive, particularly so since it is so easily relatable to simplicistic psychological models about man. It is a fine model of certain aspects of a telegraphic system, of a telephonic or radio message system, but it is not about the structured behavior which constitutes *social* communication—or, at least, as a model it relegates to "noise" such a major proportion of all social communication as to make the model, as it stands, of little value to the communication theorist as a device for the investigation of the significant elements of human communication. Information theory has been of incalculable value in delineating fields for investigation for the student of communication analysis. It has been an efficient instrument for the location of communicational problems—it is not a tool for the solution of many of them. Its greatest utility has come from the fact that it serves to desentimentalize the message process. With such an outline of our universe of investigation, we are freed to tackle problems which had not been seen before. Moreover, information models provide excellent tools for the description of myths about unilateral transmission of knowledge. It can make especially clear those situations which are so constructed that the respondent can only inform the sender about imperfect transmission. We shall return to make use of this model later in our discussion.

One of the reasons that inappropriately borrowed models such as these—and there are many which are more popular and far less descriptive—have come into usage as ways of describing human communication is that they stand the test of naive review. That is, such models "feel right" to us. Or to say it another way, this kind of stimulus-response model is descriptive of communication in a way in which we were taught to reflect upon it. When we introspect about an interaction, a conversation, an interchange, our memory is that

Time: T¹   T²   T³   T⁴   T⁵   T⁶   T⁷   T . . .

A: —   —   _____   — —   —   ___

B: —   —   —   ___   —

Behavior

FIGURE 3.

our discussion was a dialogue during which silence was interrupted by vocalization, followed by silence, followed by silence, followed by vocalization, and so on (see Fig. 3 above).

Our memory (or an observation which is made in terms of this preconception) tells us thus that communication is, at its simplest, a dialogue. It seems to be structured like a play, made up of more or less serial messages which are punctuated by silences in which nothing is happening. This is a folk reflection which happens to coincide with an overextended information model. Emerging social communication theory based upon behavioral research, however, maintains that this is not the case at all. We get an entirely different picture of communication if we recognize that communication is not just what happens in one channel. We cannot investigate communication by isolating and measuring one channel, the acoustic (that is, the sound-sending and sound-receiving channel). Communication, upon investigation, appears to be a system which makes use of the channels of all of the sensory modalities. By this model, communication is a continuous process utilizing the various channels and the combinations of them as appropriate to the particular situation. Figure 4 abstracts this model.

If we think of Channel 1 as being in Fig. 3 the audio-acoustic (vocal) channel, Channel 2 as the kinesthetic-visual channel, Channel 3 would be the odor-producing–olfactory channel, Channel 4 would be the tactile and so on. Thus, while no single channel is in constant use, one or more channels are always in operation. Communication is the term which I apply to this continuous process.

Time: T¹   T²   T³   T⁴   T⁵   T⁶   T⁷   T⁸   T . . .

Channel 1   —   —   —   —   —   —   —

Channel 2   ___   _____   _____   _____ ___   ___

Channel 3   _____   _____   _____
etc.

FIGURE 4.

The structured and systematic organization of the behavior of the individual channels I describe as infracommunicational. Thus, the scientific discipline of linguistics examines language in its broadest sense. Language and paralanguage is that formal behavior which utilizes the audio-acoustic channel and is an infracommunicational system. We can no more understand communication by exhaustive investigation of language and paralanguage than we can understand physiology by, say, the exhaustive investigation of the circulatory or nervous system.

Channel 2, the kinesthetic-visual channel, is utilized by communicative body motion. Kinesics is the discipline concerned with such behavior. Communicational body motion, like language and paralanguage, is organized into an infracommunicational system. I and other students of the infracommunicational systems have been studying the structures of these systems and have been trying to discover how they interact or combine in the communication process. This is not the occasion to discuss the technical problems involved here. Let me say only that as experimentation proceeds, the intimate relationship between them becomes more evident. Certainly by the time one deals with phrases or sentences, their roles are inseparable. Since we have only the most preliminary knowledge about the tactile, the gustatory, or the olfactory channels, it is impossible at this time to predict their special contributions to the communicative process. It is already clear, however, that they are ultimately inseparable in the larger system.

What led to the decision to abandon the older model which maintained that communication was essentially a verbal (and lexical at that) process, modified by gestures, pushing and holding, tasting and odor emitting and receiving? As late as 1955 a leading scholar told me that he thought of communication as a picture—language being the image-figure, body motion being the frame around it. Certainly the traditional version makes good sense. It has the further virtue that it requires no new special training for the investigator. A trained philosopher or psychologist or a team of judges equipped with a good dictionary can study a verbal transcript, hold all other behavior as constant, and derive a judgment about communication. This is a perfectly useful and limited conception of *derived* human behavior. From my point of view, such a conception as: "Verbal (actually lexical) material when modified by other behavior (which is not examined, but assumed constant or trivial) equals communication," builds in an experimental error exactly as one which would describe the physiological system as endocrine or circulatory behavior with the other component systems held constant or as of trivial influence. One of the unfortunate results of this kind of thinking has been a plethora of discussion of "nonverbal communication" which is no more than an inversion of the earlier model. Experimentation using such a model has been interesting but largely noncontributory. The simplest answer is that the data of interaction, once examined, demanded a reorganization of basic theory. The old theories were just too limited to explain the observed behavior. In short, they are insufficiently productive theories.

Traditionally, as outlined above, communication has been discussed as a psychological process. The emphasis has been placed upon the individual sender or receiver. Logically, such investigations have stressed mechanisms of central concern to the psychologist. Perception, afferent-efferent nerve systems, and learning studies have dominated research from this perspective. From the point of view of the analyst of social communication, these studies are more directly relevant to the nature, state, and activity of the sensory modality and perhaps to the channel. They are of concern to him in communication research only when he seeks to understand particular distortional behaviors in particular interactional situations. For him, communication is a social, not a psychological phenomenon; psychological reductionism serves only to obscure the central issues involved in the investigation of human interaction.

Albert Scheflen has elucidated this point, in lecture, by analogy with the impossibility of understanding a baseball game by the summation of the behavior of the individual players. As he has pointed out, even if it were possible to exhaustively describe the behavior of each of the eighteen men involved, such a technique would be so inefficient as to indefinitely postpone our comprehension of the game. On the other hand, he continues, once we understand the regularities imposed by the game, it is relatively easy to measure the individual performances of the players. Such an operation will not *explain* individual variations in behavior, but it does point them up for further examination.

Research on human communication as a systematic and structured organization could not be initiated until we had some idea about the organization of society itself. So long as we conceived of communication as merely a mechanical process of action and reaction—either trial and error or the result of some kind of contract between individual men—its systematic nature remained as hidden from investigation as was that of physiology a hundred years ago.

Physiological processes could not be detected so long as all research upon the body was predicated upon the proposition that the behavior of the body was to be described as the sum of the behaviors of the individual organs plus some mysterious implanted force called life. Vesalius tells how medieval anatomists, sitting high on a chair above the cadaver of a pig, pointed out to faithful students the "natural" parts of the body. His philosophical ruminations about the functions of these parts effectively prevented any but the most heretical from suggesting that this was not a particularly productive exercise. Even when grave robbers provided the anatomist with human cadavers and the anatomist himself wielded the dissecting knife, his preconceptions precluded discovery.

It is well to remember that physiology as we know it is less than a century old. The discovery of electricity led to the development of information about neural processes; the emergence of modern biochemistry laid the groundwork for endocrinology; clinical and, particularly, military medicine established a basis for the comprehension of the circulatory system. However, until the living system as a whole was examined, modern physiology with its complex considerations of homeostasis, balance and organization of its subsystems, could not be conceived.

As long as the investigation of communication was limited to the dissection of the cadaver of speech, writing—by anatomists who used imperfectly understood Latin rules of grammar to describe its parts—and relied on introspectively derived dictionaries to determine its meanings, the communication process could not be detected, much less understood. This operation, like the researches, psychological or sociological, that depend on its products, can do no more than prescriptive or deceptively elaborate but clearly inconclusive correlation studies. No statistical procedure can assemble bark, dead leaves, maple sugar, and the ashes from a burning log into a comprehensible tree.

The accumulating scientific behavioral investigations of many societies, human and animal, over the past half-century have led us to the point where we have had to recognize that for both men and animals society is a natural habitat, that both are by nature social. When growing sophistication carried us beyond either simple instinct theory or equally simple learning theory to the point that we could recognize the necessary interdependence of members of social groupings, animal or human, atomistic explanations no longer sufficed to elucidate either individual or group behavior.

This has occasioned major revolutions in theory. It has made us recognize that man did not, in his special wisdom, invent society. We have been forced to see that even the earliest complex animals were born into a social system to which they had to be adapted if they were to subsist—that these social groupings were organized so that the functions of sustaining life are complexly distributed. The individual member could not sustain life without certain special relationships with his fellows. Within the past decade the old formula of evolution (from inanimate to animate—from single-cell to multicelled animals—from sea dweller to land dweller, through the amphibians—to man—to society) has been restated. Today we know that while man *may* be the only animal to have culture, he is certainly not the first to be social.

We have had to re-turn our attention to social learning; if animals were not merely systems which responded to the genetic, the instinctual, imperative, how did they become part of the complex behavioral systems which the ethologists and comparative psychologists have described for us? We have no clear evidence yet of any animal engaging in teaching, but (if we do not allow ourselves to be misled by charming studies of bees, termites, and ants) it is clear that they learn.

The psychologist has made tremendous strides in delineating some of the mechanisms of animal learning—there are even studies that contain suggestive ideas about certain aspects of human learning—but we are here concerned with the transmission system between the members of a social grouping, rather than with its particular mechanism within the organism. Our attention has been redirected toward that process by which the member of the group makes and maintains contact with his fellows so that patterned participation is possible. There is an increasing body of evidence that not only do animals signal relational states like anger and sexual readiness to one another (and even these in a far more complex manner than hitherto surmised) but that age, grade, status, courtship, territoriality, play, mood, states of health and of alarm or well-being are completely and intricately patterned and learned. To be viable members of their social groupings, fish, birds, mammals, and man must engage in significant symbolization—must learn to recognize, receive, and send ordered messages. In other words, the individual must learn to behave in appropriate ways which permit the other members of the group to recognize and anticipate his behavior. Society is that way in which behavior is calibrated so that existence is not a process of continuous and wasteful trial and error.

As we came to see how continuously important this was for living creatures, we were forced to take another look at human communication. The new informational aspect of communication, while certainly significant to human communication, is relatively limited in occurrence. We may describe communication as containing two kinds of messages—one rare and intermittent in occurrence—the other continuous. The first I came to think of as the *new informational* aspect, the other, the *integrational* aspect of communication. I am, of course, suspicious of the dichotomies imposed by these definitions. I assume that as we learn more, our categorizations will become more complex and precise. However, this construction freed us from earlier biases which limited the communicational process to the point of incomprehensibility and allowed us to take on the task of the exhaustive analysis of interactional behavior. From a research situation which had limited our vision to such a small portion of the process that its investigation gave trivial results, we were now inundated with data of myriad shapes and sizes. Unless some way could be found to order this data for investigation, we were in an even less profitable position than before.

Groundwork for the avoidance of the psychological fallacy in the study of language was laid by the European linguistic scholars of the last century who recognized that language is ordered and has a structure which changes independently of the culture or personality of its member speakers. Yet these insights were not fully exploited until the American linguists, Leonard Bloomfield and Edward Sapir, following the lead of Ferdinand de Saussure and the early Sanskrit grammarians, insisted that language could not be understood until adequate descriptions of spoken language behavior were developed. Bloomfield, Sapir, and their students have insisted upon rigorous descriptions of language behavior without recourse to *a priori* psychological or historistic explanations. The success of their investigations has had a controlling influence upon the development of kinesics. Not only have the descriptive linguists conclusively demonstrated the systematic, learned, and patterned nature of the linguistic process, but they have met Occam's criterion by the search for simpler, rather than more complex, explanations for the phenomena which they were observing.

However, there was no easy way to transform linguistic procedures, so effective in the description and delineation of audible behavior, into an instrument for the investigation of the communicative aspects of body motion behavior. The observer of human body motion soon recognizes what a contribution silence has been to the student of language. As a starting point, at least, the linguist can define his subject matter as that audible behavior which terminates silence and is, itself, terminated by silence. (A number of modern linguists are becoming increasingly curious now about the patterned shape—the duration and the special order of appearance—of silence. However, this interest in silence has been stimulated by exhaustive investigations of sound. The linguist did not start with a preconception of a field of continuous sound.) The student of body motion behavior, as he becomes a more practiced observer, becomes increasingly aware of the apparently endless movement, the shifting, wriggling, squirming, adjusting, and resituating which characterize the living human body in space. If the entire human body becomes the organ for communicative movement as an analog to the vocal apparatus as the organ of speech, how can he hope to deal with the flood of information which he observes? His would seem to be an impossible task.

The solution is almost absurdly easy. If we examine the functioning of the lips, the tongue and teeth, the palate, the esophagus, the larynx, pharynx, and lungs, we become quickly aware that to call these the "organs of speech" is to disregard their continuous function as related to breathing and swallowing. The fact that they are adaptable to operations whereby the stream of air passing through them is sounded, impeded, or stopped and that these sounds are utilizable by the language system does not limit them to being organs of speech, nor is all of their behavior speech behavior. Laryngescopes, pharyngescopes, and X rays may make us better able to understand the relationship between somatic behavior and that collected on some kind of sound frequency recorder. However, the data which we derive from this examination are not about speech or language but about physiology or acoustics.

(Let me hasten to say that I do not regard the study of acoustics or speech physiology as trivial. I think that such studies when correlated *with similarly manipulable data* from linguistics or sociology are of prime importance to our understanding of human communicative behavior. All too often, however, elaborately precise machinery is utilized to produce elegant and quantifiable data which are then naively correlated with or extrapolated to descriptions of speech behavior of a type already discredited by the turn of the century.)

Comparably, all of the observed shifts of the human body are not of equal significance to the human communicational system. As the organs involved in breathing and swallowing are *also* involved in vocalic communicative behavior, so also is the activity of the skin, musculature, and skeleton involved in communicative behavior. Which particular behaviors are of patterned communicative value, and thus abstractable without falsification, can be determined only by the systematic investigation of the behavior in the communicational context. Obviously, just as much of the audible activity produced by the oral-pneumatic cavity is prelinguistic, so is much of visible body motion prekinesic. Our problem is to describe the structure of body motion communication behavior in a way which allows us to measure the significance of particular motions or complexes of motions to the communicational process.

To continue our analogy with the study of spoken language, in research the student of communicative body motion finds that he cannot rely upon his informants to tell him which behaviors are of communicative significance or what is the meaning of this behavior. Certainly he cannot rely upon the informant to tell him how to perform these behaviors in a meaningful manner. Such information is simply not available to even the most successful untrained speaker or actor. We may recall that although English has been spoken for hundreds of years, only within the past twenty have we come to recognize that spoken English utilizes tone and loudness variations to make it a stress and pitch language. Any native speaker could tell when a speaker misused these aspects of the language but he could not report accurately *what* was wrong in the speech he heard. That is, for instance, a child of five would have no difficulty in distinguishing between a dirty dog-catcher and a dirty dog catcher. He could report that the first was a dirty (with a variety of connotations possible for "dirty") catcher of dogs. He'd have not too much difficulty in recognizing that a dirty dog *catcher* was one who caught dirty dogs. He might even be able to extend this patterned recognition to the production of other jokes. A 10-year-old once told me: "A king sits on a shaky throne; President Kennedy is on a *rocking* chair." However, he'd have no way of abstracting the structural principles which underlie these two examples. It is unnecessary to know the abstract nature of a pattern in order to behave in a patterned manner. Nor is it necessary to know the nature of a pattern to recognize that someone is behaving in an unusual manner. However, only if we know something about patterning can we determine whether any given piece of behavior is idiosyncratic or pathological, or is, rather, representative of normal behavior from a different system.

Children, as do recent learners of a second language, often play with its pieces as this patterning strikes them. One such joke, which became a comedian's standby, occurred when someone took a stem form from the word "uncouth" and described an elegant man as "couth." The fact that we've had no "couth" since the days of the Anglo-Saxons did not prevent a child from making a patterned joke on a model whereby /able/ is removable from /unable/ or /attractive/ from /unattractive/.

Comparably, while an informant can tell us when a person from his culture moves "wrong" or "badly" or "awkwardly," his descriptions of what was done wrong are likely to be highly unreliable. Certainly, no informant that I've worked with has been able to detail reliably what a mover did when he was moving correctly. By extension of this, all informants may have a common misconception about items of movement. Not only can fifty million Frenchmen be wrong but they are highly likely to be wrong the more they are in agreement. This is one of the reasons why the linguistic or kinesic anthropologist distrusts the "judging technique" so dear to the hearts of some other behavioral scientists.

A case in point here is that behavior called "gestures." Almost any informant from most societies can quickly be taught to give the investigator an extensive set of examples of stylized body motions and their "meanings" upon request. For instance, it is relatively easy to get an Arabic informant to stroke his beard to represent a gesture which he will tell you means "there goes a pretty girl." A South Italian will be able to tell you that to pull the lobe of his right ear with his right forefinger and thumb is a gesture which has the same meaning. An American male informant when requested to give you a gesture which has this meaning may make two out and in movements with his paralleled hands while moving his hands downward from the shoulder level. (Try starting at the bottom and working upward in the gesture to feel how stylized and kinesthesiologically patterned this movement is.) Or, your American male may make a circle of his right thumb and forefinger and kiss the air behind it to give an alternate form with the same "meaning."

The "gesture" is deceptively easy to abstract and there is an extensive bibliography of gestures from a variety of cultures.* Often

---

* See Francis Hayes, "Gestures: A Working Bibliography," *Southern Folklore Quarterly* Vol. XXI (Dec. 1957), pp. 218–317. For an unusually lucid gestural inventory, see Robert L. Saitz and Edward J. Cervenka, *Columbian and North American Gestures: An Experimental Study* (Bogota, Columbia, Centro Columbo Americano), Carrera 7 # 23–49, 1962.

these gestures are arranged with their meanings listed in diction-arylike form. Like dictionaries, these are useful assemblages of data for certain purposes. However, such lists, like dictionaries, can be quite deceptive when overliteralized as though they described pre-cise, exclusive and inclusive, meaning-carrying forms of behavior. To see examples of such inappropriate usage one need only review the literature on signs and symbols (including much which has been written about the deaf-and-dumb sign language). A number of scholars, too sophisticated to contend that any word has a precise and invariable meaning, will maintain that there are gestures which carry an absolutely denotative message.*

12. Gestures: Signals or Partials†

As ANTHROPOLOGISTS have become increasingly aware of the im-portance of comparative body motion studies, evidence has accumulated to support the proposition that "gestures" are culture linked both in shape and in meaning.

During World War II, I became at first bemused, and later in-trigued, by the repertoire of meanings which could be drawn upon by an experienced United States Army private and transmitted in accompaniment to a hand salute. The salute, a conventionalized movement of the right hand to the vicinity of the anterior portion of the cap or hat, could, without occasioning a court martial, be performed in a manner which could satisfy, please, or enrage the most demanding officer. By shifts in stance, facial expression, the velocity or duration of the movement of salutation, and even in the selection of inappropriate contexts for the act, the soldier could dignify, ridicule, demean, seduce, insult, or promote the recipient

*[This selection is continued in the following pages, after a few more examples of gestures from another article.—B.J.]

†The first two paragraphs are excerpted and adapted from "Communication without Words," in "L'Aventure Humaine," *Encyclopédie des Sciences de l'Homme* Vol. 5 (Geneva: Kister; Paris: De la Grange Batelière, 1968), pp. 157–166. The rest of this section is from "Communicating on Purpose," presented to the Virginia Personnel and Guidance Association on March 21, 1965.

of the salute. By often almost imperceptible variations in the performance of the act, he could comment upon the bravery or cowardice of his enemy or ally, could signal his attitude toward army life or give a brief history of the virtuosity of a lady from whom he had recently arisen. I once watched a sergeant give a 3-second, brilliant criticism of English cooking in an elaborate inverted salute to a beef-and-kidney pie. It was this order of *variability on a central theme* which stimulated one of the primary "breakthroughs" in the development of kinesics.

My own research has led me to examine extensively American gestural behavior and I have done preliminary work with German, French, Italian, and Spanish gesture behavior. From this work I can say conclusively that in the American and English movement system, and it looks likely to be the same for these other less well-studied cultures, "gestures" not only do not stand alone as behavioral isolates but they also do not have explicit and invariable meanings. Under analysis, those aspects of body motion which are commonly called gestures turn out to be like stem forms in language. That is, these are bound forms which require suffixual, prefixual, infixual, or transfixual behavior to be attached to them to determine their function in the interactive process. Like /couth/ they cannot stand alone.

The isolation of gestures and the attempt to understand them led to the most important findings of kinesic research. This original study of gestures gave the first indication that kinesic structure is parallel to language structure. By the study of gestures in context, it became clear that the kinesic system has forms which are astonishingly like words in language. This discovery in turn led to the investigation of the components of these forms and to the discovery of the larger complexes of which they were components. At least as far as English, American, and German kinesic systems are concerned, it has become clear that there are body behaviors which function like significant sounds, that combine into simple or relatively complex units like words, which are combined into much longer stretches of structured behavior like sentences or even paragraphs.

This does not mean that even for American movers we have exhaustively studied communicative body behavior. We do know now that it can be studied.

The other direct result of the original survey of gestural behavior was the fact that even this limited kind of survey dispelled another primary misconception about body motion material. This is the "more natural" conception of the body. We have, over the years, come to recognize that the "mind" and its products are subject to training. Only the most ethnocentric can believe that theirs is a natural language while other societies speak some distortion of it. However, there is a prevalent belief which maintains that, beyond certain motor skills which are specially developed in particular societies, there is a natural pattern of movement which other peoples have either learned badly, not evolved to, or lost. Or, alternately, it has been assumed that there are universal, core movement patterns characteristic of all men. It is, of course, self-evident that with a common somatic organization, men will stand with their legs, lift with their hands and arms, manipulate with their fingers, turn, lift, and lower their heads, and so on. However, although we have been searching for 15 years, we have found no gesture or body motion which has the same social meaning in all societies. The immediate implications of this are clear. Insofar as we know, there is no body motion or gesture that can be regarded as a universal symbol. That is, we have been unable to discover any single facial expression, stance, or body position which conveys an identical meaning in all societies. I am unprepared, as yet, to conclude from this that the relationship between various body motion systems is parallel to (or different from) the traceable relationship between language families. However, I think that not only can we dispense with so-called "natural" gestures as being single-culture bound, but we can be prepared to discover that the methods of organizing body motion into communicative behavior by various societies may be as variable as the structures of the languages of these societies.

There is one last item which we must deal with at this time. This has to do with "expressive" behavior. Almost as soon as the linguist or the kinescist meets someone he is asked, "What can you tell about me from my speech or my body motion?" More fearful or more coquettish respondents manifest considerable anxiety that their behavior is going to reveal their deepest secrets to the expert. Unless the specialist is in a particularly playful or vindictive mood, he has a proper answer to these queries. It is quite true that the individual member of the society has had special experiences which make his performance differ from that of his fellows. To use Ted Schwartz's useful distinction, the special idiolect or the idiomovement system of any individual is a product of the special experiences of his idioverse. However, the specialist cannot determine how distinctively individual any particular performance is before he knows the structure of significant ranges of behavior for a particular behavioral area. When he makes such judgments in an *a priori* manner, he abdicates his professional role and interprets as an amateur, as do other members of society. Because such behaviors are communicational, as members of society, we use the pattern of another's behavior to anticipate and to react to him—but the scientific study of expressional behavior as a reliable test for determining underlying personality dynamics must await extensive experimentation before we can test productive value and reliability of clinical judgments. It is the hope of the anthropological linguist or kinesicist that he will some day be able to describe the kinesic or linguistic pattern in a way which will make individual variations more evident and understandable. It is his hope, too, that by the analysis of communicational behavior, he will be able to develop objective descriptions of behavior which will replace present impressionistic categories. However, his primary concern is with interaction, with social and not with individual behavior.

13. *Handicaps in the Linguistic-Kinesic Analogy**

THE DEPENDENCY of structural kinesics (that is, those aspects of kinesic research which deal with infracommunicative, structural matters) upon structural linguistics is evident throughout this volume, and some of the thoughts evolving from this relationship and some examples of the application of linguistic techniques to the study of body motion are presented in the essays which follow. However profitable this dependency has been, it is not without handicap. The universes of sound and of light, of hearing and seeing, and of sound production and light pattern production may appear coextant in nature but they occupy very different strata. The fact that afferent and efferent pathways are traversed by roughly the same

*[These observations were written in 1969 for this book.—B.J.]

physiological and sociological processes does not make the various communicative channels or the behavior of which they are composed identical. Techniques and theories developed over the last 2000 years of linguistic research are now and may in the future remain quite relevant for kinesic research and are absolutely necessary to communicational research. However, these techniques are not all immediately and without adaptation transferable to kinesic research. For example, the informant technique, so basic to research on spoken language, is difficult to control in the investigation of kinesic material. It has been our experience that informants are so easily influenced by the researcher concentrating on body behavior (perhaps because we have still not invented a concept like "silence" for body motion) that an informant often learns in a single trial. Moreover, while an informant, in most cases, can quickly adapt to the tape-recorded sample of speech and help the linguistic investigator in his isolation procedure, viewing habits (particularly of the Westerners whom we have been studying) intrude upon, if they do not actually determine, the data we are trying to isolate.

There are other more serious difficulties involved in the comparison and intercorrelation of linguistic and kinesic data. As discussed below, perhaps one of the most productive ideas resulting from the interdisciplinary work at Palo Alto was that of nonsimultaneity of communicative signals. When the stream of data derived from kinesic research was placed in association with linguistic data on a score sheet marked off in squares representing sequential time, there was no one-to-one time correlation between the visually received events and those received acoustically. That is, structural moments in kinesic time were not coextant with structural moments in linguistic time, when *time* was subdivided into shapes measured by motion-picture film frames or by horological convention. True, at the level of kinesic stress superfixes, discussed on pages 132–142, spoken phrases and syntactic sentences were marked by contemporaneous kinesic structure. And, kinesic *demonstratives* (the behavior by means of which the oral description of events is supplemented by conventionalized "air pictures") are normally coextant in time with vocalic behavior. Certain oral ejaculations and single lexeme interjections may also be accompanied by coextant kinesic behavior. What I think of as "closed emphasis" statements, in which the message carries with it a statement to ignore other statements in the communicative context *while commenting upon the content of these statements,* may also carry temporally congruent behavior from the two channels within the same horological boundaries. Furthermore, the kinesic markers (isolated movements described on pages 119–127, which operate in connection with or in substitution for certain pronouns, adverbs, and adjectives) often occupy clock time spaces coextant with the words with which they coordinate.

These behavioral shapes, the stress superfixes, the demonstratives, the kinesic markers, and the isolates (of closed emphasis) constitute only a small portion of the events present in the body motion stream. That these represent a *minority* of the events which contribute to the communicative stream is no measure of their importance to the stream. If we follow the basic tenet of linguistic-kinesic procedure which demands the exhaustion of data, the non-contemporaneous linguistic and kinesic events need explanation, too.

Although a majority of the descriptive linguists recognize that *interactional discourse or conversation is the natural situation of language usage,* linguistic techniques have focused upon structural abstractions in the shapes of phones, phonemes, morphemes, phrases, and syntactic sentences. The restraint which they have shown in the careful specification of their universe of investigation is one of the great methodological achievements of the social or behavioral sciences. By this methodology linguists have been able to avoid, or at least to make explicit, certain semantic problems which have burdened more philosophical and psychological discussions of language behavior. However, for those who would comprehend social interaction, communication, and the relationship between language and communication and culture, this discipline has exacted a price. The linguist has tended, like the schedule- and questionaire-bound psychologists and sociologists (as well as anthropologists), to live in a sentence-shaped universe. Men speak sentences to one another, just as they speak words to one another; neither are final units, both are dependent upon larger communicative structures. Those who would seek meaning *inside* sentences can learn from the experience of those who sought meaning *inside* words.

14. "Redundancy" in Multichannel Communication Systems*

PERHAPS ONE of the most elusive and thus most debatable concepts in emerging communication theory is that of "redundancy." Many of us will recall the concept from our schoolday classes in rhetoric. Webster defines redundant as "more than enough; over abundant; excessive." Pejorative in implication, "redundancy" is in criticism applied to any "unnecessary" duplication of words within a sentence.

When information theorists such as C. E. Shannon and W. Weaver began to construct models for the investigation of informational passage and exchange, they modified the meaning to cover all signs, that is, behavior, that served to reduce the ambiguity of a message. Colin Cherry in his useful book, *On Human Communication,* defines redundancy as "a property of languages, codes and sign systems *which arises from a superfluity of rules* [our italics] and which facilitates communication in spite of all the factors of uncertainty acting against it" (1957, p. 19).

These two definitions, the first based on conventionalized precepts for rhetorical style, the second, on modern informational theory and research, hold in common the primary assumption that communicational systems contain superfluous behaviors which do not directly contribute to the comprehensibility of a communicational incident. Let me hasten to say that I have no quarrel with this term as a descriptive concept useful to the critic of composition. Furthermore, it is an exceedingly useful tool in experimentation on single-channel message systems (or, even, in the comparison of two or more channels). The information theorists have used the concept to advantage in the investigation of telephone, telegraph, and written message systems. However, this concept must not be brought *carelessly* into the laboratory of the scientist concerned with communi-

*Presented to the American Orthopsychiatric Association on April 24, 1962, with a brief introduction, as "An Approach to Communication"; in slightly different form it was published in *Family Process* Vol. 1 (1962), pp. 194–201.

cation as a central aspect of human interaction. Cherry issues a warning that should be attended to by those overimpressed with information theory as a source of models and concepts for the investigation of social interaction:

> When we speak to a friend, we carefully construct our words and phrases, building in redundancy, as we judge to be necessary for him to understand; with speech this is a running affair, because we are watching and listening to his reactions, and redundancy may be put in, in a changing manner, moment by moment. . . . Writing must make up for the lack of gesture or stress, if it is to combat ambiguity, by introducing redundancy through a wider vocabulary and closer adherence to grammatical structure. [1957, p. 120]

If we can use the term "redundancy" without the normative judgment of unnecessary, superfluous, extravagant, emptily repetitive, nonfunctioning signals, it will focus attention upon the richness of the communicative process. If however, out of awareness, we permit the concept a pseudotechnicality, we may infect our research procedure in a manner which will preclude any real comprehension of the structure or function of communication. It is all too easy to assure ourselves that there is in any social interchange a *central,* a *primary,* or a *real* meaning which is only modified by a redundant environment. It is all too easy to move from the position that describes certain behavior as redundant to one which defines such behavior as *only* redundant.

Our temptation to classify certain aspects of a transaction as the central message and other aspects as serving only as modifiers rests upon untested assumptions about communication. One of these assumptions is that communication is about the passage of new information from one person to another. Certainly, this new-informational activity is one aspect of the communicative process. But if the research at Palo Alto by Bateson, Birdwhistell, Brosin, Fromm-Reichmann, Hockett, and McQuown and at Eastern Pennsylvania Psychiatric Institute by Austin, Scheflen, and the writer is valid, the conveyance of new information is no more important than what we call the *integrational* aspect of the communicative process. In the broadest sense, the integrational aspect includes all behavioral operations which:

1. keep the system in operation

2. regulate the interactional process

3. cross-reference particular messages to comprehensibility in a particular context

4. relate the particular context to the larger contexts of which the interaction is but a special situation

I recognize that the conceptual contrast of new informational and integrational does not preclude distortion by the investigator appalled by the apparently limitless signal activity present in any isolated interactive scene. By some kind of sleight-of-hand, the investigator, flooded by data, can predefine the qualities of novelty, record the behaviors so defined, and lump the residue as integrational. He will not be isolated from his academic fellows by such an approach. He will find methodological companionship among those who separate the communicational stream into the cognitive and the affective (or emotive). Review of the literature is persuasive that some researchers have used far less rigorous methods for describing the behavior defined as affective than they do for the so-called cognitive aspects of the interactions. Nor will his efforts be unsympathetically received by those who are quite disciplined in their descriptions of linguistic behavior (which they recognize as digital in shape) but who become poetic and indistinct as they deal with other behaviors which they predefine as analogic.

The view of communicational reality which underlies this tendency to divide the universe into the definitive and specific and the general and modificatory gains support from introspection. It seems "natural" to believe that words or words plus grammar carry meaning in interaction and that all other behavior is either modificatory, expressive of the individual personality differences of the particular participants (and thus nongeneralizable) or just incidental and accidental noise. It does "feel" as if communication is a stop-and-go intermittent process of action and reaction. To be asked to view communication as an altogether ordered and continuous system is anathemic to most of us. The suggestion that the idiosyncratic elements of the process are only to be detected *after the isolation of structure* comes as an insult for those of us who find our individuality most clearly demonstrated or proved by our communications. We think of communication as centrally verbal—centrally cognitive and centrally willful and only laterally and by imperfection influenced by the other modalities of interaction. It is no surprise that our research designs will mirror this structure of conventional reality.

I am not completely convinced that such descriptions as these will not in the final analysis provide models which contribute to the description of the communicational structure. I insist, however, that they cannot be assumed to be descriptively correct, simply because they are popular. In fact, I am suspicious of such characterizations as these simply because they are so familiar. Such suspicions approach certitude as I inspect the regularity of multilevel and interdependent patterning in a 10-second or 1-minute transcript of a sound film recorded session.

The investigator gains a certain freedom by the willingness to concede that the communicational stream can be made up of multiple behavioral patterns existing on different time levels. Under such analysis both the specific structural meaning of an event at a given level and the cross-referencing function of it at other levels of analysis become manifest. Furthermore, although at first glance such a methodology seems laborious and prohibitively time-consuming, as we gain analytic control of these levels, the communicational process becomes increasingly simple and increasingly ordered.

It has been our experience that even preliminary research, using structural linguistic and kinesic methods, lends confidence to a description of communication as being a continuous process made up of isolable discontinuous units. These units are always multifunctional; they have distinguishable contrast meaning on one level and a cross-referencing function (meaning) on others. Under inspection, each level of behavioral activity is discontinuous—that is, is made up of a series of discrete, arbitrary elements—and none of these elements has explicit or implicit social meaning in and of itself. However, when, following analysis, our levels are reassembled in observational time, the whole becomes a continuous process. The exciting thing about such an assembled, multilevel description of the communicational process is that it becomes immediately clear that it is just as easy (and unrewarding) to describe the lexical material as modifiers of the remainder of the behavior as it is to define the remainder of the communicational behavior as modifying the lexical.

It may be possible to demonstrate on a simplified model certain aspects of this process as operative in communication. I use a model for this discussion because a real situation would require too much explication to permit abstraction here. Charles Hockett's provocative example of Paul Revere and the lights in the church tower can be used for our demonstration. To use the example I shall have to distort it beyond Hockett's original usage as a trivial two-message system—lone light signaling that the British are coming by land; two lights conveying the warning that they are coming by sea. This is a clean informational model. To modify this into a communicational model requires the recognition that as soon as there are a body of communicants united by *the knowledge* that *one* light means "by land" and two means "by sea," the communication is in operation. The message introduced by the recognition is: "as long as there are no lights the British are not coming." There are thus immediately a series of elements isolable but interdependent in this structure:

1. The continuous signal, no light: "no British."

2. Presence of light: "British are coming."

3. One light (which cross-references absence of one light): "British are coming by land."

4. Two lights (which cross-references as absence of one light): "British are coming by sea."

Now, however, let us make our communicational world more real. Let us imagine two contingencies which are statistically probable for eighteenth-century New England. Let us suppose that Farmer Tutt looks up at the tower of North Church and sees no light but begins to worry lest the light has blown out. Or, let us suppose that Farmer Jones, an excellent rifle shot and noted for his eyesight, becomes so anxious that he hallucinates a light. Our case is not simplified if he is also able to hallucinate the fact that it has blown out.

While we are reconstructing history, let us take further liberties with the situation. Let us conceive of the breakdown situation which would occur if mischievous Boston teenagers decide to get the farmers out of bed from time to time by stealing into the church and lighting lanterns in the window.

Even with minimal uncertainties introduced into the system, it is clear that the farmers will soon fail to be appropriately soothed, but alerted by darkness in the tower, and be insufficiently aroused by a light in that tower. Our alerting alarm system is simply too simple and brittle to meet the needs of the group.

Let us contribute to the reliability of the system by cross-referencing it from a second church tower. In this second tower we will place a lantern which sends the message that as long as it is *not* lit the message sent by the other tower *is correct.* That is, as long as there is *no* lantern in church tower number 2 the absence of light in church tower number 1 indicates that the British are *not* yet coming. However, if there is a light in church tower number 2 the absence of light in number 1 means that the British are coming. If number 2 is lit and there is one light in number 1 this means that the message is a lie. However, we cannot yet know the content of the lie. We do not know whether this translates (a) The British are not coming or (b) The British are not coming by sea.

Obviously, our system is still too simple. Furthermore, it is sensorily inefficient. It is too dependent upon the vigilance of a group of watchers who maintain all-night vigils. Too, because of the non-penetrating qualities of light, other sensory modalities must be readied (alerted) for stimulation and communicative activity. To meet these and similar problems we arrange with a sexton to ring a church bell as a signal to look at the lights in the tower of churches 1 and 2. However, this church bell is already employed as the channel for a message system which sends both the integrational message "all is well" and the specific message denoting the hour, the quarter, and the half hour. Now, upon the approach of the British, the sexton is instructed to do one of two things. If the British arrive within a period 5 minutes prior to the time of striking, the sexton is to omit the next ringing of the bell. If, on the other hand, the British arrive during the 10 minutes immediately following the ringing of the bell, he is to ring it again. Either the ringing or the absence of ringing, if appropriately performed, send the signal "look at the bell towers."

We have now introduced an aspect which demonstrates how much of a communicational system depends upon the proper internalization of the system. A listener would not be alerted by the unusual bell unless he had already internalized the rhythm of the time-clock bell. Any mislearning or distorting of this piece of pattern would leave the individual unwarned and vulnerable. And what of the viewer who confuses the identity of the two towers?

We must not oversimplify our example. Boston sextons ring the bell for weddings and funerals, the rate and rhythm of ringing conveying the happy or tragic message. The sexton must be instructed upon the approach of the British to ring the bell at a different rate and velocity than for either of these occasions. I have left the example purposively simple. We are dependent in this example for British stupid enough to agree to come by night so our lights can be seen. Finally, and, in these times, I cannot resist this. This system has built into it the assumption that the British can only approach with malevolent intent. What if they are landing on a peaceful excursion? Further, suppose the French decide to take advantage of this situation or are mistaken for the British.

This is an exceedingly simple model of one phase of the communication process. It is intended only to direct attention to certain problems of communicational analysis. Yet, if we use even this simple example and imagine it multiplied astronomically, we gain some insight into the task faced by a child in becoming a sane member of his society. Finally, it enables us to focus on the fact that if the child internalizes the logic of such a flexible, dynamic, and ultimately uncomplicated system, he has learned to solve the problems solved by normal children of every society. This process may tell something about the nature of sanity and, by extension, insanity.

I should like to close this discussion by a quote from the great physicist Michael Faraday, who in 1846 said:

> I think it likely that I have made many mistakes in the preceding pages, for even to allow to myself my ideas on this point appear only as the shadow of a speculation, which are allowable for a time as guide to thought and research . . . how often their apparent fitness and beauty vanish before the progress and development of real natural truth.*

*Faraday, "Experimental Researchers in Chemistry and Physics," *Philosophical Magazine,* 3rd series, Vol. XXVIII (May 1846), p. 372.

PART 3

Approaching Behavior

15. *Social Contexts of Communication**

U NLESS THE student of structural analysis of communication is so omnivorous in his conception of communication that he defines it to include all of culture, he must have distinct, or at least heuristically distinguishable, *contexts* for measuring the behavior which he is attempting to order. If he is going to study the communicated shifts of behavior in groups, he must know the contexts of these occurrences. Only in this way can he isolate the strictly communicational behavior from the idiosyncratic, on the one hand, and from the institutionally internalized, on the other.

For the purpose of this paper, communication can be regarded in the broadest sense as *a structural system of significant symbols (from all the sensorily based modalities) which permit ordered human interaction.* We are not, as students of communication, concerned with the army, for instance, as subject matter but we are concerned with the militarily influenced situation as a structure which gives special meaning to a symbolic act. Similarly, we are not concerned with the family as a communicative activity—we are concerned with the family as a matrix which elicits, permits, or prevents certain kinds of symbolic acts which we are better able to understand if we know the structural pressures imposed by the system. We are not concerned with either schizophrenia or psychiatry or even with Dr. Miller, psychiatrist, or Mr. Smith, patient, when we examine the doctor-patient interaction; we are concerned with the situation as an ordered matrix which makes the delineation of communicative acts or systems more comprehensible.

As behavioral scientists we are, of course, hopeful that by the delineation and description of communicational behavior, we can shed light on military, familial, or therapeutic matters. However, we have made the methodological judgment to study the communicational system itself.

*Adapted from "Research in the Structure of Group Psychotherapy," *International Journal of Group Therapy*, Vol. 13 (1963), pp. 485–493.

As anthropological linguists or kinesicists or, emergently, as students of communication behavior, our primary task is that of isolating structural meaning. That is, we seek to order vocal and body motion behaviors in a way which will make it possible for us to understand their structural properties. We must, if we are to do more than impressionistic or lexical studies of the meaning of the events that make up the communicative process, understand the nature of the linguistic or kinesic systems themselves. We need to know how these are related to each other and what the emergent communicational units are. We do not, as yet, know enough about words or gestures or their association to know the shapes and sizes of the presently only vaguely conceptualized semiotic or communicational units. Nor do I believe that we are going to be able to weigh the effect of either words or body motion complexes in interaction until we know enough about the matrices of their occurrence to study them. As our studies approach the point where we must deal with *social* meaning, we need clear statements regarding the structure of the *social* contexts of communicational occurrences. It is difficult, if not impossible, to answer the question: What does this symbol or that gesture mean? Meaning is not immanent in particular symbols, words, sentences, or acts of whatever duration but in the behavior elicited by the *presence* or *absence* of *such behavior* in particular contexts. The derivation and comprehension of social meaning thus rests equally upon comprehension of the code and of the context which selects from the possibilities provided by the code structure.

As Hockett has so clearly pointed out, if it is to accomplish the many tasks inherent in its role as a primary communicative channel, no language can be merely an assemblage of signs—each sound having a specific and exclusive referent: "One of the most important design-features of language is 'productivity,' . . . the capacity to say things that have never been said or heard before and yet be understood by other speakers of the language." * I think that this design-feature is also possessed by body motion language. Even at this preliminary stage, it is apparent that body motion behavior, like vocalic behavior, is composed of a limited (society by society) list of distinctive elements that are, by rules for coding, combinable in a virtually infinite number of ordered combinations which order the communicative aspects of human behavior.

* Charles Hockett, "The Origin of Speech," *Scientific American,* Sept. 1960, p. 90.

It is not enough, however, to know that both body motion and vocalic behavior are ordered systems of isolable elements. To repeat, the most comprehensive knowledge of linguistics and kinesics (*qua* linguistics and kinesics) will not permit us to analyze the precise social meaning of the content of an interactional sequence. On the other hand, we can, from the stream of audible sounds and the visible motions interchanged by the membership of the group, detect, isolate, and describe the nature of the linguistic and kinesic behavior. Thus we may be able to discover and describe our discoveries in ways which make it possible to test our judgments of the following:

1. The social genesis of the behavior (if from known systems). That is, we can determine, within certain limits, the dialectic and areally defined body motion background of the speakers.

2. We can determine whether these are "standard" or "nonstandard" communications. That is, we can make certain inferences as to the socioeconomic background of the participants.

3. We can, within limits, define pathology in the performance as evidenced in internal inconsistencies of performance.

4. We can say something as to the *range* of activity occurring in the interaction. That is, is this a highly limited and controlled performance or is it a loose, relatively unstructured and malleable one?

5. We can determine the extent to which there is adaptation or resistance to communicative adaptation among the members.

6. We can determine signaled internal inconsistencies or consistency in the social performance, and often we may be able to detect signaled reactions to this degree of consistency.

And most importantly, we can say these things in a way which makes it possible to test our judgment.

However, if we want to discuss social meaning of any particular element of behavior, if we want to distinguish appropriate from inappropriate behavior in a given scene, if we want to discuss how much information passes between the membership, if we want to know whether effective accomplishment of therapeutic or educational purpose results from the interaction, or if we want to talk about the effects of this particular interaction upon the participants in other situations—we must know a great deal about the nature of the social context within which the particular communicative acts take place.

I stated above that I object to any attempt to subsume all social behavior under a linguistic, kinesic rubric. I do not think, as presently conceived, that all interactive behavior should be relegated to a communicational or "semiotic" frame. However, I equally object to any conceptual scheme which could suggest that the linguist or kinecisist should only be concerned with single utterances or movement sequences. Whether studied from the point of view of the performance of a single actor or from the equally atomistic position of those who conceive of the world as made up of people who alternately speak and listen or move and watch, focus upon the actor and the reactor serves only to obscure the systematic properties of the scene. And this stricture holds whether the scene is viewed from the sociological or the linguistic-kinesic-communicational point of view.

At the present writing it seems likely that styles of communicating, orders of choice of communicative items, and, even, orders of choice of sensory modality for participation may very well be so structured and so related in a hierarchical manner to linguistic and kinesic systems that they will fall within the province of the linguistic-kinesic analyst. It seems, moreover, that communication and interaction situations must, for comprehension, draw from psychiatric, social psychological, sociological, and anthropological research. As each discipline develops explicit descriptions of the order of the phenomena at each level of organization, they should contribute crescively to delineating the range of social meaning of a particular activity of the interactants in a particular society.

16. *Toward Analyzing American Movement**

I T WOULD be wonderful but premature to report that we have completed the kinological analysis of the American movement system. A number and, hopefully, the majority of American kinemes (see p. 229) have been abstracted and withstood the test of contrast analysis. It seems safe now to predict that the kinemic catalog will probably contain between fifty and sixty items. At the risk of being dully repetitive, it must be reiterated that these are building blocks with *structural meaning*. As these units are combined into orderly structures of behavior in the interactive sequence they contribute to social meaning.

For purposes of demonstration, it seems useful to list the kinemes found in the face area of the American system. Two warnings must be included. First, these vary "dialectically." In America, there exist body motion areas with locally special variations of movement as distinctive as the variations to be heard in the varied speech communities. Second, tentative and preliminary research upon French, German, and English movers suggests that the body motion languages vary comparably to the range of difference heard between these in their spoken language. However, this remains suggestive rather than definitive. Only when full kinesic analyses exist from each of these cultural communities can we speak of national kinesic systems with any confidence.

American Kinemes

Physiologists have estimated that the facial musculature is such that over twenty thousand different facial expressions are somatically possible. At the present stage of investigation, we have been able to isolate thirty-two kinemes in the face and head area. (I am

*Adapted from "Communication without Words," in *Encyclopédie des Sciences de l'Homme,* Vol. 5 (Geneva, Editions Kister, 1968), pp. 157–166.

reasonably confident that this is accurate within two or three units.) There are three kinemes of head nod: the "one nod," the "two nod," and the "three nod;" two kinemes of lateral head sweeps, the "one sweep" and the "two sweep;" one of "head cock" and one of "head tilt." There are three junctural, that is connective, kinemes which use the entire head (but with allokines from the head and brow regions), one of "head raise and hold," one of "head lower and hold" and a third of "head position hold." All of these full head kinemes have allokines of intensity, extent, and duration.

We have thus far isolated four kinemes of brow behavior: "lifted brow," "lowered brows," "knit brow," and, finally, "single brow movement."

Extensive and technically difficult research reveals that there are four significant degrees of lid closure: "overopen," "slit," "closed," and "squeezed." There are besides these a series of circumorbital kinic complexes that have resisted analysis. For instance, contraction of the distal aspects of the circumorbital area gives us the familiar "laugh lines." We have not yet been able to determine whether this distal crinkling has kinemic status. It is clear that its absence significantly varies the "meaning" of a smile or laugh, but until we can demonstrate that it is not merely an allokine of lid closure, we must withhold its assignment. Less difficult is the order of problem occasioned by lower lid activity. Extensive research has revealed that its usage in the United States seems to be reserved to certain ethnic groups originating in Eastern and Southeastern Europe. If so, it would have only diakinesic significance in the American movement system. That is, the lower lids seem to be of no more (or less) significance than the absence or presence of the /ŋ/ phoneme in the repertoire of New York City speakers.

The nose is the anatomic locus for four significant behaviors: "wrinkle-nose," "compressed nostrils," "bilateral nostril flare," and "unilateral nostril flare or closure."

The mouth has been very difficult to delineate. The seven kinemes which make up the present circumoral complex are tentative. Only continued research will give us confidence that these represent complete assessment and that the list is composed of equivalent categories. The list includes "compressed lips," "protruded lips," "retracted lips," "apically withdrawn lips," "snarl," "lax open mouth," and "mouth overopen." I am particularly doubtful about the first two of these. Both may belong to some general midface category which we have thus far been unable to isolate.

To this list must also be added "anterior chin thrust," "lateral chin thrust," "puffed cheeks," and "sucked cheeks." "Chin drop" may gain kinemic status but at present is seen as part of the behavioral complex discussed under parakinesics below.

Kinemorphology

These kinemes combine to form *kinemorphs,* which are further analyzable into *kinemorphemic* classes which behave like linguistic morphemes. These, analyzed, abstracted, and combined in the full body behavioral stream, prove to form *complex kinemorphs* which may be analogically related to words. Finally, these are combined by syntactic arrangements, still only partially understood, into extended linked behavioral organizations, the *complex kinemorphic constructions,* which have many of the properties of the spoken syntactic sentence. Only extensive further research is going to give us full understanding of the formal structuring of kinesics. This summary, admittedly skeletal, is presented only to amplify the larger problem undertaken in this chapter.

Much of the research that went into the initial isolation of the microkinesic structure was done on behavior captured on film for slow-motion projection and study. As each new unit was abstracted, it was tested both in multiple universes provided by thousands of feet of interactional film and in the direct observational situation. Whenever possible, each generalization was tested by the employment of live actors in a test situation.

For the purposes of the present chapter, the most significant finding was that these complex microkinesic behaviors could take place without obvious accommodation to the presence or absence of a vocalic accompaniment. Furthermore, while increased velocity of interpersonal vocalic activity *usually* led to increased kinesic behavior at *this* level, increased kinesic activity did not seem nearly as likely to occasion increased vocalic activity. The reader is warned that this may be the result of the choice of the familial and the psychiatric interview contexts as test situations; in more impersonal encounters, the conversational etiquette may impose a different interactional style.

The slow-motion film analyzer provided us not only with a method whereby we could repeat and test our descriptive abstraction but with a method whereby fleeting movements could be detected and timed. In terms of duration, kines have been recorded in sequences that ranged from $\frac{1}{50}$ of a second (significant lid, finger, hand, lip, and head movements faster than this *seem* to be allokinic within a range from as fast as $\frac{1}{100}$ of a second to as long as a full second) to over 3 seconds. These extended performances seem rare, usually such a held position has a double utility: on the one hand, a kine, say a "head cock," serves as a kineme in a series of kinemorphemes *within* the complex kinemorphic construction; on the other it has a suprasegmental and syntactic function as a transsequence juncture which ties together a stream of behavior into a single extended behavioral unit.

Speech-Related Body Motion

As indicated above, the descriptive structural methodology takes the exhaustion of the data stream as a cardinal rule. In a sense, we peel off layers of data. More accurately, we lift out layers of structure. Since the behavior can have multilevel functions, as in the "head cock" mentioned above, we are not merely cutting out and discarding pieces of anatomy as inconsequential to further analysis. As analysis proceeded on particular interactional sequences and the micro-kinesic elements abstracted, once again we had the experience of discovering that we amplified more data in the residual corpus than we had eliminated. Microkinesic analysis left us with two orders of data of differing size: the first of these data were of relatively short duration and were characterized by the fact that they were normally associated with a vocalic stream. At first we dismissed them as "fall-out behavior," the effects of the effort involved in speaking. As their regularity became more manifest, we recognized that we move as well as speak American English. Immediately, a tantalizing problem which had been with us since the inception of kinesic research became illuminated, if not solved.

Just after World War II, I had had access to newsreel film files and had found there strips of film depicting that beloved New York politician, Fiorello La Guardia. La Guardia spoke Italian, Yiddish, and American English. As a public speaker, he was fluent and effective. To me, at that time, the astonishing thing was that even with the sound removed, any observer who knew the three cultures could immediately detect whether he was speaking English, Yiddish, or Italian. The significance of this phenomenon was buried under the deceptive generalization: "La Guardia is a great actor; he knows how to *look* Italian, Jewish, or middle class American." Nor did the point become apparent when George Trager and I, working with one of his Taos (Amerind) informants, found an equally manifest shift in the behavior of the informant when speaking Taos and English. Later, I had an opportunity to study in a preliminary fashion a Lebanese who was similarly transformed when switching from English to Arabic and from Arabic to Parisian French. The partial error I made was to subsume all such ethnically and linguistically tied behavior under a broad parakinesic description (discussed below). Accumulated research is convincing that, while ethnic groups do display differential parakinesic behavior, there is, besides this (at least for Western European languages), a set of necessary and formal body motion behaviors which are tied directly to linguistic structure. The old joke, "She couldn't talk at all if you made her hold her body still," seems to be literally true.

Kinesic Markers

Two orders of kinesic behavior interdependent with speech have been isolated for American talkers. The first of these are the *markers*, which are particular movements that occur regularly in association with or in substitution for certain syntactic arrangements in American English speech.*

*   *   *

Conventions such as these seem to extend with minor variations, say, in body part reference, to the Romance and Germanic languages. Many African, Asian, and Amerind groups, on the other hand, find these confusing, incomprehensible, or insulting when used in combination with their own language.

Kinesic Stress

During the same period that research was delineating these semantically bound markers, systematic observation revealed that a second series of behaviors, previously dismissed as speech effort behavior, were regular and orderly. Slight head nods and sweeps, eye blinks, small lip movements, chin thrusts, shoulder nods and sweeps, thorax thrusts, hand and finger movements, as well as leg and foot shifts proved to be allokines of a quadripartite kinesic *stress*

---

*[The discussion omitted here covers the material treated at length in the next selection.—B.J.]

system. These formed suprasegmental kinemorphemes which, when associated with speech, served a syntactic function by marking special combinations of adjectivals plus nominals, adverbials plus action words, and, furthermore, assisted in the organization of clauses, phrases, and finally, connected specially related clauses in extended and complex syntactic sentences. The four stresses include:

Primary stress	V	A relatively strong movement normally concurrent with loudest linguistic stress. One occurrence for each spoken American English sentence. In contrast with
Secondary stress	∧	a relatively weaker movement occurs in association with the Primary in certain spoken American English sentences. In contrast with
Unstressed	—	the normal flow of movement associated with speech may occur either before or after Primary and before or after and between Secondary.
Destressed	O	Involves reduction of activity below normal over portions of a syntactic sentence. (Sometimes confused as "dead pan" or "poker face" which are maintained kinemorphs which extend over one or more syntactic sentence; destressed normally occurs over phrases and clauses.)

To illustrate these stresses, two sentences are presented in contrasting form below.

In spoken English we detect a loudness contrast between the adjective plus noun in the form "hot *dog*" (heated canine) and the name form for a popular American sausage, the "hot dog." Conventions of writing in English, whereby we can capitalize and/or omit the space between "hot" and "dog" to indicate the close relationship between the subforms, reduce the ambiguity in such forms just as does capitalization of the noun in German or the special article forms for French. Rulon Wells (1945) brilliantly demonstrated that spoken English utilizes four phonemically significant degrees of loudness to assist the communicant in making these same distinctions.

The appropriate response to the question, "What is the term for that sandwich?" is:

That + is + a + hótdòg   (Primary plus tertiary stress)

The appropriate response to the question, "Is that a *cold* dog?" is:

(No) that + is + a + hót + dôg   (Primary plus secondary stress)

The appropriate response to the question, "Is that a *cold cat?*" is:

(No) that + is + a + hót# dóg   (Primary plus terminal juncture plus primary)

In each of these cases we have abstracted partial sentences from the full stream of behavior to demonstrate the stress point. Using a different set of words, perhaps, we can demonstrate how the kinesic stress system operates to make a comparable point. Let us suppose that we have an uninformed speaker of English who does not know that Americans use the form "hot dog" to indicate a wiener or frankfurter. Sent for a "hot dog" by his hungry employer, he returns with a poodle and says, "I've found a dog for you, but we'll have to exercise him for a few minutes to make him warm." The employer laughs and says:

I + want + a + hotdog/not + a + hot + dog#

Kinesic stress analysis and function can be demonstrated by depicting the kinesic activity which occurs regularly at three levels of analysis; first, the articulatory or anatomic activity level; second, the kinemic level; third, the kinemorphemic level.

Kinemorphemic line.	⌐∨	∨⌐	
Kinemic line.	— — ∨	— ∨	∧
Kinesic	oo ∨ ∧	h ∨ ∧	∨
Articulatory line.	lids ↓ ↑	head ⇅	↓
Lexical line.	I + want + a + hot dog/not + a + hot + dog #		

(movement over "dog" relatively weak)

Kinesically, at still the next higher level of organization, the complex kinemorphic construction level, we derive data which can then be used to describe kinesic-linguistic sentence types and to compare such types for the assessment of the universe of discourse. The sequence above contains no *destress*. The following sentence will demonstrate an order of context in which it does appear. In case (A) which follows, the context describes Jones, the president of a scientific society, as a leader in the scientific community. This stands in contrast with the second context (B) in which Jones is described, while admittedly functional as president of the society, as leaving something to be desired as a leader of science or of the community.

(A) Kinemic line $\vee$ /– $\vee$ / –   – $\vee$ *

      Lexical line   Jones as + a + president is + a + good + leader #

(B) Kinemic line $\vee$ / o   o / –   – $\vee$ *

      Lexical line   Jones as + a + president is + a + good + leader #

The use of kinesic destress /oo/ in the included phrase in (B) calls attention to the special emphasis on this phrase. Incidentally, when spoken, (A) and (B) will also stand in linguistic pitch and stress contrast. In spoken (B) after a primary linguistic stress on "Jones," "as a president" will be marked by an even and relatively unvarying stress and pitch profile while (A) is marked by the pitch and stress expectable for a more statistically normal spoken English sentence. While this example is fresh in the reader's mind, let us review an analytic point. In the discussion of kinesic stress above, it was pointed out that the inexperienced kinesicist may confuse a de-stressed passage with one which is accompanied by "poker-faced" behavior. An informant can produce this sentence with an accompanying kinemorphic construction of "poker face" which involves perceptible reduction of facial activity. The actor still must move the necessary kinesic stresses. Informants have no difficulty with the contrast between (B) above and (C) below, which puts special emphasis on the included phrase of (B) *within* a sequence of "dead pan or poker face." Thus:

(C) *Kinemorphic*   Face + O   K/ T + O . . . . . K/ TZ . . . . K#
     construction TZ

     Kinesic stress $\vee$ o   o   –   –   ∧   –

     Lexical   Jones/   the president/   is + a + good + leader #

The frozen body (T+) over "the president" is a clear example of the use of various parts of the body to code separate pieces of information for the communication. While the face is immobilized to form the complex kinemorph $\left(\frac{H + O}{Face + O} \right)$, the (TZ) in hands, fingers, shoulders, and so forth can produce the stress markers. One warning must be given to those who would quickly jump to assuming that destress has a *particular* meaning. In this special case, taken from an observed interaction, the context was one in which the actor-speaker was casting doubt on the ability of Dr. Jones. Destressed clauses, depending upon the larger context, have wide ranges of social meaning. Destress over a vocalized stretch has a *syntactic* function and indicates some order of *inclusion*. In contexts other than the one discussed above, such an inclusion could serve to draw attention to the unusually *high* esteem in which the referrent is held rather than to his deficiencies.

Multichannel Redundancy

The reader may very well, at this point, exhausted by the technical and unfamiliar gymnastics of these paragraphs, ask if one point being made here is the conventional one: communication is, by nature, redundant. The answer to this is, "Yes, we have been trying to show how kinesics at this level of analysis can operate in a redundancy role." However, I would immediately reject the suggestion that multichannel reinforcement of structure is *merely* redundant. Part of the objection would be to the implication that a reinforced message has the same content as a simple message; *there is no reason to assume that nature is haphazard in the selection of certain messages for emphasis and reinforcement.* All of the available data, derived from extended observations, indicate that apparent redundancy is often an agent of reinforcement which serves, at one level, to tie together stretches of discourse and interaction that are longer than sentence length. Of equal importance is the fact that behavior which appears merely repetitive at one level of analysis demands further analysis. Such behavior always seems to be of very special social and cultural significance at other levels.

In the larger evolutionary sense, the possession of physiological equipment which permits multichannel redundancy increases man's adaptive potential. Multichannel reinforcement is positively adaptive, if for no other reason than it provides a far wider range of possibility for the utilization of individual variation within a population. Human beings do not all mature at the same rate and at maturity they are not sensorily equal. Redundancy of the type described above makes the contents of messages available to a greater portion of the population than would be possible if only one modality were utilized to teach, learn, store, transmit, or structure experience. Multichannel reinforcement makes it possible for a far wider range within the population to become part of and to contribute to the conventional understandings of the community than if we were a species with only a single-channel lexical storehouse. We must not allow the fact that it seems easier to recover the data stored in words and sentences to blind us to the vast storehouse of conventional usages, to the multiple arenas of exploration that are the heritage of a multisensory species. We are aware of this with relation to music, graphic art, and the dance. We need to recognize that these art forms are special derivations of deeper and more basic human mechanisms.

Speaking of language in its broadest sense, Margaret Mead has written:

> . . . all natural languages that survive are sufficiently redundant that they can be learned by the members of any *Homo sapiens* group.
> . . . we would say that any language developed by a human society can be learned by the members of another human society, and that this learning is possible both because of the redundancy, which provides for a whole range of individual differences in sensory modalities, memory and intelligence, and because language has been conceptualized the world over as a part of culture that can be learned by members of different cultures.*

No society has a monopoly on observation, reflection, or invention. Transmission of experience from society to society multiplies the opportunity for experimentation, for innovation and development. And, since societies place differential stress on sensory reliability, a multichannel system maximizes the opportunities for transmission between unlike societies. Multisensory redundancy and channel reinforcement thus not only increase the social viability and potential contribution, both to innovation or conservation, of a wider range of individuals within a specific society, but contribute to intersociety communication and, thus, to the opportunities for viability of the species.

Paralanguage

The abstraction of the microkinesic structure and the circumverbal kinesic material does not exhaust the body motion behavior observable in any interactional sequence. Complex kinemorphic constructions are seldom more than 4 or 5 seconds in duration. The

---

* Margaret Mead, *Continuities in Cultural Evolution,* Terry Lectures (New Haven, Yale University Press, 1964), p. 45.

markers, even when complexly bound in "syntactic" sequence, are only, at the most, slightly longer than the vocalized sentences they accompany. The suprasegmental morphemes of kinesic stress are usually of clause length. Besides these, there occurs body motion behavior which can be almost instantaneous in appearance or can extend for minutes, hours, or, perhaps even for portions of a lifetime. Obviously, further investigations will reveal portions of this behavior which properly belong in the microkinesic structure. At the present writing, however, most of it defies microkinesic analysis. I am here referring to that behavior which is covered by categories like *stance, posture,* and *style.* Such matters of muscular and skin action as *flaccidity, rigidity,* and *tone,* because they shift contextually in what seems to be a regular manner, belong here, too. Visibly variable *vascularity* and the *oiliness* and *dryness* of the skin seem, under observation, to have communicative consequence, and this kind of learned activity should be scrutinized for more formal properties. General categories of behavior like *appearance, self-presentation, beauty* and *ugliness, gracefulness* and *clumsiness,* seem likely to have regular, abstractable qualities. (These latter, usually only considered as normative categories, gained communication analysis status when the examination of extended stretches of interaction—an hour or more—showed these to be far more transitory and regular than we had formerly assumed.)

Because this behavior, when parallel research was undertaken with descriptive linguists, was revealed to be so similar in occurrence to behavior on the vocal level, we have described it as *parakinesic* to maintain the terminological parallel with the earlier linguistic concept of *paralinguistics.* Such terminological borrowing seems increasingly appropriate as we move from the study of the communicational subsystems of linguistics and kinesics to the analysis of the communicational system itself. Thus far, because of the time and labor involved, only a limited number of long interactional sequences have been exhaustively studied. However, such body motion and vocalic behaviors seem so intimately and systematically interdependent that they can only be heuristically separated. Present evidence is convincing that while canons of descriptive care must be adhered to, in the recording of each modality, parakinesics and paralinguistics may be comprehended as a single system, *paralanguage.* And I have no reason to believe that paralanguage will be fully understood until the other channels of communication—tactile, olfactory, gustatory, and proprioceptive are analyzed and comprehended. Furthermore, I feel most of the communicational data sketched by Hall (1959, 1962) and Wescott (1960) ultimately will be structured somewhere in the complex paralanguage area.

Fifteen years of extended and increasingly systematic observation is persuasive that paralanguage is too gross a category to be final. It, too, theoretically should emerge as a structure composed of a series of ordered levels of communicational behavior. It seems likely that as we discover how sentences are linked together to make up discourse, as we, following Scheflen's lead (1965c), delineate the conventionalized structures which order two- and three-member and group discussions, that as we decode the signals that compose a system whereby we can leave and return to topics in an interaction without strain, that as we learn how humans can separate and return to each other to maintain continuous interaction, we will absorb into structural categories much of the material now preanalytically assigned to paralanguage.

17. Movement with Speech*

EARLY IN my investigations, research made it clear that it was going to be impossible to develop objective interviewing techniques before much more was known about the detailed structuring of body motion and about the relationship between this structuring and that of other communicative processes. Furthermore, even preliminary evaluation of the data made me face the difficulty of the simulta-

*Presented at the Second International Symposium on Communication Theory and Research, March 23–26, 1966, under the title "Some Body Motion Elements Accompanying Spoken American English"; at Kansas City, Missouri; Reprinted with minor revisions from *Communication: Concepts and Perspectives,* Lee Thayer, ed. Chapter III, pp. 53–76. Copyright Spartan Books 1967. This is a slight revision, with an added introduction, of an earlier paper "Some Relationships between American Kinesics and Spoken American English," presented to the American Association for the Advancement of Science on December 27, 1963, and partly published in *Communication and Culture,* by Alfred G. Smith. Copyright © 1966 by Holt, Rinehart and Winston, Inc. Reprinted by permission of Holt, Rinehart, and Winston, Inc. [I have omitted the introduction and included three passages in double parentheses, which Birdwhistell included in the early version.—B.J.]

neous observation of linguistic and kinesic material. In fact, neither I nor my linguistic associates could reliably distinguish the linguistic behavior from the kinesic in the interactional sequences we observed.* To hold the sound steady while we observed the visible behavior or vice versa, or to observe and report on both at the same time, required perceptual and reporterial skills beyond our capacities. At this point my interest in the *relationship* between kinesic and linguistic processes was postponed and was concentrated upon body motion behavior. This was a methodological decision. Before I could hope to understand communication, I had to know more about the operation of the kinesic structure. Fortunately, a methodology existed for such investigations. The productivity of the analytic techniques employed by the descriptive linguists held promise that similar rigor and discipline, if applied to body motion behavior, might provide the information prerequisite to correlative studies between the spoken and moved communicative processes. However, the linguistic method is a complex and often tedious one. And, more importantly, it requires long training before the investigator can use it. I had hopes that there were short cuts to information and insight about body motion behavior.

Preliminary work had seemed to justify the conviction that body motion communication behavior is both learned and structured (Birdwhistell, 1952). The decision to deal exclusively with visible body motion encouraged the fantasy that years of research might be saved by the investigation of the communicative behavior of the sensorily deficient. Research funds were available and I was optimistic that by the study of the necessarily silent, those incapable of speech and/or hearing, kinesics would be isolable in a "pure" state. Comparably, it seemed reasonable to study the behavior of the blind. By evaluating sensory function subtraction, the function of visible communicative processes might be isolable. At that stage of theory it seemed logical to assume that the study of those who could not see might enable me to discover what the blind missed in interaction.

Preliminary and limited, but nonetheless systematic, observation of the interaction between blind adults and the interaction between blind parents and children dissolved any hopes about the efficiency

---

*Several years were to pass before it became evident that much of the data abstractable by linguistic and kinesic techniques could not be observed simultaneously because the units were not coextant in time.

of this approach. The research immediately so involved us in problems of patterned learning and in intricacies of perception theory beyond our skills and interest that I dismissed any thought of extensive exploration of the communicational behavior of the blind or blinded.

The interactional patterning of the deaf, at the time, seemed a more relevant area for study. Even though it was already evident that gestures and signs had a logic systematically different than that which prevailed for the kinesic material, circumsign-language behavior seemed temptingly evident and easily abstractable. Again, as soon as I began to systematically observe the interpersonal behavior of the deaf it became obvious that this strategy was not going to simplify the investigatory problem.

Fortunately, I had opportunity for consultation with physiologists at the University of Louisville and at the University of Chicago. These experienced researchers convinced me that it was experimentally naive to assume that by the study of either the congenitally or the traumatized deaf (or the blind) I could comprehend normal patterning. Even a few relevant examples from the history of experimental endocrinology were persuasive that the function of either *aspects* or the whole of nonmechanical systems cannot be determined by simple subtractive devices.

There are other objections to the use of the behavior of the deviant to illuminate that of the normal. Margaret Mead pointed out (in a personal communication) that blindness and deafness are not merely physiological phenomena. The blind and deaf in any given society are able to live in the society because the culture is in some way structured to accommodate to their infirmities. In some societies there are no deaf and in others no blind individuals. Apparently, it is not that defectives do not appear in these societies; rather, they do not survive. In certain cultures the viability of the physiologically deficient seems to be limited to certain age ranges within the society. In others, the choice of the viable seems to depend upon the particular gender-linked socioeconomic adjustments of the particular society. In short, the sensorily deprived are permitted to live *if* they adapt to a system of communication structured to handle their specially defined function within the particular society. That is, if the deaf or the blind in any culture can be adapted to established roles within the society, they are viable. Such roles structure, if they do not determine, the communication behavior of both the sensorily deficient and those who interact with them.

These preliminary investigations reinforced the recognition that stylized behavioral systems such as the sign language of the deaf could not be studied as exemplary of the kinesic system. The deaf-and-dumb code is transmitted along the kinesthetic-visual channel. But it is not, even upon first examination, a first-level communicational system. Such stylized codes, like writing, are *derived* systems. Furthermore, all available data lead me to doubt very much that the deaf-and-dumb sign languages are directly derived either from the kinesic or the linguistic system. These, like other derived body motion complexes, dancing, gaming and miming, are going to resist communicational analysis until we know more about the various component sensory modalities, their transmission channels, and their emergent interrelationship in the communicational system.

((While derived communicational systems are clearly inappropriate as models for primary communication analysis, there are contemplated or in progress a series of studies, the results of which should be exceedingly valuable for the student of communication. One of these which is especially promising is Alan Lomax's* present investigation on the relationship between the distribution of folk music forms and the body behavioral styles which accompany them. It will be extremely valuable to know whether the singing style has a different distribution than the movement style of the singers (or their audience). Such data can have real importance as guides toward understanding the dynamics of learning communicative behavior.† Are such behaviors learned and transmitted as multimodal packages or can the derived systems in the various modalities be learned and transmitted separately? Do different societies have special techniques for teaching these, and what is the range of individual variation in this area?

A second example of promising derived communicational system research is provided by the on-going investigations of Max Beberman and Gertrude Hendrix at the University of Illinois Mathematics Project.‡ My observation of their work indicates that by utilizing sound films of teachers and students of mathematics, these mathematicians are effectively demonstrating that even such a spe-

* Alan Lomax, personal communication.

† For studies of infrahuman, multimodal learning, see Peter H. Klopfer, *Behavioral Aspects of Ecology* (Englewood, N.J., Prentice Hall, 1962).

‡ Max Beberman, personal communication. Gertrude Hendrix, unpublished communication at University of Indiana Conference on Paralanguage and Kinesics, 1964.

cially derived system as mathematics can be more readily learned by a greater proportion of American students when its formulas are performed in moved and spoken American English. Traditionally, mathematics has been communicated through a jargon which over the years has been reduced to a spoken written language, easily accessible only to those who learn through reading. Further studies like these would have immeasurable value of a basic and an applied nature in the study of learning and teaching.

Finally, I'd like to mention still another area of investigation which would seem to be of real consequence. At the Indiana University Conference on Paralanguage and Kinesics, Father Bernard Tervoert reported on the invention and utilization of a special language by a group of deaf-and-dumb children during World War II. It would seem of great importance to compare such a language as this, invented by the sensorily deprived for use in their own sub-society with the usual deaf-and-dumb conventions invented for the purpose of relating the sensorily deprived to the membership of the larger society. Such a study could throw light, too, on the relative efficiency of the two as communicative systems. Perhaps, furthermore, in this way some light could be thrown upon the process of derivation. What orders of experience are excluded from incorporation by these two differing methods of code production? Finally, and probably ultimately more important, are there orders of experience expressed in either or both of these codes which are not explicit in the spoken language?))

Linguistic and Kinesic Research

Consistent with the decision to limit attention to kinesic activity, most of the early research on body motion was done with silent film or with silent projection of sound film. And, while there was no recourse but to have informants vocalize as I worked with them on particulars of kinesic structure, their judgments were tested in the silenced universe. I must confess that my decision to study kinesics as a separate and discrete system was, in part, a result of my limitations as a linguist. While I had studied linguistics as a graduate student and had continued with my training following graduation, I was technically incapable of either recording or analyzing much of the linguistic behavior of obvious consequence to any relationship between spoken and moved "languages." This deficiency made it necessary for me to collaborate with experts.

In 1956 came an opportunity for multidisciplinary correlation of speech and body motion. This was provided by the association with the "Palo Alto team"* and with Henry Lee Smith, Jr., and George L. Trager at the University of Buffalo. Working largely with the "Doris Film" (see p. 227) (with controls provided by other Josiah Macey, Jr., films and by the Syracuse Veterans Administration Hospital films), it was possible to establish a working abstraction of the American macrokinesics structure. From this work and from earlier research at the Foreign Service Institute, we could speak with some confidence of basic macro- and microkinesic units. Analysis of the body motion communicative stream early yielded the kine and the kineme. Continuing contrastive study soon revealed the higher organization of these into the kinemorph and the kinemorpheme. In turn, these forms could be seen to combine into complex kinemorphic constructions. That is, research revealed that it is legitimate to speak of body motion, at least insofar as American English is concerned, as having a structure comparable to that of spoken language. The kinesic system structures body behavior into forms comparable to the way the linguistic system structures the speech stream in "sounds," "words," "phrases," "sentences," and even "paragraphs." The word "comparable" is carefully chosen—only future research will reveal whether these formalized aspects of body motion communication are indeed analogous to spoken language. I suspect that the linguistic and kinesic systems as totalities have shapes more analogous than do their components.

((During this same period, the descriptive linguists were becoming more confident that they had isolated the general area, if not the particulars, of paralinguistic behavior (Trager, 1958). And, once the initial structuring of American kinesics had been laid out and corpora of data analyzed by means of this framework, a residue of body motion behavior comparable to the paralinguistic material became manifest. Much of this data was tentatively categorized as "parakinesic." This is not the place to go into the theoretical and practical difficulty of analyzing this material into tested orders of significance. Largely matters of variations of intensity, duration, and style of kinesic performance, these data still remain insufficiently analyzed for any final assignment (Birdwhistell, 1961a).

* Norman A. McQuown, Charles Hockett, and the psychiatrists Frieda Fromm-Reichmann and Henry Brosin, Fellows at the Institute for the Advanced Study in the Behavioral Sciences, invited Gregory Bateson and me to join with them in the multidisciplinary investigation of a nontherapeutic interview.

It is at least hypothetically possible that the "para-" designation is less a statement of the nature of such phenomena than of uncertainty as to the extent of "emic" (meaningful class) structuralization possible here. There are strong indications from interactional data that parakinesic and paralinguistic data are but aspects of more comprehensive units which somehow combine the behavior of both channels. It has been methodologically justifiable and necessary to heuristically abstract macrokinesics and macrolinguistics as systems subject to isolation and analysis in and of themselves. However, it may very well be that what we have been describing as *para*-phenomena may organize only at the communicational or the semiotic level. If future investigations support this contention, body motion and vocalic behaviors now designated as *para* to the more structured kinesic and linguistic material will be seen as inseparable at the interactional level. It seems likely that as research develops, they will be subsumed under a cover classification. Furthermore, as research has proceeded, not only do the vocalic and body behavioral data at this level of description appear to be interdependently organized, but there are considerable data emerging to indicate that the macrolinguistic and macrokinesic structures may not be as finally independent as originally conceived. The discussion to follow will describe one section of the data which is attracting me, at least for working purposes, to this theoretical position.))

Charles Hockett and Norman A. McQuown, in their work on the linguistic data for use in *The Natural History of an Interview* (in preparation) analyzed and transcribed extensive stretches of the vocalic behavior of the participants in an intensive sequence, while I did the kinesic analysis of smaller but usually associated stretches of body motion behavior. ((McQuown, as organizing editor of this multidisciplinary research, had insisted on fine-grained and exhaustive recording of both the linguistic and kinesic material. This recording was done as independently as possible; McQuown and Hockett working with tapes, while I recorded from the silently projected film. Later, McQuown and I, by careful listening and viewing, gave frame numbers (thus, timing) to the material from the two modalities.))

Inspection of the working transcript of the linguistically and kinesically recorded data revealed repetitive and apparently systematic body behaviors directly associable with the vocalic stream. That is, there seemed to be some systematic regularity in the movements people made when they talked. These in both shape and structural activity seemed distinguishable from the clearly structural kinesic particles which occur both concurrently and apart from the flow of speech.

Two classes of phenomena appear in the kinesically analyzable stream. One class includes the *formal* kinesic phenomena which appear in interactional sequences whether there is speech present or not. This behavior, as its structures become analyzable, was assigned to macrokinesics proper. Macrokinesics supplies, to repeat, the structural elements of complex kinemorphic constructions: the wordlike, the phraselike, the sentencelike, and the paragraphlike forms of the kinesic communicative stream.

Associated with these highly structured forms is the range of behavior, largely characterized by distinguishable degrees of intensity, frequency, extent of movement, and duration of movement which still remain only partially analyzed. Since this behavior is analogous to that vocalic behavior linguists tentatively summarize as "paralanguage," these are termed "parakinesic." Such behavior cross references, in a variety of ways, the kinesic or linguistic messages emitted or received (Austin, 1965). These cross-referencing signals amplify, emphasize, or modify the formal constructions, and/or they make statements about the *context* of the message situation. In the latter instance, they help to define the context of the interaction by identifying the actor or his audience, and, furthermore, they usually convey information about the larger context in which the interaction takes place. However, the cross-referencing signals differ systematically from those included in the discussion to follow in that while they occur with speech, they are also present in inaudible interaction.

Macrokinesic and parakinesic elements appear in interactional streams both concurrent with and *apparently* independent of the flow of speech. "Apparently," because we still know so little of the structure of silence as a linguistic phenomenon that these elements may appear independent only because the investigator sees them that way. I suspect any formulation which on the basis of linear observation denies channel interdependence. We know something about the shape of spoken sentences and about the shape of intricately structured kinesic strings, but we have only begun to envision the shape of communicative blocks. Certainly, everything we have come to know about utterances and conversations indicates that communicational behavior is multilinear in time, but observational conventions screen much of the dynamics of this process from analytic view.

For the purposes of this paper and because the material reported below may have a special relationship to spoken sentence production (and have special import for those who seek to comprehend derived systems), the following material is distinguished by its intimate association with spoken language.

As collaborative research proceeded on interactional scenes, it became evident that a series of movements, previously discounted as artifacts of speech effort, were regular, orderly, and predictable. Varisized head nods and sweeps, lid blinks, small chin and lip movements, variations in shoulder or thorax adjustment, hand, arm and finger activity, as well as foot and leg nods and sweeps became separable from the kinic stream in which they appeared. Systematic analysis revealed these to be allokines of a relatively simple four-part stress kineme structure. These are reported elsewhere (Birdwhistell, 1968f). These allokines (see p. 132) form kinemes of stress which are organized at a higher level into suprasegmental kinemorphemes which at this writing seem absolutely necessary for the production of American English speech. While analysis is still in progress, these suprasegmental kinemorphemes can be demonstrated to have syntactic functions related to the production of speech. Already isolated is their function of marking special combinations of adjectivals plus nominals and adverbials plus action words. These stress forms appear to assist in the organization of clauses, phrases, syntactic sentences, and, finally, to connect specially related clauses in complex and extended utterances.

At the same time that analysis was revealing the kinesic structures mentioned above, another order of data took shape in the records. Because these data were so specifically related to particular classes of particular lexical items and because they showed no indication of the structural properties so characteristic of the remainder of the kinesic stream (I am still unconvinced as to the amorphic structure of parakinesic behavior) the isolated items were termed *kinesic markers*. However, these cannot be made comprehensible to an audience unconversant with general kinesics, without reviewing our earlier discussion of gesture. Early in the investigation of body movement patterning, that deceptively transparent set of phenomena commonly called "gestures" had to be assessed and analyzed. A considerable body of ethnographic data was extant demonstrating that "gestures" varied from culture to culture. An even larger body of philosophical and psychological literature maintained that these could be understood as "signs" as distinct from less transparent or easily translatable "symbols." * Examination of these phenomena in context, however, soon revealed that this was at best a dubious interpretation of their activity or function.

Under kinesic analysis (once I had gotten some idea of how items of the stream are systematically linked to other items of the stream) it became demonstrable that so-called gestures are really *bound morphs*. That is, gestures are forms which are incapable of standing alone—except, of course, where the structural context is provided by the questioner. Just as there is no "cept" in isolation in American English, an informant may be taught how to produce it together with "pre-" or "con-" and "-tion." As bound morphs, as stem forms, gestures require infixual, suffixual, prefixual, or transfixual kinesic behavior to achieve identity.

Gestures are characterized by the fact that informants can easily recall them and attach a general order of meaning to them as recognized. However, this easy access to their form or meaning proves illusory when they are examined in the actual interactional flow. Although they have an apparent unitary and discrete quality, they prove consistently to carry the instruction to look elsewhere in the body behavioral stream for their modification or interpretation. A "salute," for example, depending upon the integrally associated total body or facial behavior, may convey a range of messages from ridicule and rebellion to subservience or respect. A "smile" can have at least this range, as can a "wink," a "wave," or a "bow." To call these "signals" is to indicate a specificity such behavior lacks in actual practice.

To return to the kinesic markers: regularly around certain kinds of audible syntactic items, kinic behavior appears which resembles the gestural bound morph except that its shape seems to be dominated by particular linguistic contexts. The term for such behavior, *kinesic marker,* represents a tentative compromise between a position that would definitively designate such behavior as macrokinesic and that of prematurely (in terms of kinesic methodology) assigning

* For a limited and generalized bibliography see Francis Hayes, *Gestures: A Working Bibliography,* reprinted from *Southern Folklore Quarterly,* Vol. 21 (Dec. 1957), pp. 218–317. For a more precise and modern study see Robt. L. Saitz and Edward J. Cervenko, *Columbian and North American Gestures: An Experimental Study,* (Bogota, Centro Columbo Americano, 1962).

them some kind of supralinguistic and suprakinesic position in the semiotic system (Sebeok, Hayes, and Bateson, 1964). For purely heuristic purposes I have made the admittedly questionable decision to classify them according to the classes of lexical items with which they are regularly associated. It is regrettable that such a classificatory device may signal an unintended priority to the linguistic form. However, since these data have resisted placement in the macrokinesic structure and since semiotic analysis is only in its earliest stages of conceptualization, it is, perhaps, permissible to store them in pigeonholes from which future research can easily retrieve them.

Marker Qualities

The units abstracted below have four characteristics.

1. They have articulatory* properties which are abstractable into *contrastive* behavioral classes.†

The articulations themselves are not distinctively and exclusively related to specific functions. The particular articulatory behaviors may in other environments have other functions, for example, a lid closure articulation may be, at one level, a kineme in a kinemorpheme; at another, a stress kineme in a suprasegmental organization. Here we locate it as a marker.

2. These units appear in distinctive syntactic environments; that is, the lexemes with which they appear belong to distinctive syntactic classes.

3. The articulatory behavior, if two or more of these units appear in series, is always sufficiently varied to reduce signal confusion; that is, we have situational articulatory contrast.

4. Since the articulatory behavior is not definitively distinctive, in and of itself, the abstraction of the unit depends upon the isolation of contrastive sequences of behavior in contrastive syntactic neighborhoods.

---

*The term "articulation" is used to refer to any abstractable movement or position. It is prekinesic in the sense that articulations are unanalyzed for *structural* properties.

† It is characteristic of structural classes at the level of microkinesics that articulatory performance has a wide range; a given abstracted unit, say, a distal movement of a body part followed by pause in position may range from a total body-involved movement with extended arm and finger to a movement involving only a single finger. Style, diakinesic patterning, structure, and parakinesic emphasis may be involved singly or collectively to govern the range.

Thus, a marker is a *contrastable* range of behavior in a *particular* neighborhood.

Kinesic Pronominal Markers

First, and most easily recognizable, were what I called the K^P group, so identified because they are normally associated with or may be, in certain environments, substituted for pronominals.

In address or reference, the head, a finger, the hand, or a glance may be moved so that a *distal* extension of the movement can be interpreted by members of the movement community as moving *toward* the object or event referred to. These K^P's may be found in association with the verbalizations, "he," "she," "it," "those," "they," "that," "then," "there," "any," and "some."

The *proximal* movements of these same body parts are used in association with "I," "me," "us," "we," "this," "here," and "now."

In recording, I originally ignored the distal-proximal distinction and listed the behavior associated with "I," "me," "he," "she," "it," "we," "they," "here," "there," "now," and "then" as K^P's, *pronominal markers.** It soon became evident that the more complex patterning of the K^P distinguished kinesic marker behavior from kinesic stress behavior.

As the investigation of larger and varied corpora of data proceeded and the methods for tying body motion and vocalic behavior improved, it was clear that what had at first been seen as an indicator over a single lexeme was more complex both at the articulatory level and as a functioning structural unit. First of all, a lateral sweep often appeared at either the proximal or the distal end of the act. This sweep distinguished *pluralization.*

---

* Traditional grammarians may quarrel with the classification of "here," "there," "now," and "then" as pronominals. However, when a lexeme behaves syntactically like a pronominal, from my point of view it is a pronominal. My judgment was based on interactional data which contained the contrast items: "this," "this here," "this here dog;" "that," "that there," and "that there woman."

In the items "this here dog" and "that there woman," "this here" and "that there" are kinesically stressed as are adjectival items. When "this" and "that," and "this here" and "that there" stand without a following name form, they act as pronominals and are so marked. It is of significance that the K^P behavior is initiated during the latter aspects of "this" and continues through part of "here." The same occurs over the "that there" pronominal. Thus, /this K^P here/ and /that K^P there/; the junctural phenomena pulls the K^P to the medial position just as the stress kineme is pulled in forms like /rocking $\vee$ chair/ and /lamp $\vee$ post/.

Pluralization Marker

Pluralization is indicated by a slight sweep of the moved member over "we," "we's," "we'uns," "they," "these," "those," "them," "our," "you" (plural), "you all," "you'uns," "youse," "their," and "us." "Any" and "some" show the same contrast from the singular as do "many," "several," and so forth. Since, however, a similar sweep often takes place in association with name forms which are ambiguous ("fish," "sheep," "deer," and "bear," etc.), or overpluralized name forms, it seems necessary to make a double annotation over plural pronominals of K^p followed by a *marker of pluralization* (K^{pp}).

In association with a phrase like "all of them" or "none of them," "all" or "none" may have a head sweep or lid close (K^{pp}) in association. "None" is a particularly interesting form as kinesically marked. It varies in articulation (perhaps dialectically) from a K^p of a single lower nod to a sweep K^{pp}. When the hand or the foot is involved, a single sweep may alternate with a single nod.

I have never seen sweep, thus K^{pp}, parallel to the spoken "none is" but sweep, as K^{pp}, is common in the environment of "none are." Depending upon stress in the sentence, "them" in either of the phrases "none of them" or "all of them" may or may not be marked. Examination of several hundred examples of this phrase has indicated that we will find, if the phrases "all of them" or "none of them" do not have a primary vocalic over "all" or "them" or "none" or "them," the entire phrase is covered by the behavior of the (K^{pp}) pluralization marker.

Verboid Markers

The distal and proximal aspect of the movement became increasingly important after the pluralization sweep was isolated. At this point the microkinesic recording indicated that such a proximal or distal movement was not limited to the sound stretch of the pronoun but rather linked the subject form to the verb form. Thus "I went" has a proximal movement over "I" which, *without interruption,* moves distally over "went." /I went to the house/ may well be marked by a proximal movement over "I" which moves, *without interruption,* over "went." Then the movement combines, *with a change of direction,* over "to the house." These movements are clearly distinguishable from the kinesic stress markers which take place in either the same or other body parts.

In a form like /I gave it to him/, the marker movement is very much the same as in /I went to the house/. /He gave it to me/ reverses the action, the movement terminating in a proximal position. The demand, /Give it to me/, logically enough, has the same shape as /You give it to me/.

Such sentences stand in sharp contrast to sentences of the form /The book is red/ in which there are no markers. /The dog is barking/ requires no markers, while /He's barking/ has the characteristic distal movement followed by a continuous move. On the other hand, /The dog barked/ or /The dog was barking/ are customarily accompanied by a distal movement to the rear of the body, whereas /The dog will bark/ has a distal movement toward the front of the body. These examples indicate the presence of *tense markers*.

Let us attempt to diagram our articulations and see whether we can abstract certain regularities:

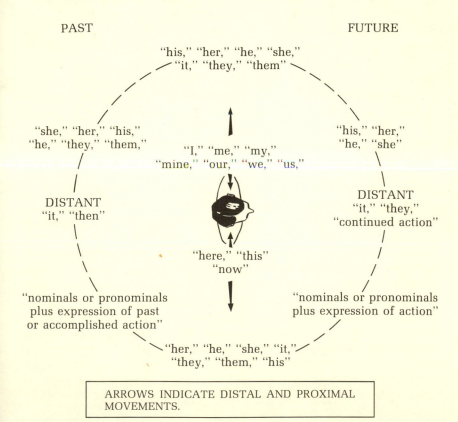

ARROWS INDICATE DISTAL AND PROXIMAL MOVEMENTS.

FIGURE 1.

With the application of Fig. 1 to the data it was possible now to distinguish the first person pronouns K^{p1} from all other pronouns K^{p2}. By extending the K^{pp} convention of pluralization, K^{pp1} and K^{pp2} could be distinguished. Tense is clearly signaled here. Futurity is signaled by an anterior progression of the movement; the past, in general, is signaled by a posterior movement. Thus, /He will give it to me/ involves: (1) A distal extension K^p over "he"; (2) a K^v (verboid marker) of continuous movement over "will give it"; (3) a K^t of tense supplied by the direction of the movement over "will give it"; (4) a K^p, the proximal movement, over "to me." Exhaustive repetitions with parallel forms demonstrate that these operate apart from the kinesic stress system.

By contrast /He gave it to me/ utilizes position and proximal movements to carry the parallel message. In all cases a sweep over the K^p changes it to a K^{pp}. These rules seem to hold for all actor action sentences although the behavior is most easily detected in actor-action-object sentences. However, in forms like /He *was* a red/ or /She *was* crazy/ in which the emphasis is on completed action, a K^t may be the only marker. Comparably, /*She* is crazy/ usually has only a K^p. Under certain circumstances /*She* is crazy/ will carry both a K^p and a K^v. In both of the former cases there is, of course, a kinesic primary stress concurrent with the K^t or the K^p.

Area Markers

Besides these we have the *area markers,* "on," "over," "under," "by," "through," "behind," "in front of," and the like, which, when accompanied by verbs of action, usually take a K^a. The articulations are particularly noticeable when these items are under primary linguistic stress. I am indebted to Harvey Sarles and his associates at Western Pennsylvania Psychiatric Institute and Clinic* for pointing out the distinction in this regard between sentences like /Put it behind the stove/, which requires a K^a over "behind," and /He arrived behind time/, in which "behind" requires no marker. Or, /He arrived in the nick of time/, where the "in" requires no marking in contrast to, /Put it in the can/, where "in" is customarily marked. ((When the Western Psychiatric group completes its analyses of

*Harvey Sarles, the linguistic anthropologist, worked with two psychiatrists, Joseph Charney and Felix Loeb, and with a philosopher, William Condon, in the examination of phrase and sentence forms and their associated body behavior.

American English prepositional phrases, we shall have excellent data for the final isolation of this type of marker.))

Manner Markers

In parallel fashion, I mark the behavior which is associated with such phrases as "a short time" or "a long time," and with "slowly" and "swiftly." These I annotate as K^m for *kinesic manner markers*. Also as K^m's are listed the behaviors associated with forms like "roughly," "jerkily," "smoothly," and so on.

This delineation may seem to imply that kinesic markers are moved adjectivals or adverbials or pronominals or verbals. Even if such a description seems satisfactory, we should take care to avoid assuming that this *proves* that kinesic markers are derived from spoken language. There is no more evidence for this than there is that syntactic activity is not ultimately a derivation from body movement. From my point of view, it is premature at this stage of analysis to conjecture about origins. Our central concern is how such behaviors operate, not where they come from.

Before concluding, let us take up one point of general theoretical interest. Our discussion has led us to the point that we need to ask whether there is a qualitative difference between such behavior as we have been describing here and the elaborately descriptive behavior that accompanies certain kinds of story telling and technical instructions.

There will be a temptation, when the kinesic markers are first examined, to somehow feel that all of these markers are no more than "gestures" which designate or modify the morphemes, the lexemes (the words), with which they are associated. At one level of description this is a supportable, if not a very productive, contention. However, such description may well lure the student into the kind of assumptions about universal symbolism in body motion that earlier thinking about onomatopoeia led to in language description. Even the most cursory cross-cultural examination reveals that such behavior varies from group to group at least as much as does the spoken language of these groups.

How can we best analyze the behavior of a woman telling another woman about the intricacies of dressmaking? Her apparently imitative demonstrative movements, like those of a man discussing his exploits in playing and landing a trout, seem qualitatively different than the behavior which surrounds other orders of discourse.

At one time, I used a cover marker which I termed a K^d or *marker of demonstration* for such extended and elaborate gesticulation. Analysis of these, however, revealed that this convention would overextend the concept of marker. For while such demonstrative behavior is clearly distinguishable, it is not unitary; it is made up of complex kinemorphic constructions, kinesic markers, and para-kinesic behavior. At the moment I am inclined to regard such behavior as examples of derived communicational systems. As such, they are not the primary subject matter of kinesics at the present.

Summary

If it seems helpful to describe the kinesic markers as "analogic" as contrasted to other signals which seem more "digital"-like, I have no objection so long as these terms are used descriptively. However, if in any way assignment to a digital or an analogic category tempts us toward premature closure of descriptive structural research, such phrasings are just too expensive and I oppose their usage. Models are only justifiable so long as they are productive. All too often informational models developed as research tools have been prosti-tuted into "explanations" of the behavior they were designed to isolate for investigation.

Originally we made a methodological and theoretical decision to exhaust linguistic and kinesic descriptions to avoid premature "explanations" from one system to another. Terms like "moved adverbials" or "moved pronominals" are sloppy. There is no good reason why the linguistic and kinesic systems cannot interrelate at this, or at an even lower, level of analysis. Pluralization and tense markers indicate a morphemic point of conjunction. There is no good reason why, when we began to look more carefully at the semiotic impact of linguistic phenomena, we should not find certain vocalized behavior assignable to a position of linguistic markers. Some of the material presently described as vocal "segregates" may be of this order.* There is no justification, however, at this writing to restrict such markers to segregate type behavior. In fact, a number of vocalic interjections, under preliminary scrutiny, seem to behave in this manner, being semologically more intimately associated with the

---

* Trager has used the term vocal segregate to describe vocal behavior like that present in "hunh," "uh-uh," "eh," "ah," etc. See Birdwhistell (1961a).

kinesic behavior than with the verbalizations appearing in the same context.

Finally, both the kinesic and the linguistic markers may be alloforms, that is, structural variants of each other, at another level of analysis. The more research we do upon the structure of inter-action, making use of sound films, the more attractive as a next arena of investigation this last conception becomes for me.

My own research has led me to the point that I am no longer willing to call either linguistic or kinesic systems communication systems. All of the emerging data seem to me to support the conten-tion that linguistics and kinesics are infracommunicational systems. Only in their interrelationship with each other and with comparable systems from other sensory modalities are the emergent communi-cation systems achieved.

The kinesic markers do not supply the central evidence for hypothesizing this relationship between kinesics, linguistics, and the communicational system. Review of the suprasegmental kinemor-phemes is even more convincing as to the inseparability of vocalic and body activity as communicational phenomena. Only further research in American communicational patterns as well as extensive cross-cultural evidence can give this position more than hypothesis status. If we assume its correctness, we are dealing with a re-evaluation of communicational theory of the same dimension as that which occurred with the recognition that the neural, the circulatory, or even the metabolic processes are infraphysiological systems.

What I am trying to say is that men have not communicated with each other by spoken language alone any more than they have lived by metabolism. Speech contributes to the total communication process; the metabolic process is but one aspect of the vital process.

One last, practical note: if this is so, there is a good reason why Johnny has so much trouble learning to write. Writing must derive and abstract both spoken and body motion activity. If Johnny is taught that he is only dealing with lexically bound speech material, he has to deny reality to be literate. The multimodal universe of television may teach him this and he may very well revolt against the teacher who overbelieves in words. If our formulations are correct, the grammarian must turn to body motion for data to make sense out of a number of areas now hidden in the parts of speech.

18. Kinesic Stress in American English*

IN THE discussion to follow, I would like to present data which demonstrate at greater length and technicality an intimate and possibly necessary relationship between certain structured body motion and spoken language forms. Although technical, the data should be, with effort, comprehensible to native or skilled speakers of American English. The example *abstracts* certain behaviors from the spoken and moved stream; the reader is again urged to remember that these abstracted pieces of structure do not exhaust the communicative activity in an interaction.

Among the more important linguistic investigations in spoken American English of the past 25 years have been those concerned with pitch,† stress, and juncture. Contrastive research revealed that structurally significant variations in loudness and intensity are required for the production of meaningful lexemes, clauses, phrases, and syntactic sentences. These discoveries, when combined with new insights into the junctural conventions of American speech, expedited the behavioral examination of utterances. Since stress and juncture are technical phenomena, a brief and very simplified introduction follows.

Linguistic Juncture

A number of linguists now agree that American English can be described as having three *terminal* junctures. These are often relatable to punctuation conventions in writing.

---

*From "Communication: A Continuous Multi-Channel Process," presented in April 1965 in a lecture series sponsored by the University of California; published in a slightly different version in *Conceptual Bases and Applications of the Communication Sciences* (New York, John Wiley & Sons, 1968).

†For clarity and simplicity little attention is given in this example to intonation patterns. The relationship between kinesic behavior and linguistic intonation behavior is still undergoing analysis. It seems likely from preliminary data that some kind of systematic relationship exists between certain stretches of kinesic be-

The first, usually at a cessation point in phonation, the /#/, is described as an off-glide in pitch, plus some elongation of terminal phonemes (characteristic of, but not limited to, a standard "declarative" sentence).

The second, usually at a cessation point in phonation, the /‖/, is described as a rise in pitch, plus some elongation of terminal phonemes (characteristic of, but not limited to, certain "interrogatory" sentences).

The third, more difficult to handle, the /|/, is described as sustained pitch (with some shift in phoneme length). (/|/, is often, but not always, at a pause point and anticipates continuation of phonation.)

Linguistic Stress

Many linguists agree that the speaker of American English utilizes combinations of four significant degrees of loudness in the production of various lexemes, phrases, clauses, and syntactic sentences. These, from loudest to most weak, are: primary/ˊ/, secondary/ˆ/, tertiary/ˋ/, and weak/ˇ/. These four degrees of American English stress are relative, not absolute, distinctions. The auditor makes his contrasts within a given utterance on the basis of the points of relative loudness in the particular stream of speech as measured against his internalized code.

In the discussion to follow, it is hoped that by a series of contrasts of the phrase "forty five," uttered in a variety of contexts, the reader unacquainted with linguistic and kinesic conventions can be sensitized to some of the relationships which have been discovered between linguistic and kinesic structure. In each case below, "forty five" is to be tested as a complete sentence, the response to an appropriate question. To orient the reader, the linguistic stresses and junctures are isolated in contrast exercises. Next, the kinesic stresses and junctures are noted. After some tentative correlations, the frame will be enlarged to demonstrate how utterance strings are tied together, linguistically and kinesically. Finally, the intimate relationship between body motion and spoken behavior will be demonstrated by some contrastive examples from spoken and moved

---

havior and certain aspects of American English intonation behavior. However, the data are exceedingly elusive and must be investigated further before even tentative generalizations can be made.

mathematics. For the reader easily (and understandably) wearied by the detail and technicality of this discussion, the following generalization can be made as the point of the exercises to follow. *Since regularities appear in the stream of movement and in the stream of audible behavior around certain syntactic forms, it is possible to state that body motion and spoken "languages" do not constitute independent systems at the level of communication. By a logic, not yet known, they are interinfluencing and probably interdependent.*

An Exercise in Linguistic-Kinesic Analysis

1:0   (a) "forty fives"   (as in a list made up of forty numerals of the shape of five)

from

  (b) *"forty* fives"   (as in the case where the speaker is distinguishing between a list made up of forty, not thirty, fives)

and from

  (c) "forty *fives*"   (as in the case of a list of forty numerals in the shape of fives, not forty numerals in the shape of sixes)

and from

  (d) "forty-fives"   (as in the case of guns of a particular caliber)

and from

  (e) "forty-*fives*"   (as in the case where the speaker is distinguishing guns of .45 caliber from guns of a .44 caliber)

The question is how (in the sense of what code does he possess) does a normal speaker of English (without recourse to larger contexts in which these appear) make these distinctions when he *perceives* them as total sentences in response to a direct question. If we attend only to degrees of loudness and annotate them with the linguistic symbol, we get some immediate contrasts*: In examples (a), (d), and

---

*According to linguists concerned with American English structure, every stretch of phonation bounded by terminal junctures contains a primary stress against which other stress activity can be weighed.

(e) our informants spoke "fives" louder than "forty." We assign primary stress /ˊ/ to "fives."

When we then compare the production of the initial lexeme in these three forms, we can perceive that "forty" in (a) is in contrast (stronger than) with "forty" in either (d) or (e). We assign secondary stress /ˆ/ to the stronger "forty" in (a). Thus, (a) is recordable as /fôrty fives/. The "for-" in "forty" in (d) and (e) is demonstrably not under weak stress and can be recorded as tertiary /ˋ/. We now have (d) and (e) as /fòrty fives/.

1:1 (a) fôrty fíveš   (as in a list of the numeral fives)

     (b) fòrty ⁺ fíveš   (as in the guns of a given caliber)

     (e) fòrty ⁺ fíveš   (as in .45's not .44's)

Further information is required to distinguish (d) from (e). One solution is to note that some informants hear "fives" in (e) as having a higher pitch than in (d) and to note this by an arbitrary convention (∗).∗ Thus (e) is recorded as /fòrty ⁺ fíveš/. However, since a number of informants cannot, when listening to tape, distinguish (d) from (e), we will pay special attention to this later when we combine the linguistic and kinesic data. Thus, (d) /fòrty ⁺ fíves/; (e) /fòrty fíves/.

We find that when stress only is attended to, "forty" and "fives" appear equally loud in (b) and (c). Thus: (b) /fórty fíves/ and (c) /fórty fíves/. The single bar juncture, described above, is involved and we get /fórty | fíveš/ for both (b) and (c). Again, pitch seems to play a special role and, even though a number of our informants cannot hear it, we add our pitch distinctions as one solution to the problem. Our corpus now reads:

1:2 (a) /fôrty fíveš/   (d) /fòrty ⁺ fíveš/

     (b) /fórty | fíveš/   (e) /fòrty ⁺ fíveš/

     (c) /fórty | fíveš/

These represent the most common responses in the informant test situation. However, the informant may vary his responses, and

---

∗The fact that we do not attend to pitch *patterning* in these examples does not make them artificial but incomplete. However, for purposes of explication, we omit such data. It must be emphasized, however, that no informant did *or could* omit the intonation profiles from his speech. The inclusion of (∗) and the linguistic junctures are only part of the significant intonational material necessary to the production of syntactic sentences.

some informants seem to prefer alternate contrasts. These are linguistically contrasted below.

1:3   (a) /fôrty fíveš/   (a′) "fórty | fíveš"

     (b) /fórty | fíveš/   (b′) "fórty fíveš"

     (c) /fórty | fíveš/   (c′) "fórty fíveš"

     (d) /fòrty + fíveš/   (d′) "fôrty + fíveš"

                               (d″) /fórty | fíveš/ (rare)

     (e) /fòrty + fíveš/   (e′) "forty + fíveš"

It must be remembered that these are only several of the possible vocalic variations. If the original questioner gives some signal that he has not perceived the distinctions between (b) and (c) or between (d) and (e), the informant may add paralinguistic or parakinesic behavior as he repeats for clarification. For instance, he may put *drawl, overhigh,* or *overloud* on the lexeme shown above marked by the arbitrary pitch symbol (∗) or he may put *oversoft* on the weaker stress to emphasize the stronger stress.

Kinesic Stress and Juncture

Early work in kinesics concentrated on the isolation of kinemes, kinemorphemes, and complex kinemorphemic constructions as discoverable in silenced interaction. As research proceeded, body motion behavior of a different order was detected in association with vocalization. Embedded in the complex stream, they were noted as part of the microkinesic record. At first, as they seemed inconsequential to the structure of the kinesic stream, they were dismissed as artifacts of muscular, skeletal, or skin involvements in speech production. They were to take on new significance when research energies were turned to the correlation of spoken and moved behavior in sound-filmed sequences of interaction. The regularity and the systematic nature of these eye blinks, nods, and hand and foot movements became apparent, and they could only be accounted for by analysis in the larger frame. At first, these segments were assigned to a general category of kinesic *markers* (see pp. 119–126). But, when research revealed that these could be analyzed into classes of movements (in intensity or body position) in free variation, they were elevated to the status of kinemes of stress.

There are four kinesic stress kinemes: *primary* /∨/, *secondary*

/∧/, *tertiary* or *unstressed* /−/, and *destressed* /○/. Earlier research in *kinemorphology* had demonstrated that American kinesics has at least four kinesic terminal junctures. The first, which terminates a complex kinemorphic stream with a lowering, plus a slight lengthening of movement, is termed *kinesic double cross*, /κ∗/; the second, *kinesic double bar*, /κ‖/, has a raise and hold of body part; the third, *kinesic single bar*, /κ׀/, involves a hold in position. Finally, the *kinesic triple cross* /⧣/, which usually but not always occurs coincident with a kinesic double cross, following a series of passages marked by double crosses, involves a major shift in body position.

As we shall see in the examples below, there are one and perhaps two *internal* kinesic junctures. The first, a *kinesic plus juncture*, /+/, occurs to change the positioning of the primary kinesic stress as it binds certain forms. The second, still under analysis, has been termed a *hold juncture*, /⌢/. The hold juncture, under special conditions, ties together two or more kinesic primary stresses or a primary and a secondary.

As in the case of linguistic phenomena, theoretically, there can only be one kinesic primary stress between any two kinesic terminal junctures. However, the hold junctures /⌢/ may subsume a kinesic single bar juncture between two primary kinesic stresses. The hold juncture also operates to tie several syntactic sentences together—that is, it can cover several stretches bounded by terminal /⧣/ or /‖/ junctures. I suspect the hold juncture category as too inclusive. It may, under further study, in certain situations be an allokine of a single bar, in others, a separate terminal juncture which operates across /׀/, /‖/, and /⧣/ but *within* triple-cross junctures.

As this data developed, we were suspicious of the parallel to linguistic phenomena. It seemed quite possible that we were forcing the body motion data into a pseudolinguistic frame. However, the more experience we have with the recording and analysis of utterance situations, the more confident have we become of the utility it not the final validity of this formulation. There is, after all, no reason why the systems must, at this level of structure, have two different logics.

The kinesic stress and juncture material customarily concurrent with our five contrast examples is presented below. First, stress and juncture kinemes, as derived from the behavior of informants in the question-answer environment, are presented. There is insufficient space here to detail the articulatory variations which are involved in the performance of either the kinesic stress or junctures. The reader who is a native or skilled speaker of American English, interested in perceiving these, however, can speak the examples *in response to the appropriate questions* and, by restricting his movement to his head, "feel" the body involvement.

Kinesic Stress and Juncture

2:0 (A) "fôrty fĭves" (as in a list made up of forty numerals of the shape of five)

(B) "fŏrty—fîves" (as in a case where the speaker is distinguishing between a list made up of *forty*, not thirty, fives)

(C) "fôrty—fĭves" (as in a case where the speaker is distinguishing between a list made up of forty *fives*, not sixes)

(D) "fôrty v fîves" (as in the case of guns of a particular caliber)

(E) "fôrty v fîves" (as in a case where the speaker is distinguishing between guns of .45 caliber, not .44 caliber)

These represent the most common responses in the informant test situation. However, the informant may vary his responses and some informants seemed to prefer alternate responses. These are kinesically contrasted below.

2:1 A) "fôrty fĭves" (or) A') "fŏrty | fĭves"

B) "fŏrty⌢fîves" (or) A") "fŏrty⌢fĭves"

C) "fôrty⌢fĭves" (or) B') "fŏrty# fĭves"

D) "fôrty v fîves" (or) B") "fŏrty | fĭves"

E) "fôrty v fîves" (or) C') "fôrty⌢| fĭves"

Some informants characteristically utilize parakinesic "overstrong" or "overintense" or parakinesic "drawl" in making distinctions; others appear to turn to parakinesics only when the questioner seems confused. Some informants characteristically use paralinguistic phenomena; others seem to employ parakinesics as a primary tool for contrast distinctions. Still others "pile up" para- behavior from both channels. There is some temptation to regard these variations as items of "style," personality, or as functions of larger inter-personal relationship patterns. Until we know a great deal more about the structure of both parakinesic and paralinguistic behavior, such psychological or sociological extrapolations must remain un-justified by our evidence.

Kinesic-Linguistic Correlation

When the data from the linguistic analysis and from the kinesic analysis are assembled and correlated we get interesting, if incon-clusive, results. While the general form of the kinesic material is predictable from knowledge about the linguistic form and the general form of the linguistic material is predictable from knowledge of the kinesic, there is some variation in the subshapes. There do not seem to be *absolute* and nonvariable correlations between particular junctures or stresses at the phonemic and kinemic level. However, some correlations are possible when regular combinations of stress kinemes are examined. Certain combinations of the stress kinemes form regular structures which under analysis are revealed to be members of form classes, the suprasegmental kinemorphemes.

In 3:0, below, the allokinemorphs of stress, and the kinemor-phemes of which they are members, are listed.

3:0 Allokinemorphs of Stress	Kinemorphemes
/v/	= /v/
/ʌv/ or /-v/ or /-ʌ/	= /⌣̃/
/vʌ/ or /v-/ or /ʌ-/	= /⌣̄/
/-v̄-/ or /v̄/ -v̄ʌ	= /⌣̂/
/v|/ or /v≠v/ /v⌢v/	= /⌣̃⌣̃/ *
/ook|/ or /ooᴷ⁑/ or /ook‖/	= /-o-/
/oov/	= /̃⌣/
/voo/	= /⌣̄/

When we analyze our corpus, noting the suprasegmental kine-morphemes, the interdependent patterning becomes clearer.

---

*/⌣⌢/ may, as research proceeds, turn out to be a syntacteme or even an "ut-tereme." Only as we know more about kinesic junctures can we be sure about its form and function.

3:1

A ⌒⌣ K#	A′ ⌣⌢⌣ K#	A″ ⌣⌢⌣ K#
(A) ∧ ∨ K#	(A′) ∨ | ∨ K#	(A″) /fôrty⌢fǐves̆/ K#
(a) /fôrty fíves̆/	(a′) /fórty | fíves̆/	

B ⌣⌐ K#	B′ ⌣⌢⌣ K#	B″ ⌣⌢⌣ K#
(B) ∨ ¦∧ K#	(B′) ∨ ⌢ ∨ K#	(B″) /fŏrty | fíves̆/ K#
(b) /fŏrty | fíves̆/	(b′) /fórty#fíves/	

C ⌐⌣	C′ ⌐⌣ K#	C″ ⌣⌢⌣ K#
(C) ∧ ¦∨ K#	(C′) ∧ ¦∨ K#	(C″) /fŏrty⌢fǐves̆/ K#
(c) /fórty | fǐves̆/	(c′) /fórty#fíves/	

D ⌣⌐ K#	D′ ⌣⌢⌣ K#
(D) − ⌣ − K#	(D′) ∨ ÷ ∨ K#
(d) /fòrty + fíves/	(d′) /fôrty + fíves/

E ⌣⌐ K#	E′ ⌣⌐ K#
(E) − ∨ ∧ K#	(E′) ∨ ∧ K#
(e) /fòrty + fǐves/	(e′) /fôrty fǐves/

Further perspective is provided upon (d) /forty fives/ and upon (e) /forty fives/ when we put them in contrast with another form. In these we are dealing with an example in which crescendo stress sequences of tertiary-plus juncture-primary operate. Let us contrast them with a form in which we invert the stresses to the diminuendo sequence of primary-plus-tertiary. This is characteristic over forms like "tenpins," "suitcase," and "baseball." We will singularize both forms.

3:2

D ⌣⌐ K#	F ⌣⌐ K#
(D) ∨ K#	(F) ⌘ K#
(d) /fórty + fìve/	(f) /báse + b̀all/

In both cases the kinesic /+/ juncture pulls the primary stress to tie the two lexical items into a "nominal." Let us extend this example:

4:0

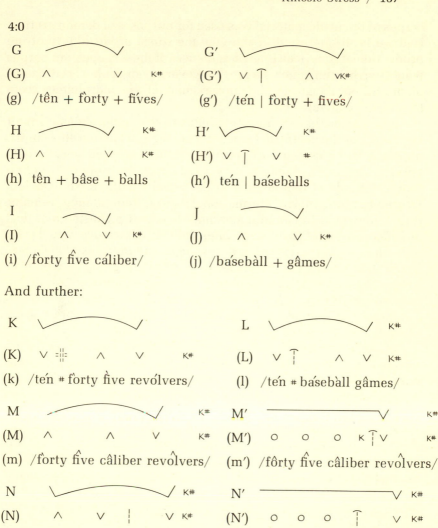

G

(G) ∧   ∨   K#   G'   (G') ∨ ⌐̄   ∧   VK#

(g) /tên + fòrty + fíves/   (g') /tén | fòrty + fivés/

H   K#   H'   K#

(H) ∧   ∨   K#   (H') ∨ ⌐̄   ∨   #

(h) tên + bâse + b̀alls   (h') tén | básebàlls

I   J

(I) ∧   ∨   K#   (J) ∧   ∨   K#

(i) /fòrty fîve cáliber/   (j) /básebàll + gâmes/

And further:

K   L   K#

(K) ∨ ≡||≡   ∧   ∨   K#   (L) ∨ ⌐̄   ∧   ∨   K#

(k) /tén # fòrty fîve revólvers/   (l) /tén # básebàll gâmes/

M   K#   M'   K#

(M) ∧   ∧   ∨   K#   (M') o o o K ⌐̄ ∨   K#

(m) /fòrty fîve câliber revôlvers/   (m') /fôrty fîve câliber revôlvers/

N   K#   N'   K#

(N) ∧   ∨   ⌐   ∨   K#   (N') o o o ⌐̄   ∨   K#

(n) /básebàll gâme | stréetcàr/   (n') /básebàll gâme | stréetcàr/

From these examples it becomes clear that *linear* survey of particular body movements as related to particular degrees of loudness does not yield significant data about phrase, clause, and sentence formation. However, examination of the relationship between the patterning of the linguistic material and the patterning of the kinesic material illustrates how each contributes structure to the comprehensible utterance. In these examples an exceedingly limited corpus of linguistic material was used for purposes of demonstration. Had we been interested in showing the *range of variability* of the production of American English sentences of these shapes, our corpus would have been much larger. However, even with variations of pitch and paralanguage, the suprasegmental kinemorphemes seem to remain relatively stable.

That kinesic patterning contributes to the comprehensibility of utterances at the syntactic level seems evident. Whether this contribution is to be assessed as "redundant" will depend very largely upon the definition of redundancy—and particularly upon the definition of the role of redundancy in the social situation. An excellent term and a useful tool in informational theory, "redundancy" remains little understood in communicational theory. It makes a great deal of difference whether we are interested in *a message* sent by *an individual* to *an individual* or in *messages* and *patterns of messages* transmitted among the membership of a human group of whatever shape. Multichannel contributions not only support continuity in ordered performance by overlapping codes of various sizes and durations but increase the likelihood of message reception from variably readied sense perceptors.

In the examples above, the lexemes, "forty" and "fives" were selected as relatively colorless, numeral lexemes. The five examples with their varying semological contexts were used to show how simple constructions and clauses are structured morphologically and syntactically. As a final example, a series of contrasts will be drawn from our continuing research on "spoken and moved mathematics." Association with Max Beberman and Gertrude Hendrix of the Illinois Mathematics Project studies and examination of their very good films on the teaching situation led to the conviction that there was considerable range of skill (or technique) to be seen in the performance of mathematics teachers. This range, from my point of view, cannot be understood by such subjective and crude or poetic descriptions as "a matter of personality" or in paradigms which define "good" teaching as a matter of "innate" skill or of the even looser concept "experience." Even less rewarding are discussions of degrees of "motivation."

It seemed to me that we need to be able to objectively describe certain differences in the *behavior* of a "successful" teacher as contrasted to that of the less "successful" teacher. ("Success" here is measured either by professional reputation or by the comparative performance of groups of pupils.) Thus far, I have been concerned as an investigator with only one very limited aspect of this monumental problem. Preliminary examination of a film made of one teacher regarded as an excellent teacher led me to observe other teachers (but, unfortunately, without benefit of film) whose teaching performances seemed to leave room for improvement. One of the behavioral differences which I observed between these teachers was that the "better" teacher enunciated his mathematical propositions as though he were speaking standard American English, while the others varied between such enunciation and a peculiarly stilted and thus ambiguous variety of spoken "written" mathematics. It seemed likely that this would occasion some distress in students who perceived mathematical concepts in other than the written frame.

At best this was an impressionistic conclusion. Since that time, as part of other research into the structure of American movement patterns, the behavior which is characteristic of spoken formulas has been under scrutiny. The research is far from completed, but certain of the findings may be illustrative of the points being made here. The examples below will serve to illustrate certain organizational functions of kinesic stress and juncture. The linguistic data are incomplete for these contrasts. Data thus far analyzed are consistent with that presented in sections (1), (2), (3), and (4) above.

Common responses given in the context of "answers to particular mathematical problems."

5:0

$$V^{K\#}$$
$$V^{K\#}$$

(a) "A" as in A

(b) "A squared"   or   "A squared"   as in A^2

(c) "A plus B"   or   "A plus B"   as in $A + B$

(d) "A squared plus B" as in $A^2 + B$

or

(e) "A plus B squared" "A plus B squared" as in $A + B^2$

(f) "A plus B squared" as in $(A + B)^2$

(g) "A plus B squared minus one" as in $(A + B)^2 - 1$

(h) "A plus B squared minus one" as in $A + B^2 - 1$

or

(i) "A plus B squared minus one over two" as in $A + B^2 - \dfrac{1}{2}$

(j) "A plus B squared minus one over two" as in $A + \dfrac{B^2 - 1}{2}$

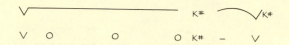

(k) "A plus B squared minus one over two" as in $\dfrac{A + B^2 - 1}{2}$

Some students, when shown these examples, suggest that the body motion behavior evident in these performances may be an artifact of eye movement or head movement in reading or writing behavior. While some informants do "move" in their reading, they appear to be about as rare as those who move their lips while reading silently. Others, upon viewing these examples, tend to view them as "mathematical behavior." Some evidence that these are special cases of more general principles of organization may be demonstrated by the following paired contrasts. For simplicity, only the suprasegmental kinemorphemes are shown. Punctuation conventions are coded to assist the reader.

5:1

(a) "A"   =   "John"

or   or

(b) "A²"   =   "John Smith"

or   or

(c) "A + B"   =   John and Mary

(d) A² + B   =   John Smith and Mary

∨ᴷ| ⌄#   ∨   ᴷ| ⌄   ᴷ#

∨ᴷ# ⌄   ∨ ᴷ#   ⌄ ᴷ#

(e) $A + B^2$ =   John (Jones) and Mary Smith

−o−| ∨ᴷ#   −o−   ᴷ| ∨ ᴷ#

(f) $(A + B)^2$ =   John and Mary <u>Smith</u>

⌄ | ⌄ᴷ#   ⌄ᴷ |

(g) $(A + B)^2 - 1$ =   John and Mary <u>Smith</u>,

                                ⌄   ᴷ#

                                when married

∨ᴷ# o ᴷ| ⌄ᴷ#

∨ ᴷ# ⌄ | ⌄ᴷ#   ∨   ᴷ#   ∨ ᴷ|

(h) $A + B^2 - 1$ =   John (Jones), and Mary <u>Smith</u>

                             ⌄   ᴷ#

                             when married

∨ᴷ# ⌄ᴷ# ⌄∨ ⌢ ⌄ᴷ#   ∨   ᴷ#   ⌄ᴷ#

(i)* $A + B^2 - \dfrac{1}{2}$ =   John (Jones), and Mary <u>Smith</u>,

                          ⌄   ⌢   ⌄   ᴷ#

                          when married, and willing

∨ᴷ# −o− ⌢⌄ᴷ#   ᴷ#   −o−

(j) $A + \dfrac{B^2 - 1}{2}$ =   John (Jones), and Mary <u>Smith</u> when

                          ⌢   ⌄   ᴷ#

                          married and willing

⌄   ᴷ# ⌄ᴷ#   ⌄

(k) $\dfrac{A + B^2 - 1}{2}$ =   John and Mary Smith when

                          ᴷ#   ⌄   ᴷ#

                          married, and willing

∨ᴷ#   ⌄   ᴷ#   ⌄ ⌢   ⌄ᴷ#

* "A plus B squared minus one over two."

Conclusion

These examples have been designed to illustrate certain definable relationships between body motion behavior as kinesically analyzed and spoken American English.* A more complete treatment would have to deal with the relationships between the body motion during silence as related to other modalities as well as that which is demanded for the performance of spoken language. We know far too little about the other communicative modalities to do more than hypothesize about such relationships. However, if we extrapolate from even the limited data presented above, it would seem that we have good reason to be deeply suspicious of any theory of human communication which accounts only for the behavior carried on the audio-aural channel.

I can do no better than conclude with the words of Colin Cherry from his excellent study *On Human Communication.*

> In all experiments carried out upon people, involving their sensations, it is of the greatest importance to record all the conditions of the test; only too frequently, results are vitiated because an experimenter has failed to record some significant attribute of the stimulus or of the environment. The human senses . . . do not possess one set of constant parameters, to be measured independently, one at a time. It is even questionable whether the various "senses" are to be regarded as separate, independent detectors. The human organism is one integrated whole, stimulated into response by physical signals; it is not to be thought of as a box, carrying independent pairs of terminals labeled "ears," "eyes," "nose," et cetera. [p. 127]

*The author is indebted to the linguistic anthropologists Norman A. McQuown, Harvey Sarles, Henry Lee Smith, Jr., and George L. Trager. These men have listened to and corrected his other crude attempts to abstract the linguistic data from these examples. However, they must not be held responsible for this particular recording.

PART 4

Collecting Data: Observing, Filming, and Interviewing

```
ЛЛЛЛЛЛЛЛЛЛЛЛЛЛЛЛЛЛЛЛЛЛЛЛЛЛЛЛЛ
```

19. *Still Photographs, Interviews, and Filming**

Paul Byers and Ken Hymen have worked on ideas about still photographs which influenced our view at Eastern Pennsylvania Psychiatric Institute of the extended present, recorded and signaled by the still photo. I have always been wary of the still camera as a research tool for the study of movement, expression, and, even, for the study of stance. While research with movies has made us increasingly aware of the intrusive role of the movie cameraman and his technology, this has not reduced my bias regarding the use of the still camera as a device for the establishment of base lines for research. The selective power of the still photo is more coercive than is that of movie film. The string of pictures adds movement to position and for me reduces the chance that a point photographed in transition will be mistaken for position. However, Byers and Hymen have demonstrated to me that in the hands of a trained and sensitive observer who carefully records the conditions of photography, one still photo is of more value than thousands of feet of film taken by a movie man who takes moving *pictures* and who is not trained to record human events and activity. The work of Alan Lomax, while not directly applicable to formal kinesic research, has been important to us. In his concern with the study of folk songs as human social events (and not merely as nostalgic curiosae), Lomax has forced me to study ritual and conventional practice as communicational contexts. His work with Conrad Arensberg and Irmgard Bartenieff on the correlation of song styles with dance styles sets a standard for cross-cultural research in derived (secondary) communication which must be met by future communication research (Lomax, 1968). It was not only in his finished work that Lomax was to influence linguistic-kinesic thinking. In long research conferences Lomax, Scheflen, and I worked together to try to make sense out of the three languages of the artist, the research clinician, and the scientist. Perhaps the

---

*[The following essay was written in 1969 for this volume. The other selections in this section describe some methods of collecting data.—B.J.]

most important thing which came out of these discussions was the realization that many of the failures of communication between workers of such different orientations are not the result of parochial stubbornness, of ill will or resistance, but stem from the fact that mutual understanding about nature is not merely a matter of translation. Unless ignorance can be pooled in a way which reveals the shape of that ignorance, the discomfort occasioned by interdisciplinary noncommunication can mask the absence of substantial knowledge to be communicated. This is often the final source of the failure to communicate.

Margaret Mead, who, with Gregory Bateson, had pioneered the use of film as research documentation, was working on her lectures for Yale at this time. She and Rhoda Metraux served as consultants and consistently forced us to a broad perspective of the E.P.P.I. project. As but one example, it was at her insistence that we looked at the work of Gertrude Hendrix and Max Beberman. Hendrix was using the training of horses to demonstrate mathematics teaching and Beberman and his group, as part of their work in the "new math," were making a brilliant attempt to examine the communicational variables in the teaching of mathematics. These workers took two movie cameras, one directed toward the student and the other focused upon the teacher. We had previously thought that two films projected at the same time would be confusing, but as we watched other people watch their movies it became clear that again preconception had led us to underestimate human adaptability. To watch two synchronized images at the same time required far less effort than we had predicted. This offered us a method of presentation which reduced the distortions introduced by earlier camera angles which, at least, were compromises developed to avoid the deluding and conventionalized swing of camera from speaker to speaker.

Less tangible, but no less important influences were exerted upon our work at Eastern Psychiatric by the way in which these educationists from the University of Illinois Mathematics Project looked at their material. It was not that they were more "scientific" or that they were tougher and less sentimental in intellect. Rather, the nature of their preoccupations and the data at their disposal permitted them to trivialize the fears of shallowness that often led us to read information into our data. Less burdened by the need to look for "hidden meaning" or to search for "deeper motivations," they concentrated upon the classroom situation in a way alien to those of us who had been working in a psychiatric context. In saying this I am not suggesting the recruitment of mathematicians as communication research scholars instead of young social scientists or humanists. I am saying that sensitivity to human motivation and to social organization may need special disciplining, if the *problem* being investigated does not demand the direct application of such sensitivity. Systematic inattention can be highly useful in the process of investigation. On the other hand, the possession of skill in mathematics is hardly sufficient to prepare the student to study human communicational *behavior*. One need only review the work of those exclusively preoccupied with information theory and with computer programming to see how crippling can be the substitution of even exquisite logics for trained and sophisticated observation. This is particularly true when the situations that scientists seek to rationalize have gained their structure from the "noise" which theoretical preconception has excluded from investigatory scrutiny. Skill in abstraction and theory manipulation can mask myopia the moment our model world precludes the inspection of the world we seek to comprehend. It would be a misuse of talent to depend upon the world's greatest monetary expert to search for rare metals. On the other hand, his perspective is hardly irrelevant. The amount of hay we have to sift is greatly reduced if we have guide lines to tell us where the needle is *not* hidden. The connection between the rigorous attention to the details of classroom interaction by teachers of mathematics and the theoretical manipulations of skilled information analysts may seem tenuous to the reader. However, both contributed to our conviction that to be understood communication situations must be investigated at a series of behavioral levels *and* that the context itself must be investigated as an integral aspect of communication projects. That is, neither the isolation of individual motivations nor the discovery of the logic of message transmissions and/or reception (regardless of how important for other problems each may be) can substitute for the exhaustive investigation of the structure of communication itself.

At Eastern Pennsylvania Psychiatric Institute, assisted by the work of Condon at Western Pennsylvania Psychiatric Institute and Scheflen and Kendon at Bronx State Hospital, we have been experimenting with the production of sound movies and of television tapes as devices to record kinesic communication as well as to communicate about it. I have mixed feelings about these media. Several things make them less useful for communicating about communication than one might think. First, we have discovered that viewing and listening habits ingrained by a half-century of audience behavior learning tends to control the shapes and sizes perceived by even the most highly motivated research or student spectator. For example, we will tend to register experience in chunks. That is, there seems to be a rhythm of pieces of given shapes and sizes which we, unaware, perceive as the "something" in "something has happened." McLuhan, in nonbehavioral terms, has pointed out that the media control the message. I should, rather, in comparably nonbehavioral terms, say that audience and producer have, without being aware of it, over the years negotiated a conventional telecommunicative structure. Performer, recorder, receiver, and spectator accede to a convention. This is difficult to penetrate if one is an investigator, or to vary if one is an artist, and almost impossible to talk about if one is an unconventional spectator.

For well over a century, pundits have viewed the passive audience with alarm—as though increased audience participation automatically would bring on more creative change. Some have even seen audience participation as the key to communicative freedom. I would submit that this can do no more than create a different form. The performer-audience ritual is dependent upon a conventional structure. To destroy that structure and to replace it with another *implicit* structure does not necessarily enhance the creative excellence of the specially talented—it may only spread the activity and limit creativity by an implicit structure geared to the capacities of a majority (or of the most coercively active). I suggest that there is a Gresham's law of creative communication which would operate here.

The relationship between actor and audience, speaker and auditor, whether viewed as complementary, mutually influencing, or, as I see it, as an aspect of larger communication structures, is not well understood either by those who are concerned with telecommunication or by those of us who are primarily interested in "direct" communication. Allen Trachtenberg, with whom I have discussed these matters, says that I am being ambiguous and, furthermore, offer little hope to those who feel that only the audience-auditors can finally influence the quality of the communication. Moreover, he stresses the fact that I seem to give the performer-speaker little control over the process either. I submit that we cannot have *control* if we do not have knowledge—all members of a communicative stream influence the shape of that stream but control can only be exerted if we have information about the stream itself. In the long run it would seem to me that, disregarding the economic investment in our present technology which would obviously influence any changes we might anticipate, if we are to change telecommunicative boundaries either for education, amusement, or science, we must comprehend the artifacts of the structure and attempt to hold them in mind, or change the structure to fit our needs.

This is not a book about telecommunication. However, insofar as telecommunicative devices are necessary for either kinesic or linguistic teaching and research and thus for education about communication research, it seems advisable to stress the instrumentation problem a bit further. A movie film or a tape ties together a string of behavior—and can include in its record more people and behavior than can other telecommunicative devices: still pictures, blackboards, or books—or, by the way—all of the conventions of lecture and recitation. At the same time, in a sense, in its record of the unidirectional stream, the movie and television screens give a more primitive record. To the extent that the stream of behavior which we apprehend seems "realistic" it lacks the explicit warning about selection more manifest in other devices. This leaves us defenseless against our conventional habits of observation which seem so natural because they are customary.

Not only does the movie and television screen reinforce, by the very velocity of its image and sound presentation, our preconception of past, present, and future in a single line, but only the most sophisticated are aware of the coercion of the technology which prepares the record. It is not difficult for the thoughtful viewer or producer to be aware of the exigencies of conscious censorship in the preparation of a script. It is extraordinarily difficult to be constantly alert to the extent of control exerted by the focus and the selection of the cameraman and his recording team. Close-ups feel right to experienced viewers, the shift of camera from speaker to auditor, or from speaker to speaker seems natural, too. They influence all of us trained by Western and, particularly, American dramaturgical conventions which see communication, the interpersonal situation, and interaction itself, as action-reaction sequences.

This is particularly serious because, with the exception of the very expensive machinery present in a few laboratories, we lack the devices necessary for instantaneous review. We cannot, without considerable expenditure of time and energy, review an event, as it passes before our eyes, to test the shapes and sizes which make up the scene. We can pause in our reading and return to earlier sections of the text and re-examine an idea presented to us. We can look and relook at pictures and at diagrams on the blackboard. And, if we can reach him, ask the lecturer for repetition or restatement. Even the most naturalistic film streams past our eyes and ears at a rate which can accelerate and obscure as we learn more about the events which we see as significant to it.

This velocity and volume of data, and the unidirectionality of the record, make the sound film or tape a difficult medium to analyze. A thousand pictures may not, unless the viewer is specially trained, carry the *effective* information of a single word. And yet, this is not an irremediable situation. If the investigator or the teacher can forego the assumption that a sound film is a labor-saving device, he and a few students can learn to use a time-motion analyst projector and can learn to replay tapes to choose segments for re-examination. To re-view requires a discipline at least as inexorable in its demands as the discipline required to be selective in viewing. There is little evidence that a preponderance of students (or teachers) will acquire that discipline. However, in the teaching situation, a teacher who has thoroughly prepared himself by the study of a film can direct the attention of his students to anticipate a sequence, replay that sequence, and then, by reviewing it before reshowing it, gradually reshape the viewing habits of his students. We require more of a teacher of literature than the ability to read and turn the pages of a book without tearing them. Eventually we may set higher standards for audio-visual teaching.

The possession of a durable and reliable projector and tape playback or a closed television system provides the educator or the investigator with a tool, but such paraphernalia are no more than tools. A microscope, a telescope, a linear accelerator are useful to the teacher or investigator as long as he has control of them. They are otherwise elegant and expensive badges of office. A printing press cannot provide us with poems or ideas, a computer cannot do more than process input. The telecommunication tools, tape recorders, cameras, films, and projectors can do no more. They are necessary, they require skill to make them useful, and they place an inevitable shape upon the data. From the outset these tools have their own limitations and these limitations must be recognized or the shapes they record or transmit can become so real as to obscure the very nature they were designed to abstract. One need only look at linguists trapped by their methodology within the narrow confines of a syntactic sentence to see that even the best tools can become straitjackets.

The paragraphs above have stressed the arbitrary nature of annotation systems and the shapes and problems imposed by recording devices. They were in no way intended to depreciate the value of these tools. I have intended only to stress the fact that annotational conventions and instrumentation cannot substitute for systematic training. Neither can common denominator observation substitute for disciplined recording and recheck. It has become acceptable among some investigators to substitute a jury technique for training or skill in perception as a test for reliability (and validity). A necessary canon in scientific procedure has been the demand that results be duplicatable, that investigators agree on the shapes of the reality they manipulated. This important principle has been vulgarized, as has operational definition, by procedures which accept as valid the perceptions of the naïve, as though they were either innocent of common preconception or, through the combination of repeated observation (or observers) equivalent to the trained and disciplined investigator. The fact that with retrial naïve observers (whether college sophomores, army privates, or colleagues) get high agreement scores is a measure of the educability of man—not of the categories to which he assigns nature. I am highly suspicious of categories which elicit high agreement among naïve observers (and by naïve I mean *not specifically trained* in observation techniques). Agreement is a measure of similarity of training and thus response; it is not necessarily a measure of the external environment observed.

There is one other *caveat* which must be included here. This has to do with the teacher or analyst as an actor. The teacher or member of a research team who can abstract and repeat a sound or an action can (with an audience prepared to accept the point) specify and dramatize particular facets of the communicative stream for special attention. The ability to abstract and reproduce a sound (particularly if it is an exotic one) or an action or stance (particularly if the behavior is bizarre, or overfamiliar and thus "invisible") facilitates the search for the location, isolation, and substantiation of minimal distinctive units and their measurement. However, the capacity to reproduce a signal or a complex of signals to the satisfaction of an audience can lead to a confusion of reproducibility with comprehension, on the part of both the investigator and of his colleagues. Although the general public may confuse the polyglot with the analytic linguist and the actor or the mime with the kinesicist, it is important that the student of communication remain vigilant to the difference.

The distinction between the performance of an act, audible, visible, or otherwise perceptible, and the comprehension of the nature and functional significance of the act in context must at all times be kept in mind by the investigator. To imitate another successfully requires a cooperative audience; the actor establishes an agreement with his audience to attend to certain aspects of a performance. That agreement is seldom open and explicit. In fact, it is often so embedded in the conventionalized context as to be as difficult to analyze as the signal behavior itself. The fact that an audience agrees to the reliability, the "realism," of a presented signal may validate the *performance* but this does not necessarily contribute to our knowledge about the signal or the context.

If the context of a given encounter limits (as it must) the "meaning" variants to be attended to in any sequence, and the audience commits itself, by participation, to this limited repertoire (as it usually will), it should not be surprising that we can achieve a high degree of agreement among the audience members about the accuracy of the performance and its assessment. Nor, by extension, should we be surprised by a considerable agreement about *incomprehensibility* of other signal events presented in the same sequence. The difficulty for the investigator comes when he attempts to distinguish audience responses to structural properties immanent in the signal complex from those which are derived from the conventionalized structure of the action-audience reciprocal.

There is little difficulty in comprehending that the vocalizations of a parrot are not isomorphic with the vocalized salutations of one man to another. It is somewhat more difficult to see that an actor greeting a fellow actor as part of a play does not perform isomorphically with the man on the street. It is extremely difficult to keep this absence of isomorphism in mind when we observe a role-playing group, a group therapy performance, or a linguist or a kinesicist presenting an example to a class (or to an informant).

To reiterate, it is not only useful but necessary to abstract and isolate bits and strings of signals for identification, test, and analysis. The danger arises when we make the assumption that any given structural context exhausts the conditions of natural performance. The fact that a kinesicist or a linguist can produce a reasonable, that is, "acceptable," abstracted facsimile of the signals observable (by certain restricting agreements), by using certain rules which he has discovered, does not mean that he has demonstrated the *communicative* distribution or contribution of the events. A phone or a kine, a word or a kinemorph, a sentence or a complex kinemorphic construction can be produced at will by a sufficiently skilled analyst or actor. This performance demonstrates the fact that a facsimile can be produced which will satisfy an audience *in a particular context*. The abstraction is a facsimile—our knowledge about it is limited by our comprehension of the *contexts* in which it appears.

This is being written at the Center for Advanced Study in the Behavioral Sciences at Stanford. One of the most valuable aspects of working here comes from the opportunity to exchange critical reading with the other Fellows in residence. Charles Tilly, after listening to the last segment of these remarks, gently cautioned me that while I was doing a reasonable job of chiding other investigators, I seem to pretend an omniscience about solutions to the problems which I have raised above. He asked whether I felt that either linguistics or kinesics as disciplines had developed a methodology which is sufficiently bias-free to avoid the pitfalls of ethnocentric observation and extrapolation. Clearly, no method of search can ever be free from bias. And, comparably, any method of data assessment on review is shaped by the logic chosen for the ordering procedure. However, to the extent that human interaction is dependent upon spoken and moved signal structures, there is an advantage to methods which seek to investigate such structures instead of assuming them. It is not nihilistic to discard unproductive models.

Descriptive linguistics has developed, and descriptive kinesics is attempting to develop, a methodology which demands explicit operations in its unit-deriving procedures. Both of these methods insist upon investigators trained to recognize as many of the artifacts of observation as have already been isolated—and to be vigilant for others not yet detected. Indigenous to these methods is the insistence upon constant check on context within particular cultures before specific generalizations are made—and upon extensive and appropriate cross-cultural investigation before universal generalizations are attempted. These strictures have been productive of insights about methodological preconception and bias, and about the need for new conceptions of communication which in turn demand new techniques for investigation.

20. Body Signals*

U NDERLYING most social science procedures is the relative incidence fallacy. We are all too inclined to confuse rarity or low
incidence of an aprioristically isolated phenomenon as, by definition,
"abnormal" and high regularity or incidence of an isolated piece of
behavior as "normal." Such definitions become increasingly malig-
nant in mental health research when "normal," thus derived, is
normatively extended to become "health," "abnormal" to become
"pathology." This is aggravated when the researcher, unclear about
the levels of organization from which he selects his data, counts, in
a single series, diverse elements like muscle tension, tics, toe taps,
and kinemorphic constructions. These varying elements do not constitute a class of components at the same level any more than do
cells, tissues, and organs. No counting procedure can make a cell
and organ into members of the same physiologically functioning
class. Almost a half-century ago, Franz Boas is reported to have
responded to an overenthusiastic young devotee of Karl Pearson by
saying, "The death of a given man is a rare occurrence in history
but a given funeral is but a special incidence of a social regularity.
The confusion of deaths and funerals can lead to nothing but further
confusion."

21. How Much Data Do You Need?†

I F THE 30 years of work described for the leveling and analysis of
American English had to be repeated for every society with
which we might be concerned, microanalysis would offer little of

---

*From "Body Signals: Normal & Pathological," presented to the American Psy-
chological Association in September 1963.

immediate value to cross-cultural research. This is hardly the case. The analysis of American English provides us with a model which should make it possible for skilled analysts to order the communicational behavior in a much shorter time than seemed possible before. And, once analyzed, the control of patterned communication sharply increases both the acuity and the reliability of the observer.

If the experience gained within the past 3 years is a guide, one of the most important questions raised by microanalytic studies is related to the amount of data required for the description of personality. All students of personality, particularly when people in exotic societies are being considered, are plagued by the question of how long they should stay in the field, how much material and what orders of materials they should collect. This is an absolute parallel to the task confronting the clinical researcher. How much tape does he need? How many hours must he analyze? How much reliance can he put on his own sensitized intuition to tell him what aspects of an interview to stress? Like other students of personality, we have been impressed with the sheer repetitiousness of human behavior. We have observed the same pattern of behavior repeated hundreds of times within a 20-minute period. A stretch of sound film 20 seconds in duration will often, when adequately analyzed, reveal patterns so basic to the base line of an actor that intensive descriptions of these 20 seconds will often prove more productive than hours of interviewing. Without longer stretches of film, say an hour, and without perspective on the social and cultural matrix in which the activity occurs, such a record provides little more than an extended set of candid closeups or, at best, a piece of ethnographic curiosae. But in a familiar context even very brief pieces of behavior provide us with extensive generalizations *which can be systematically tested.*

Another methodological implication of this work relates to the use of linguistics and kinesics as coordinate tools for the analyst using projective techniques. We have done no *systematic* investigation in this area, but even our preliminary tests reveal that microanalysis of the noncontent aspects of the interaction involved in testing multiplies the emergent data and provides reliability checks on it. This is particularly important for those working with nonliterate peoples. Our present guess is that in pseudostatistics proba-

†From "Paralanguage: Twenty-five Years after Sapir," in *Lectures on Experimental Psychiatry,* Henry W. Brosin, ed. (Pittsburgh, University of Pittsburgh Press, 1961).

bly no more than 30 to 35 per cent of the social meaning of a conversation or an interaction is carried by the words. Microcultural analysis offers objective measures of at least a portion of the remainder.

Finally, and this is for the future, the microculture approach should, as research proceeds, make it possible for us to use the derived systems, jokes, games, folklore, dances, and drama as controlled laboratories for the measurement of the participants. We do not as yet have control of these derived systems—we do not have the research necessary to understand what special structuring these systems exert on language and body motion. But it is clear from even our most limited investigation that the sound camera and the tape recorder can now be regarded as necessary field tools. With carefully planned filming and taping, the field worker or the clinical researcher can come back with a record for extended laboratory analysis. It may take some time for schools to include courses in sound photography in their curricula; an even longer period of demonstration may be required before foundations and other fund-granting institutions recognize the necessity for these tools, but such research can now be justified for those with sufficient training to do the analysis.

22. *Sequence and Tempo**

As we have grown more sophisticated in social research, especially in interaction and communication research, we have become more and more concerned with the difference between timing and clocking. As I use the term, "timing" refers to those operations which relate abstracted events in an explicitly defined sequence to other events within that sequence. We are concerned with asking whether or not given events can occur together, in parallel or in series, in some kind of repetitive order. We are not, in this sense of timing,

---

*From "Critical Moments in the Psychiatric Interview," *Research Approaches to a Psychiatric Problem,* Thomas T. Tourlentes, ed. (New York, Grune and Stratton, 1962), pp. 179–188.

attempting to place the data in calendrical or horological frames. We are attempting to isolate the structure of continua.

By way of example, it is a common human experience to begin associations in childhood (with only intermittent contacts during much of the courtship, marriage, and childbearing periods) which are resumed with no sense of break in the later years of life. This is a patterned experience which can be played through without disruptive derangement from other life themes. The steps in such a pattern can be isolated and compared, without reference to actual time periods, to those of similar structures with other participants.

A few years ago as part of a larger study at the University of Louisville, the Interdisciplinary Committee on Culture and Communication attempted to isolate the steps in the American adolescent "courtship dance." We found it quite easy to delineate some twenty-four steps between the initial tactile contact between the young male and female and the coitional act. These steps and countersteps had a coercive order. For instance, a boy taking the girl's hand must await a counterpressure on his hand before beginning the finger intertwine. The move and countermove, ideally, must take place before he "casually" and tentatively puts his arm around her shoulders. And each of these contacts should take place before the initial kiss. However, there seems to be no clockable duration necessary for each of these steps. The boy or girl is called "slow" or "fast" in terms of the appropriate ordering of the steps, not in terms of the length of time taken at each stage. Skipping steps or reversing their order is "fast." Insistence on ignoring the prompting to move to the next step is "slow." In other words, we found in this situation, as in others in the American scene, that order is often sensed as time. The courtship dance, in clock time, is probably as short as an hour or as long as several years. I have oversimplified this example. It's hard to imagine anything duller than a clock-watching lover. Skill in love-making involves the utilization of minimal physiological signals from both partners and this is probably basically definitive in the "fast" and "slow" designations. However, this does not change the generalization. Such behavior is communicative, is patterned and learned, and is part of the interactive ritual.

We are now and probably will for some time be doing basic research in a number of disciplines before we can do more effective research on human interaction. We still do not know its significant intervals and moments and we are certainly not yet prepared to make more than preliminary statements about the function of the elapse of varying amounts of clock time in such interactions. In projects throughout the country various investigators are attempting to isolate significant intervals and their moments in the psychiatric process. Those who are using sound film and frame-counter equipped analyzers are working on absolutely clocked sequences. It has been our experience at Eastern Pennsylvania Psychiatric Institute that clocking can become an end in itself if one does not carefully tie such operations in an explicit manner to the general design of the research. It is so easy to count the frames of a given sequence and divide by 24 (the number of frames per second at sound speed) that unless we reassess our selected moments by strict methodological procedures, we end up with little more than a catalog of behavioral categories of different clock periods. At times, this procedure has proved useful as a screening device, but, generally speaking, it obscures by reverse procedure. Timing should precede clocking.

The investigator needs to know what it is that he wishes to find out from his data. He must then use those timing operations which will best give him manipulable entities. Only after this can he do his clocking to discover the triviality or significance of precise ranges of clocked durations, velocities, and accelerations. Let me take as an example an aspect of interactional phenomena which I have been investigating. In the course of a series of filmed intervals, psychiatric and otherwise, a piece of behavior appeared: the anterior lowering of the head from its erect position to some point and the return to the erect position.

The methodology employed in kinesics in this kind of research is quite comparable to that used by the linguist. As soon as the investigator suspects that a regularity has a unitary value, he abstracts the unit from the continuum of activity. Having isolated it, he seeks other instances of the same articulatory shape. He then compares the contexts of these instances to see (a) if he has a unit, (b) whether it occurs in comparable behavioral matrices, and (c) whether the presence or absence of the isolated event occasions comparable shifts in these contexts.

To return to the head nod (n): as I reviewed head nods in my filmed material I noted that certain moments contained one head nod, others two head nods, and still others from three to nine such nods. Certainly, on the level of prekinesic, skeletomuscular activity, the individual nods involved in these activities seemed the same. That is, prekinesically we had a situation which included one head nod, two one-head nods, and three or more one-head nods. However, context analysis quickly revealed that one head nod was distinguishable as a stem form (so-called gestures have proved to be stems requiring modifying kines for production) from a two-head nod (when there was no sustained rest at either the highest or lowest point of the down and up and down and up movement sequence) as a stem. Both of these proved to be in sharp contrast to the form: three or more head nods. All of these nod forms were measured with the same accompanying kines, that is, with the same facial and body components. Then by context analysis we could isolate the contextual meanings of the stem forms as auditor behavior.

The first, //n//, repetitively occurring during the vocalization of a *vis-à-vis,* appears to sustain the interaction without significant change in the level or content of the communication. The second, //nn//, occurring during such a vocalization, is seen to stimulate elaboration of a previously established point or to be followed by an increased or decreased rate of vocalizing. Finally, the form //nnn// as an auditor response, like //n// and //nn//, occurs during the vocalization of a *vis-à-vis.* //nnn// is usually accompanied and/or followed by vocalic hesitation, change of subject, or gradual fadeaway of phonation on the part of the speaker.

Interestingly enough, in certain yet undetermined contexts //n// seems interchangeable with //nn// for certain respondents. We have three occasions when //nn// accompanies the sentence "No#...#" on the part of actors who make //n// substitutable for //nn//.

The fact that some movers tend to use //n// and //nn// interchangeably seems to be idiosyncratic and related to their image of self as encouraging listener. We have thus isolated three separate mutually distinguishable stem forms. When we now begin to clock //n//, //nn//, and //nnn// we get significant data. For instance, we discover that if the duration of //n// is less than .4 second and does not coincide with a primary linguistic stress on the part of the speaker, it seems to act as strong affirmation of the speaker's behavior. If it coincides with the speaker's primary stress, $//n - .4//$ acts to emphasize the interdependence of speaker and auditor. If //n// has a duration of .8 of a second or longer, the velocity of vocalization may well shift. In several instances $//n + .8//$ occasioned the interruption of the flow of vocalization for interpolation and elaboration of earlier points. After a $//n + .8//$ one patient interrupted his flow, shifted his stance and said, "I was only joking." Another said, after a similar self-interruption, overloud and rasping, "God damn it, why don't you believe me# " The therapist blinked three times . . . held his face in "dead pan" and said:

"Whŷ do yôu belíeve/I doñ't belíeve yôu# "

The patient focused on the eyes of the therapist and with his face in dead pan said:

"Yoû kêep intérrúpting mè/when I wañt to têll yôu sômething//"

I have not completed clocking operations with //nn// and //nnn//. However, at the risk of making my illustration overlong, one more item might be added. I have been attempting to ascertain how far apart in chronological time three or more //n//s might be from each other in order not to be kinesically identical to //nnn//. Thus far I have not been able to arrive at a definitive clocking of the //n// interstices. However, I can make the following three generalizations. (a) More than two //n// acted by an auditor within a vocalization marked by linguistic terminal junctures is normally followed by hesitation behavior on the part of the speaker. (Unless the //n// are coincident with the speaker's primary stresses.) (b) More than four //n// if equidistant from each other within a 30-second stretch have been seen to be followed by searching behavior on the part of the communicatively normal speaker. That is, marked rhythmicity on the part of the auditor, if apparently unrelated to a parallel or counterrhythm on the part of the speaker, seems to communicate self-stimulation and lack of attention. (c) If //nnn// is made up of //n// of less than .4 second, the communicatively normal speaker may stop vocalizing entirely or ask a question like "What's the matter? "

Nearly every interviewer whom we have observed uses //n// repetitively as part of his response behavior. Our study of the item was implemented by my access to films of residents taken at the Upstate Medical School of New York. Several of these inexperienced therapists handled the "understanding nod" like an overheavy baton, often beating time to the pulse of their own anxiety rather than to the rhythm of the patient's story. We called this the "sore thumb" nod. Since that time we have come to recognize the "sore thumb nod" as a special case of either //nnn//, //n − .4//, or //n + .8//.

In summary of this illustration of kinesic research, aimed ultimately at a methodology for studying communication between patient and therapist, it should be re-emphasized that timing must precede clocking. Initially, tentative units were abstracted. Only after certain classes of these units were isolated and tested in context was it possible to discover that our classes were overbroad. At that point it became evident that further units with clocked value were required. Through these operations it has been possible to derive five kinesic stem-forms. Two of these, //n// which is the common "nod" and //nn// which writers refer to as the "nod of agreement or encouragement," are in the awareness of all speakers and movers of English. //nnn// is marginal in this sense. Writers may indicate such behavior as "continuing to nod." The other two forms //n − .4// and //n + .8// require more elaborate literary devices for explication. However, at present writing it seems likely that they will prove to have a kinesic function of comparable value to that of the other three forms. The fact that they are less explicitly definable by the nonkinesicist is trivial.

One final technical point: the notations (−.4) and (+.8) are, in a sense, time boundary markers for the shape of //n// for a normal mover. It must be remembered that if the general base line of a given speaker is characterized by overall slowness or speed, these clockings will undergo a shift relative to the usual pacing of the speaker. That is, even though in this instance we have been able to achieve a high degree of measurement precision, clocked behavioral units remain relative, not absolute, entities. I have the feeling that we are on the verge of making comparable discoveries with both larger and smaller intervals and moments.

23. *Head Nods**

KINESICS is no more concerned with specific body movements than it is with specific body parts. It is concerned with the derivation of ranges of movement with equivalent function. On the articulatory

*From "Kinesics Analysis in the Investigation of the Emotions," presented to the American Association for the Advancement of Science, December 29, 1960; published as "The Kinesic Level in the Investigation of the Emotions," in *Expression of the Emotions in Man*, Peter H. Knapp, ed., pp. 123–139. Copyright 1963 by International Universities Press, Inc. [On head nods, see also the preceding selection.—B.J.]

level no two body shifts are ever identical, but kinesic analysis reveals that it is possible to derive variants of behavior which can be used interchangeably. Usually such variants are located within a given region of the body.

It can be demonstrated that the head-nod kine //Hn// is a kinesic unit covering a class of down and up movements of the head. This class is made up of a series of movements which are called kine variants. In a population of American movers in comparable contexts, it is possible to show by contrast analysis that the kine //Hn// covers a range of kinic variants (Hn)[1,2,3,] etc. These kinic variants differ from each other along two axes, breadth and velocity. Our present measurements indicate that informants (interactants) respond to any down and up movement of the head (in the median sagittal plane) utilizing any portion of an arc extending from approximately 5 degrees to about 15 degrees as "meaning" the same thing. That is, the structural meaning of $(Hn)5° \equiv (Hn)8° \equiv (Hn)13° \equiv (Hn)15°$. Comparably, clocking has revealed that a similar population of movers will make a full 15-degree nod in moments which can extend from about .5 seconds to around 1.5 seconds. While we have not exhaustively clocked the intermediate arc utilizations, the evidence indicates that velocity, not duration, is significant here. That is, we have kinic variants (Hn) with a velocity range of from about .8 degrees per frame (or $\frac{1}{24}$ second) to around 3 degrees per frame. When kine variants of this velocity range have been checked out in their structural contexts, they may be recorded as the kine //Hn//. As such //Hn// stands in contrast to head movements with higher and lower velocity and incidentally with movements of greater and lesser breadth. The role of //Hn// as combined in kinemorphs and kinemorphic constructions of varying size can now be investigated. The fact that we have abstracted //Hn// from our kinic variants and do not need to attend at this level of analysis to the particular breadth or velocity of these variants does not mean that we ignore such variations in behavior. The fact that such variation is kinesically insignificant does not mean that these variations are communicationally insignificant. We carefully store our descriptions of such data as reminders for parakinesic analysis. Investigation of the American movement system has revealed that it is possible to isolate a series of ranges of variation which "modify" the kinesic structures and which have an analytic identity separate from these structures. These variations I have termed the *motion qualifiers*. This category includes:

Intensity: Which delineates the degree of muscular tension involved in the production of a kine or kinemorph. It has been possible to subdivide intensity into five relative degrees of tension; overtense, tense, N, lax, and over lax. It is obvious that intensity variation in //Hn// is a function of the activities of the neck muscles. (For American movers it is possible to record a //Hn// as having degrees of tension without referring to the neck where we are recording //Hn// as a single kine kinemorph. If, however, a full kinemorph including eyebrows, eyes, etc., is structured, the degrees of intensity must be recorded as occurring in the neck.)

Range: Width or extent of movement involved in performance of a given kine or kinemorph. Range is subdividable into narrow, limited, N, widened, and broad.

Velocity: The temporal length (relative to the range) involved in the production of a kine or kinemorph. Thus far we have been able to isolate only a three-degree scale for duration: stacatto, N, and allegro.

Although it is possible to get absolute range and velocity measurements, such measurements give us little more than central tendencies. The ascription of "overtense," "staccato," or "broad" to a piece of behavior is assigned only after the base line of the interactants has been established and the general qualifier behavior of the actor has been noted. Thus, while informants tend to react to head nods of .8- to 1-degree movement per frame as allegro and to 2- to 3-degree movements per frame as staccato and to 1- to 2-degree movements per frame as normal, these velocities shift in value depending upon whether the overall movement pattern of the interactant is slow or fast. Comparably, an arc of from 5 to 8 or 9 degrees is reported as limited and one from 12 to 15 degrees is regarded as widened. The viewer makes his judgment of these in terms of his own diakinesic system, depending upon the normal range of movement in the actor.

It should be clear from the foregoing that the communicational units are not absolute bits of articulations but are always parts of larger cross-referencing contexts. The system of which they are a part is sufficiently ordered that its patterning can be internalized by all members of the social system who must interact through it. At the same time the values of its particles and forms must be sufficiently flexible to permit adaptation on the part of the viewer to both individual and situational variations.

24. *Similarities and Differences**

$\mathbf{S}$EEMINGLY identical body movements supply the activity for quite different cue classes. Within the space allotted here it is difficult to illustrate this necessarily technical point. To keep the example as simple as possible, the eyebrows are selected for discussion and only the variables of context and duration are described. The specialized kinesic terminology and annotational conventions may prove confusing to the reader but the examples chosen should be sufficiently familiar to soften the technicality of the illustration.

One of the more easily detectable *kines* (least perceptible units of body motion) is that of eyebrow lift and return (bbʌv). At times such movement is fleeting; I have been able to detect and record brow movement lasting but thousandths of a second. For instance, the brows may be raised in certain contexts and held for a short duration before returning to the zero or base position. Such positioning may operate as one of the *allokines* (members of a class of events substitutable for each other) of the junctural *kineme* (the least cue class) of /k//. This bilateral eyebrow raise is quite comparable to, and may during phonation co-occur with, the linguistic single bar of terminally raised pitch, appropriate to the context of "doubt" or "question" or as a signal to repeat a message. If we ignore the duration of the action and attend only to the spatial movement of the brows, an identical movement of the brows may be seen in the circumvocal behavior of speakers who select the brows for kinesic stress functions. Intensive experimentation on the relationship between spoken and moved American has demonstrated that there are 4 degrees of kinesic stress (Birdwhistell, 1965e). The brows form one of the positional allokines of the kinemes of stress. Other allokines

*From "Body Behavior and Communication," published as "Kinesics." Reprinted with permission of the publisher from the *International Encyclopedia of Social Sciences,* David L. Sills, Editor. Volume VIII, pages 379–385. Copyright © 1968 by Crowell Collier and Macmillan, Inc.

are provided by the head, hand, foot, or body nodding or the lid closure that accompanies speech.

Thus, the kine "eyebrow raise" (bbʌ) may be allokinic with the kines of superior head nod (hʌ) or hand nod (/ʌ), members of the class kineme of kinesic single bar /k//, in one context position and an allokine of the form degrees of kinesic stress, /primary, secondary, unstressed, or destressed/ in another. These two allokinic roles do not exhaust the cue potential of the brows. Furthermore, with the same muscular involvement, the (bbʌ) may be an allokine of the kineme, the first degree of eyebrow raise, /bb^1/, which combines with other circumfacial kinemes to form a kinemorph.

I fully appreciate the reader's difficulty in picturing these abstractions. It is as hard to put movement into words as it is to move words. The point made here may be comprehended if the reader will conceive of a conversation in which an animated speaker is being attended to by an interested auditor. The eyebrows of the speaker rise and fall as he speaks (kinesic stress kinemes). From time to time, the speaker's eyes "focus" upon the face of the auditor and he pauses in his speech and raises his brow, /k//. He may continue vocalization following the single head nod, /hn/, of the auditor. During one sequence of the conversation, the auditor may "de-expressionalize" into the complex kinemorph of dead pan, //O//; the speaker, without signaling response, may continue vocalization until the auditor raises his brows /bb^1/ while sustaining the dead pan //O// to form the kinemorph // $\frac{\text{bb}^1}{\text{O}}$ //. At this point, the speaker hesitates in his speech flow, drops his head and lids. // $\frac{\text{h} \quad \text{v}\wedge}{\bullet\bullet \quad \text{v}\wedge}$ // and, after several vocal false starts, repeats part of his lexication. In the situations which we have observed, several conversationalists returned in discourse correction to the topic under discussion at the onset of the auditor's dead pan, //N→O//.

These three kinesic activities do not exhaust the cue potential of the eyebrows. Like the scalp, the eyebrows, while mobile in position in the young, gradually become relatively stationary in *base* placement (the point from which movement is initiated and the point of return following movement). As measured at the most superior aspect of the hirsute brow, there is a possible range of almost ½ inch for brow placement. While the diakinesic (comparable to dialect) range is less marked in Americans, any observant traveler in England can mark the contrast between the high brow placement of certain regional and economic groups (so that many Englishmen look to the American as though they were perpetually surprised) as contrasted to the low brow placement in other areas and at different socioeconomic levels (so-called beetle browed). Such brow and scalp placement is learned behavior and is, on the one hand, an aspect of unique identity (as part of signature behavior), and, on the other, contributes to the common appearance of family, group, and regional members (signature behavior at another level). From this example of certain eyebrow behaviors and from this view of communication it becomes clear that communicative units may vary in duration from milliseconds to years. It may be argued that individual appearance, like diakinesic variation, is not to be classified as communicative behavior. Such a position, focusing on short sequences, would deny, too, the communicative role of dialect and individual speaking style. However, any regular and systematically variable, learned behavior which redundantly contributes to the definition of an aspect of the code is in itself part of a larger code and must be understood if we are to comprehend the structure of the interactive process. As we have long realized intuitively, there is more that goes on in any conversation than is present in the immediate interaction. It is the researcher's duty to adapt his observations to the shapes of nature.

25. *Body Motion Research and Interviewing**

IN THE process of training ten interviewers for an extended study of a Kentucky hill community, I noted that there were considerable differences in the abilities of these interviewers to note, recall, and/or record either gestures or less explicitly defined motion complexes. Several of the interviewers were quite visual-minded and seemed anxious to pursue the leads they got from their observations. However, the majority of the interviewers, while evincing considerable interest in the method, were less capable in gathering or

*Excerpted from *Human Organization*, Vol. II (1952), pp. 37–38.

organizing such data. Although the reports of all the interviewers showed signs of increasing sensitivity in observing body motion, only two could be described as skillful.

As the study proceeded and the group became more objective concerning their interviewing experiences, a tripartite scheme was developed for describing movement in the research conferences. The broadest generalizations concerning the relationship between the interviewer and those interviewed (or in less formal situations, interacted with) we termed "syntactic," that is, they helped to classify sex, marital status, age, and social position, as well as such patterns of interaction as "stranger," "friend," "acquaintance." At least half of the interviewers became sufficiently sensitive to these signals to see shifts occurring in relationships and to orient the interview accordingly. These shifts are common in everyday experience. Anyone who has ever observed (or participated in) an intersex situation which has changed from being "just friends" to "courting" is aware of this. The problem for the interviewer is to observe this quickly and so be able to react to the shifting situation.

Closely related to the first category, but requiring more elaboration in description and more effort at recall, were behaviors which were listed as "tonal." By carefully observing long muscle activity, hand-mouth patterning, movement of the hands and feet, "cues" could be observed which indicated aspects of an interview to stress or repeat. "Rigidity" or "shift," even without noting the particular part of the body which moved was found to be easily recordable and was exceedingly fruitful in suggesting areas for intensive interviewing. In fact, it was our conclusion that such cues were at least as significant as verbal "slips" as an indication of primary attitudes. If we keep in mind the fact that the person interviewed is not insulated from the interviewer, that there is a social relationship extant between the two at least for the duration of the interview, a case could be made for having the interviewer making an oral instead of a written report. Often in the dramatization of a critical interview, an interviewer will "act out" cues that he may not have noticed consciously during the actual interview. While this is obviously not feasible for all interviews, we found that the dramatization provided an excellent training device for the team. It was particularly successful when a male and female of comparable backgrounds replayed an interview in which they had jointly participated. When roles were interchanged, both became aware of the importance of cross-cultural perspectives. Out of the "silent playback" came some of our most important cues for re-examination of a critical interview.

The third of the three categories is the least well defined and, at the present time, largely dependent upon the peculiar aptitudes of the interviewer. This third concerns the symbolic meaning of what might be called arrested motion sequences. Some interviewers will pick up a variety of informational levels in any interviewing situation. Some will even go so far as to report statements that the recording machine or the verbal report specifically contradict. In a sense, such an interviewer "hears" kinesthetically. Although it is dangerous, methodologically speaking, wholly to trust such abilities, there have been a sufficient number of cases where later and more intensive interviewing justified such "projective" statements and convinced me that it is this kinesthetic reaction that constitutes one of the primary differences between the highly "intuitive" observer or interviewer and his less-skilled counterpart.

We must recognize the inherent difficulties in body motion research. How are we to identify the "whats" of body motion? How do we isolate, differentiate, and measure a body motion? What are the initiation and end points of a particular motion or motion sequence? Until we can find devices whereby we can isolate units for quantification, it is evident that we are going to have great difficulty in determining particles of motion which serve as symbols and have meaning. I believe that this is not an impossible limitation. However, research in this area will be exceedingly expensive. A sound camera, observation laboratory, and specially designed electromechanical recording devices will probably be necessary for any definitive research in the "grammar" or "syntax" of body motion.

This paper is much too limited to permit a more adequate discussion of this aspect of interviewing and social interaction research. It has been my experience that interviewers may be taught certain aspects of this kind of research relatively easily. Anyone with some degree of visual acuity and cultural sensitivity can train himself, if he will start with one aspect of the body, accustom himself to its patterning, and then gradually enlarge his gestalt to include the total body motion system.

PART 5

Research on an Interview

26. Body Motion*

WHILE body motion behavior is based in the physiological structure, the communicative aspects of this behavior are patterned by social and cultural experience. The meaning of such behavior is not so simple that it can be itemized in a glossary of gestures. Nor is meaning encapsulated atomistically in particular motions. It can be derived only from the examination of the patterned structure of the system of body motion as a whole as this manifests itself in the particular social situation. It is the task of this essay to review the present status of kinesics, in such a manner that the nature of the relationship between the two communicative systems can be recognized—if not entirely revealed. Based on the same assumptions, the two modes, kinesic and linguistic, have parallel, even at time analogous, structures. They are, however, infracommunicational systems, not directly meaningful in themselves, and the reader should not be surprised to discover that their correlation brings difficulties into the analysis of the communicative process.

In the pages to follow an example of a communicative system without words will be presented. This is designed to sensitize the reader to the kinesic scene. The second subsection will contain a general review of the present status of kinesic theory and research. Finally, we discuss the problems of systematic interpretation.

Example

Just west of Albuquerque on Highway 66 two soldiers stood astride their duffle bags thumbing a ride. A large car sped by them and the driver jerked his head back, signifying refusal. The two soldiers wheeled and one Italian-saluted him while the other thumbed his nose after the retreating car.

*[Birdwhistell wrote this chapter and the next one for *The Natural History of an Interview* (edited by Norman A. McQuown), whose publication has been delayed. In this volume a group of contributors from several disciplines examine a film of the Doris-Gregory interview, described on pages 227 ff., in which a mother discusses her son with an interviewer. The first chapter includes a passage in double parentheses added from an earlier version.—B.J.]

Soldier No. 1:

		Car passes	
Head	H > 1°	$\cdots$	
Forehead-brows	Hfb-b	$\cdots$	Hffbbz
Eyes	$\dfrac{oo}{dnuer}$	$\cdots$	$\dfrac{=oo=}{car}$
Nose	Mz	$\cdots$	oMo
Cheeks		$\cdots$	
Mouth	L-L	$\cdots$	tl-l.
Chin		$\cdots$	
Neck		$\cdots$	
Shoulders	11 $\geq$ 1°	$\cdots$	//
Trunk	TpTp	$\cdots$	Txpivot
Hips		$> \quad > \quad >$	
Right arm	RAN[RA2:45$\leq \geq$3:45n	N $\quad$ N $\quad >$	RAn(4 $\leq$ 5)n $\qquad$ RA25n
Hand and fingers	R/1?4P	$\cdots$	R/14-p
Left arm	LAn-15'3u\[A:TA]	$\cdots$	LAn $\quad$ 3n
Hand and fingers	L/1c2C3C4C5C belt	$\cdots$	L/14c(on R. biceps)
Right leg	Y45Y	$\cdots$	RY $\leq$ 3°(Y45 + 30'Y)
Foot	Y45Y	$\cdots$	
Left leg		$\cdots$	(Y45 + 30'Y)
Foot		$\cdots$	Ly5 $\geq$ Ly3°

Soldier No. 2:

Head	H > 1°	H > 1°
Forehead-brows	Hfb-b	Hffbbz
Eyes	$\dfrac{oo}{driver}$ $\quad$ Mz	oooo
Nose		oooo
Cheeks		oooo

Soldier No. 2: *Continued*

Mouth	L-L	.	.	.	.	.	.	.	.	.	. oooo
Chin											
Neck											
Shoulders	‖ ≥ 1°	.	.	.	.	.	.	.	.	‖	
Trunk	TpTp	.	.	.	.	.	.	.	.	Txpivot	
Hips											
Right arm	RAN[RA2:45≤ ≥3:45n	N	N	<	<	<	>	.	RAn(5<∨n)n		
Hand and fingers	R/1↑4p							.	R/?↓1-5	R/14c	P≥/o̲
Left arm	LAn-15'3ul A;TA	.		>	>	>		.	LAnn		RAnn∩
Hand and fingers	L/1c2C3C4C5C belt	.		\				.	L/14cP≥		
Right leg	Y45Y	.	.	.	.	.	.	.	RY ≤ 3°(Y45 + 30'Y)	Ly5≥	Ly3°
Foot											
Left leg	Y45Y	.	.	.	.	.	.	.	) (Y45 + 30'Y)	Ly5≥	Ly3°
Foot	.	.			.	.			.		

Driver:*

Head	H≥.	.	H.nq <	>	.	H≥ .
Forehead-brows	Z .	.	Hfb-b .	>	.	Z .
Eyes	oo road.	.	oo soldiers	≥ —	.	oo Road .
Nose						
Mouth	Z .	.	oMo .		.	Z .
Cheeks	L/L .	.	tL-L .	>	.	Z .
Chin						
Neck						
Shoulders						

*Driver maintains upright, bimanual driving position throughout scene.

Time: Estimated 5 seconds. Characters: Soldier No. 1, Soldier No. 2, and Driver.

FIGURE 1. *Highway scene.*

MACROKINESIC TRANSLATION

The two soldiers stood in parallel, legs akimbo with an intra-femoral index of 45 degrees. In unison, each raised his right upper arm to about an 80-degree angle with his body and, with the lower arm at approximately a 100-degree angle, moved the arm in an anterior-posterior sweep with a double pivot at shoulder and elbow; the four fingers of the right hand were curled and the thumb was posteriorly hooked; the right palm faced the body. Their left arms were held closer to the body with an elbow bend of about 90 degrees. The left four fingers were curled and the thumb was partially hidden as it crooked into their respective belts.

The driver of the car focused momentarily on the boys, raised both brows, flared his nostrils, lifted his upper lip, revealed his upper teeth, and with his head cocked, moved it in a posterior-anterior inverted nod which in its backward aspect had about twice the velocity of the movement which returned the head and face to the midline and, thus, to driving focus.

Without apparent hesitation the boys right-stepped posteriorly, one of the boys moving in echo following the movement of the other. Facing the retreating car, one of the boys raised his upper lip to expose his teeth, furrowed his forehead, lowered his brows, contracted the lateral aspects of his orbits, and flared his nostrils. His right arm swept from its posteriorly thrust position, on a shoulder pivot, to rest, fist clenched, upper arm across the right half of the body and the lower right arm thrust up and slightly anterior to the body line. The left hand left the belt and the lower arm swept right and upward to meet the descending upper (right) arm. The left hand grasped the right biceps as, fist still clenched, the right arm moved quickly in an anterior-superior thrust in line with his shoulder and the retreating automobile.

The other boy dropped his face into "dead pan," pivoted his right arm at the elbow, flared and straightened his fingers into crooks, and, as the already-hooked thumb crossed the midline of the body in the lower arm's downward sweep, the apex of the thumb made contact with the apex of the nose. Without hesitation the arm completed its sweep across the body and came to rest hanging, palms slightly forward, at his side. The left arm, on an elbow pivot, swept downward and came to rest mirroring the right.

DISCUSSION

These three portrayals, the brief statement, the macrokinesic transcription (Fig. 1), and the kinesic description derived from the macrokinesic recording, all tell the same story with varying degrees of fullness. Some readers may feel like the little boy who received a birthday book about penguins from his aunt and felt it contained more about penguins than he ever wanted to know. However, such a record as is provided by these kinesic descriptions makes it possible for us to do extended analysis of the transaction. The initial descriptive statement is totally inadequate for such purposes.

This scene contains much more than three men gesticulating at each other. In the time it takes an auto to pass a fixed point at 70 miles an hour, a communicational transaction has taken place. In 5 seconds a social group is established, a social ritual is performed, and, presumably, the lives of three human beings are somehow affected. This is patterned activity; its components were learned in many comparable but differing situations by the participants. Yet this is no mere mechanical performance. We cannot, for the moment, "explain" it; nevertheless, it is a piece of microculture whose natural history we may attempt to relate.

We have no way of telling how the driver felt or what he thought about as he approached the soldiers. Our only evidence comes from the driver's compressed mouth (L/L). Our experience with other American scenes suggests that this orifice compression scarcely indicates receptivity to their plea. We have for the purposes of this example elected to limit the scene to that period during which all members of the transaction could "see" each other. The "why" of the transaction may rest upon the boys' previous experience that day which occasioned the particular stance which they maintained. Perhaps as the car came into view it swerved almost imperceptibly toward the soldiers, thus alerting them to the driver's attitude. Interpersonal space variations are in part extensions of kinesic activity and are often definitional of communication situations. Within the range of our abstracted scene, the driver's face was clearly visible to the soldiers for scarcely 2 seconds, and his head and face movement took less than a half second to complete. The observer has no way of finding out exactly what the soldiers "saw." Yet their unhesitating reaction indicates that the driver's analyzable act was transmitted to them. Both soldiers responded with acts of the same class as that used by the driver. Further, the second boy selected his movement complex from the same South European (post-World War II American male overlay) diakinesic system as that expressed by the driver. This supports the conclusion that theirs was a response to the driver's activity and not simply an idiosyncratic reaction to being refused a ride.

Further questions arise from the analysis of this microcosmic scene. Was the driver initially stimulated to his insultingly rejective activity by the spread-legged stance of the boys? And/or were the left thumb in the belt combined with the spread-legged stance (often part of the prefight or presexual advance behavior of adolescents) dominant as parts of a definitional act which challenged him, a male, into his negative response? Obviously, only by observing this driver and these soldiers or their counterparts in a series of contrasting scenes would such questions as these be answered. There is a strong suspicion, however, that if the driver had responded with a back nod of less ascending velocity, raised his eyebrows bilaterally, and lowered the corners of his lips in a "I would if I could, but if I can't, I can't" manner the boys would have carried out their activity in a considerably less hostile manner.

This scene is illustrative of the extent to which a human communicational event, a transaction, can be completed without recourse to verbal behavior. At the same time it demonstrates the fact that communication within even one modality is seldom a simple affair. The student of body motion behavior is not always so fortunate as to have a scene so clearly defined for him. Nor do most transactions have their interactional tempos so neatly marked, as in this case, by the explicitly conventionalized "gestures."

Notwithstanding its relative simplicity, the scene provides a useful point of departure for our present discussion. The ritual of "thumbing a ride" is familiar in American culture, yet a closer analysis of this special incident is illustrative of the hidden complexity of such scenes. In the soldiers' persuasive activity with the "thumbing a ride" gesture as the ostensible action proposition of this scene, we are provided with an excellent example of the extent to which an act can be modified by incongruent movement complexes which complete it. The spread-legged stance, congruently modified by the thumb-in-belt complex, contains two components which combine in a larger act. At the same time this act is, at one level, incongruent with the gesture of thumbing. Such components may modify, that is, may constitute commentaries on, each other. What they mean is another matter. At the moment we are concerned only with their relationship to each other and to the package act of "thumbing."

By careful cross-context analysis, we can derive a series of working hypotheses concerning the soldier's initial act and its incongruent components. The stereotypic "thumbing" gesture is deceptively familiar.

We must remember that the same gesture in another actional setting is conventionalized as the insulting or mock-insulting directive to "Get lost!" In fact, the complex act described above, if it took place on a street corner in Los Angeles or Chicago, could have just this explicit interpretation. Through contrast analysis, we are able to say that the "thumbing" action as produced is itself incongruent with its context—*if* we postulate that the dominating purpose of the boys was to persuade the driver to give them a lift. The recognition that communicational behavior can be congruent in one setting and incongruent in another should serve as a warning against any theory of meaning which suggests that the particles carry meaning in and of themselves.

Contrast analysis permits us to define this particular combination of movements in this context. We postulate the arm and thumb as an "appeal for a ride," the spread-legged stance modified by the thumb-in-belt as "male defiant," and the whole as an act conveying a "defiant appeal for specific assistance." This complex of behavior is consistent with the role of these late adolescents, in uniform, who are avoiding "begging." These young soldiers are in no position to play the role of the college boy who "thumbs" a ride but whose college sticker and clothes belie the ingratiating stance and head cock plus smile with which he modifies his petition.* We could pursue such contrastive examination throughout the entire scene, and in the final analysis the social meaning of the individual movements, gestures, acts, and action must be phrased in terms of the entire scene. These are all susceptible of analysis if the activity is seen as a transaction, in the context provided by the various participant social roles as defined by American male subculture. The scene may be viewed as a role-stating ritual in which the component activity is such that it negates the central gesture. The boys must wait for another car and driver in order to get to Los Angeles. It is probably safe to say that the boys either must amend their activity or wait until a driver with a different set toward such messages comes along if they hope to get a ride.

* For an interesting analysis of the complex social psychological aspects involved in such "presentations," see E. Goffman (1959).

Background to Kinesics

The methodology of kinesics is still extremely crude. At its present stage of development, kinesics may claim to be a science only by virtue of the canons which dominate its operations and by virtue of the postulates upon which these operations depend. As a body of knowledge, it cannot yet be judged worthy of the appellation *kinesiology*. Yet 5 years of research which has utilized and constantly refined the methodological procedures of kinesics have been so fruitful that it is without qualms that the present investigation (see pp. 115–116 and 228n) employing those procedures, is attempted.

It is entirely fitting that psychiatrically oriented interview material be the subject matter for this initial attempt to apply practically the data derived from kinesic investigation. Psychiatrists and psychologists have for over a century been aware that body motion and gesture were important sources of information regarding personality and symptomatology. Allport, Dunlap, James, Krout, Lersch, Ombredane, Groddeck, and Wolff are but a few of the students of personality who have contributed to a considerable body of literature concerning expressive movement. The brilliant observations of Felix Deutsch on what he calls "posturology" must be especially noted. His is one of the clearest statements concerning the diagnostic value of body motion and posture. Kinesics, however, represents both a theoretical and a methodological departure from studies such as these which stress personal activity and individual performance. It is our hope that communicational research and, particularly, kinesic research, will provide a methodology, an annotational system, and a set of norms against which these kinds of intuitional systems can be checked. It is our conviction that significant statements concerning the behavior of particular individuals must be based on an understanding of the patterns of intercommunication of more than one actor. The significance of particular individual variation can be assessed only when the range of permissible group variation has been established.

There is nothing new about the recognition that formalized gestures play a role in communication. Theatrical performances, whether centering around dancing, drama, opera, or the mime have long emphasized the role of gesture, particularly in its stereotyped or conventional form. Integral to every religious ritual, the gesture is stressed in all novitiational training. A considerable bibliography has been collected with representation from almost every literate country and extending back in time to early India, which evidences the international character of the interest in gestures, and their *proper* performance. Most of these writings are of collateral interest to the kinesicist.

The concentration upon the particular gesture and its meaningful performance leaves most of these writings of primary concern to the folklorist. Perhaps when extended research into the kinesic systems of particular areas has provided a body of background material, much of this earlier material will become relevant in a new way, just as linguistic research consistently opens new perspectives upon old data of a verbal nature.

Of these earlier publications, most relevant have been those which have dealt with the development of systems for annotating body movement. Before the publication of the *Introduction to Kinesics* (Birdwhistell, 1952) we carefully reviewed a series of annotational systems and were particularly impressed by those of Craighead (1942), Lifer (1940), and Pollenz (1949), and these no doubt influenced our system of microkinesic recording. These annotational systems are all extremely useful for recording the conventionalized patterns present in the dance—modern, classical, or folk. They are, however, somewhat too limited in scope for use as instruments of broad kinesic research. Perhaps the most complete and extensive recording system in usage today is that provided by the Laban school. Used principally for industrial studies, this system has been used effectively both for stage and for general movement recording. The decision to develop the specialized system presented here rests finally upon the conviction that annotational conventions which signal the specific operations governing their abstraction are probably desirable. In short, recording systems should derive, in the first instance, from considerations of theory and methodology, rather than the reverse. As research and theoretical re-evaluation continues, such recording procedures must necessarily be revised.

The microkinesic system and the macrokinesic system demonstrated in Fig. 1 (both outlined in Appendix III) have been revised a number of times and must be further revised as body motion research continues. Certainly any system which is as accurate and which would permit still easier and swifter notation would be more desirable. As the annotational system for microkinesic recording now stands, only a relatively large, well-trained (and thus expensive) team could record live microcultural material with any degree of completeness and accuracy. Designed for the analysis of filmed material, the kinegraphs are useful only for checking kinesic research with live subjects. They are insufficiently flexible for primary microkinesic research on such subjects.

The interdependent nature of linguistic and kinesic research is anticipated by Edward Sapir, who, a little more than a half century after Darwin, says:

> Gestures are hard to classify and it is difficult to make a conscious separation between that in gesture which is of merely individual origin and that which is referable to the habits of the group as a whole . . . we respond to gestures with an extreme alertness and, one might almost say, *in accordance with an elaborate and secret code that is written nowhere, known by none, and understood by all* [italics ours, R. B.].*

Sapir did not follow up his own lead, but his students and other linguists strongly influenced by his work have contributed most to the systematization of body motion research. George L. Trager and Henry Lee Smith, Jr., at the time doing research in the structure of American English at the Foreign Service Institute, provided an atmosphere and the special guidance which encouraged the original formulation of kinesics as a science. John Broderius, another student of Sapir's, worked cooperatively with me at later stages of the refinement of kinesic principles. His constant insistence that kinesics be firmly based in prekinesic research and not be lost, as he phrased it, "in the thin stratosphere of intuition," helped to maintain the frame which early association with Smith and Trager had produced. The research with linguists on the study of an interview is another logical step in the necessarily interdependent companionship of descriptive linguistics and kinesics.

Parallel to these influences and consistent with them have been the writings of a series of anthropologists whose field experience, as did my own, led them to the conclusion that body motion and facial expression were strongly conditioned, if not largely determined, by the socialization process in particular cultural milieux. While affirming the ultimate biological basis for all human behavior, they left little doubt that out of the vast range of possible combinations of muscular adjustments, perhaps a quarter of a million in the

---

*Edward A. Sapir, "The Unconscious Patterning of Behavior in Society," in *Selected Writings of Edward Sapir in Language, Culture, and Personality,* ed. David G. Mandelbaum, (Berkeley, Univ. of California Press, 1949), p. 556.

facial area alone, each society "selects" certain ones for recognition and utilization in the interaction process.

Probably the pioneer anthropological analysis of gestural activity is Efron's (1942) test of the hypothesis that there is a direct correlation between the previous social environment of European immigrants to America and their gestural systems. Concentrating largely on the range of movement in the arms and hands, Efron contrasted the gestural systems of Italian and Southeastern European Jewish immigrants. Although his thesis correlating certain ecological factors with the respective gestural systems remains inconclusive, his work effectively demonstrates the social genesis of the evident variation in the gestural systems of these two groups.

While Efron's experimental approach has not been pursued by other investigators, Labarre (1947) and Hewes (1955, 1957) with quite different emphases, have directed the attention of field workers to the importance of recording and analyzing the gestural behavior of human groups. However, the most important anthropological contributions to the development of the study of body motion as a communicational system have come from the work of Mead and Bateson (1942). Their concern with the relationship between socialization and communication, assisted by considerable skill with and appreciation for the camera as a research instrument, set the stage for the development of kinesics as a behavioral science. Not only has their field work provided a body of materials for cross-cultural study, but their insights into the systemic quality of the communicational process have prevailed upon the writer to take up his profitable association with the linguists.

[The next four paragraphs, from an earlier draft, will serve as a convenient summary of the following section.—B. J.]

((All of these influences have contributed to the basic assumptions which underlie kinesic research. The methodological section which follows is strengthened by Bateson and Hockett's suggestions with special reference to body motion analysis.

1. Like other events in nature, no body movement or expression is without meaning in the context in which it appears.

2. Like other aspects of human behavior, body posture, movement, and facial expression are patterned and, thus, subject to systematic analysis.

3. While the possible limitations imposed by particular biological substrata are recognized, until otherwise demonstrated, the systematic body motion of the members of a community is considered a function of the social system to which the group belongs.

4. Visible body activity, like audible acoustic activity, systematically influences the behavior of other members of any particular group.

5. Until otherwise demonstrated such behavior will be considered to have an investigable communicational function.

6. The meanings derived therefrom are functions both of the behavior and of the operations by which it is investigated.

7. The particular biological system and the special life experience of any individual will contribute idiosyncratic elements to his kinesic system, but the individual or symptomatic quality of these elements can only be assessed following the analysis of the larger system of which his is a part.

Propositions 1 and 2 may seem to many readers to be somewhat overobvious. Most scientists and many laymen are—at least by credo—prepared to consider any aspect of experienceable nature as subject to ordering by scientific procedures. Yet, the scientist who attempts to communicate about the raw materials of communication finds, as in perhaps no other area, the ghosts of dualism, of "accident," and of atomistic conceptions of the peculiarity of the particular event, rising to haunt and distort the discussion. Propositions 1 and 2 represent, at least for now, the stable foundations upon which the remaining five propositions rest. In fact, the latter five propositions are particularizing refinements of the first two.

This is too often forgotten when the descriptive analysis of kinesic material reaches the point where interpretation becomes possible. It is all too easy to forget the interdependent and systematic nature of the physical universe and to engage in "explanations" of behavior which treat an *abstracted* unit as though it were by nature a thing in itself. The question "What does X mean?" can have two quite different, but within their respective frames, equally legitimate answers. When the question is asked without reference to the role of the specialist and within the framework of folk or "everyday" ideology, the answer is of necessity a statement of the respondent's personal history. Such an answer, selected and ordered by the more or less invisible patterning in which the respondent participates, is a folk answer. The folk answer is likely, at least in American culture, *to act as though* the event under discussion had a special integrity and, in fact, carried its own motive power with it. Such an answer is not, however, legitimate when "What does X mean?" translates "How do you know the place of this phenomenon in that larger pattern which you are describing?" It is this question that the methodology of kinesics is designed to answer. Whether the answer given is acceptable or not is less important than the fact that the questioner can re-examine the investigatory procedure and confirm or deny the role assigned to the particular event under discussion.

Before turning to the presentation of the methodology of kinesics, one other of the propositions should be given special attention. Proposition 7, which deals with the evaluation of idiosyncratic or symptomatic kinesic behavior is of eminent concern in the present undertaking. Novelty, like peculiarity, has a lure of its own for even the most cautious investigator. All too often the excitement of experimental isolation and of discovery can lead the analyst to assign undue significance and peculiarity to an event which a larger frame would make comprehensible. The fact that a given kine, kinemorph, or act does not seem to "fit" a given interactional situation may only signal the need for a larger frame of investigation. The *idiokinesic* system of any actor is derived from a multiple of experiences with a wide variety of exposures to often quite differing systems. As a speaker of English may use pronunciations characteristic of a variety of dialects, so the actor may from time to time, stimulated by the special situation, put into motion responses which signal a different milieu. For instance, while the actor cannot, of course, simultaneously sit like an upper status New Englander and sit-slouch like a recent migrant from the Appalachians, he may, in the course of a given scene, utilize both of these postures. The fact that he sit-slouches but once in a long scene is obviously of special interest to the investigator. But whether this is a slouch of "despair or rejection" can only be determined by extensive contrastive analysis. With no more information than that provided by the kinemorph count, we have no more justification for such an interpretation than we do for the contradictory assumption that the sit-slouch signals the only time he "really relaxes" in the whole scene. It is at this point that the value of the examination of all modalities of communication becomes evident. As Bateson has stressed, each of the modalities is a commentary on each of the others. The isolated event has significance, finally, only in the perspective provided by the full investigation of the various modalities, in context, and through extensive contrast. Counting is an important part of any investigatory procedure, but the final measure of the importance of the event is not its rarity or statistical normality but the *shift* evoked within a milieu by its appearance or absence.))

In seeking to comprehend and to make intelligible those aspects of human body behavior which contribute to the communicational process, the kinesicist-anthropologist employs a set of procedures which are special only in the sense that they must be adapted to the peculiarities of the system under examination. Because he deals with a universe which he has predefined as ordered and interdependent, his primary task is that of developing a methodology whereby units and subsystems can be abstracted and manipulated. From the seminal insight that kinesic activity constitutes an infra-communicational system is derived a plethora of data which, unless explicitly and methodically ordered, drowns the investigator in myriad shapes and sizes and orders of behavioral pieces. Having fixed his eyes upon the behavior which constitutes the human interactional scene and having adjusted himself to the outrage of the recognition that communication is continuous, he must resist a series of temptations which would short-cut and, coterminously, predetermine the results of the observational process. Some of these temptations are suggested in the discussion above, but their subtle influence upon the work of those concerned with "nonverbal communication" has been such that they are probably worthy of explicit delineation.

Temptations

THE "CARRIER" TEMPTATION

This derives from a linguistic naiveté which assumes that each gesture, whether as gross as a thumbed nose or as tiny as a first-degree right lid droop, has a "real" meaning just as "words" are supposed to have. If the investigator succumbs to this, his attention is directed into a kind of "lexicon" wherein he draws up lists of moves and their meanings only to discover that most human beings are kinesically illiterate and move improper English.

THE "CLOSER TO NATURE" TEMPTATION

This category really covers two companion but differing hidden assumptions. One of these is that body movement is somehow more primitive and thus closer to biological nature than is verbal behavior. Animals move and animals don't talk. Humans move *and* talk. *Ergo,* moving and kinesthetic-visual communication came earlier in evolutionary history than did talking and thus remain unpatterned. Depending upon the predispositions of the writer, this same assumption has permeated the work of the *individualists,* who feel that body motion and facial expression reveal the "true" feelings of a communicant, the writings of the *racists,* who confuse social variation in response pattern with genetically determined "stoicism," "vivacity," or even rhythmicity, and the *universalists,* who assume that since there is minimal biological variation in man and since moving came early, there is species-fidelity and universality in all movements. The way in which these assumptions are expressed varies from that of some of the individualists who say that everyone is so different from everyone else as to preclude generalization at all to that of some of the universalists who optimistically anticipate a movement catalog. Whether simply nihilistic or modern pastoralist, these assumptions do not hold up as we examine the communicational situation. Not only is kinesic activity systematically patterned but this pattern varies significantly from culture to culture and even from subgroup to subgroup. While eventually we may find that the special physiological patterning of special groups may influence to a considerable degree the characteristic tone of the kinesic activity of such groups, we expect also to find a reciprocity of influence between the biological and social systems rather than any pattern of basic priority of a simple genetic nature.

More subtle and more seductive than these assumptions which deal largely with the total membership of society are those which see infantile behavior as more natural than adult behavior. Those so persuaded see maturation as somehow artificial and distortional of infantile naturalness or, accepting maturation as a natural process, these writers seem to feel that those behaviors which are characteristic of the infants of a group (or of all infants?) are somehow truer representations of the feelings of the communicant than are those more characteristic of adolescence or maturity. As long as generalizations such as these are related to the examination of individual responses and deal with the documentation of personal histories, they are not of direct concern to the kinesicist. However, if they are permitted the dignity of becoming basic to all systemic interpretation, it is well to point out that our knowledge of the ontogenetic development of individual kinesic systems is less than fragmentary. There exist a number of suggestive—even exciting— studies of maturational behavior. But we lack the cross-cultural longitudinal analyses which would permit any safe generalization of "how" humans learn to become communicators or give us more than an intuitional feel for the sustaining strength of infantile response.

It must be pointed out that this does not in any way affect the validity of the regression hypotheses. It is evident to any observer that adults will in special situations behave incongruently with their level of maturation. However, to assume in an *a priori* manner that this proves the strength of the infantile response is to ignore the communicational function of the act.

As we shall discuss below, while a *body curl* or a *thumb suck* may on one level of analysis be incongruent with other kinesic behavior being exhibited by an actor, such behavior may be quite congruent in the total communication situation. In the sections below on *body-set* and *motion quality* the differences between "ageing" and "age grading" will be discussed. For the moment it is sufficient to say that it is the present premise of kinesics that considerable research on the social learning patterns of infants and children must precede any security on our part concerning "basic" behavioral manifestations.

THE "MODIFIER" TEMPTATION

As professionally literate members of a culture devoted to literacy, we are strongly tempted to believe that words carry meaning and that all other nonword behavior merely modifies it. Thus, there are those who feel that words form the natural center of the communicational universe and that all other modes of communication are to be studied as subsystems subordinate to it. Such a decision predetermines the nature of the communicational process and I am as yet unwilling, from the situations which I have examined, to assign any such priority to any of the infracommunicational systems. For the kinesicist, silence is just as golden as are those periods in which the linguistic system is positively operative.

Correlated with the process of verbalization, kinesic markers, whether an aspect of the speaker's production of the message or the listener's contribution to the transaction, deserve special attention in an assessment of communicational exchange. Indicating position, temporality, special emphasis, subject, object, and so forth, the markers, like many gestures, are often so closely bound to linguistic behavior as to seem like extensions of it. Further research may well force a special categorization of this kind of kinesic behavior. At present, however, with the recognition that during much of human interaction verbalization is absent, it seems proper to study the two systems as of comparable weight in the communicational process.

This temptation has received stress because of its implications for communicational theory and research. When do humans verbalize? Is there a correlation between intimacy, for instance, and a reduction of conversation? Is there a correlation between the culture of a group and its dependence upon one mode of the communicational process? What are we talking about when we say that one person is verbal and another taciturn? Even such a subjective term as "good listener" may now be within the reach of objectification. It seems unlikely that such questions as these can be answered until we have considerable understanding of the nature and the role of the infracommunicational systems and their relation to each other. To assume priority for one or the other subsystem prior to such research would be to oversimplify the problem in a manner already too familiar in so-called "content analysis."

THE "CENTRAL MOVEMENT" TEMPTATION

Somewhat more technical than these temptations is the tendency on the part of the investigator to assume that one part of the body "carries the meaning" and other parts "modify" this central message. This is particularly seductive because we "know" intuitively as a member of a particular diakinesic system that certain movements seem to take precedence in the presentation or reception of a message. The eyes, the mouth, the face, the hands, the posture, the shoulders have all been listed by informants as being the primary carrier of meaning. To accept such statements would be a little like accepting an informant's conviction that nouns or verbs or even consonants or vowels are the most important part of language. Further, as is true in linguistic analysis, simple particle counting does not give us a score revealing system importance. I have no doubt that research will reveal that given cultures will, by sheer count, tend to produce more movements from one body area than from the remainder. Such counting does not, however, permit the investigator to assume a correlation between the incidence of usage of a body area and its functional importance either to the infracommunicational system or to the communicational process. Redundantly, I must again insist that only following systematic analysis of kinesic units and patterns can so-called central movements be established.

Even with the minimum of cross-cultural data at our disposal, the evidence is clear that cultures will tend to concentrate activity in certain body areas and permit the activity of others only under certain very limited circumstances. It seems evident that this will have momentous implications for students of national character. However, it does not follow that we can make statements like "Spanish women use their eyes and Russian Jewish women their hands and American stenographers their feet to say what they really mean." Such statements as these will remain at best brilliant intuitions until we comprehend the respective kinesic systems of these women and the role of these systems in the communication processes of their respective cultures.

THE "ANALYTIC INFORMANT" TEMPTATION

Kinesics, like the other behavioral sciences, uses informants as well as direct observation in gaining control of the data of the discipline. Like linguistics, however, it insists that the informant be an informant and not a fellow analyst. The young investigator is particularly prone to ask the informant what he has done or what the movement meant and to forget that the answer provides further data for analysis, not an acceptable conclusion to his analytic research. Even those investigators too sophisticated to rely on such subjective contributions may in lieu of behavioral description and analysis substitute the "multiple judge" technique. Often little more than a pooling of ignorance, such a technique is perfectly valid if the investigator is concerned with questions of establishing patterns of recall; it contributes little to the final abstraction and analysis of the kinesic system.

Kinesics is concerned with the abstraction of those portions of body motion activity which contribute to the process of human interaction. Much, if not the overwhelming proportion, of such behavior is learned by a member of any society without being aware of the learning process. It is my belief that not only is much of such behavior not within the range of easy recall but that the learning pattern may carry within it positive prohibitions to such recall. Kinesics is not concerned, as such, with the movement potential of the human species, but rather with those portions of the movement spectrum which are selected by the particular culture for patterned performance and perception. At the same time, as is true with other cultural behavior, much of what happens and which is necessary to the proper performance of a social act cannot be recalled by the actor or the untrained spectator. I have long had the belief that as the child is taught to move, to view and meaningfully to reproduce movement, an integral part of this education is concerned with enhancing or preventing recall of much of this activity. Preliminary observation of "flat-land" Southern contrasted with New England children in Louisville from comparable socioeconomic positions supports the conclusion that, even within a single culture, subgroups may experience socialization processes sufficiently different to create misunderstanding between them. Not only was the child socialized in the South encouraged to engage in gender-identifying behavior earlier than his or her Yankee cousin, but the Southerner had far greater recall in this area both as actor and as viewer than did the Northern child.

The need for skilled observers in kinesic research is evident, but even training is at times insufficient guarantee of objectivity in certain situations. One of the critical scenes of the Doris-Gregory interview contains extensive intrafemoral hand play on the part of Billy. I must confess that it was only after some thirty viewings and with the demand for microkinesic recording that I allowed myself to see that his hand play was patterned. I venture to suggest that early training which precluded my "seeing" male play in the genital area contributed to my concentration of attention on the little boy's eyes and head.

An informant should be used as a window into a culture. As shall be seen below, his contribution to the research is indispensable. The investigator must constantly remind himself, however, that his informant is an adherent, not an objective interpreter, of his communicational system. The report of an informant about his behavior is itself behavior; such reports are data and not evidence. And, the fact that all informants agree does not make their statements true, except insofar as agreement indicates conventional understanding.

Methodology

Having determined the systematic nature of human interaction and having recognized that membership is attained in a social system only after patterned experience in this system, it is the task of the behavioral scientist to ascertain *what* it is that is learned which provides any particular system with its particular dynamic. It is not my task, but that of the psychologist, to determine *how* the organism incorporates the experiences which make him a human being. Neither is it my task to map the internal relationships of the physiological systems out of which emerge the perceptible shifts in the various parts of the body. As an anthropological kinesicist I am concerned with the learned and visually perceptible shifts in the body which contribute to the peculiar communication systems of particular societies. Kinesics is concerned with abstracting from the continuous muscular shifts which are characteristic of living physiological systems those groupings of movements which are of significance to the communicational process and thus to the interactional systems of particular social groups.

The human body is capable of producing literally thousands of distinguishable positional shifts per second. Even at "rest" the body is not inactive. A high-speed movie camera, the so-called slow-motion camera, as it is speeded up, records more shifts or motions the faster it is set. Obviously, on some level of analysis these are of significance. The question which immediately confronts the kinesicist is whether or not his minimal unit of activity is in the last analysis to be determined merely by the speed of his film and camera and the patience of the recorder.

There is a considerable body of data concerning the speed of neural transmission. An even larger bibliography is concerned with the psychological study of visual perception. Neither of these, unfortunately, provides us with a statement of biological potential which might in any *a priori* way delimit the raw material of kinesics. In short, the body of one human being produces a volley of signals, an indeterminate proportion of which may excite the optical nerve of another human being. Observation of the two over any extended period of time will reveal that, if the two are selected from a common social group, each adapts his behavior to the activity of the other. The intrapersonal activity which results in such adaptive muscular shifts and electrochemical activity in the visual area is *prekinesic* in nature.

This does not imply that the behavior of the physiological system is isolated from the social environment. Even the most cursory examination of the cross-cultural or ontogenetic data indicates that the developing system is influenced, if not shaped, by its patterned interaction with its environment. The reverse is equally evident. In the same way, the knowledge that member X of society A will tend to be more active in one area of the body than is member Y of society B is of obvious concern to the kinesicist, but such interest is still prekinesic. The data of kinesics are not derived from the observation of intrapersonal behavior. A product of systematic social interaction, the kinesic system is a social system. Out of the range of muscular adjustments produced by a human being, some are utilized by the social system for communicational purposes. Thus, to say it simply, no human body produces a *kine* (least kinesic unit); it moves or adjusts in a set of muscular relationships. In social interaction, certain of these have demonstrably special utility in the communicational process. That is, under analysis, they emerge as kines. Every visible body movement, accordingly, is not a kine any more than every audible noise made by the vocal apparatus is a phone. Only after analysis has revealed that the presence or absence of a given movement in a particular context systematically affects the interactional process do we assert that that movement has kinesic significance.

The Kine

A kine is an abstraction of that range of behavior produced by a member of a given social group which, for another member of that same group, stands in perceptual contrast to a different range of such behavior. While, theoretically, within certain limits provided by the physiological structure, a given complex of muscular reactions may produce a continuous series of positions, in actuality, any social system patterns these into a discontinuous or discrete series for reception or reproduction. Thus, while, for example, the membership of culture A will report only 2 degrees of lid closure, culture B may recognize as many as five. As a skilled spectator under optimal conditions, I can record or reproduce 15 degrees of lid closure quite distinct from each other, but most middle majority informants "see" only three. Similarly, while a portion of even the distal joint of the finger can produce a continuous arc of position in relation to the remainder of the finger or hand, 4 degrees of finger position on this axis are all that elicit the report of a perceptual contrast from a middle majority informant.

Thus, a kine is not a point or position of articulatory activity; it is a range which the unsophisticated informant reports as "the same." In a previous publication (Birdwhistell, 1955) points within this range were described as being in *allokinic* relation to each other. I propose now that these be called *kine variants,* since they may be substituted for each other and are, thus, symbolizable by a single class-denoting symbol. At the risk of being repetitive, I must restress the point that these equivalences are culturally defined. Each kinesic system will have differently shaped kinic classes. As a demonstration, we may use laterality as a special test of kinic significance. All indications are that, at least on the level of the kine, American movers do not necessarily, in awareness, distinguish laterality. Given individuals may favor the fingers of the right hand, the right eye, or the musculature of the right side of the face. Two American middle majority movers, one favoring the right side of the body, the other the left, can, *as far as we now know,* interact without translating "right lid droop" into "left lid droop" or vice versa. This seems to hold for all body parts considered on the kinic level. This does not deny the obvious fact that handedness is of social significance. What we are here concerned with is whether we can record, say, the movements of the right or left lid as variants of the same kine. We must test whether $R\sim$ is equivalent to $L\sim$ and whether they can be regarded as variants of a kine class. It is obvious that they are distinguishable on the level of articulation. The test is not, however, whether the informant tells us that the right or left lid is used. What we need to discover is whether they function interchangeably in larger kinesic contexts.

As a test let X stand for a specific brow kine; Y stand for a specific lid kine; Z stand for a specific lateral orbit kine:

$$\text{Are } \frac{\overline{LX}}{\overline{RY}}, \frac{\overline{RX}}{\overline{LY}}, \frac{\overline{LX}}{\overline{LY}}, \text{ and } \frac{\overline{RX}}{\overline{RY}} \text{ equivalent}$$
$$\overline{LX} \quad \overline{RZ} \quad \overline{LZ} \quad \overline{RZ}$$

to each other in a manner which permits us to establish a class of

$$\frac{X}{Y}$$
$$Z$$

covering all four of these as class variants? If it is inconsequential whether the right or left eyelid is involved in each of these structures, we have no need to establish RY and LY as members of different classes since they are variants of (Y). The fact that the difference between R and L may not be of significance on this level does not, however, preclude the possibility that on other levels of analysis they may function contrastively.

Kinemorphics

In earlier formulations of kinesics, to expedite recording, yet with the intuitive feeling that the particular division of the body "made sense," I arbitrarily divided the body into eight specific areas. Systematic investigations, utilizing contrast analysis, have since justified this body division when applied to American movers. However, even a few hours of work with Indonesian and Bombay Indian informants makes it clear that the specific divisions will not hold up cross-culturally. The eight areas, head and neck, face, shoulders and trunk, right arm, left arm, pelvic region, right leg and left leg, will probably be differently subdivided according to the body conception of a given social system. The particular range of such segmentations can only be determined by further research. Nevertheless, the *kinemorph* was defined then as an assemblage of movements (kines) in one such area.

A kinemorph, however, is not merely an assemblage of movements in a given body area. A moving picture of such an area would not provide the investigator with a kinemorph. Such a picture or abstraction from it in the form of an exhaustive list of microkinegraphs or articulations would provide us with relatively little concerning the kinesic system of the actor. We must again use the method of abstraction and contrast analysis. As soon as we begin to contrast, with the aid of an informant, a series of kine assemblages, it becomes possible to abstract those which form unitary complexes. To return to the example which we used in the test above: We may find that we cannot set up a single kinemorph to cover

$$\frac{RX}{\overline{LY}}, \quad \frac{RX}{\overline{RY}}, \quad \frac{RX}{\overline{RY}}, \quad \frac{LX}{\overline{LY}}.$$
$$RZ \qquad LZ \qquad RZ \qquad LZ$$

Further, we may discover that

$$\frac{\overline{\frac{RX}{RY}}}{RZ} \quad \text{and} \quad \frac{\overline{\frac{LX}{LY}}}{LZ}$$

are kinemorphic variants to which informants react as substitutable for each other at this level. Similarly,

$$\frac{\overline{\frac{RX}{LY}}}{RZ} \quad \text{and} \quad \frac{\overline{\frac{LX}{RY}}}{LZ} \, , \qquad \text{etc.,}$$

may also be found to be substitutable for each other. We may then conclude that we have two kinemorphs, which may be recorded as (XYZ) for all variants which are monohanded and (X-Y-Z) for all mixed-handed variants of this assemblage. Thus eight possible assemblages have been reduced to two significant kinemorphs.

While this example gives some idea of how the kinesicist deals with contrast analysis, it will be exceedingly misleading if it is not seen as oversimple. For while all of the kines which compose a kinemorph are to be found within a given time frame (which will be discussed below), they are not necessarily coterminous. I have thus far been able to abstract three kinds of kinemorphic constructions, their definition dependent upon the order behavior of the component kines:

(1) synchronic kinemorphs; in which the component kines are simultaneous and of equal duration;

(2) series kinemorphs, in which the kines follow one another in time; and

(3) mixed kinemorphs which have both synchronic and series features but in which all component kines are not of the same duration.

Each of these meets our definitional criterion of taking place within one body area and each forms a complex in which all components are necessary for the production of the unit and all are to

(1) $\underline{X}$ (2) (3)

$\underline{Y}$ $\underline{XYW}$ $\underline{XY}$

W W

FIGURE 2. *Kinemorphic Constructions.*

be found within a given time frame. In the discussion of the kine we did not deal with the durational aspect of its definition, since by extended test, it is clear that performance, not duration, determines the kine.

A raw movement becomes classifiable as a kine at any time that its performance (of whatever duration) suffices to change the contrastive function of the complex in which it operates. The same kind of test is utilized on the kinemorphic level since the kinemorph is more than an arbitrary grouping of kines. We can establish the kinemorph, not only because the informant tells us that "these movements fit together," but also because we find transition devices which mark its initiation and terminus, and because we are able to establish its unitary function in larger contexts.

The most readily apparent kinemorph is one which begins with the body at zero (Z) and ends with it at zero (Z). Zero is defined as attention without specific movement, or, in the appropriate context, as an arbitrary norm from which all kines are traced. Such kinemorphs can be described as *pause-marked* (=). A second type is characterized by onset of activity in one body part and is terminated by the introduction, from zero, of activity in another part. The term *areal transition* (×) seems useful here.

There is a third type of transition, the *bound* transition (+), which marks kinemorphs which can only be detected by extended contrastive research. This occurs when one kinemorph is replaced in the same body part by a different kinemorph which utilizes the same points of articulation but by rearrangement of order and/or duration establishes a complex with a meaning demonstrably different from that of the previous complex. The fact that these types of kinemorphs are differently marked by differential transitional behavior indicates that future analysis may reveal their special roles in the kinesic system. On the other hand, it is within the range of possibility that they are functionally equivalent and are merely contextual variants.

The linguist will see that the kinemorph and the morpheme are in some ways comparable. For several years I have been hopeful that systematic research would reveal a strict hierarchical development in which kines could be derived from articulations, kinemorphs from complexes of kines, and that kinemorphs would be assembled by a grammar into what might be regarded as a kinesic sentence. While there are encouraging leads in the data, I am forced to report that so far I have been unable to discover such a grammar. Neither have I been able to isolate the simple hierarchy which I sought.

While, by count, a major proportion of the kine assemblages of the American kinesic system may be meaningfully segmented in one body area, there are many occasions when the restriction of contrast analysis to one area leads only to confusion. This occurs when kines from two or more areas form a complex, which, under contrast analysis, behaves precisely like a kinemorph. These I have chosen to call *complex kinemorphs*. The complex kinemorph and the simple kinemorph seem to be on the same level of analysis in that they may both be directly and in one stage analyzed into kines. By definition, of course, the complex kinemorph differs from the simple kinemorph both in its placement and in the fact that we cannot utilize simple shift of body area as a transition marker. Letting (a), (b), and (c) stand for kines in one body area and (x), (y), and (z) stand for kines in another, we may specify the shape of the complex kinemorph as (A, Y, B), while the shapes of simple kinemorphs are (A, B, C) or (X, Y, Z).

To complete the description of this level of analysis, I must include those single kines which emerge as kinemorphs: thus (a) becomes (A), (x) becomes (X), and so on. The test for kinemorphic function continues to be one of abstraction and contrast analysis. Our testing context is the kinemorphic construction. The raw unit of body motion is classifiable as a kine when it is seen to have differential value in a kinemorph. Ultimately, the existence of the simple kinemorph, the complex kinemorph, and the kine as kinemorph must all be established in the kinemorphic construction.

In Figure 3, the reader will note the succession of two-way arrows. This indicates that at each level of analysis a unit not only

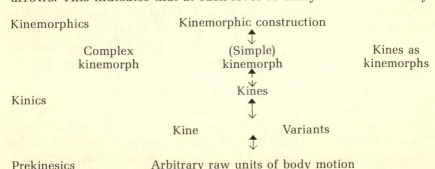

FIGURE 3. *Kinemorphic Constructions.*

must be abstractable from nonsignificant variation, but must be seen to have differential meaning in the complex in which it operates.

The term *kinemorphic construction* is suggested to cover the next order of combination in kinesic behavior. As kines combine with other kines to make isolable units (the kinemorphs), or as single kines emerge as kinemorphs, these forms combine with each other in a variety of *kinemorphic* constructions. The simplest of these is the *kinemorphic combination*. A kinemorphic combination is constructed of two or more kinemorphs—either in parallel or in series. Recorded initially as (A, B, C) (X, Y, Z), if the combination can be tested for unit existence, i.e., as having differential meaning in a wider context of body activity, it can be recorded as /(A, B, C,) (X, Y, Z)/. We further find that complex kinemorphs can combine with other complex kinemorphs in complex kinemorphic complex combinations /(A, X, C) (Y, N, Z)/, and with single kinemorphs to form *kinemorphic compounds* /(A, B, C) (X, N, Z)/. Finally, constructions of the shapes /(A) (X, Y, Z)/ and (A) (X, N, Z)/ have been abstracted.

The existence of a kinemorphic construction is determined by exactly the same procedure as has been utilized in the abstraction of the kinemorphic or kinic combinations. We abstract an assemblage in which the components repetitively appear in conjunction with each other. Then by substituting behavioral events of a comparable shape within the combination, we establish the kinemorphic function of the components and, by extension, the reality of the morph, on one level, and that of the construction on another. Thus, the kinemorphic value of kines is revealed when we discover that /(A) (X, Y, Z)/ stands in contrast to /(B) (X, Y, Z)/ in exactly the same way as /(A) (Z, Y, Z)/ stands in contrast to /(A) (M, N, D)/. Thus, recording /(A, B, C) Z (X, Y, Z)/ signifies that the construction has been abstracted from a larger action sequence and that during its duration the rest of the body has remained at what one of my students aptly referred to as "ready rest." The (Z), in this case, serves to remind the analyst that he is dealing with an *included* construction. When a full actional sequence is dealt with, (//)'s are utilized to mark the initial and terminal aspects of the sequence and all segments within the double slashes are *bound* constructions and form a unit on the next level of analysis.

I have not yet found any way of determining whether or not there is a conventional limitation, in terms of the number of component morphs, to the size of a kinemorphic construction. In the examples above, two-part constructions were used. The reader must not be misled by this. I have seen kinemorphic constructions which contained as many as seven morphs. The test for the unitary nature of a kinemorphic construction takes place in the larger field of body movement which we call *action*.

Action

Analysis of the American kinesic system has led to the tentative conclusion that in the probable absence of cross-referencing systems similar to those of linguistic grammar and syntax, meaningful segmentation and binding together of kinesic construction sequences is handled, in all likelihood, parakinesically (Birdwhistell, 1960) through the medium of *stance*. *Stance* is a term designed to cover a pattern of total body behavior which is sustained through time, within which one or a series of constructions takes place, and which contrasts with a different stance. *Stance* subsumes *position* (p), (which is a statement of the relative position of all the body parts in space), *locomotion* (l), (the movement of the body through space), and *velocity* (v) (which covers sustained velocity of movement of the total body).

A stance change is said to occur when any one of these or combinations of these is varied to such an extent that there is a marked shift in the total message. In a major proportion of the interactions which we have observed, these shifts coincide with a transition $(+)$ $(\times)$ or $(=)$ on the construction level. Our problem would be a good deal simpler if we could say that action-sequence transitions always coincide with interconstruction sequences. Certain of these stance changes, however, take place within what appear to be bound constructions as well as within an included construction. Such stance changes may or may not be coterminous with morph transitions. The term *stance shift* is used to indicate this variety of stance variation which may, as research develops, turn out to be parakinesic in nature.

While our research in this area is far from exhaustive, it seems probable that stance variation may serve at least a dual function. On the kinemorphic level, stance serves to mark the beginning and end of action sequences. In such cases $(//)$'s mark the action sequences and all elements included within are analyzed as *bound* components in an interactional system. Thus, we might record a typical action sequence according to the notational logic, $//(A, B, C)$ (N) (X, O, Z) (etc.)$//$. The type of stance change is marked by a small letter at the upper right of the double slash notations: $(//^p)$,

$(//^l)$, or $(//^v)$. When a stance shift occurs within a sequence of bound constructions, a capital S is used with the identifying marker. Thus: $^v//(X, Y, Z) (N) (P, Q, R) S (A, F, C) (etc.)//^v$ indicates an actional sequence bounded externally by two perceptible shifts in velocity and containing a stance shift (S) of one of the other two variants (position or locomotion).

Only further research can reveal the functional nature of these internal shifts for the action sequence. As shall be seen below, the gross behavior noted on the microkinesic level as stance contains behavior which, on the macrokinesic (i.e., probably parakinesic) level, emerges as posture, demeanor, pose, and presentation. It would be desirable to have the evidence which would give assurance that all internal stance shifts can be ignored on the microkinesic level. However, for the time being such a conclusion must be postponed. In discussing the interpretation of kinesic systems more will be said about the incidence and relative placement of stance shifts and changes. The fact that communicants react unfavorably toward "too many" or "inappropriately" placed stance shifts suggests that these are especially patterned.

Interaction

While it is hardly the function of this section to develop a social psychology of human interaction, the data to follow are perhaps illuminated by establishing exactly what it is we mean by interaction. Review of the existent literature on social animals gives us some security in making a generalization which states that *when social animals of a common species make sustained sensory contact with each other they must engage in behavior which identifies each to the other as a species member, a group member, and as being in a particular state of readiness.* Ethologists and comparative psychologists have presented us with an impressive array of behavioral data which indicates that some term like "learned" or "conditioned" or "released" must be applied to this behavior. That is, behavior of identification is not only necessary for the adaptation of the species but is apparently patterned by the particular experiences of the group. This is hardly the place to review the evidence, but it seems clear that a member of any social group must "recognize" and "emit" certain signals in order to sustain association with that group. The data are at the present time too sparse to indicate the range of discrimination of in-group and out-group identification signals.

The fact that animals engage in species-, group-, and state-readiness signals does not give us the right to call this complex of identifying signals "animal" behavior with the implication that it is somehow instinctual. I prefer to call such behavior *social*, since it emerges from the patterned association of species members with patterned activity systems. The fact that we use the same term to cover an aspect of kinesic behavior does not make such behavior "more biological." It rather emphasizes its functional importance to the social system.

The term *encounter* will be used to cover that communicational situation which occurs prior to interaction. The duration of an encounter will depend upon the nature of the communication systems exhibited by the participants. An encounter becomes an *interaction* when the participants become communicants. That is, the participants interact rather than counteract when they find it possible to introduce cross-referencing signals into the scene in such a way as to sustain continuing adaptive association.

This difference between an encounter and an interaction is stressed because it so clearly sets boundary lines between those situations in which mutual cross-referencing signals are appropriately used and those in which none yet exist or, if they exist, are inappropriately used by the participants. It is probably evident to the reader that with this definition few encounters are ever of sufficient duration to be recordable. It may well be that "encounters" have no real existence and that "encounter" (or noncommunication) refers to the subjective feelings of distress which we have when we do not comprehend the communication situation in which we are participating. There are cross-cultural situations in which an "encounter" becomes an interaction by the introduction of the cross-referencing signal that the participants shall search for cross-referencing signals. Such a sequence may be no more complex than the joint presentation of palms followed by squatting, buttocks resting on heels, with the weight balanced on the ball of the feet and the toes. This set of signals gives evidence of the willingness to participate in some sort of sustained interaction. This simple action sequence stands in sharp contrast to a scene in which participants may not engage in a sustained encounter because one or more of the participants uses only *internal* cross-referencing signals and thus prevents the emergence of an interaction.

Kinesics and linguistics provide recording and analytic techniques which should give new insight into the processes of acculturation and group formation. At the same time such situations should provide microcultural laboratories for sharpening the tools of these disciplines. *The Natural History of an Interview* team working closely with Smith and Trager, who had originally suggested comparable though by no means identical classification of similar vocal phenomena, developed a methodology for the analysis of visual recognition patterns. The skeletal structure of this aspect of communicational behavior is presented below with full recognition of its crudeness. However, even in this unrefined state, such abstraction provides a tool which has proved invaluable in the establishment of *actor base lines.*

Visual Recognition Patterns

While we do not wish at this time to become involved in status and role theory, we must note that the broadest cross-referencing behavior in the communication system relates directly to these aspects of interaction. In the section above we discussed the function of stance shift (or change) in providing structural frames for extended stretches of kinemorphic constructions. Such cross-referencing behavior gives us data for recognizing that even on the kinemorphic level, human beings do not communicate through an additive series of independent messages. In kinemorphics we were concerned with demonstrating that the system contains a variety of behavioral shapes which tie together least pieces of activity. We are now reversing our procedure to examine those cross-referencing signals which tie together the broadest possible amount of interactional behavior. Among such behaviors, that which we call *body-base* is, theoretically, sustained throughout any interactional sequence.

This list of body-base types has been derived from a set of recognition behaviors some of which probably occur in all social groupings, animal or human. As we originally worked with these categories, it seemed to us that not only were these the broadest of

Position	Rhythm phase
Sex	Territoriality
Age	Mood
State of health	Toxic state*
Body build	N-states

*And organic confusional and deficit states.

FIGURE 4. *Body-Base Types.*

the cross-referencing patterns, but also that they were somehow "closer" to the physiological *base* of the species. Certainly, with the exception of "position," which related to the order participation of a member of a group *vis á vis* his or her group associates, and "territoriality," which refers to systematic space occupation, all of these types *seemed* to have primary, physiologically constituted accompanying behavior. It seemed justifiable, therefore, to refer to these as "primitive"—somehow implying priority in an evolutionary sense. As I worked with these categories, increasing confidence was gained that such states are characteristic of *social* groups—at least of mammalian groups—and probably of a number of fowl groupings. I had the opportunity to talk at some length with Konrad Lorenz, who concurred in the tentative conclusion that these are probably requisite to sustaining the basic division of labor necessary for adaptation in animal groupings. In light of this, it may be suggested that if we are justified in calling these recognition states "primitive," it is with reference to the order of their appearance in social groups rather than in terms of anatomical characteristics.

The detailed description of the body-base types has been purposely avoided since these types are kinesic categories—not behaviorally specific constructs. *Body-base* constitutes the basic image of other members of the social group which must be internalized by the group member in the socialization process. *Body-set* constitutes behavioral derivatives from the expectancy pattern of an associated member against which are measured the *body qualities* or situationally variant signals basic to any interactional sequence. Body-base, then, constitutes the zero line which any communicant must have internalized in order to recognize the special cross-referencing message carried by the body-set signal-complex.

No member sends or expresses any of the types as a unitary activity to the exclusion of others. Even the limited survey of films which I have attempted makes it clear that these types are neither specific (in an organic sense) nor independent from each other. In every case that we know anything about there is a complex relationship between the various types. Until further extensive cross-species research has been carried out, we can only say that body-set is complexly patterned and learned. As we gain more knowledge cross-culturally, both about the patterning of these types and the predominant shapes of body-set in particular cultures and in particular individuals within the group, we shall be able to provide a more substantive base for cultural character and temperament studies.

Body-Base	Body-Set
Body-Base	*Body-Set*
Position	Status
Sex	Gender
Age	Age grade
State of health	Health image
Body build	Body image
Rhythm phase	Rhythm image
Territoriality	Territorial status
Mood	Mode
Toxic state	Toxic image
N-state	N-status

FIGURE 5. *Body-Base and Body-Set.*

In the discussion above, body-base was described as the patterned, learned zero-line against which body-set is measured. Body-set represents the particular cross-referencing signals introduced in the *particular* interactional scene. A brief glance at Figure 5 will make clear the relationship between the body-base zero-line and the body-set which appears in the communicational sequence. It will be noted that for each of the body-base types we have derived a parallel body-set of social recognition value.

Before a discussion of body-set states, a word of caution must be introduced. While it is possible heuristically to abstract the ten states and to use these as frames for the collection of data, such abstracted units are never behaviorally isolated categories. Communication, intrinsic to culture, is patterned and systematic. As such it is constituted of a number of interacting subsystems, the appearance of which is determined by the complex demands of the particular interaction situation. Since a particular (in space-time) cross-referencing system is shaped by the exigencies of a particular interaction system, it would be surprising if any specific state could be reacted to without modification by other state representations.

In the process of the establishment of actor and interactional base lines, I have found it necessary to analyze large stretches of behavior on a base-set model. In every case, at least five and at times all ten set-states categories are represented. The particular kinemorphs or kinemorphic constructions, the organization of stance shifts and postural positions, as well as the selected body *motion qualifiers* (to be discussed below), all combine to give us a cross-referencing statement of the quality of the interaction.

To avoid confusion, I have purposely avoided examples in the preceding discussion. However, the reader may gain more perspective if a somewhat stereotyped example is presented at this point.

If we were to consider a situation in which a 35-year-old junior vice president talks to the 63-year-old chairman of the board of his firm, we might find the following states manifested in the two participants in the interactional scene. These states cross-reference the discourse within the situational frame. While the problem of representation makes the diagram below appear like parallel or contiguous individual behavior, the reader is again reminded that the behavior of each is a function of reciprocation—the cross-referencing signal is reciprocal, i.e., part of an interaction—not an individual expression.

This scene, which is purposely oversimplified by having its opening and closing phases eliminated, covers the length of a discourse, marked at its beginning by "settling in" behavior and terminated by interruption and departure behavior. We are concerned neither with the content of the scene nor with the linguistic or kinesic detail of these cross-referencing signals. The signals above are internally congruent—the young man's overyouthful, clear-eyed "sincerity," with appreciative humor, is consistent with the slit-eyed

Categories	Vice president's behavior	Chairman's behavior
Status	Ұ4 K ″	4 Ұ
	p T p	b T b, AxbA
	Hq or Hq	Hn . . .
	—LL— alternating with L/L	Hfbb, sOOs
	OO : : : :(intermittent)	
Age grade	+OO+ Hqn Hq + N −LL− ∼L/L	Set + 3
Gender or		
Sex grade	Ұ4 K ″ (XX − XX)	4 Ұ + intermediate R 2 p
Health status	p T p	
	Qualifier!!! / + . . . +	Set + 3
Mode	+ OO +	Hfbb, sOOs
	− LL −	AxbA
Body image	_____ _____	_____ _____
Territorial		
image	interaction centered	movement projection to whole room
Rhythm phase		
image	+ OO +	s OO s
Toxic status	_____ _____	_____ _____
N-status	_____ _____	_____ _____

FIGURE 6. *Body-Set States.* (*See Appendix III for the symbols used in the macrokinesic recording*)

belly holding and genital scratching of the older man. The (¥4K")
(knee over knee leg cross) is the congruent seating posture reciprocal
for the older man's (4¥) (broken or open 4 leg cross). The seeming
reversal here in which the older man uses a leg cross customarily
seen in younger men is modified and tempered by his (AxbA) (bimanual belly hold)—just as the (4¥K") (knee over knee) which is
formal and at the same time within the range of the feminine leg
cross arc is tempered by the (+OO+) (eyes with distal aspect
crinkled) and the (Hq) (head cock).

These body-set cross-referencing signals may be seen as overall
frames for the system of interaction occurring within their boundaries. The example above is simplified in that the interview portrayed contains no major shifts; that is, this complex of behavior
extends throughout the interaction. Body-set signals are extremely
important in assessing interaction topography; often the first signal
of a parameter shift in an interaction is signaled by a set-shift—either
in the linguistic or in the kinesic area, or in both. As our understanding of the dynamics of interaction increases, it is clear that in
body- and voice-set shifts we have one method for measuring
"movement" in psychiatric as well as other interviews.

Returning to the example, it is to be noticed that under territorial
image the younger man's behavior is described as "interaction centered," whereas the older is noted as "movement projection to whole
room." The absence of macrokinesic recording here relates to my
own uncertainty. However, at the moment it seems likely that space
control has something to do with eye focus and convergence behavior modified by activity discussed below under motion qualifiers and
motion markers. Of theoretical and methodological importance is
the fact that while such behavior may be experimentally "located"
in one rubric of the kinesic and parakinesic system, it may nonetheless be multifunctional.

Using the above as a background for recognizing the interdependence of quality behavior, the role of base and set as related
to health and health image may be elaborated. Pathological conditions in the muscular, skeletal, and neurological system can emerge
directly as limitations or specific underlying determinants of motor
or dermal behavior. There can be little doubt that the form of the
message sent or received is often strongly influenced by the state
of the organism. Probably the largest section of the bibliography
concerned with visible body movement is related to the specific or
generalized symptomatology of neurological disturbance. Theoret-

ically, all specifically idiosyncratic body behavior lies outside the
field of kinesics, whether such behavior gains its peculiar cast from
organic sources or from some special conditioning experience on the
part of the actor or viewer. Yet it is essential to the methodology
of kinesics, as it is for linguistics, that the behavior of any participant
in an interaction situation be described as idiosyncratic only after
the patterned aspects of the behavior have been exhaustively described. That is, in the process of classification and testing, individuality is assigned *after* not *before* the fact of data exhaustion. Our
theoretical framework provides us with an approach to the problems
of allocating data to prekinesic or to macrokinesic levels, but only
when cross-cultural research provides us with clear indications of
symptomatic activity concurrent with specific organic malfunction
can we be secure in our assessment of particular pieces of behavior.

While anthropologists have long been aware of differing cultural
emphases on disease or accident, the literature is exceedingly thin
with regard to the specific variations in symptom presentation. Discussion of this problem with physicians whose practices are limited
to the ethnic variations of an American city has convinced me that
practitioners are aware of the difficulties involved in treating symptoms expressed by various groups as though there were a common
and universal symptom structure for a given disease. This point was
repeatedly stressed by M.D.'s whose practice included the range of
variation provided by a Santa Fe or an Albuquerque hospital. Yet
to my knowledge the data remains essentially impressionistic. Perhaps as the World Health Organization expands its research area,
specific and extensive attention will be given to the cross-cultural
examination of the social structuring of symptoms. Such data as
would be supplied by these studies—properly organized—should
help us to be more explicit about the separation of prekinesic and
kinesic behavior.

My own convictions in this area derive from experience gained
while doing research on the social structure of two adjacent but
differing subcultures in central Kentucky. Not only did the "Bluegrass" and "Hill" Kentuckians differ in their attitudes toward disease
in general, but their choices of favorite ailments varied as systematically as did other aspects of their social organization. This research was done prior even to the preliminary systematization of
kinesics, yet we were aware of the fact that there were styles of
symptom presentation in both verbal and kinesic statements of illness which were sufficiently different in the two areas as to lead to

misunderstanding between them. The discussion to follow is based on insights gained during this community research project, measured against the material gathered by a number of investigators in the cross-cultural sphere, and reinterpreted through the recent formalization of communication research.

Although Dry Ridge was only about 15 miles into the hills from the Bluegrass community Green Valley, the health set of this area is markedly different from that characteristic of the valley. As a culture, more rigorously individualistic and puritanical than Green Valley, sickness was patterned in Dry Ridge into "nonreference to health" and "critically ill." Ideally, any variation between these two states is to be ignored or, at least, should remain a private matter. Ideally one is *forced* to go to a doctor, take medicine, or go to bed. The kinesic message that one is critically ill (although conscious and not yet bed-ridden) is best covered by the gestural reference, "stiff upper lip." This includes retraction of the scalp, tightening the skin of the forehead (with a significant reduction of brow markers), reduction of smiling, carrying the torso hyper-erect, reduction of velocity in hand and arm movement, increased precision in gross movement (decreased overkick—anterior and posterior—while walking) and increased "foot-planting" (both feet—heel and ball—on floor while standing or sitting). If this does not elicit response from responsible kindred, this general quality is sporadically interrupted by "sag" behavior of about 2 to 5 seconds' duration followed by "pulling together" behavior of about 2 to 4 seconds' duration. The sag and pull-together should not take place very often or the quality shifts and the behavior is reacted to as malingering or as an infantile appeal. I have never, in over a year of watching this behavior, seen the sag and pull-together used by males more than once in 15 minutes except by the very young and the very old. Females, on the other hand, sag and pull-together more frequently—several as often as two or three times in 5 minutes. This statement of variation is probably overprecise, but there is quite obviously a difference in expectancy here. A child, an old person, or a woman may engage in sag and pull-together at greater frequency within a time span without being considered as malingering. It is perhaps unnecessary to stress the point that in Dry Ridge the full cross-referencing system is made up of "stiff upper lip" plus "sag and recover." It is perhaps of interest to note that the health image quality behavior of "stiff upper lip" differs from the mood image of anger in Dry Ridge in only two behaviorial aspects that I have been able to trace. First, in eye convergence and focus—in anger the Dry Ridger avoids focusing on the eyes of others—looking to either side of other communicants, whereas, in sickness, he looks at his communicant with in-and-out-of-focus variation. Second, in aspiration presentation: in sickness he engages in intermittent pronounced chest presentation with audible aspiration (usually through the nose). Paralinguistically this is very close to a sigh. In anger, he uses deep, measured, visually perceptible breathing which is usually inaudible.

In Green Valley the situation differs both linguistically and kinesically. A kith and kin community, health is used as a device for establishing interdependent interaction. Ill health is discussed and, in a manner of speaking, "enjoyed." A public affair, any manifestation of physical malaise occasions group diagnosis and comparison of symptoms. Accompanied by extensive verbalization, the kinesics of all communicants are characteristically directed with kinesic area markers. The etiquette of illness even in Green Valley (both of these communities are, after all, American) demands that the viewer initiate verbal discussion of the actor's debility. Thus, the community member introduces a cross-referencing appeal which is sustained until it is responded to by other participants in an interactional scene.

In Green Valley the kinesic illness behavior is characterized by first- to third-degree medial compression of the brows accompanied by first-degree brow raise. The lids sag and there is tensing of the lateral aspects of the orbit plus upper cheek sag. The lips fill and the lower lip falls slightly away from the lower teeth. The neck is out of tonus, often with a forward or forward and lateral thrust. The upper torso sags anteriorly as do the shoulders. Belly may be presented. Arms and hands may hang at the side or move in overslow velocity with lower arm performing any arc at greater velocity than do the hands. Feet drag while walking, or rest anteriorly on heels while sitting. There is, of course, variation in completeness or duration of this quality behavior—but it is my conviction that this variation is a function of the lack of response on the part of the other communicants rather than of the seriousness of the debility represented. This is supported by the fact that as soon as the malaise of the initiator is responded to, the body moves into tonus and a verbal recital of symptoms is accompanied by pointing—touching—rubbing—caressing of the ostensibly involved body parts. Even persons who are apparently (from doctor's diagnosis) quite ill become animated, with eyes in focus—mouth at zero, and body at increased frequency of response during such conversations. Such activity is intermittently interrupted by "sag and recover," if the responses get "too" general in nature. I am somewhat unsure about this, but it is my feeling that malingering is suspected in this community when the "sick" person does not interrupt his or her performance with sympathy and empathy activity, when the traded symptoms are introduced by other participants in the conversation. An actor's preoccupation with his own health is a signal that his appeal is not simply a statement of illness.

These are neighboring systems and there is some intermarriage between the two groups. With this range of difference, it is easy to see that some misunderstanding arises in an intermarriage situation. It is perhaps of no consequence to this present chapter, but it is interesting to note that Dry Ridge, an economically poorer region than Green Valley, has produced four doctors since 1890 while Green Valley has produced but one.

Further discussion of body-base and body-set must await a more extensive presentation. These examples should serve, however, to illustrate the general propositions concerning the function of this aspect of the parakinesic system as a cross-referencing system. This discussion and these examples may be somewhat misleading for they do not properly underline the point that while we are able to abstract some fairly precise movements as central indicators here, such behavior may congruently or incongruently be modified on the macrokinesic level, which contains kinemorphic constructions, the constituent behavior of which may function on both levels of systematization. Further, our analysis must not omit what is probably the most critical (and least adequately analyzed) level of *parakinesics*. This area includes that behavior which I have termed the *motion qualifiers,* and the kinesic *action* and *interaction modifiers.* Although they in general refer to shorter stretches of behavior than do the base and set cross-referencing systems, these parakinesic qualifiers and modifiers may cover activity as limited as a kinemorph or a single kinemorphic construction or stretches of behavior of such duration as to make us feel that they may ultimately be relegated to the base-set level.

Motion Qualifiers

The stream of body motion behavior has thus far been discussed as though there were a somewhat mechanical all-or-nothing quality to the production of the components of the kinesic system. The student analyst in his training tends to move from a period of concentration on the "expressive" or personality indicative, or idiosyncratic behavior, to one of atomistic recording of the finite particles. It soon becomes evident that the range of variation in production of body motion interaction is not a simple matter of idiosyncracy or "style," nor, on the other hand, is it as highly patterned as is kinemorphic construction. Out of an extended range of production behavior, three aspects of the *motion qualifiers* deserve special attention because their performance seems so intimately tied to the structure of the most complex arrangements of kinemorphic constructions. These include *intensity* behavior, *durational* behavior, and *range* behavior. For most middle majority American movers these seem each to be distributed on a 3- to 5-degree scale, which is outlined below with the symbols I am presently employing for their notation.

These motion qualifiers are roughly analogous to suprasegmental

Intensity (or degree of muscular tension or production of kine (or kinemorph)	Overtense	
	Tense	
	N	
	Lax	
	Overlax	
Duration (or length) of kine (or kinemorph)	Staccato	
	N	
	Allegro	
Range (or width) of movement in performance of given kine (or kinemorph)	Narrow	
	Limited	
	N	
	Widened	
	Broad	

FIGURE 7. *Motion Qualifiers.*

phenomena in language; that is, they may occur across or cover segments of a complex construction. They function to modify the kinesic meaning of the construction, but so far as I am able to ascertain, an increase or decrease of intensity, the rate of production or the breadth of the performance of any kine or kinemorph in a kinemorphic construction *cannot serve as a substitute* for one or more of the kines or kinemorphs in that construction. In other words, the modification function of one of the qualifiers, regardless of its extent of distribution within a bound form, seems to extend over the full kinemorphic construction. Or, to say it still differently, at least as far as our examination of American movers is concerned, there are no kinemorphs composed of variation in intensity, duration, and range.

If we try to evaluate these phenomena with relation to the present or allied research, the motion qualifiers take on special significance. While present research indicates that the 5 degrees of intensity and range and 3 degrees of duration have kinesic significance for all middle majority American movers, the "distance" covered by a particular mover in the performance of the qualifiers will vary widely. This distance is of significance in the assessment of motion qualities. Further, the qualifiers seem to be especially related to that area of psychiatric symptom description called "flattened affect." Flattened affect in the kinesic behavior seems, at least in part, to be an *incongruent* narrowing of qualifier extent, the term incongruent, in this case, being related to the general or interactional system. Not altogether in jest we have been using another term "fattened affect" which occurs when the spread of qualifier extent becomes incongruent with the interactional sequence. This discussion of interpretation may seem somewhat out of keeping at this point in the chapter but I think the reader must be warned with respect to a methodological point. The qualifiers may be looked at from two analytic points of view: first, as patterned modification phenomena which vary the kinesic meaning of a kinemorphic construction and, second, in their extent aspects as part of the general cross-referencing system of the full interaction. In analysis these must be kept separate since in their discovery quite different operations are involved. The particular qualifier behavior noted for a particular construction is of kinesic significance and is determined as variations of behavior within the base line of the actor. The quality aspect of the qualifier behavior is determined by comparative analysis and has interactional significance.

Action Signals

Since one of the purposes of this chapter is to serve as a progress report on the attempts at data exhaustion in kinesic raw materials, it is perhaps justifiable to include in this already programmatic section a series of behavioral categories whose position and function are far from worked out. Something of a catch-all category, the action signals include the *action modifiers* which are descriptive of an entire body in motion, the *interaction modifiers* which involve the full body behavior of two or more participants in an interactional scene, and the *action markers*. Perhaps the material at present handled under these headings will become data for the description of motion quality and/or for the analysis of the base line, but for the time being I am more comfortable in recording them under these less definitive categories.

The literature covering "expressional behavior" contains a number of sets of more or less descriptive categories of individual behavioral types. Many of these provide useful concepts based on careful observation and brilliant intuition. In the training situation, however, such borrowed concepts prove the adage that one can never get a borrowed bucket clean. Since we have attempted to make sure that each of the concepts utilized in kinesics and parakinesics relates both to a specific order of behavior and to the operations by which such behavior is abstracted, a new set of terms and categories is required. The following outline includes those modes of behavior which have been sufficiently examined to give us some confidence in their presentation. Such a systematization does little more than scratch the surface of possible categorizations. The nine modifiers listed below are what remain of forty-one paired types which I worked with in 1955. As systematic research proceeded, most of these were discarded as overgeneralization of kinemorphic constructions. As it became clear that the "gesture" was a closely bound stemlike morph which signaled a constructional core, it also became evident that the classification of gesture types as indicators of cultural character tendencies must await systematic cross-cultural research. Furthermore, the development which followed the recognition of the cross-referencing function of the base-set activity further limited this list. I have no doubt that this list will be lengthened and rearranged as research proceeds, but I present these categories as they now stand in the hope that other workers will find them useful. All of my testing indicates that they have some kind of communication function, but I am not at all sure how they fit into the remainder of the data.

Action Modifiers

The categories listed in outline below under the action modifiers include a series of paired types that cover the mode of behavior of the body as a whole. In all cases these are included because they elicit patterned responses from communicants and because they seem in "normal" movers to vary from situation to situation within the behavioral system of the particular member.

Action modifiers

Type	Behavior
Unilateral—Bilateral:	Mover favors right or left side of body, contrasts with inclusion of both sides in performance (not just handedness).
*Specific—Generalized:**	Mover tends to utilize one body area for major proportion of kinesic activities as contrasted to more extensive utilizations.
Rhythmic—Disrhythmic:†	Mover tends to adopt a definite rhythm within which he moves (often marked by kinemorphic or stance shift junctures) as contrasted to a clearly defined pattern of rhythm interruption (not just nonrhythmic).
Graceful—Awkward:	Mover tends to make major proportion of movements in a directed, minimally interrupted manner, as contrasted to a start-stop-proceed action with a series of abortive inclusions. (Grace

---

* There is probably a closely allied pair which covers "lost" or avoided body parts. This is not now included since cross-cultural research is needed to determine how idiosyncratic or set-quality patterned this is.

† See the section on interaction modifiers.

is characterized by containing minimal "searching" behavior in contrast to awkwardness where searching is maximized.)

Fast—Slow: (Not to be confused with the duration qualifier.) Mover tends to high velocity of production of kinemorph and kinemorphic constructions as contrasted to a low production rate.

Integrated—Fragmented: Integrated mover tends toward harmonic organization of various body parts (whether generalized or specific) whereas fragmented mover may divide body into nonharmonic—even apparently contradictory—parts. A finger, a hand, or an eye may seem to have existence independent of remainder of body activity. May involve the full division of the body into two spheres as: above and below pelvic girdle or (in one case) right through the middle of the body, leaving a right and left sphere.

Intertensive—Intratensive: Intertensive mover tends to be highly responsive to behavior of other communicants—engages in consistent check and modification behavior as contrasted to the intratensive mover, who appears to engage in extended autostimulation but with minimal apparent strenuous rejection. At first these seemed aspects of the encounter-interaction process but, as research continued, it became clear that such behavior continued even after an interaction was clearly in progress. As in the case of the "self-possessed-self-contained" type which follows, this typology has special significance for clinical observation.

Self-possessed–Self-contained:

A dubious category (see discussion). These types are easy to recognize once seen but are difficult to objectify. I suspect that this is a complex category and perhaps should not be included in this list of modifiers. However, this category is so useful in the analysis of psychiatric interview material that it is included.

The self-possessed mover is characterized by a reduction of qualifier width without incongruence, by the harmonic organization of the body parts, by minimal searching behavior, and by what might be loosely characterized as "poise." Only the fact that self-possession seems to appear intermittently within or beyond and apparently quite independent of the qualities persuades me that this is a category of another order than quality. Self-possession appears to relate to social "ease" and "confidence" in interaction (neither of which terms have more than impressionistic value in this presentation). Our description of self-containment is equally impressionistic, characterized by seeming intratension; the general feeling is one of restraint and "avoidance" of stimuli. Category by category the behavior is congruent, but it is best characterized as systematically resistant to any change in the interaction beyond narrowly established limits.

Only extended research can establish a clear perspective on this pair of types. The difficulty may lie in the pairing which I have used in the modifier assignment. Self-possession may be a special complex more adequately described under the body qualities, while self-containment may be a special pathological condition paired with another poorly defined pattern that I have been calling "identity loss." *Identity loss* has been characterized by a high incidence of "echo" behavior or of pieces of behavior that have no *apparent* relevance to the interaction situation. If self-containment is characterized by exclusion or avoidance of stimuli, identity loss seems to be made up of overreactivity to them.

Interaction Modifiers

While, by definition, kinesic research is only concerned with body motion behavior with a demonstrable communicative function (and this implies an interactional frame), the action modifiers are concerned with the behavior of a *given* actor (in an interactional context). The interaction modifiers are concerned with the classification of comparable and shared behavior which appears in a sequence involving two or more actors. In the outline below is presented a series of three paired types of interaction modifiers.

Interaction modifiers

Mirror-Parallel:

Mirror behavior is characterized by one or more actors acting in mirror image of a central actor. Parallel behavior occurs when two or more actors move in parallel.

It is recognized that when more than two actors are involved, some by limited possibility are in parallel, others in mirror, interaction. Our very limited observation of group interaction has not revealed any particular patterning to this variation.* Perhaps when kinesic observation is combined with the linguistic and studied in association with devices like Chapple's (1949) chronograph, this material will have more consequence.

Rhythmic-Disrhythmic:

When the interactional behavior of two or more actors contains a

---

*Albert Scheflen and Adam Kendon at Bronx State Hospital have made significant advances in this area recently. (Personal Communication, 1969.)

clearly perceptible beat, introduced either in parallel or in
series, such interaction is termed
rhythmic. *Disrhythmic* interaction occurs when established
rhythms are repeatedly interrupted.

Open-Closed: An interaction is termed *open*
when the behavior is charac-
terized by searching the environment for other stimuli. To the
extent that the participants are so
highly interactive that they do not
respond appropriately to other
stimuli in the milieu, the interaction is *closed*.

"Searching" as used here refers to focusing the eyes or ears, or
other sensory receptors, on objects or people outside of the interaction area, "squirming" (noncongruent shifts in stance), foot
shuffling, finger drumming, and so forth.

Systematic research has thus far been directed almost exclusively to the examination of two- and three-person interactions. Even
within this limited universe, there are a number of other interaction
modifiers which are being examined. Their behavioral limits are not
yet clear, however, and discussion of them should await further
analysis. Needless to say, the interaction modifiers appear both in
association with speech behavior and through periods of silence.

Motion Markers

The discussion of that aspect of body motion behavior which
is classifiable only in direct association with verbal behavior has
been saved until the remainder of the material had been presented.
Up to this point, with few exceptions, body movement has been
treated as a universe different from that of speech behavior. The
internal consistency of language has been revealed by systematic
research based on the proposition that linguistic phenomena are
organized into a system which can and should be examined without
reference to other social systems. This rigorous abstraction provided

both a model for kinesic research and a set of clear frontiers which facilitated the abstraction of kinesic material. This entire discussion has rested upon the proposition that every interaction is based upon continuous communication carried on through the medium of patterned, discrete, but interlocking and cross-referencing symbols. Looking only at the two modalities, speech and body movement, but inspecting them from the point of view of the kinesicist, we might construct a model to illustrate the temporal aspects of this process.

Observational time T^1 T^2 T^3 T^4 T^5 T^6 T^N

Parakinesic behavior   _____

Kinesic behavior   __ ____ _____   _____   _____ __ __

Audible speech behavior   _____   _____   _____

FIGURE 8. Model of Continuous, Patterned Speech and Movement.

"Gestures" and "posture" and "facial expression" are probably the body motion events most accessible to the American "folk"-viewer. That is, these phenomena represent public abstractions or shorthand notations for the much more complex behavior described in the pages above. As such they may be included in literary description, stage instructions, and even in etiquette prescriptions. As our discussion above has demonstrated, these are derived sytems and are to be finally analyzed only in the complexity of the full communicational process. The motion markers, while less public in the sense that only a portion are sufficiently abstracted to be taught, seem very close to awareness in American speakers and movers. At least, an American audience seems to have relatively little difficulty in seeing them and "explaining" their function, once they are demonstrated. Yet, as with "gesture," "posture," and "facial expression," their apparent accessibility creates confusion and pseudounderstanding when we attempt to analyze them. Special attention is given here to the motion markers, because of their tremendous importance in measuring the congruity of the linguistic and kinesic systems and because, in the interview situation, they are immediately available to the observer.

The kinesicist, recording, let us say, from a muted sound film of hitherto unanalyzed material, records a stream of kines. As his analysis proceeds, he orders these into kinemorphs and kinemorphic constructions. As he enlarges his procedure to include the qualifier behavior, he develops a multilevel record which is internally consistent. Yet, as he scores this record, he can detect a particular distribution of kines as kinemorphs, and he can observe narrowly limited stretches of qualifier shift which combine to punctuate certain portions of his data sheet. Upon turning up the sound, it becomes clear that these specially marked passages are very frequently coextant with speech phenomena, although this is not always true, for under a variety of circumstances a communicant may verbalize subaudibly, so that his speech behavior is visible rather than audible. At this stage in the research, the kinesicist's abstraction of such phenomena will provide him with a data series which resists systematization except insofar as it constitutes discernible patterned movement that occurs in association with speech behavior. Such body motion behavior tends to have a different shape if the mover is speaking. Auditor behavior often includes the same order of punctuating events. The model shown in Fig. 8 may now be expanded to:

Observational time	T^1	T^2	T^3	T^4	T^5	T^6	T^N

*Parakinesic behavior

Kinesic behavior

Audible speech behavior

FIGURE 9.

*Including kinesic stress behavior.

Until some of the linguistic and paralinguistic analysis is completed, however, we have no way of explaining this evident intersection of the linguistic and kinesic systems. When we turn to protocols which include both the linguistic and kinesic material, it is possible to abstract a series of linguistic situations which seem to demand a particular kinesic accompaniment. A more explicit description of some of the punctuation behavior is probably called for, therefore, before we proceed with the analysis. Utilizing our abstracted figure of kinemorphic construction, a record may read:

$$//(X \overset{\uparrow\cdots\uparrow}{Y} Z)(N)(O P \overset{\uparrow\cdot\uparrow}{Q})/ \quad /(L M \overset{\downarrow\downarrow}{N})(O)(\overset{\circ\!\!-\!\!\circ}{P} Q R)//$$

In this example the kine Y, in the kinemorph (X Y Z), stands for brow rise which is held for 1 degree of overlong as compared to X and Z. Q, which may stand for lip pursing, is comparably overlong in the (O P Q) kinemorph. In contrast, N in the (L M N) kinemorph, here standing for head nod, is overshort, and (P Q R), here a mid-face kinemorph, is marked by first degree of overlaxness. Since nothing *never* happens, this variation must be accounted for in the process of data exhaustion. The kines (as kinemorphs) (N) and (O) cannot from this record be abstracted as potential punctuation. However, when we match this record with a record of the speech events, we may well discover that either or both have a punctuational function as well as an observable bound place in the kinemorphic construction.

Theoretically, it should be possible to analyze this punctuational behavior without recourse to the linguistic or paralinguistic behavior which accompanies it. At the present time, however, our knowledge limits us to the conjecture that these events will eventually be orderable into some kind of suprasegmental form, analyzable in purely kinesic or parakinesic terms. Certainly the events do have a certain regularity of occurrence and individual shape. Until either or both a binding or a linking kinesic principle is detected in their operation, they must be considered punctuation forms to be classed—since they are abstracted both behaviorally and functionally—as motion markers.

The motion markers, behaviorally, seem to fall into two general types: those constructed from qualifier variation, and those composed of kines-as-kinemorphs and of "gestures" as bound kinemorphs in a kinemorphic construction. Either type may appear in the behavior of a speaker prior to and at the cessation of phonation—but not at the beginning or end of *all* phonation. They also appear in conjunction with special internal arrangements of complex sentences, but a speaker may very well emit (although this is probably quite rare) certain complex sentences without punctuating them with markers. Similarly, an auditor may or may not modify his speech-related behavior with motion events of the order of markers. In other words, while the punctuational behavior can be located in the speech context in certain positions, the analysis has not yet reached a point where we can posit obligatory binding between linguistic and kinesic events. With this caveat, we may list a series of derived functions that markers play in the interaction sequence. By "derived function" I mean an observable set of behaviors in a given context which can be abstracted and interpreted as related. Since my confidence in such interpretations is, at the moment, relatively low, I prefer to use "derived function" rather than some kind of "meaning."

These five markers (Q), (S), (D), (A), and (P) represent contextual appearance of a wide variety of punctuation behavior. Assignment

Types by derived function	Punctuation behavior	Motion marker

I. CUE
  A. Signaling anticipations of interruption
  B. Signaling anticipated termination of phona-tion
  C. Signaling anticipated initiation of phonation
  D. Signaling "proceed, I'm listening."
  E. Signaling "completed phonation."
	Examples would include hand, foot, and head nods, raised eyebrows, stance shifts, lid closure and dura-tion to second degree, sustained incomplete kine-morphs, palm presentation, pursed lips, visible breathing, eye focus shifts.	(Q)

II. SELECTION
  A. Selected item in series of items
  B. Selected connection between items in series
  C. Selection of certain items as related to other items
	Examples would include qualifier shift, head nod, head sweep or arc, special lip protrusion or retroflection, torso nod, hand nod, foot nod, digit nod, brow nod.	(S)

III. DURATION
  A. Increase
  B. Decrease
	Duration qualifier shift to staccato or allegro; lateral sweeps of hands, feet; eyeball sweep.	(D)

IV. AREA
  A. Nearby locale
  B. Distant locale
  C. Traversing distance
	Range of "gesture" including "pointing," with head, hands, feet, torso, hand sweeps, head sweeps, etc. (always en-cased in construction)	(A)

V. PRONOMINAL REFERENCE
  A. Speaker
  B. Auditor
  C. "We"
  D. "They"
  E. "It"
	Same as in IV above except that pointing is directed toward subject with support-ive construct.	(P)

FIGURE 10. Motion Markers.

of marker status to any particular punctuation thus represents an abstraction from context. Only extended contrast research in interaction situations can strengthen our confidence in the organization of the marker categories. For the present, the five-point system represents a tentative working base which has proved useful in the examination of interview material. A sample recording of kinesic marking following extensive analysis might read:

(Q) (P)   (S)   (P)   (A)
   I told John, Mary, and Bill to put it in the back part of the big,
(S)   (Q)
red barn.

The reader will note that the markers here are added to the simple English orthography. The position of the marker may be seen to have even more significance when the full linguistic-kinesic protocol is assembled for the assignment of symptomatic and diagnostic features.

[The following statements, along with the earlier discussion of methodology, define the procedures used to isolate the kinesic markers and kinesic stress described in Part III (pages 103–143).]

Interpretation

At this stage in the development of kinesics, interpretation must always rest upon the adequate measurement of the context of an occurrence. Throughout the preceding discussion I have stressed the fact that no kinesic event, whatever the size or the shape, is a *carrier* or invariable stimulus with its own emergent causal component. From the point of view taken within this discussion, no kinesic form is a vehicle with a constant load, no kinesic event, an encapsulator of meaning. I have tried to make it clear that the question "What does X mean?" is nonadmissible unless the system within which X operates has been subjected to sufficient analysis so that X in its multiple of transforms can be described. However, to reject the oversimple question is not to repudiate the responsibility for weighing the role of the event within the system. Perhaps a summary of certain aspects of our discussion will make this position less ambiguous.

When we have repetitively isolated the forms A, B, and C, established within the preliminary descriptive frame of the investigator, as least discriminable variations from an established zero point, we can say that for the investigator the meaning of A is not that of B and is not that of C. This procedure provides us with units whose value for the subject is yet to be determined. If repetitive manipulation of the forms A, B, C demonstrates that, for the subject, they are in fact not substitutable for each other in all frames, it is then necessary to describe them as having (for the subject) *discriminational meaning*.

If, on the other hand, we establish the fact that the preliminary units which the investigator distinguishes in a given position (e.g., A_1, A_2, a_1, a_2) are substitutable for each other in that context without (for the subject) varying the function of the form, we may then say that these units are in this context in *free variation* and have, for the subject, the same perceptual value. That is, the *kine variants*, while having for the investigator discriminably different values, have for the subject identical perceptual value. They belong to the same class of events and they derive their meaning from their class membership. Thus A^1, A^2, a^1, and a^2 have a single perceptual meaning A. Yet we have said nothing as to the meaning of A as a kine. We can, however, discuss the structural value of A when we systematically examine the kinemorph and kinemorphic-construction bound forms which contain A. Again we are not saying what A in and of itself means. What we are saying is that A will occur in certain kinesic contexts. While our analysis has not yet gone this far, in the future we may very well be able to list those kinds of constructions in which A does not appear. There is also the possibility that we will discover a systematic nature to kine positioning which will allow us to perform the complementary distribution analysis so characteristic of linguistic analytic procedures.

On the next level of analysis we can determine the relationship between certain groupings of kines and their complex associations under some kind of suprasegmental binding system. Through analysis we can determine that certain of these bound forms will exist in association with other bound forms under some kind of cross-referencing system which serves to distinguish one complex bound series of movements from another comparable but differing cross-referencing series.

But the question still remains, once these forms have been distinguished, ordered, and conceptualized in their complex organization, how do we then determine their significance in the interactional sequences in which they appear? Throughout the sequences discussed above, our procedure has been dominated by a series of methodological canons: (a) Establish and maintain a given level of analysis. (b) Isolate units for manipulation. (c) Establish the independent identity of these by contrast analysis. (d) Weigh the analytic value of these newly established units by the examination of the contexts in which they regularly appear or never appear. These same canons prevail in the analysis of the *social meaning* of any form or series of forms. The social meaning of a form is established by the description of the shift in a field or context occasioned by the presence or absence of a given *complete* form. However, let us re-emphasize one point. This procedure cannot be accomplished before the full analysis of the form—which includes the assignment of the form to its role within a pattern—has been carried out. We cannot simply count the forms present and derive the special meaning of the forms. Unless we carefully separate our levels of analysis, we shall be unable to deal with those patterned arrangements in which the value of a pattern is shifted by the absence of a component which is normally internally bound. In other words, no running list of kine variants will ever inform us as to the role of the kine in the interactional sequence. Only in a pattern, composed of complex bound forms, does the form enter into associations on the social interactional level.

Because we are dealing with a patterned system, our analysis, once completed, serves to make it possible to see incongruities* which appear within the system at any given level. The statement that the behavior which we are analyzing at any given level contains incongruities, however, does not permit us to assume that these incongruities will introduce incongruities into the social interactional sequence. One of the most important functions of parakinesic activity is that of introducing cross-referencing signals that indicate that what appears to be an incongruity is congruent within some larger system. Such statements as "Everything to follow (or everything just said) is a joke," or "I am imitating" or "to quote so and so" or "this is play" provide us with examples which can be kinesically rendered in such a manner that apparently incongruous statements are cross-referenced into congruity. As we shall see in later discussion, this is the very area in which personally distorted systems become maloperative. Only systematic research with contrast

---

*These are often termed "ambiguous" when observed in a single stream of behavior, e.g. the lexical—or when, *within a time frame,* events in one stream seem to contradict events in another, e.g., lexical items or vocalic behavior differing in apparent content from kinesic items.

analysis in multiple contexts will permit us to evaluate the particular incongruity. Within our basic assumption that "nothing *never* happens," the incongruity is itself a message if it remains uncompensated for within the larger system. Its interpretation, again, will rest upon its repetitive contextual appearance.

The data do not permit final analysis of the relationship between the two communicational systems, language and body motion. We already have considerable evidence that these systems cross-reference each other and establish full patterns of conversational performance which operate in the social interactional sequence. Man does not merely move and see movement, or talk and hear, in an interaction. Body motion and language, on this level, form a complex pattern in which they are only analytically separable. The full pattern must be assessed before we can hope to weigh the role of either within the interactional sequence.

Finally, even the most exhaustively analyzed conversational pattern does not exhaust the systems in operation in any sustaining association. That is, communication analysis as discussed here does not constitute a final analysis of culture or its component situations. The final answers to "What does X mean" *can only be arrived at when all of the other social systems interacting in any situation are equally thoroughly analyzed.*

27. A Kinesic-Linguistic Exercise: The Cigarette Scene

Doris and Gregory, as the camera is reloaded and again begins to record the scene, are reseated upon the sofa. Each has a stein of the homemade beer supplied by Doris. Doris looks from Gregory to her beer stein and at the matches which Gregory is holding. Her left hand carries the cigarette to her mouth after her right leaves the stein on the coffee table before them. Gregory continues: "He's a very, very bright four-and-a-half-year-old. Why, that drawing that he brought in is very advanced for four-and-a-half." As he talks, he opens the match folder, extracts a match, strikes the match under the closed flap, moves the lighted match into position and makes contact with her cigarette as he terminates his vocalization. As he talks, Doris moves in concert with his match manipulations until her cigarette is lighted. She speaks: "I suppose all mothers think their kids are smart, but I have no worries about that child's intellectual ability." A $\frac{3}{8}$ second lag between "child's" and "intellectual" was equaled by another between "intellectual" and "ability." Gregory speaks, his first words coterminous with the latter hesitation and "ability": "No, that's a very smart one." As Doris talks, her right hand drops to the table edge and then past it slightly to the left to adjust her shoe strap before she drops her hand backward to the couch. This movement, with its momentary shifts, are still in concert with Gregory's, who, after Doris' cigarette is lighted, forms a triangular movement in the air which terminates with the extinguishing of the match and its disposal in the ash tray. This scene begins at (plus or minus ten frames) #12529 and is concluded by (plus or minus 10 frames) #12784.

Introduction

"The Cigarette Scene," an interactional sequence of some 18 seconds in duration, has remained a type site for linguistic-kinesic analysis throughout the decade following the original work on the Doris-Gregory films.* Filming techniques have improved, budgets have become sufficiently large to permit extensive recording on sound film of half-hour and hour-long sequences of conversation, interview, and interaction, and, with Jacques Van Vlack's development of the frame count B Roll, the correlation of the vocalic and the movement stream has become more precise. Other films have attracted our research interest, but this scene, in which Gregory and Doris contemporaneously discuss the merits of Doris' four-year-old son, Bruce, and engage in a ritual dancelike lighting of Doris' cigarette, has remained a rich, only partially analyzed corpus. The spe-

*From *The Natural History of an Interview*. Norman A. McQuown, ed., in preparation, 1956– . The research for this still unpublished report was initiated at the Center for the Behavioral Sciences, during the summer of 1956. Gregory Bateson, Henry Brosin, Charles Hockett, Norman A. McQuown, Frieda Fromm-Reichmann, and the author selected 10 minutes of sound-filmed interview taken earlier by Bateson for examination. Research of the scenes from this corpus given special attention has continued sporadically by McQuown and his students, Birdwhistell and his students, and by Henry Brosin until the time of this writing (June, 1967). [Since a large part of this essay deals with kinesic stress, the reader would do well to review the selection on pp. 128–142.—B.J.]

cial cadence of this piece of interaction, which Gregory (frames 12756–12786 and 12786–12826) terminates by a batonlike change of pace, marks the scene as critical and relevant to any final appraisal of the Gregory-Doris reciprocal. The seeming irrelevance of the body movement to the content exchanged by the participants and the glove-fit coherence of the rhythmic movements of the two participants to the instrumental act of cigarette lighting has made the scene useful for demonstration purposes. In our earlier assessments, the dramatic quality of the interchange masked out the significance of other behavior in the performance. The parakinesic category, "Rhythmic-Disrhythmic," in the first appraisals, subsumed data that, as our analyses became more refined, were to be analyzable as stress kinemes and suprasegmental kinemorphemes. This present exercise attempts to bring the earlier research in line with some more recently developed techniques.

Kine to Kineme

As reported elsewhere (Birdwhistell, 1952, 1958, 1961a) the theory and methodology of kinesics has been consistently influenced by that of descriptive and structural linguistics. From the initial morphological discoveries, it has been clear that visible communicative behavior exhibited formal properties at least analogic to those describable for audible behavior. I have been fortunate to be in constant consultative contact with linguistic researchers, and this contact shaped the research design and terminology constructed for kinesic research. At the same time, because of a deep appreciation of linguistic discipline and rigor, I have reacted against the fashionable and often careless preemption of the "etic-emic" distinctions. Throughout kinesic research, every attempt has been made to be cautious about the abstraction of isolable elements of body motion (kines) into manipulable classes of allokines (kinemes). "Complementary distribution" is an idea of great methodological force for the linguist and has proved to be an efficient tool for phonologic analysis. Because of the multiple layering of body motion behavior, both in body part and temporal arrangement, the distributional qualities of units of kinemorphology are more difficult to assess in the empirical data. At the present writing, a kineme is:

a class of allokines *which can be demonstrated in kinemorphs* to be substitutable.

Note: *If more than one allokine is discovered to be present in the same structural neighborhood,* the kine representing it may be either:
   a. a member of more than one kinemic class
   b. an insufficiently refined kine, or,
   c. the morphology has been insufficiently analyzed and we are probably dealing with an intersection of levels in the behavioral stream.

The distinctions between kine and kineme, kinemorph and kinemorpheme, remain useful and efficient. However, these terms are heuristic devices. Until we become much more secure as to the morphology and syntactics of kinesics (even for American English movers) our emic assignments must be registered as tentative. The history of phonological research is reassuring to the kinesicist timid about working models; tomorrow's research will validate the model or obliterate it.

Sight and Sound

The earliest work in kinesics attempted only the crudest correlation of body motion and speech behavior (Birdwhistell, 1952). I had yet to comprehend either the feasibility or necessity of sound film recording and was, in fact, resistant to the idea early suggested by McQuown (1951) that the future of kinesic-linguistic research as related to social processes depended upon intensive and parallel phonetic and microkinesic recording and analysis. As an anthropologist, I was attracted by grosser elements which I felt could be abstracted and organized by the careful scansion of the complex message stream. The isolation of these, I believed, would lead to the understanding of communication—for me then, as now, the dynamic structure which sustains order and creativity in social interaction.

The complex data which began to emerge as body motion research became involved in cross-cultural comparisons of human body motion, and the encouragement of Henry Lee Smith, Jr., and George L. Trager to study body motion as a structure with its own rules of order combined to force me to concentrate upon the visible and silenced behavior of human beings. Small stretches of films and access to a slow-motion projector by 1956 laid the groundwork for the analysis of the American kinesic system. As research proceeded, the presence of vocalization or auditor behavior was not ignored.

However, it was recorded at the articulatory level as body motion behavior—not as speech behavior. Even the preliminary attempts to abstract this data, however, made it clear that beyond the circumoral activity involved in speech production, behavior appeared which seemed related to or was at least usually modified by the presence of vocalization. It was not until the Palo Alto group* began its research conferences that the delineation of such behavior became relevant to kinesic research.

Out of these conferences, out of the co-research with Smith and Trager, and out of the subsequent ongoing research at Eastern Pennsylvania Psychiatric Institute and at Western Pennsylvania Psychiatric Institute and Clinic† came ideas which led to the isolation of a variety of circumspeech body behavioral abstractions. These abstractions cover behavior characteristic of conversation, but which seems to have differing structural properties than those which could be traced for the phenomena assigned to kinesics proper.

In the Cigarette Scene, the acts of lighting the cigarette, Gregory's manipulation of the match, and Doris' adjustment of her shoe strap may be termed *instrumental behavior*. Moreover, the fact that Doris and Gregory are seated for an extended conversation is, at one level, instrumental. To say that an act is instrumental, however, does not define it, in itself, as without signal or message value. The performance of any act in the presence of others must be comprehended as having the stamp of individual and social practice. Yet, at this writing, acts such as walking, smoking, eating, knitting, woodworking, still must be filed as "instrumental" and/or "task oriented" until we know more about their communicative structure.‡ However, as we can see from the analysis of the scene, the assignment of instrumentality to the larger frame of behavior must not preclude the examination of concurrent behavior, whether such behavior is at first glance integral to or apparently trivial to the immediate task accomplishment. There is a temptation to see instrumental acts in a social

*Gregory Bateson, Ray Birdwhistell, Henry Brosin, Frieda Fromm-Reichmann, and Charles Hockett.

†The work of Harvey Sarles, William Condon, Felix Loeb, and Joseph Charny at Western Pennsylvania Psychiatric Institute and Clinic has been invaluable both as a check upon and as a creative incentive to the work here at Eastern Pennsylvania Psychiatric Institute.

‡The work of Marvin Harris is an approach to this problem. See *The Nature of Cultural Things* (New York, 1964). See also the review by Duane Metzger in the *American Anthropologist* 67, no. 5, pt. 1 (1965), p. 1293.

situation as "carriers" of other messages. Yet there is an equal justification, from another point of view, of assigning priority to the communicational act. At the moment, I am using the concept of *alternating context*. Either can be the context for the other.

There is a second type of customary behavior which resists kinesic analysis while having patterned form and discernible message value. Included in this category, the *demonstratives,* would be such acts as gestural mapping, the illustrative movements customary as accompaniments to female discussions of dressmaking and design or of cosmetological arrangements of the hair. To the same category belong the illustrative movements which accompany male discussions of fishing or cabinet making and which often accompany male discussions of sporting events. From the limited cross-cultural data available it is clear that demonstratives are conventionalized forms, but they do not appear to follow kinesic rules, at least among American movers. No definitive demonstratives appear in this particular scene. However, the limited tridirectional sweep which is employed by Gregory as he extinguishes the match and which is followed by the larger cigarette movement to change the cadence of the scene may, as we get more comparative data, be both "instrumental" and "demonstrative." The act is clearly, at one level, instrumental. However, without supporting data, we cannot define the *act* itself as demonstrative—the change of cadence may very well be at times, in and of itself, demonstrative.

The durations of both instrumental behavior and demonstrative behavior are often longer than that of the accompanying syntactic sentences. This need not be so. For example, a speaker may circumscribe a shape in the air while describing an object and the air picture may be coextant with the nominal clause. Comparably, an instrumental act, whether referred to in the context of accompanying speech or not may be completed within or beyond the stretches of the speech behavior.

There is a third type of body behavior which, while still only crudely understood, should be mentioned here. This behavior is characteristic of all conversational and nonconversational interactional situations. *Interactional behavior* includes a variety of behaviors of part or whole bodies as they move toward or away from, or maintain careful spacing among, participants of an interactional scene. Hall (1959, 1965, 1966) has done pioneering work in the isolation of certain aspects of these phenomena in his work upon proxemics. Scheflen's (1965c) analysis of the movement patterns in the psychiatric interview provides still another dimension to the understanding of body shifts as messageful. His study, related to Bateson and Mead's (1942) earlier work of complementary, mirroring, and parallel movements of participants, indicates that there is a discoverable logic which marks segments of interaction. The work of Condon on "synchrony" and "dissynchrony" in interaction is further suggestive of overall interpersonal movement patterns which promise, as analysis proceeds, to supply us with measures of interactional communicative signals.* A number of behavioral categories are reported as relevant to the examination of the interaction. Often this behavior, which ranges from the presence of a rhythmic cadence to the interaction to a disassociation in the behavior of the actors to the extent that they appear to be in isolation from one another, seems almost to be a running comment to the participants about the interaction (see also Birdwhistell, 1961a). Bateson's concept of "metacommunicational" is of relevance here. Perhaps the term "metainteractional" would leave the function of such variations in behavior more open for further investigation. In the case of the Cigarette Scene, going beyond the data provided by our corpus, Doris' activity might be interpreted as a demand upon Gregory for a relationship more interpersonally involved than he has seemed to engage in before. As hostess, she has provided beer. Her nonlexical request for Gregory to light her cigarette *may* be no more than an act to elicit a formalizing etiquette. At some level of analysis his act can be seen as the reciprocal of hers. The cadence of which we spoke above, which distinguishes this part of the scene from the remaining 20 minutes, sustains itself until Gregory cuts the beat in half with the waved match and cigarette. This action is special and must ultimately be accounted for in any description of the interaction. However, the point being made here is that while Doris moves her hands and arms and shifts her body, and while Gregory moves his hands and body in a concert beat, other things are continuing to happen. The "dance" is no more exclusive than is her "shoe fixing"—interaction is multidimensional in time and structure.

To return to the data, Doris, while continuing to talk about her son, turns away from Gregory, "reaches" for a glass which she does not take, drops the heel of her shoe away from her foot and then

---

*Personal communication with William Condon. His analysis of fine-grained movement reveals that there is very close coordination in the fine movement of interactants in conversation.

adjusts the strap and lets her hand fall away from the shoe before it swings back to touch the table again. Meanwhile, she has "closed" her body, moving her torso closer to her legs as she talks about "all mothers think their kids are smart". . . Her hand touches the table on "but." She then turns back to Gregory and focuses upon him as she says, "I have no worries about that child's intellectual ability" while shaking her head with animation. Here again is a "layer" of behavior which cannot be accounted for either in strictly kinesic structure or in either of the categories laid out above. The quality of the film makes it impossible for us to confirm the impression that as she talks the tonus of her face changes. Nor can we determine whether the tight mouth-limited smile with which the scene began, taken together with the tonus shift, forms a cross-referencing signal that calls attention to the signal value of the complexity of her utterance. These phenomena which are recorded as parakinesic are detectable when we contrast these scenes with others in the larger film. However, "interpretation" of these would require more data than are supplied by all of the film and tape at our disposal.

Since the stretch which we are examining contains no clear examples of *kinesic markers,* these movements, which seem to be tied to particular semologic forms, require no discussion here. These movements (see the discussion above, on pp. 121–126) customarily but irregularly appear in utterance situations in conjunction with ambiguous pronominals, in situations where the lexeme is ambiguous about tense, position, possession, and plurality, and in situations where adverbial clauses appear to require reinforcement or modification. The fact that these are lacking or submerged within other phenomena in this stretch may or may not be of significance. The string upon which we will concentrate in this discussion is Doris' "I suppose all mothers think their kids are smart, but I have no worries about that child's intellectual ability." When compared to comparable strings within the larger corpus, there is a kind of stereotypy here to her speech behavior. It is impossible from the available data to determine whether this stereotypy arises from the fact that she has used this sentence before in her dealings with the outside world, whether her words are somehow fillers for a critical relationship shift, or, whether what we hear is not stereotypy at all but what Fromm-Reichmann once described in conference as the "voice of despair." At any rate, regardless of our rationalization, the absence of discernible markers is worthy of note and may become of significance as we come to know more about the codes of interaction.

The Problem

In this exercise our focus is upon what Doris *says* in this situation. It is not our present problem to determine what she *means*. At the same time, operating upon the assumption that description approaches explanation as it deals with a greater proportion of the available data, it should be profitable to describe our corpus more adequately. Charles Hockett originally transcribed this string, and his transcription was modified only slightly by an independent analysis by Norman McQuown. Trager-Smith conventions are used here, although modified slightly for Hockett's purposes.

In an attempt to get some kind of perspective upon the lexical aspect of this piece, twelve women of comparable age and social class background to that of Doris were given a typescript in standard English orthography and asked to comment upon it. All except one commented that this was standard "woman talk," i.e., a preliminary apology followed by a proud statement about the child, unusual only in the presence of the "but" rather than the expected "and." The one exception to the "woman talk" generalization came from an informant who said, "It's a sentence to hide the 'but.' She is very concerned about her child." The general attitude of these informants

CHART 1A. *Linguistic Transcription: "I Suppose All Mothers Think Their Kids Are Smart But"*

1c***				͡͡							͡͡
fn**<										⌢—	
VSg*?m											?
Int	3		2						<u>3</u> 2 3	‖	
StrJ	∧	∧	∧	∧	∧		∧		/		
Sgm	ay +	spoz +	ɔhl +	maðərz +	θink +	ðer +	kidz ər +	smart		bət	
	I	suppose	all	mothers	think	their	kids are	smart		but	
	(673)	(676)	(683)	(688)	(694)	(705)	(711) (716) (719)	(724) (730)		(732)	
		676	683	686	691	698	702	706 710	718	725	

* ?,h,r,ə,m, Vocal Segregates (Trager)
** <, Crescend (Hockett); ⌢ Drawling (Trager)
*** ♀, Rasp (Trager)

Phonetic transcription omitted. Circled numbers are numbers assigned 1956. Open numbers are from edge reading of sound film 1967.

CHART 1B. Transcription: "I Have No Worries About"

*In   ʌ–

VSg   hr ?ə?m?—?

Int	2		3	3	2	2
StrJ	\		ʌ	ʌ	/	
Sgm	ay +	haev +	now +	wəriyz		əbawt +
	I	have	no	worries		about
	⑦⑤⑥	⑦⑤⑦	⑦⑥④	⑦⑥⑦ ⑦⑦③	⑦⑧⓪	⑦⑧⑤
	752	755	760	763	778	

* ʌ Overloud, (Trager)

CHART 1C. Transcription: "That Child's Intellectual Ability"

*In/fn   –ʌ   >
                  –ʌ

VSg		hr			r		
Int		: :			3̲	1	#
StrJ	ʌ	: :\	ʌ	/			
Sgm	ðæt + cayldz:	:intilekcuwil + əbilitiy					
	that childs	intellectual ability					
	⑦⑧⑥ ⑦⑧⑧ ⑦⑨① ⑦⑨⑤ ⑧⓪⑥	⑧①④ ⑧②⓪ ⑧③③					
	783 789	804	831				

* > Fading (Hockett)

about the "but" was consistent with the appraisal of the psychiatrists, Henry Brosin and Frieda Fromm-Reichmann, who saw the
central lexical signal of the sentence in the conjunction. (It is worthy
of note that four of a control group of six women, when showed
this sentence among five other sentences and asked to recall them
5 minutes later, wrote this sentence as "I suppose [one case 'guess']
all women think their kids are smart [two cases, 'bright'] and I have
no worries [one case 'I'm not worried'] about that child's [three cases,
'my child's'] intellectual ability.")
    Careful review of the linguistic evidence (see Charts 1A, 1B, 1C)
provides the following discussion. Doris' customary discourse
pattern contains long strings of secondary stress. Moreover, the

tertiary on "I" at the start of the string is not unusual. What is more unusual are the two double cross junctures within such a short string. Doris customarily has very long strings without terminal junctures. This is a phenomenon common in psychiatric interviews (this is not ostensibly such an interview) and has been interpreted as a device to avoid interruption or interpretation. The segregates here again are not unusual in her speech patterning. The paralinguistic rasp over "think their kids are smart" is consistent with other portions of the larger protocol. The drawl over "are smart but I have no worries about that child's" is not, in the fact that it conveys portions of two syntactic sentences, a common device for her. *If we were trying to assess her meanings,* the use of drawl here would deserve further comparative attention. Studies of silence remain preliminary among linguists. "Hesitations" and "pauses" have been remarked upon by a number of students as worthy of study, but even when they are statistically appraised, we still know relatively little about the conventional use of the devices. However, in the case of Doris, the roughly $\frac{1}{4}$ second between "worries" and "about" and between "child's" and "intellectual" seem worthy of note, particularly if we are in pursuit (consciously or not) of some kind of evidence that the utterance implies that she does have worries and among those worries, some about her child. Even though we are not here preoccupied with meaning, it is always with us, and an increase in our data might amplify our understanding of the situation. Let us see how this sentence is marked kinesically.

Kinesic Junctures

From the beginning of the systematic investigation of American movement patterns it was evident that we were not dealing with a set of isolated and disconnected gestural forms. The discovery of kinesic junctures in the behavior of American (including American-English-speaking Canadians) movers laid the groundwork for structural kinesics. Not only were movement segments tied together morphologically, but longer segments and complex forms were joined or separated by junctural conventions. The fact that streams of body behavior were segmented and connected by demonstrable behavioral shifts analogic to double cross, double bar, and single bar junctures in the speech stream enhanced the research upon kinemorphology and freed kinesics from the atomistic amorphy of earlier studies dominated by "gestures" and "sign" language. More-over, when we attempted to study interactional situations, by means of context analysis (Scheflen, 1965b), the need for rigor demanded markers to give us some way of explicitly breaking the behavioral stream, of segmenting out sections for special comparative attention. The fact that the kinesic markers, while at times coextant with the linguistic markers, often gave us a very different shape contributed to our assessment of data that did not seem to fit within linguistic terminal junctures. This became particularly evident when the major body shift which I termed the kinesic triple cross juncture served to relate and segment much longer stretches of conversational behavior. While not entirely accurate, we have come to see the behavioral stretch marked by kinesic triple cross junctures as com-parable to paragraphing or stanzaing in writing. We have not at-tempted the systematic research necessary to relate this juncture to content but, as of this writing, the best statement possible is that it is often but not always related to shifts in content or to shifts in relationship patterning. Only further research will permit security as to whether such phenomena as these are separate, interdependent, or in free distribution.

During the past several years, research upon complex strings of speech taken from conversation and compared with the production of simple and complex statistical formulas (Birdwhistell, 1968f) has provided us with two other junctural forms. The first of these, the "tie" juncture, has been detected only in conjunction with spoken nominal constructions and will be demonstrated (page 240). The second, the "hold" juncture, occurs regularly in conjunction with complex strings of discourse and apparently has a discretely semo-logic function. The hold juncture, involving a particular body part which holds a position while other parts continue to perform other functions, connects included and apparently intrusive variation in content, maintains the coherence of complex themes, and bridges apparently trivial diversionary or explanatory discourse excursions. These six kinesic junctures are working tools. The primitive state of kinesic research does not permit us at the moment to see them either as structurally equivalent or as of more than one level of activity. My *hunch* is that the single bar and the tie juncture will turn out to be at a different level than are the double cross, the double bar, the triple cross, and the hold. However, this may be a result of the types of data I have been analyzing rather than a matter of structure.

Tentative Kinemes of Juncture

Symbol	Term	Gross behavioral description
K#	Double cross	Inferior movement of body part followed by "pause." Terminates structural string.
K//	Double bar	Superior movement of body part followed by "pause." Terminates structural strings. Homomorph in initial and medial or parallel positions may be a kinemorpheme which permits K# in terminal position. We have no data which illustrate coexistence of a terminal K// in conjunction with a complex kinemorphemic construction containing "K//" in other positions.
K##	Triple cross	Major shift in body activity (relative to customary performance). Normally terminates strings marked by two or more K#s or K//s. However, in certain instances K## may mark termination of a single item kinic construction, e.g., in auditor response, may exclude further discussion or initiate subject or activity change.
K=	Hold	A portion of the body actively involved in construction performance projects an arrested position while other junctural activity continues in other body areas.
K/	Single bar	Projected held position, followed by "pause." Considerable idiosyncratic variation in performance; "pause" may be momentary lag in shift from body part to body part in kinemorphic presentation or may involve full stop and hold of entire body projection activity.
K·	Tie	A continuation of movement, thus far isolated only in displacement of primary stress discussed below, pp. 245ff.

The Stress Kinemes

Three of the junctural kinemes were isolated prior to the initiation of serious research and analysis designed to *integrate* kinesic and linguistic data. K#, K//, and, although not given separate status, K## were easily detectable as operative forms in complex kinemorphic constructions. Only as linguistic-kinesic analysis proceeded, however, did K/, K=, and K· emerge in that order from the behavioral stream. From this time on, work proceeded, in a sense, in two directions. Microanalysis permitted the abstraction of the kinic stream from articulatory description to the point that complex kinemorphs could be abstracted. Fortunately, early hunches that shifts in body part, of intensity or breadth of movement, marked movement from kinemorph to kinemorph held up in a sufficiently large number of cases that, as the "terminal" junctures were isolated, their function in relation to strings of kinemorphs could be postulated and a primitive syntactics could be derived to permit the investigation of bounded sequence of behavior. This proved immediately productive.

The Cigarette Scene as a unit for study was originally chosen because of the unique interactional cigarette lighting. While the film was being changed, Doris reported to Gregory that a psychologist had examined her son and felt that he did not need any special attention. The sound made by the camera starting seemed to trigger Doris and she makes a major body shift which is recorded as a kinesic triple cross. The termination of the scene is marked by Gregory's body shift and match lid closing which follows directly upon his triangular cigarette wave. The cameraman shifts his focus and we are precluded from determining whether Doris acquiesces to his juncture. The fact that after a 34-frame duration of silence she places her hand firmly on the table as she shifts indicates that she has. It is worthy of comment that even after this major shift they continue to discuss the little boy's personality.

Doris' string, with which we are concerned here, is marked:

$$K· \quad K/ \qquad K\# \; K\# \qquad\quad K=$$
$$K/(?)$$

//I suppose all mothers think their kids are smart but I have no
$$K/ \qquad\qquad K· \qquad\quad K\#$$
worries about that child's intellectual ability//
(See Charts 3A, B, and C below for correlation with linguistic transcription.)

The kinesic single bar, noted in the phonational gap between "worries" and "about," is questioned because while her head activity is the only part in manifest movement, it, *in its activity,* meets the minimal articulatory requirement for held part. However, there is no manifest (in relationship to her ongoing movement pattern) stop in that activity. Analysis of the film does not lead me to see the presence of the morpheme of "dead pan," nor can I find any evidence of "destressed," discussed below under the stress kinemes. The "hesitation" in the head sweeps is assigned single bar status, but I hold little confidence in the assignment. It may be simply that kinesics, like linguistics, must learn how to deal with cessations of activity which are not codable by any prevalent classification system. The $K=$ is manifest; her very active torso holds over the remaining stretch. I suspect that it is the $K=$ which gives the impression of the presence of a $K/$.

McQuown and I had insisted that the analysis of human communicational behavior was in such a primitive state that, insofar as time permitted, we could not afford either in the linguistic or kinesic transcriptions to dispense with the most microscopic recording achievable within the state of the art. We felt that it would be more profitable in the long run to do shorter stretches in an intense fashion than to do longer stretches of macrorecording. In the annotated transcript which accompanies *The Natural History of an Interview,* the reader will find that the kinesic "macro" is often crude and arbitrary. Unlike linguistics with its background of research, kinesics had no canons which would regulate the size and relevance of shapes which we termed "macro." On the other hand, the past 10 years have given me little reason to vary my decision that microanalysis is, *for our purposes,* sufficiently fine-grained if every third frame of a movie taken at 24 frames a second is recorded.* As the years have passed, the micro line has continued to supply data to and confirm hypotheses made about conclusions derived at much higher levels of analysis.

Data have a way of hiding in a corpus and have in themselves little power of resistance to false, overfine, or overgross retrieval techniques. In the case of the behaviors that were to become the kinesic stress phonemes, two factors served to obscure them. The

---

*The elegant work of Condon, Sarles, Loeb, Charny, *et al.,* to my mind constitutes a partial affirmation of this position. Moreover, there seems every reason to believe from their reported data that an articulatory kinesics is developing which will ease the microrecording of exotic movement systems.

first of these factors came from an all-too-available classification called "speech effort" into which I placed the nonkinemorphic activity which occurred between the isolated junctures. Naively and innocently influenced by the fact that these activities were roughly correlatable with shifts in vocalic pitch and stress and reinforced in my conclusions by introspective support as I mimicked the speech patterns, I at first dismissed such evident variations in movement as artifacts of speech production. The difficulty of matching speech and movement because of the crudity of our correlational techniques contributed to the artifact theory. It was only later when Henry Lee Smith, Jr., and George L. Trager worked to strengthen my knowledge of descriptive linguistics and to sharpen my ear did it become evident that, while clearly production of speech strings requires effort or at least is not laborless, the regularities I was becoming aware of could not (because of their systematically variable appearance) be so dismissed.

Kinesic stresses are discussed at length elsewhere (see above pp. 128-147). It is enough to say here that four distinct variations in movement pattern, usually with the head, the hand, or the brows, serve to mark the flow of speech. These have been termed "primary"/ ∨ /, "secondary"/ ∧ /, "unstressed"/ — /, and "destressed" / ○ /. At least one stress occurs between all kinesic terminal junctures. By definition this is a primary stress. The following example from a film may serve to illustrate the stresses. In response to the question //What was John's last name?//, //Doe// is marked by a single movement, //Doe//. If the emphasis is upon John (not Harry), in the question, the question itself would be marked with //John// under primary kinesic stress and //last name// either has a secondary plus unstressed, two secondarys, or two unstressed:

thus:

   ∨   ∧   —   ∨   ∧ ∧   ∨   — —

//John's last name// or //John's last name// or //John's last name//.

The stressing is reversed if "name" not "John" is being emphasized.

Thus:

   ∧ —   ∨   ∧   ∧   ∨   —   —   ∨

//John's last name// or //John's last name// or //John's last name//.

The third stress of "unstressed" was derived following the isolation of "destressed," the fourth stress which is a reduction of stress below the norm of the produced string. In the filmed corpus was discovered:

$$\overset{\wedge}{//\text{What}} \ \overset{-}{\text{is}} \ \text{Johns} \ \overset{o}{\text{you}} \ \overset{o}{\text{know}} \ \overset{\wedge}{\text{Bills}} \ \overset{\vee}{\text{friends}} \ \overset{\wedge}{\text{last}} \ \overset{\vee}{\text{name}}//.$$

The string takes on more form when the kinesic junctures are added:

$$\overset{K//}{//\text{What}} \ \overset{\wedge}{\text{is}} \ \overset{-}{\text{Johns}} \ \overset{\vee}{\text{you}} \ \overset{K=o}{\text{know}} \ \overset{o}{\text{Bills}} \ \overset{K/\wedge}{\text{friends}} \ \overset{\vee}{\text{last}} \ \overset{K\#\wedge}{\text{name}} \ \overset{\vee \ K\#}{}//.$$

Although several thousands of exercises have been run from sound filmed data, it is still not possible to establish a rule which states an absolute relationship between these kinesic stresses and junctures and the linguistic stress and intonation patterns (by the Smith-Trager conventions) which accompany them. In general, a primary kinesic stress tends to coincide with the primary linguistic stress. Yet, in more than 20 per cent of the cases it does not. Perusal of the data indicates that the highest point of loudness and pitch, when these points coincide, is usually marked by a kinesic primary. However, this does not always occur. A long string of linguistic secondary stresses or a long string of phonation at a pitch 2 level is usually marked by destressed, but not always. In nominal phrases which are often marked by kinesic secondary-primary or kinesic primary-secondary or kinesic tertiary-primary, the kinesic stress may be consistent with or differ from the linguistic stresses. To summarize: while, statistically, kinesic stress patterning tends to be consistent with linguistic stress patterning, this is not invariable. I assume that further research at the semologic level and greater refinement of research with relationship to both linguistic and kinesic stress patterning will provide more perspective upon these phenomena. I am attracted by a conception of communicative structure which would include the possibility that, at least for American English, kinesic and linguistic suprasegmentals may be in free variation. However, I would hasten to say that the burden of proof for such a proposition would at the present state of knowledge rest upon me.

The concept "free variation," a useful one for structural analysis, may be misleading to the reader concerned with either psychological or sociological considerations of meaning. All that the term is intended to designate is the fact that forms of a given level are substitutable without special structural adaptation *at that level*. Throughout the structures of either linguistic or kinesic phenomena, "emic" forms are abstracted from class members, which are described as being in free variation with one another. However, there is no implication here that the choice of one of a series of alternatives (defined in structural terms) at any level of structure is not of consequence at the level of social interaction. The difference between /ðə/ and /ðiy/ (thuh and the) may at one level of analysis be seen as trivial but at another be of great consequence. These forms, under certain morphological or syntactical analyses, may be seen as identical, but, at the semological level, as well as at the phonological, as absolutely distinct. Comparably, the fact that in a stream of action the movement of the head may be seen to transport all kinesic stress signals, while in another stream a movement of the brows or, in another, the hand is utilized for this activity, is of little consequence in kine-morphological analysis. However, this may be of definitive significance for questions asked of this data at the level of social interaction.

When the tentative hypothesis is established that at certain levels of analysis we may discover, as research proceeds, structural forms from kinesics which are substitutable for structural forms from linguistics, there is no suggestion that the "choice" made by the conversant is not of consequence to the *interaction.* We are postulating an interdependence of linguistic and kinesic *structure,* not a final equivalence of semological or interactional function. In the discussion to follow, it will be seen that structural distinctions are made in the abstracted speech stream which do not appear in the abstracted movement stream and *vice versa.* At one level of analysis it is possible to say that the kinesic suprasegmental activity is functioning to make distinctions that *might* have been made by the linguistic suprasegmentals, and that we could not have been aware of these distinctions if we examined only the audible aspects of the activity stream. It is furthermore possible to say that these same (at this level of analysis) distinctions *could* have been made in the linguistic stream without an alteration in the structural activity in the kinesic stream. All that we are saying is that *unless we analyze both the linguistic and kinesic stream* we have no way of knowing *what distinctions* have been made by the conversant.

There is a temptation to say that when one channel carries a distinction which is not made by the other, the fuller channel carries the "real" meaning. This implies that a given performance has *a* particular meaning. Under no circumstances must the reader be misled by the heuristically limited corpus which we are examining in this exercise. From the examination of extensive sound-filmed interactional sequences, I have every reason to posit the proposition that in human experience there are at all observational times many streams of meaning in process. The particular section of the stream we analyze is always a partial one, and only as we come to comprehend the larger rules of communicational structure will we be able to determine the relevant meanings in particular sequences. In short, it is my hope that as we gain more complete control of the vari-sized forms of both linguistics and kinesics, we shall be able to examine limited sequences with an increased control over the data we ignore when we limit our corpus. I think a great part of the arguments popular in linguistics today about "grammar," syntax, and meaning are viable only because of the limited universe which is under scrutiny.

The kinemes of stress combine to form a set of suprasegmental kinemorphemes which have tested in studies of complex sentences and statistical formulas. These are:

Stress Kinemes		*Suprasegmental Kinemorphemes*
/ᵛ/	=	/ᵛ/
/ᴧᵛ/ or /-ᵛ/ or /-ᴧ/	=	/⌒/
/ᵛᴧ/ or /ᵛ-/ or /ᴧ-/	=	/⌣/
/-ᵛ̌-/ or /ᵛ̌/ or /-ᵛ̌ᴧ/	=	/⌄/
/ᵛᴋ│ᵛ/ or /ᵛᴋ╪ᵛ/ or /ᵛ⌒ᵛ/	=	/⌣⌣/ *
/ₒₒᴋ│/ or /ₒₒᴋ╪/ or /ₒₒ│││/	=	/-o-/ *
/ₒₒᵛ/	=	/⌄̣/
/ᵛₒₒ/	=	/⌣/

Charts 2A, B, and C, below, will demonstrate the kinic, the kinemic, and the kinemorphemic levels of analysis of Doris' circumlexical stress behavior. The structural balance of this selected segment is immediately obvious. The /ᴋ=/ is the added factor in the latter section of the utterance. However, ignoring this, if the suspected /ᴋ/ / is added, our type becomes:

$$//⌣/⌣\text{─}* ⌣ \# ⌣/⌣\#//$$

This balance could be related to the cadence in which Gregory and Doris are moving in their interactional dance. On the other hand, this may be a stylistic factor related to the production of a stereo-

---

*/⌣⌣/ and /-o-/ may as research develops turn out to be at a higher level of structure. The fact that the form crosses terminal junctures may or may not require such placement.

CHART 2A. *Kinemorphic, Kinemic, and Kinic Transcriptions.*

K_1 ⌣̇ | ⌐   ⋕   ∨ ⋕
K·

K_2 —   —   ∨   K| —   ∨   ∧   — —K⋕ ∨K⋕

K_3 hn   <u>hn</u>   hn   an

     I suppose all mothers think their kids are smart but

K_1 KINEMORPHIC
K_2 KINEMIC
K_3 KINIC

CHART 2B.

                       $K = K/(?)$

K_1 ⌒̇ ✓

                       $K = K/(?)$

K_2 ∧   —   —   ∨   —

K_3 hn   <u>hn</u>   (torsohold)

    I   have   no   worries   about

CHART 2C.

K_1 ⌣̇   K⋕
                K·

K_2 —   —   ∨   ∧   —   K⋕

K_3 <u>hn</u>   hn   —(torsohold)

    that   child's   intellectual   ability

typic utterance. At this stage of kinesic and communicational research, however, such statements remain little more than conjecture. (One of my assistants who was proofreading this paper points out that the sentence above, when spoken aloud, has the same quality of balance in its accompanying suprasegmental structure.)

    A final task remains for this exercise. In Charts 3A, 3B, and 3C, the linguistic and kinesic materials are assembled for comparison.

    A linear examination of the charts points up a series of items for special examination:

    1. The movement of the kinesic stress from its expectable position, either over /mothers/ or over /all/ as in //a̬ll mo̭thers// or //a̭ll mo̬thers//, gives us a form //all mo̬thers// as in //hot do̭g// which contrasts with //ho̬t do̭g// and //ho̭t do̬g//.

2. The form //thĕir kîds// in the string is specially marked by the kinesic primary-secondary form.

3. Neither of these distinctions appear to be marked either in linguistic stress or intonation. (verboid marker?)

4. The kinesic single bar between /mothers/ and /think/ is unmarked in the linguistic stream.

5. The linguistic stress and intonation appearing over /smart/ is absent in the kinesic line but may be subsumed under the kinesic /#/.

6. The kinesic primary stress over /but/, bounded by kinesic double cross junctures, in emphasis seems comparable to but not identical with the rather complicated linguistic situation in which /but/ is not specially denoted in either pitch or stress but is followed by a "pause" and glottal stop, and is the nexal point for the paralin-

CHART 3A. *Linguistic and Kinesic Transcriptions.*

K_1			⌣					#	∨ #
			K						
K_2	—	—	∨	K|	—	∨	∧	— —K#	∨K#
K_3			hn	hn	hn			an

I suppose all mothers think their kids are smart but

K_1 KINEMORPHIC
K_2 KINEMIC
K_3 KINIC

1c***				♀—					♀
fn**<									⌢—
VSg*ʔm									ʔ
Int	3		2				<u>3</u> 2 3	#	
StrJ	∧	∧	∧	∧	∧	∧	/		
Sgm	ay + spoz + ɔhl +		mǝð ǝrz +	θink +	ðer +	kidz ǝr +	smart	bǝt	
	I	suppose all	mothers	think	their	kids are	smart	but	

(673)	(676)	(683)	(688)	(694)	(705)	(711)	(716) (719)	(724) (730)	(732)
	676	683	686	691	698	702	706 710	718	725

  * ʔ,h,r,ǝ,m, Vocal Segregates (Trager)
 ** <, Crescend (Hockett); ⌢ Drawling (Trager)
*** ♀, Rasp (Trager)

Phonetic transcription omitted. Circled numbers are numbers assigned 1956. Open numbers are from edge reading of sound film 1967.

CHART 3B.

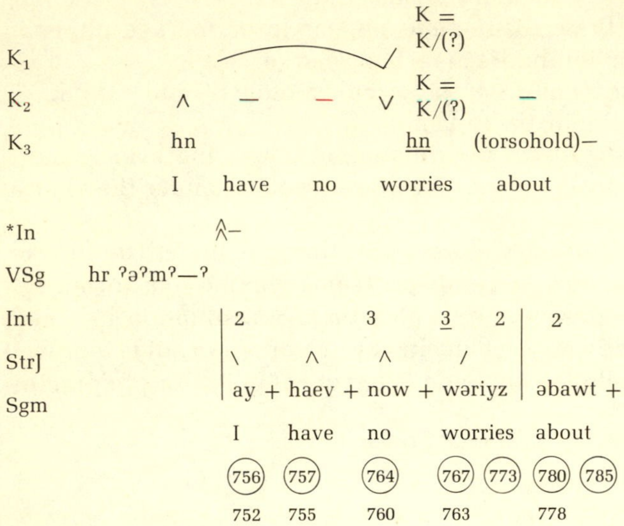

K_1

$K = K/(?)$

K_2 ∧ — — ∨ $K = K/(?)$ —

K_3 hn <u>hn</u> (torsohold)—

I have no worries about

*In ∧—

VSg hr ?ə?m?—?

Int | 2 3 <u>3</u> 2 | 2

StrJ | \ ∧ ∧ / |

Sgm | ay + haev + now + wəriyz | əbawt +

I have no worries about

(756) (757) (764) (767)(773) (780)(785)

752 755 760 763 778

* ∧ Overloud, (Trager)

CHART 3C.

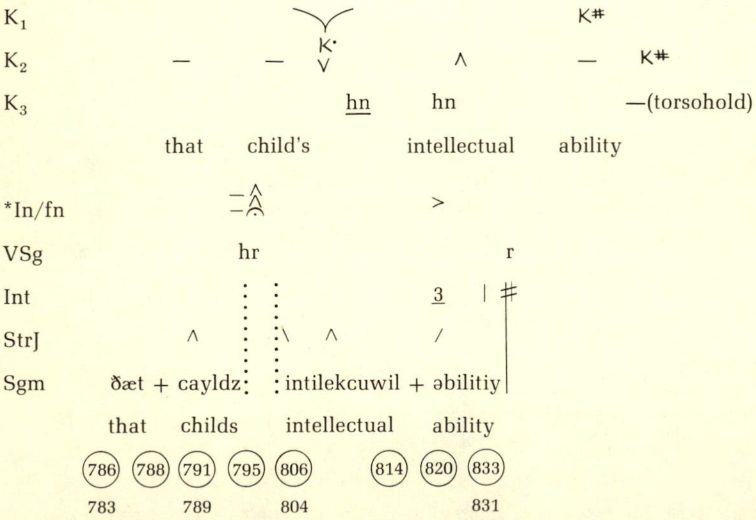

K_1 ∨ K#

K_2 — — K· ∧ — K#

K_3 <u>hn</u> hn —(torsohold)

that child's intellectual ability

*In/fn —∧ >

VSg hr r

Int | 3 | #

StrJ | ∧ \ ∧ / |

Sgm | ðæt + cayldz : intilekcuwil + əbilitiy |

that childs intellectual ability

(786)(788)(791)(795)(806) (814)(820)(833)

783 789 804 831

* > Fading (Hockett)

guistics. /But/ is included within the rasp, which marks //think their kids are smart *but*// and is, at the same time, within the drawl which covers //*but* I have no worries about that childs//. It is furthermore excluded from the overloud which extends over //I have no worries about that childs//.

7. The initial /I/ is kinesically unmarked while being at pitch 3. This may be a function of the cigarette lighting which masks either a kinesic stress or a pronominal marker. The second /I/ is marked with a kinesic secondary (perhaps flavored by a pronominal marker) while she speaks with tertiary stress over /I/.

8. The intonation pattern of 3-3-2, as marked by Hockett, over /no worries/ has some parallel in the primary kinesic stress over /worries/. I think that the kinesic stress pattern of secondary-primary or primary-secondary that might have been expected in this construction may have been absorbed in the kinemorphic construction of "head-shaking" which extends over //I have no worries about that childs//.

9. The kinesic primary stress which is pulled to a point *between* /childs/ and /intellectual/ to give us a form parallel to /all mothers/ is of special interest. More statistically normal forms would have been either:

$$//\overset{\wedge}{\text{that}}\ \overset{\wedge}{\text{childs}}\ \overset{\wedge}{\text{intellectual}}\ \overset{\vee}{\text{ability}}//\ \text{or}$$

$$//\overset{\vee}{\text{that}}\ \overset{\wedge}{\text{childs}}\ \overset{\wedge}{\text{intellectual}}\ \overset{\wedge}{\text{ability}}//\ \text{or}$$

$$//\overset{\wedge}{\text{that}}\ \overset{\vee}{\text{childs}}\overset{\frown}{\ }\overset{\vee}{\text{intellectual}}\ \overset{\wedge}{\text{ability}}//.$$

The /⌢/ recorded for the last form indicates a continuation of movement which seems to cross kinesic junctures, either of single bar or double cross. The linguistic pause, marked by Hockett, may be of consequence in the case. The segregates and the termination of the overloud and drawl are also to be noted here.

Summary

The nine points listed above are sufficient to illustrate some of the complexities which confront the linguist, the kinesicist, or the communication analyst who would attempt an assessment of the relationship between kinesic and linguistic phenomena at this level of analysis. This limited segment, containing two syntactic sentences, represents an abstracted corpus which is short enough to be subjected to intense analysis but does not seem to contain sufficient information to settle many of the questions which come to mind. One general point may be made from these data. Any discourse analysis, conversational analysis, communicational analysis, or interactional analysis which would attend to but one modality—lexical, linguistic, or kinesic—must suffer from (or, at least, be responsible for) the assumption that the other modalities maintain a steady or noninfluential state.

28. *Communication and Culture: A Limited Conclusion**

THE productivity of new approaches to human interaction and human interconnectedness should not lure us to such dependency upon the study of message systems that we subsume all human behavior under "communication." The mechanisms of information transmission are but an aspect, albeit an important one, of social experience. The fact that communicative processes are necessary to cultural continuity should not be taken to indicate that culture is nothing but communication. I find it impossible to conceive of communication as either independent of or as merely another word for culture. I realize that it is begging the question to describe communicative *behavior* as social behavior, which as process is interdependent with other social processes to form culture. But, as of this writing, I can make no clearer statement.

I have written elsewhere that it makes a great deal of difference whether we regard man as having the physiological and psychologi-

* The first excerpt is from "The American Family: Some Perspectives," *Psychiatry* Vol. 29 (1966), pp. 203–212; the second is from "Certain Considerations in the Concepts of Culture and Communication," in *Perspectives on Communication,* Carl E. Larson and Frank E. X. Dance, eds. (Speech Communication Center, University of Wisconsin-Milwaukee, 1968), pp. 144–165.

cal capacity (or ability) to send and receive symbols, on the one hand, or whether we regard communication as intrinsic to him, an adaptational minimum, on the other. In the prior case, man is seen as having the "ability" to communicate and, by logical extension, the ability not to communicate. In the latter, as human he is involved in the communication process. In the first case, communication is made up of the acts of individual men in adjustment to one another; in the second, communication (although *in part* studiable in the acts of individual men), as a system, transcends the acts of individual men. In the first case, minimal units of communication are acts of action and reaction, in the second, the least unit is a transactional act. In the first case, when humans in an interactional sequence are seen to misunderstand one another and either separate or engage in violent action, the scene is interpreted as a case of "breakdown in communication." In the latter, such events are interpreted as a different order of communication.

From the point of view represented here, communication might be considered, in the broadest sense, as the active aspect of cultural structure. Yet, even though it is useful to think in such terms, I am hesitant about such a formulation in that it may imply (in English) that communication is the behavior of the entity "culture." What I intend to convey is that culture and communication are terms which represent two different viewpoints or methods of representation of patterned and structured human interconnectedness. As "culture," the focus is upon structure; as "communication," it is upon process. Yet, again such a formulation can be misleading for it may seem to imply that process is without structure and that structure is inert. Perhaps a more illuminating way of stating the case would be to say that I believe that the studies of those who look at patterned human interconnectedness, as it were, from above and derive *cultural generalizations* from their observations will produce data which will be coextant ultimately with data derived by those who study it from below and who derive *communicational generalizations*.

Appendixes

Introductory Note*

CERTAIN portions of *The Introduction to Kinesics* are included as an appendix not merely as a historic curiosity, but as an attempt to put kinesic research into perspective. The devices included for annotation were developed to permit recording, to recheck observation, and, in the final analysis, as mnemonic artifices. The crudity of the drawing, while a direct statement of my penmanship, is still useful in conveying the idea that symbols are arbitrary and have substance only as related to specific and explicit statements of the conditions of observation. Here again kinesics owes a debt to the experience of linguistics. Linguists over the years have developed a standard orthography with which all trained linguists are familiar. Yet, few of the professional linguists with whom I have been associated hesitate to shift, adopt, or annotate any symbol when the observation or the analytic situation is made easier and more reliable and more easily communicated by such shifts.

The orthography presented below, notwithstanding its crudity, is demonstrably useful for recording unfamiliar material. Designed for kinesic research, it is hardly transferable to all body movement study. Over the years I have advised many students to use Labanotation, particularly when their problems were concerned with Western European peoples (Scandinavian, Germanic, Slavic, Romance, and Anglo-Saxon peoples)† and when they were concerned with whole body (and single body) problems. Irmgard Bartenieff and Alan Lomax, who have done the most extensive cross-cultural surveys, in their exciting analysis of dance and singing styles,‡ have found Labanotation useful. It is easily learned and is sufficiently internally consistent that they were able to achieve high reliability among their

---

*[These remarks on kinesic orthography were written in 1969 for this volume by the author.—B.J.]

†This loose, nontechnical terminology is purposive. We do not yet know how tight is the correlation between speech and movement, much less between these and political communities.

‡Alan Lomax, *Folk Song Style and Culture*, A.A.A.S. Pub. No. 88, Washington, D.C., 1968.

workers. Lomax says, furthermore, that as more detailed recording is required, Labanotation can be augmented or supplanted by other conventions.* However, I have chosen not to use Labanotation as an investigatory tool for communication analysis. Designed as a method for choreography, it is for me intrusive, when adapted to the measurement of interpersonal activity. It seems to me that it assumed that which I wish to investigate.

As a teacher I have not always been pleased by student response to orthographic conventions. An orthography inevitably achieves a reality which supersedes or at least influences the perception of the external events it is intended to record or represent. The symbols used are developed to stand for a *derived* slice of the behavioral continuum. When the conditions of the derivation process are not constantly monitored and where the *arbitrary* nature of the symbols is forgotten, investigation and analysis slip away from external reality to become operations subsumed by symbol manipulation. A symbol developed to implement the investigation of nature can, if not consistently governed, achieve its own reality.

The first task of the investigator who would invent new symbols is to develop a mutually consistent, nonambiguous system, which is sufficiently related to other kinds of symbol systems that it can be taught and is easily memorized. The fact, however, that it is easy to teach an annotational system—whether it be that presented below in the kinesic representations or in the stylized system developed by Laban—does not always facilitate penetrative analysis. The "cognitive structure" (and I use the term poetically for I am not confident of the content of the concept) or the logical style (Bateson's Eidos) of a group of communicants, exerts a control over perception and intellectual negotiation. Ease of teaching or learning is a test of convenience and not of validity or reliability. The conventions employed by kinesics have a built-in bias, some of which are sufficiently transparent as to be obvious. For instance, the use of the conceptualized clock face, and the convention of hours and minutes is clearly culture bound. The subdivisions of the imaginary space around the body into finite divisions of a series of planes along which we mark trajectories is obviously conditioned by the restriction of the drawing board, the blackboard, the photographic plate, and, thus, are part of two-dimensional telecommunicative technology.†

* Personal communication.

† The reader interested in notational conventions is directed to *The Golden Jackal, Behavior Studies* by Ilan Golani notated by Schmuel Zeidel, under the supervision of Noa Eshkol. Published by The Movement Notation Society, Tel Aviv, Israel, 1970.

I. Kinegraphs*

THE notational system demonstrated below divides the body into eight major sections. Inasmuch as most of the writer's research experience has been with American subcultures, these reflect his own ethnocentrism. The fact that he has had some opportunity to observe members of other national and ethnic groups here, in Mexico, and in Canada, and has spent some time in the field with two American Indian groups, may lessen this ethnocentrism, but it still remains. Until other workers take this or a similar recording system into the field and specifically study the motion systems of other peoples, we must continue to suspect our data.

This is reflected in the evident lack of stress on intratrunk muscles, neck, and foot activity. Most of the recording and research upon which this orthography is based has been done in clothed cultures.

This system is organized in such a way that it can be easily expanded. It is hoped that any student reading this who thinks of other kines or evident organizations of kines will communicate with the author in order that they can be listed.

It will be noted that this is a relatively static system. Only in the area of the long members is there much stress laid on movement. It is my hope that forthcoming research using motion pictures will make it possible to develop techniques which will make this more dynamic. The success of linguistics and phonetics in operating with the use of "stationary particle" recording gives some justification to the present system.

I am dissatisfied with the terminology employed for the description of types of walking, but in the absence of mobile visual aid material, the concepts used, in spite of their value-loading, have proved quite useful, with minimal involvement.

The eight sections into which the body is divided represent an arbitrary classification system which may be abandoned later. However, it has proved useful for the groups recorded thus far.

*From *Introduction to Kinesics: An Annotation System for Analysis of Body Motion and Gesture* (Washington, D.C., Foreign Service Institute, 1952), pp. 35–72.

Body Sections and Base Symbols

1. Total head: (H h ℏ)

2. Face: The selection of facial "parts" evidently reflects Western European emphases: (Symbols are pictographs of facial features) ʘ¨ʘ △

3. Trunk: To be considerably expanded as observations of pectoral, stomach, and back muscles are analyzed in context. (ℒℒ T Ƴ).

4. Shoulder, arm, and wrist: This section must be expanded to indicate muscle signals as they are located. Particularly must careful experimental work be done in localizing flows and avoidances of tension, of inception, and extension of activity. ⧣ ⟨ ⟩

5. Hand and finger activity: This complex system of numerical recording will be even further expanded when the data from more highly flexible cultures are added. (Numbers from 1 to 5)

6. Hip, leg, ankle: See shoulder, arm, and wrist (alphabetical notation of joints) ⅄ ⊥⊥

7. Foot activity, walking: The extent of foot covering present in the research situations so far have limited the kinegraphic isolation. (By addition of T before numbers, finger recording can easily be translated into toe and foot recording.)

8. Neck: The relatively few kines listed below for neck kines again reflect Western European observation situations. It is probable that, as Indonesian and other neck-active cultures are observed, a more extensive orthography must be developed. //

Utilizing this basic notational logic, the system has the advantage that it can be easily learned and may be extensively expanded.

The reader is urged to learn quickly the following "through space" indicants.

↑	To a superior position
↓	To an inferior position
→	To an anterior position
←	To a posterior position
⌒↘	To a lateral position (use R or L to indicate direction)
↙⌒	To a medial position
⊣	Indicates continuity of any particular motion or position

1. Total Head

"Norm"	Stress	Oversoft	Variants			
H	H̲	H̥	H⌢	H◡	H↙⌢	Full nod up and down or down and up
h	h̲	h̥	h⌢	h◡	h↙⌢	Half nod either up or down
ħ	ħ̲	ħ̥	ħ⌢	ħ◡	ħ↙⌢	Small "bounce"* at end of H or h (in its variations)
		ħ̲				Tense medial multiple nod, usually alone
		ħ̥				Same oversoft
Ħ	Ħ̲	Ħ̥	Ħ⌢	Ħ◡	Ħ↙⌢	Full side and back sweep (May contain nod or half nod)
ħ	ħ̲	ħ̥	ħ⌢	ħ◡	ħ↙⌢	Half sweep (may contain nod or half nod)
ƕ	ƕ̲	ƕ̥	ƕ⌢	ƕ◡	ƕ↙⌢	Small bounce at end of H or h (in its variations)
		ƕ̲				Tense medial multiple sweep, usually alone
		ƕ̥				Same oversoft
Ħ	Ħ̲	Ħ̥	Ħ'	Ħ	Ħ⌢	Cocked head

*"Bounce" is a bad term if taken literally. Head and neck muscles not necessarily in strain.

2. Face

—◯—	Blank faced
— ⌒	Single raised brow ⌒ indicates brow raised
— ⌣	Lowered brow
⌄/	Medial brow contraction
⋰⋱	Medial brow nods
⌒⌒	Raised brows
○ ○	Wide eyed
— ○	Wink
≻ ≺	Lateral squint
≻≺ ≻≺	Full squint
A	Shut eyes (with A-closed pause 2 count
⋌⋋ or	Blink⊣
B	B-closed pause 5 plus count
⊙ ⊙	Sidewise look
⋋⊃ ⊂⋌	Focus on auditor
⊗ ⊗	Stare
⊚ ⊚	Rolled eyes
⧸ ⧸	Slitted eyes
⊙ ⊙	Eyes upward
—⊙ ⊙—	Shifty eyes
"⊗ ⊗"	Glare
⊙ ⊙	Inferior lateral orbit contraction
△s	Curled nostril
s△s	Flaring nostrils
⸲△⸲	Pinched nostrils
⬓	Bunny nose
⬓	Nose wrinkle
⌒	Left sneer
~	Right sneer

◯	Out of the side of the mouth (left)
◯	Out of the side of the mouth (right)
⌣⌣	Set jaw
⌣	Smile tight — loose o
⊢⊣	Mouth in repose lax o tense —
⌐⌐	Droopy mouth
⊃	Tongue in cheek
⌒	Pout
⊹⊹⊹	Clenched teeth
⊍	Toothy smile
⊞⊞⊞	Square smile
⊚	Open mouth
s⊚ʟ	Slow lick—lips
q⊚ʟ	Quick lick—lips
⊂⊃	Moistening lips
⊂⊃	Lip biting
⌄⌄	Whistle
⋰○⋱	Pursed lips
⌄⌄	Retreating lips
⋰○⋱⊣	Peck
⋰○⋱ !	Smack
⊞⊞⊞	Lax mouth
⊔	Chin protruding
⊔	"Dropped" jaw
⊢×⊣	Chewing
⤨	Temples tightened
ℰ 3	Ear "wiggle"
⥦	Total scalp movement

3. Trunk and Shoulders

SPINE
(PROFILE)

Upright—lax—(or supported in chair) an imaginary line dropped perpendicular from spine of first thoracic vertebrae would intersect sacrum.

Upright ("stiff")

Anterior spinal curvature, thorax upright but lax, lumbar-sacral region thrust anteriorly. (If seated, buttocks firm on seat.)

Anterior spinal curvature, thorax upright but lax, sacral region thrust anteriorly. (Seated on posterior aspect of the sacrum.)

Sacral region upright, thorax thrust forward, upright

Anterior slump

"Rared back"

Leaning back

Leaning forward

In all kinegraphs concerning spine — indicates tension, o indicates overrelaxation.

SPINE
(FRONTAL)

Upright—lax—(or supported in chair) an imaginary line dropped perpendicularly from spine of first thoracic vertebrae would intersect sacrum.

Curvature right

SPINE
(FRONTAL) (*Continued*)

Curvature left

Leaning right

Leaning left

The following applies to both profile and frontal views of the spine.

Curvature beginning at base of thorax.

Curvature beginning at sacroiliac.

Curvature beginning at buttocks (i.e., involves hip axis)

SHOULDERS

Straight. Lax: o. Stiff: o.

Hunched shoulders

Shrug—for stress. Line following indicates duration.

Left shoulder raised

Right shoulder raised

Drooped (lateral) shoulders

Single drooped (lateral) shoulder (left)

Single drooped (lateral) shoulder (right)

Left shoulder forward. (Add P under right wing if right shoulder retreats coterminously.)

Right shoulder forward. (Add P under left wing if left shoulder retreats coterminously.)

Left shoulder back

SHOULDERS (Continued)

ᴾT	Right shoulder back
TA·	Left anterior thorax twist
ᴬT	Right anterior thorax twist
TᴬX	Left anterior trunk twist (from sacroiliac)
ᴬTX	Right anterior trunk twist (from sacroiliac)
ᴬTᴬ	Cupped shoulders
ᴾTᴾ	Shoulders back

PECTORAL MUSCLES

T=	Left pectoral tense
=T	Right pectoral tense
=T=	Chest tension
°T°	Chest overlax

STOMACH MUSCLES

φ	Stomach tense
φ	Stomach flaccid
₱	Stomach protruded
₿	Stomach sucked in
φ	Left stomach tense
φ	Right stomach tense

4. Shoulder, Arm, and Wrist

Note: Recording of Shoulder–Upper arm, Upper arm–Lower arm, Lower arm-wrist, unilateral or bilateral, requires considerable experience in observation. However, considerable practice (with a checking observer) can equip the recorder with sufficient facility and accuracy to meet most problems in general posture. Movement is still more difficult and the student is urged to practice "seeing in space" before trusting his records.

Warning: *Musculature and jointing are both involved in the analysis of long-member activity.* Most Americans assume *constant parallel activity* of these two interdependent physiological systems. Muscular tension does not *necessarily* flow from a medial point of inception to the most distant point. Nor does a similar movement of skeletal structure always involve the same muscles in tension orientation.

SHOULDER (AND/OR) ARM SKELETAL

#0   Chest and shoulder inceptual activity

#1   Upper arm from caput to elbow

#2   Tip of radius-ulnar complex to wrist

#3   Wrist–upper hand activity

R#0123   Activity (posture or movement) of right shoulder-arm-wrist

R#01   Activity (posture or movement) of right shoulder–upper arm angle

R#23   Activity (posture or movement) of right lower arm and wrist of hand

Either of two angle recording systems may be used—the degree of angle recorded as $\angle$ 30, 45, etc., or a clock system. Practice with a protractor (oversize) can sensitize the observer to degree of $\angle$, but this takes considerable practice. If Air Force experience can be taken here, the clock system seems practical and more easily learned. It is this which will be emphasized below.

The plane of the superior or medial member is used as the base plane. The angle formed by the shoulder plane when the upper arm is extended directly above the head is recorded R#01 (M). Movements or postures from (M) are counted clockwise. Thus when the upper arm is extended directly, medial, lateral, or anterior *in* the shoulder plane is recorded as R#01 (3) . . . direction is indicated by arrows: ⌒ indicating medial point; ⌒ indicating lateral point; ⟶ indicating anterior point.

R#01 (3)   ⟶   Figure shown indicates: right upper arm extended directly anteriorly from the shoulder.

R#01 (6)   Figure shown indicates: upper arm lax extended directly down from shoulder. (6 and M require no arrows.)

Note: For rapid recording only M to 6 is necessary. Arrows indicate mediality or laterality of gesture. Also posterior or anterior movement. R and L always recorded.

Motion clock

M

1   1

2   2

3   3

4   4

5   5

6

Following the same logic, the plane of upper arm is used to assess lower arm upper arm.

R#12 (M)   Regardless of relationship of upper arm to shoulder, this signifies the closest proximity of lower arm plane to upper arm plane.

R#12 (3)   Upper arm and lower arm at right angles. Use arrows to indicate point.

Note: Logic continues in recording wrist angle.

R#23 (6) ⟶ Hand extended to continue lower arm line.

R#23 (3) ⟶ Hand at right angles to arm line.

Note: As recorded above, ∠ is seen as anterior or posterior break at wrist. If articulation is to lateral rather than medial portion of the wrist, record as follows:

R#23 (2 ul) ⟶ Right wrist ∠ at 2 o'clock, break
R#23 (2 ra) ⟶ toward ulnar side; point; lateral.

Note: In the recording of lower arm movements it is at times significant to record the direction of the twist of the arm. Recorder should follow below:

R#2 (ul⟶) or R#2 (ul⟵)   Indicating twist at upper arm–
or R#2 (ul⌒↘) or R#2 (ul↙⌒)   lower arm break (elbow) with
or R#2 (ul ↑) or R#2 (ul ↓)   direction of ulnar region.

Note: To indicate tension or laxity of muscles of shoulder or arm section, underline arm recording wherever tension occurs. Thus

R#01 (3 —→)#12(6)#23(6) (ul ⌢)1111

> Right arm extended, lax, directly anterior ulnar portion medial, fingers extended lax, utilizing tension in the lower arm for lift and suspension.

or

R# 01 (5 ⟳)# 12(1) # 23(6)(ul —→) 1 3 1
      (table)   (check)

> Upper arm at five o'clock, elbow sharply bent to one o'clock, hand extended tense from the wrist, thumb hooked, three medial fingers extended stiff pushing against cheek with A, little finger hooked. Note subline notations indicating pressure points against table and cheek.

If arms are in complementary activity representing same activity, use double # sign: # #; otherwise record separately using R# signal and L# signal prefixing notation.

XX01 (5)# 12(3 ⇆) 23(6)(ul↓; XX1)
    (chair arms)

> Fingers intertwined, arms loosely held across stomach, elbow end of ulnar portion of lower arm resting on chair.

Note: The use of arrows within the brackets or parentheses indicates direction of placement; such usage follows segment signal. In order to portray motion, use arrows on line above signal recording. If all of arm is included in the motion:

R# 0123

> Indicating motion of hand and arm with shoulder activity moving from zero position to a lateral position.

R# 1—#2—#3

> Indicates ordinal movement beginning with upper arm followed by lower arm and hand. Initial movement lateral with upper arm, followed by anterio-lateral sweep with lower arm, upper arm remaining in position.

It may be seen that considerable practice with symbols is required before the recorder can use the full numerical system of orthography. Therefore the following is recommended in original recording situation. Two figures are conceived, one shaped ☐, the other | . These represent respectively a face view of the trunk and a lateral view. Note that the clock system is still used to record ∠.

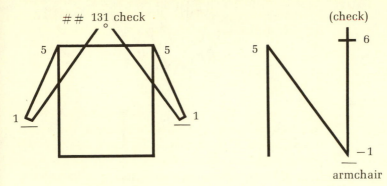

This figure represents the upper body-set of a person sitting in a chair, elbows resting on the arms and with the head held up by the fingers pressing against the cheek.

The above illustration indicates that at times it may be necessary to have more space for recording the 01, 12, 23 series. Since most of the recording and analysis of body activity will necessarily be done one area at a time, it will not impede work to any real extent if an entire page is assigned to the schematic drawing of the trunk and its extensions. Several examples will be shown of long member recording on the page to follow. The use of graph paper with pre-drawn base figures has proved efficient as a recording device. If the recorder has learned his angle clock sufficiently well, the fact that he cannot draw is relatively unimportant since he will have the angles and the *tension points* in reproducible terms. If he can draw, and I have seen few students who cannot be quickly trained to draw these simple line figures, his figure will assist him in his notations and recall later.

It must be remembered that in all cases these kines have a dual purpose. The first of these concerns actual morphological research and the second is as a mnemonic aid. Motion research, particularly once it is related to the interview or contextual observation situation, must be recalled and written up like any other interview where verbalization is stressed. It has been my experience that a sensitive interviewer can get rather complete recall with such notations. Any "written" notes that the observer can take along with his kinegraphic recording should be added.

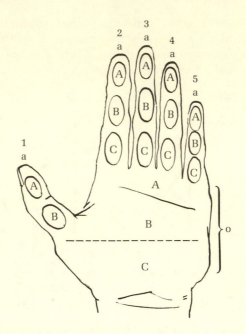

5. Hand and Finger Activity

A. Ball of finger.

a. Tip of finger.

(A), (B), (C), and (O) indicates back of finger or hand.

In notating, *when particular finger is under discussion,* list in the following order:

Hand: (R) or (L)

Finger: 1, 2, 3, 4, 5, or) for palm of hand.

Action: Hook, (or reverse; hyperextension), Curl, or Closure.

Points of contact: With thumb as 1, maintain ordinality 1A–2B, 2A–3 ⓑ, 4–5 translates "The ball of the thumb contacting the second joint of the forefinger, the first joint of which is contacting the posterior aspect of the second joint of the middle finger; the fourth and little finger being laterally separated from the middle finger and maintaining contact with each other laterally along the entire joint plane."

In notating, when entire hand is under consideration, the particular finger need not be listed. List in the following order:

Hand: (R) or (L)

Finger pattern: See below, remembering that all notation starts with the thumb as initial 1.

FINGER

(L) 1	Extended (lax).
(L) <u>1</u>	Extended, tense.
(L) ⅂	Hyperextended, posterior crook.
(L) 2, 3, 4, 5 ——⋀—	Posteriorly patterned multiangle (Until otherwise shown, angle sketch conveys sufficient variation.)
(L) 1ˎ, 2ˎ, etc.	Hook, tip of involved joint (a) contracted no further than B-c line of acting finger.
(L) 1ⅉ, 2ⅉ, etc.	Curl, tip of involved joint (a) contracted beyond inferior C line but not touching palm at any point.
(L) 1o, 2o, etc.	Closure (lax) (excepting thumb, Fl.) tip touching palm.
(L) <u>1o</u>, <u>2o</u>, etc.	Closure (tense) (excepting thumb, Fl.) tip touching palm.
(L) 1□, 2□, etc. 1⊕, 2⊕, etc.	Touching object. Pressure indicated by — and o.
(L) ~~1~~, ~~2~~, etc.	Grasping object. Pressure indicated by — and o.
(L) 1□̰, 2□̰ 1⊕̰, 2⊕̰	Finger caress. Pressure indicated by — and o. To indicate involved joint, ordinality pattern: Hand: (L) or (R). Finger number. Anterior or posterior crook signal. Joint signal. Pressure stress. Stationary object sign: □ Movable object sign: ⊕
(L) 1⋁, 2⋁, etc.	Finger drumming. Intensity and duration indicated by ___ . ___ .

FINGER (*Continued*)

(L)①   Encircling of symbol indicates posterior aspect of the finger in any of the above.

(L) ĭ   Indicates (apparent) autonomy of finger or joint.

TOTAL HAND

(L) 11111   Hand extended (lax). No finger touching another.

(L) 11111   Hand extended (tense). No fingers touching.

(L) 5   Hand extended, lax or tense (tension indicated by —). Fingers each touching neighboring finger.

(L) 131   First finger not touching second; second, third, and fourth touching along length; fifth finger not touching others. This logic may be followed as in 41, 311, 23, 122 etc.

(L) ⌐1꒐ 3꒐   All crooking notation follows logic shown above for single fingers. Figure shown illustrates "Thumb (1) crooked posteriorly and not touching other fingers; fingers 3, 4, and 5 touching along length and with a curl; finger two (2) not touching with a tense hook.

C-BC
(L) 1 2 3꒐   Notation for joint touching is placed over the numerical finger-indicating figure. Figure shown illustrates: 1 extended (lax); 2 C touching 3 at joints B and C, with 2 extended (lax); 3, 4, 5 touching along length and in curl.

(L) +4   Fist (lax), thumb outside over fingers 2, 3. (In this case conventionality eliminates necessity for 1's contact points on posterior portions of 2 and 3.) Tense indicated by —.

(L) 1̂4   Capped fist, thumb continuing radial line and touching 1A to 2BC. (Conventionality

TOTAL HAND (*Continued*)

	eliminates necessity for noting 1's contact points on 2's joints.) Tense indicated by —.
(L) 4+	Fist with fingers wrapped around thumb. (Conventionality eliminates necessity for noting contact points.)
(L) 5□	Full hand grasp of immovable object.
(L) 5⊕	Full hand grasp of movable object.
(L) 35	Radial grasp.
(L) 53	Ulnar grasp.
(L) 14)	Pull, involving 2345.
(L) 11̆111 or 11̭111	Cupped hand, fingers not touching neighboring fingers. Direction of U indicates superior or inferior direction of palm.
(L) 5̆ or 5̭	Cupped hand, fingers touching neighboring fingers. (U usage same as above.)
(L) ₀5	Hand at rest, all fingers touching on another part of own body.*
(L) 11̆111	Autonomic hand.
↑ō 5 (etc.) ↓ō 5 (etc.)	Indicates superior or inferior motion of hand. Arrow indicates direction. — and o indicates pace.†
⌐5̃ō ⌐5̃ō	Indicates lateral or medial movement of the hand. Arrow indicates direction. — and o indicates pace.†
→̃5̭ or →̃11̭111	Indicates anterior or posterior motion of the hand. Arrow indicates direction. — and o indicates pace.
	Combinations of the above may be superimposed on each other (follows hand iden-

*Experience shows that written notation of body part touched, e.g., knee, avoids confusion.

†Only necessary when wrist, elbow, and shoulder angles (see below) are not shown.

TOTAL HAND (*Continued*)

tification pattern). Illustration shows a laterally (to right) anteriorly moving cupped right hand, palms down.

35

Ulnar cupping or semicupping (in motion).

53

Radial cupping or semicupping (in motion).

a-A
1 2 3

"Okay" sign. Illustration shows tip of (la) 1 touching ball of 2 (2A) while 3, 4, and 5 touch each other and are extended lightly. Note ordinality of motion direction.

A • 131

B • 1211

C • 31,1

A., B., C., are illustrations of notating joint contacts when total hand is under notation.

BIMANUAL

One of the most important avenues of research in kinesics will probably be that of assessing degrees and situationality of bimanuality. The bimanualities listed here are restricted to some of those in which the hands are brought into close proximity with each other. This carries certain somatic-space assumptions which undoubtedly will be reoriented as research proceeds.

⑭ ⑭

Reflexive hand shake, utilizing thumb as base for either hand, R1AB curling with pressure over posterior aspects of the hand; the base of L1B making firm contact with lateral aspect of 2C and depending on thumb length, 3C and 4C; 2345 are firmly touching along length and curl around the posterior aspect of the opposing hand. This may be reversed with left hand in superior position. Note: movement from a medial to an inferior position and return. Variant; (rare) hands may be held

BIMANUAL (*Continued*)

in same plane as head and move anterior and return.

RL1X4X$_{\updownarrow}^{M}$

or

RL^{M}1X$\overset{\leftrightarrow}{4}$X

Reflexive hand hold: Right hand in primary grasp position: R1 curling around posterior aspect of L2C and 3C, R2, 3, 4, 5, curled around posterior ulnar aspect of right hand, held by R1 which is again held by L1 which curls over 1BC. May be held at rest or held in head plane (lateral) and moved in an anterioposterior set of movements. May be reversed.

RL10XX

Intermembral handhold: Firm clasp of interlaced fingers with (as illustrated R in superior position) intermembral contacts marked by joint notation (ill. Cs) and with degree of finger flexion or extension marked by crook signs.

R5^{a}L5^{a} or R5^{A}L5^{A}

Fingertip hand hold: Tips or balls of all fingers in oppositional contact.

$\underset{\circ \quad \circ}{\underline{R5^{a}L5^{a}}}$ or $\underset{\circ \quad \circ}{\underline{R5^{A}L5^{A}}}$

Fingertip hand ball: Tips or balls of all fingers touching. C aspect of palms also touching in opposition

1X1 $\wedge$ 6XX

Bimanual steepling: In this case RIB presses posterior aspect of L1B in XX pattern as are the paired 3, 4, 5; R2A touches L2A in bilateral extension.

14 $\gtrless$ 41

Four-fingered grooving: R2, 3, 4, 5 slide in and out (or rest) touching lateral complimentary member of L2, 3, 4, 5. As shown R1 and L1 are laxly extended but not touching R2BC which can be indicated by marking 1's with crooks. Note variant in motion with mediolateral arrows.

1 ⑧ XX1

Inverted four-fingered intermembral handhold: L2, 3, 4, 5 and R2, 3, 4, 5 are interlaced; R1 and L1 remain laxly ex-

BIMANUAL (Continued)

	tended; palms upward. Fingers touching posterior aspect of hand.
1 ⑧ XX1	Four-fingered intermembral handhold: Same as above, palms down. Fingers touching posterior aspect of hand.
1X3, 1X3,	Limited intermembral handhold: As illustrated R1 crosses L1; R234 curl behind L2 to posterior aspect; L2 touches and crosses R5; R5 touches L3; L3, 4, 5 remain free (note crook) touching each other. This can be varied for particular interlace pattern.
14 >< 14	Each hand firmly grips complimentary wrist.
18XX1 ⌣ or ⌢	Cupped interlace: Similar to four-fingered intermembral handhold except that posterior aspects of R and L 2, 3, 4, 5 rest within bimanual palms.
A. R5 ⊄ 5 B. L5 ⊄ 5	Right hand wring: A. Right hand strips left hand with fingerward movement involving ulnar-radial or radial ulnar twist. Can be reversed to Left Hand Wring; B.
RL5 ⊄ 5	Bimanual handwring.
14 ⟲ 41	Double-four hook: R2, 3, 4, 5 curled into L5, 4, 3, 2; L1 and R1 extended (lax).
23/1	Nail picking:
→←/55	Double five clap: Motion latero-medial; Intensity indicated by — or o. Duration indicated by . . . . . .
→←/14 5	One thumb clap: Same as above except one hand slightly turned to free thumb from direct contact.
→←/00 +	Double-palm clap (side): Superior-inferior-inferior-superior, latero-medial motion.

BIMANUAL (*Continued*)

$\overrightarrow{14}\overleftarrow{41}$

Double-four clap: L2, 3, 4, 5 slapping across R2, 3, 4, 5. Can be inverted.

$\overrightarrow{14}\overleftarrow{0}$

Four on the palm clap: L or R 2, 3, 4, 5 on complimentary palm.

$\overrightarrow{14}\overleftarrow{0}+$

Side 4 on the palm clap: Same as four on the palm except that fingers strike across rather than parallel with the palm.

$\overrightarrow{00}\overleftarrow{}$

Double palm clap: Palm to palm, fingers hyperextended avoiding contact.

$\begin{matrix} \circlearrowright \\ 5 \\ 5 \end{matrix}$ or $\begin{matrix} 5 \\ 5 \\ \circlearrowleft \end{matrix}$

Hand rubbing: Position of $\circlearrowright$ indicates superior position.

$\overgroup{11111}\ 0\ \overgroup{11111}$

Extended thumb wave: Thumb directed medially, ulnar aspect of the hand anterior and/or inferior, L or R1a contacting lateral ulnar aspect of B portion of palm, R2, 3, 4, 5 moving in complimentary fashion to L2, 3, 4, 5.

Note: $\longrightarrow$ o (above numeral) indicates one hand at rest $\longrightarrow$ $\longleftarrow$ both hands moving.

6. *Hip, Upper Leg, Lower Leg, Ankle*

Note: Recording of shoulder–upper arm, upper arm–lower arm, lower arm–wrist, unilateral or bilateral, requires considerable experience in observation. Considerable practice, with the aid of a checking observer, can equip the recorder with sufficient facility and accuracy to meet problems in general posture. Movement is still more difficult and the student is urged to practice "seeing in space" before trusting his records.

Warning: *Musculature and jointing (skeletal activity) are both involved in the analysis of long member activity.* Most Americans interviewed assume *constant parallel activity* between the muscular and the skeletal system. Muscular tension does not necessarily flow *from* a medial point of inception *to* the most distant point. Nor does a similar movement of skeletal structure always involve the same muscles in tension orientation.

Code is parallel to that used for shoulder, arm, etc., and follows same logic. Instead of # signal which indicates a given arm, etc., λ is used to indicate leg. Rλh symbolizes right leg. $\lambda\lambda$ indicates both legs.

λ 01   Hip–upper leg joint.

λ 12   Upper leg–lower leg (knee) joint.

λ 23   Lower leg–foot joint (ankle).

Tension is indicated by X under leg section number. Thus $\lambda \, {}^{2}_{X}$ indicates tensed calf.

Angle formation indicated in same way as for arm. Thus $\lambda^{m}\lambda$ 01(6)12(6) 23(3) would be the formula for standing upright, legs together.

Recorder may use the devices shown in the examples above for the arms in his recording of leg activity. However, simpler codes have been devised for certain conventional stances.

SEATED

λ λ⌐ *	Close double L. Seated, feet square on floor, 01, 12, 23 all at right angles.
λ λ₅⌐	Veed L. Legs apart (angle noted from clock) 01, 12, 23 all at right angles.
λ λ ³⤳³₄	Close extended. Legs extended 01, 12, 23 angles recorded.† Note: legs rest on heels.
λ λ₃ ³⤳³	Veed extended. Legs extended, 01, 12, 23 angle recorded. Note: legs rest on heels and interleg angle indicated by clock number in leg symbol.
λ λ◁▷	Leg box. Balls of feet touching, legs semi-extended.
λ λ↑ Ẋ	Short X. Both feet touching floor, crossed less than half of length from knee to ankle.
λ λ↑ X̣	Long X. Both feet touching floor, crossed more than half of length from knee to ankle.

*Most recorders soon abandon either the λ or the # symbols as they become more proficient with pictographs.

†Recording of angle probably arbitrary for most patterns.

SEATED

λ λ ·X   Reverse X. Lower legs crossed, feet posterior to knee point.

λ₄   Tight 4: Legs crossed: total femoral contact, knee behind knee.

λ⊔   Loose 4: Legs crossed: ankle or foot rests on opposing lower extremity of femur.

⊔λ†   Over 4: Kneecap over kneecap.

λ₈   Furled umbrella: Total femoral contact, total lateral lower leg contact.

λ8   Leg wind: Leg crosses over and then foot hooks behind opposing ankle.

Tailor: Ankles cross, legs akimbo, feet under upper thighs or hip.

Up and over: Legs crossed, lateral aspect of both feet rest on superior aspect of opposing thighs.

λ○   Body ball: Legs together, posterior portion of upper legs in total contact posterior portion lower legs. Heels may contact hip base.*

ᗷ   Half-body ball: Same as above except only one leg is pulled up.*

λⅤⅤ   Spread double Vee: Legs spread, posterior portions of upper and lower legs touching. Note angle. Note contact point. If hips make contact with supporting surface note with ᨆ .

Leg dangling or swinging can be recorded by indicating type of 4 plus direction plus member number plus stressed member.

⊔λ†↑↓ R 2 or ˥ ···⋅ ···⋅ ···⋅ ⋅ $\dfrac{2}{x}$

Leg joggling is indicated by stutter sign following leg symbol.

λ R · · · · ·

---

*Involvement of arms may be indicated by # sign (s) following figure.

Foot waving is indicated by direction symbol. In all three of these the usual stress signals may be used.

$$\lambda \ R_3 \leftrightarrow$$

7. *Foot Behavior*

STANDING

To indicate standing, feet symbols are added to leg pictograph. Short and long X symbols follow sitting logic. Angle of Vee indicated by number between legs of pictograph. Emphasis on one foot indicated by strong stress mark under foot of pictograph. If all weight on one foot, strong stress the foot and weak stress the other. The following kinegraph illustrates a person standing with his weight largely on his right foot and with his left leg crossing at the ankles in a long X.

STANDING (FEET IN MOTION BUT NOT WALKING)

Toe teeter: Standing, rising on toes and dropping back on heel and toe.

Full teeter: Standing, rocking back and forth from toe to heel to toe, etc.

Foot shuffle: Feet move back and forth but do not move body away.

Toe dig: One foot (toes) scratch surface of support while other supports weight.

Standing walk: One leg remains in place while other moves around it.

Knee bend: Involves bending of knees with feet square on ground.

Knee teeter: Knees bend while weight rests on toes.

Stoop: Same as Doubled Vee except that contact is shown at toes.

WALKING

No recording system of manners of walking has been included with this kinegraphic series. Several devices for a shorthand have been tested and thus far all have proved too clumsy for either recording or teaching. However, several general hints may be suggested to steer the observation of walking styles.

Taking first the male walker (or low-heeled shoe walker) several categories can be described. First the short chi and the long chi walker. The *long chi* (X) *walker* when taking a stride involves a swing of the body accentuating the shoulder complementary to the leg moving forward. The *short chi* (x) *walker* swings from the hip without involving the trunk to a perceptible extent. The long chi walker when adding a slight lateral swing to the movement of the leg and a slight lift to the shoulders as part of the anterior-posterior swing of them may be described as "swaggering" (∞).

Generally speaking, when the chi type has been established, further clarification is provided by the observation of the contact activity of the feet. First, we have the *overkick* in which the leg is swung forward at an angle and a velocity that the foot swings at the end of the forward motion of the foot pendulum. Normally, such walkers strike the ground with the posterior-inferior aspect of the heel when making contact with the contact surface. This same process may be seen in the *back-kick* in which there occurs a sharp posterior bend to the ankle at the completion of the foot's contact with the contact surface.

The back-kick is probably related to the force of the push. It has been noted that most walkers may be rated along a plane from pulling to pushing, some walkers grasping the ground before them and pulling it to them while others appear to utilize a push action which shoves the body ahead. At a central point may be placed the *balance* walker, whose walk is characterized by the fact that before one set of toes releases a firm grasp of the ground, the other heel is already solidly in contact.

Further classification is provided by the *bent knee* walker as contrasted with the *straight knee* walker, *straight* and *bent* knee referring to that period during which the foot is in contact with the contact surface with the body balanced directly above the legs. (There seems to be some correlation between the habitual walking on rough ground and the *bent* knee walk.)

This leads directly to the categories of *bouncers* and *gliders*. These types represent poles. The bouncer generally raises his entire body by rising on his toes as his foot passes directly below the body plane, thus his shoulders can be seen to rise and fall with each step. The glider coordinates the contact, the ankle bend, and the knee bend so that the body moves forward with the shoulders remaining in the same plane.

Further classes are provided by the *high stepper* and the *foot dragger*. The high stepper raises his foot in its swing above the ankle bone of the contact foot. The foot dragger allows the completed foot to drag as it begins its forward swing. The foot dragger is not to be confused with the *shuffler* who maintains contact with the contact surface with both feet throughout walk, or the *foot stutterer,* who allows the toes to drag in a staccato manner at the end of the contact.

The length of the stride provides one other dimension to the consideration of walking styles. Generally speaking, the earlier classifications are more important in the description of the walker than is length of stride. However, two types stand out. The *dipper* lengthens his stride to the point that his body is lowered at the end point of each stride. This may be a variation on the glide inasmuch as the length of the stride involves maintaining contact to avoid falling. The *choppy walker* may be a variation on the high stepper. The difference between the two is that the choppy walker seldom extends the forward moving foot more than a single foot length beyond the contact foot.

Since balance is maintained usually by the use of the arms, these are to be correlated with the types discussed above. There are a number of arm classes which have already been isolated. The *stiff arm* moves his arms from the shoulders and allows little break at the joints. This tends to give a staccato appearance to the walk and should be examined apart from the leg motion. The *lower arm* mover tends to keep the upper arm within the trunk plane while swinging the lower arm. Balance difficulties again give the appearance of an uncertain gait. The *chugger* should be mentioned. This concerns the arms held with #(12) at three o'clock (generally the hands are in fist). The *double swing* in which both arms move in parallel fashion is uncommon among Americans but does appear in the Far East.

As observed, American middle majority walkers seem to move the arm to about five o'clock at each step, the length of the arm swing increasing with the pace until about four o'clock may be reached by some walkers. Only two walkers have been observed to reach a three o'clock swing and both of these were former members of the Canadian Army.

The movements of the body and the head add final variables to our discussion. Several of these deserve attention. Again it must be stressed that if the observer will abstract the various parts—leg, arm, and body—and then combine them he is likely to avoid certain ethnocentric or egocentric impressions. As stances, five types have been isolated. The first of these is the *slump* in which the shoulders are lowered and/or rolled anteriorly or medially. The reverse of this is the *rared back* in which the shoulders are pulled posteriorly. Two others which may be distinguished are the *ramrod* and the *military*. Although both of these are characterized by the "squareness" of the shoulders, the ramrod involves more tension in the pectoral and upper arm musculature. The *sidle* is characterized by the fact that one shoulder is consistently more anteriorly advanced than the other. This may involve a full trunk twist or posterior-anterior placement of the shoulders.

Three other variations on trunk activity may be noted: *full trunk projection*, in which the body is held nearly perpendicular, the legs make little anterior stretch, and the feet seem to make extended contact with the contact surface behind the body plane; the *abdominal projection*, whether a resultant of hyperlordosis, the size of the abdominal region, or a combination of either of these with the rared back, projects the medial area of the body anteriorly; the *pelvic projection*, in which the pelvic region is thrust forward, the curvature usually beginning in the lumbar region and culminating at the sacroiliac.

There is less difference between male and female walking than is popularly supposed except that there is a differential selection from among the types. Most of the same categories apply to both male and female walkers. However, the wearing of "high heels" or "platform" shoes does greatly affect the general appearance of the walk. Observers are warned to record together with the physical description a statement concerning the type of footwear and the type of skirt worn. Both exert considerable influence over the walk, the stance, and the gait. Too, the breast development may give a delusory aspect to the entire walk. Only by the careful segmental analysis can this be avoided.

While *flat-footed* walkers occur among both males and females, shoe types probably lead to a higher incidence among females. In this the whole foot is placed down at once. Of these there are two evident types. The *trudger* who places his feet down flat footed and who combines flat-footedness with pulling. A second type, less common among males, is the *toe-point flat foot* in which at each step the foot is placed down squarely but the toe is always pointed in a direct anterior line. This is seldom seen with a fast gait.

Pigeon-toeing in which the toes point medio-anteriorially at each step, the *duck walk* in which the toes point latero-anteriorially, the so-called *Indian walk* in which the feet are placed directly in front of each other at each step are common enough to be noted.

The terminology used in this section is evidently ethnocentric; it is hoped that the descriptions are sufficiently nonnormative to overcome this. The terms employed were chosen because they are meaningful to most speakers of English and expedite learning and memory.

All of this section should be carefully analyzed against material taken from *observations* of other cultures. Caution is needed in making descriptions. Note that the Arab describes a woman who walks "gracefully" as "walking like a chicken." The Indian describes a "graceful" woman as "walking like an elephant." This should deter overeasy physically descriptive statements.

8. The Neck

⟶‖	Anterior projection
⟵‖	Posterior projection
‖	Right lateral projection
‖	Left lateral projection
⊔	Neck tense
⊔	Neck sag
ǀoǀ	Swallowing
ǀ◖ǀ	Adams apple jump
⌒o⌒	Neck twist right
⌒o⌒	Neck twist left

II. *Sample Conversation with Description**

HERE is an example of a recording situation taken in context on a bus in Arlington, Virginia. There was no *direct* information other than that supplied by the situation itself. Mother and child spoke with a tidewater Virginia accent. The bus route on which the event was recorded leads to a middle-income neighborhood. The way in which the mother and child were dressed was not consistent with the dress of other riders who disembarked (as did the observer) before the mother and child did. The child was about four, and his mother seemed to be about twenty-seven to thirty.

Kinesic symbols used in the transcription (see Appendix I) are given below the pertinent text.

1. This situation was observed on a bus at about 2:30 P.M., April 14, 1952. The little boy was seated next to the window. He seemed tired of looking out of the window, and, after surveying all of the car ads and the passengers, he leaned toward his mother and pulled at her sleeve, pouted and vigorously kicked his legs.

   ⌒ 3/2 ‖ ⌒ 3/2|2 ∧   ∧   ⌒ 3/ + \1 # ⌒
   1. Child: Mama. I   gotta go   to   the   bathroom.
   (mo) ⟨ ⫪ ○   ○   L35┤ ⌒   人人   ┐ ⋯⋰⋯ ⋯⋱⋰   2
            mother's   sleeve   x

2. His mother had been sitting erectly in her seat, her packages on her lap, and her hands lightly clasped around the packages. She was apparently "lost in thought."

   2. Mother:
            T "⊕ ⊕" 1ₛXX1 人m人 3-3-3

3. When the boy's initial appeal failed to gain the mother's

---

* From *Explorations in Communication: An Anthology,* Edmund Carpenter and Marshall McLuhan, eds. (Boston, Beacon Press, 1960).

attention, he began to jerk at her sleeve again, each jerk apparently stressing his vocalization.

⌒ 2/3 # ⌒2 ∧   ∧   3/1#
3. Child: Mama.   Donnie's   gotta   go.
R35⌐   R35⌐   R35⌐R35⌐R35⌐
mo. r. sleeve

4. The mother turned and looked at him, "shushed" him, and placed her right hand firmly across his thighs.

⌒ 2/ 1# ⌒
4. Mother: Sh-sh.
ọ) ọ) R5 across child's lap-firm through 5

5. The boy protested audibly, clenched both fists, pulled them with stress against his chest. At the same time he drew his legs up against the restraint of his mother's hand. His mouth was drawn down and his upper face was pulled into a tight frown.

1u + ⌒ 4 1# ⌒
5. Child: But   mama.
XX41 ↙↘ >∨<
↑↑ >⌒<

6. The mother withdrew her hand from his lap and resettled in her former position with her hands clasped around the packages.

⌒ 3/1# ⌒ (o openness; ⋁over-softness)
6. Mother: ⋁Later.⋁
18XX1   oo

7. The boy grasped her upper arm tightly, continued to frown. When no immediate response was forthcoming, he turned and thrust both knees into the lateral aspect of her left thigh.

⌒ 3/3/1/1 ‖ ⩓ (⩓over-loudness;≈whine)
7. Child:⩓ mah   mah   ≈
R5 >∧<   ⋋⋋ zz against mother's thigh
mother's   arm

8. She looked at him, leaned toward him, and slapped him across the anterior portion of his upper legs.

⩘3/1#⩘ •   (ˀrasp)
8. Mother: ? Wait. ?
　　　ꙡ ꙡ ꙡR14⊣against child's thighs

9. He began to jerk his clenched fists up and down, vigorously
   nodding between each inferior-superior movement of his
   fists.

　　　　1∪+⌒3   1#⌒4/   2/⌒ 4máh4/1máh# ⌒
9. Child: ᵥ Oh   mama,   mama, ⩘ mama.   ⩘
　　　　>§ §< XX41 ↑___H___↓↑   ↓   ↑   H

10. She turned, frowning, and with her mouth pursed, she spoke
    to him through her teeth. Suddenly she looked around, noted
    that the other passengers were watching, and forced a square
    smile. At the same time that she finished speaking, she
    reached her right hand in under her left arm and squeezed
    the boy's arm. He sat quietly.

　　　　⩘ 3/   \1#⩘⩗ 2/|3   3# ⩗
10. Mother: ? Shut up. ? ○ Will yuh. ○
　　　　>ᵥᵒᵥ< 　 h ⊙̣⊙̣ o ⊙̂ L35 child's l. u. arm
　　　　>⌒○/<　 ⇄   　 ⊞⊞ behind own r. arm

Stress and intonation are indicated above the pertinent text,
using symbols provided in Trager and Smith's *Outline of English
Structure* (1951); voice-qualifiers, e.g., the drawl (⌒), are indicated
by symbols developed by them. In a few places a phonemic transcription of the text is also provided.

⎍⎍⎍⎍⎍⎍⎍⎍⎍⎍⎍⎍⎍⎍⎍⎍⎍⎍⎍⎍⎍⎍⎍⎍

III: *Kinesic Recording**

Microkinesic Recording

In microkinesic recording, the use of a predefined staff permits
the easy recognition and timing of movie material. The microre-

*From the chapter "Body Motion" for *The Natural History of an Interview*.

cording of direct, that is, nonfilmed material, presents a much more difficult recording and timing problem. Two devices have been tried for timing specific kines or kinemorphs by a single observer or team of observers. A stop watch may be used if its presence is not a significantly interfering artifact. For more covert timing, the observer can train himself to beat time with his toe hidden by his shoe. Some practice may be required before the full beat per second is mastered, but one can learn to record one quarter, one half, single, and multiple seconds with considerable accuracy. Generally speaking, however, in the absence of words as markers, and without the use of a film record, timing is a relatively impressionistic feature for even the best trained observer.

Similarly, while a carefully trained observer can achieve an amazingly complex record of direct material, such material is not equivalent to film-based recording. Since direct material cannot be replayed for the assessment of the zero point, it is strongly advised that several hours of viewing precede even the trained observer's recording of any subject's activity.

Since microrecording is related to the notation of least particles of perceived movement, the trained observer consistently works from a zero point provided by previous analytic research with an informant using film material. This cultural zero point must be kept in mind and explicitly stated when the particular behavior of a particular subject is recorded. Since an extensive list of kines is presented elsewhere (Appendix I), only the logic of kine annotation is presented below.

Notation of State

Direction of position: (at point of central tendency)

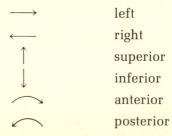

⟶	left
⟵	right
↑	superior
↓	inferior
⌢↘	anterior
↙⌢	posterior

Direction of movement: (throughout movement to point of central tendency)

>	left
<	right
∧	superior
∨	inferior
≥	anterior
≤	posterior

Position held:..........
Repeated position: ⊣   ⊣   ⊣
Scratching: zzzzzzzzzz
Feeling: o o o o o o o o o o

The relative body positions are recorded by numerals representing clock positions. (n) signals any aspect of the body when the subject is standing erect, with the nose in the midline and pointing along a parallel with an imaginary line extended forward from the feet. Each numeral refers to a clock position from (n). (1) equals a 30-degree angle, (2) a 60-degree angle, (3) a 90-degree angle, etc. to (6) which is 180 degrees from (n). Beyond (6), for convenience, recording returns to (5) and so on. To record positions of less than 30 degrees from (n), the 30-degree angle is divided roughly into 4 parts which are recorded as plus or minus 15′, 30′, or 45′. These (′) are expressed verbally as "minutes." Combinations omit ′; 3;30.

For middle majority American viewers there seem to be three significant degrees of stress recorded as (n), (—), and (o). These indicate respectively normal stress, high stress, and lax. Multiples of signals indicate impressions of overhigh and overlax: ══ and ⦵ respectively.

Notation of Body Positions or Kines

For convenience, the recording chart is divided into six staves: the head and face; shoulders, neck, trunk, and hips; right arm and hand; left arm and hand; right leg and foot; and left leg and foot. The head and face is further subdivided into four staves of: head, forehead and circumorbital activity (and, if necessary, the nose), the mouth and circummouth activity, and chin (and neck, when necessary). The arm and hand staves are divided into three substaves of arm, hand, and wrist. The leg staves are subdivided into leg, foot, and ankle.

The intrafemoral index is recorded under the left leg staves when necessary.

Whenever it is useful, English orthography may be used to append any statements not covered by the annotational system.

HEAD

h is used to cover all activities of the head. As an example, h² indicates that the head is turned left 60 degrees from (n).

h↓↑ indicates a full nod.

h⇄ indicates a full head shake.

FOREHEAD AND CIRCUMORBIT

Using the eyes, o o, as the base line, the forehead, nose, and circumorbital behavior can be quasi-realistically sketched in. ⟩⬒⬒⟨ indicates both brows raised, brow furrowed, the lateral aspects of the orbit double-lined, eyes in focus on auditor, and nose wrinkled. Lids and eyeballs may be sketched in: ⚆ ⚈.

MOUTH

⬭ is used to signal the mouth at zero. This may be varied as ⊢⊣ or ⊌ or ⌒⌄. Lining around mouth and chin is added in a quasi-realistic manner. ⌃⬭⌃, ⌄⬭⌄, or ⟨⬭⟩. Teeth may be shown ⬬.

NECK, SHOULDERS, TRUNK, AND HIPS

The neck is always recorded as //, with / / or / / used to indicate stress. Arrows provide movement and position from zero.

The shoulders and trunk are shown in a single figure:

T or T or T   which indicate shoulders straight, drooped and hunched.

Ŧ   indicates a bend at the base of the thoracic region.

Ʇ   shows trunk bend at pelvis.

T'' indicates an involvement of the left shoulder. Arrows plus clock positions are utilized to show the position of the members.

indicates that the body is bent at the pelvis to a 60-degree angle, the shoulders are rolled anteriorly for 30 degrees.

$\times\mathsf{T}_{\text{PIVOT}}$ or $\mathsf{T}_{\times\,\text{PIVOT}}.$ indicates a pivot action.

RIGHT ARM AND HAND

RL denotes the right arm.

Positional and directional notes can be made:

$\mathsf{R}^{\text{N}}|_{\text{B}}$ indicates that the right arm is extended at the elbow, with the upper arm held close to the body and the wrist at n.

The logic for the hand gives the thumb a numeral 1, the forefinger 2 and so on. The final joint is a, the second b, and the third c. The full hand without the fingers touching and the fingers extended at n is $|\;|\;|\;|\;|$. The thumb hooked, forefinger crooked (bent at a and/or b, but no lower than the joint of b-c), and with 3, 4, and 5 curled

(fingers bent beyond joint b-c) is recorded $\big)\!\big|_{3}$. The use of R and L to indicate which hand is necessary only when staved paper is not used. R is used to indicate palm and direction.

LEFT ARM AND HAND

The same logic is used as for right hand and arm. Bimembral and bimanual activity may at times be signaled within a single staff, as here:

$\big(|\!\!/\!\!\cdot.\,/\big)$ signals crossed arms, right over left.

RIGHT LEG AND FOOT

The annotational logic for leg and foot parallels that utilized for the arms and hands.

$\mathsf{R}^{|}_{\mathsf{L}}$ or $\big)$ denotes the right leg.

indicates that the ankle is bent back toward the lower leg, two hours above n, and the toes are hooked, pulling the loose shoe away from the heel and sole.

 illustrates an ankle bent to four o'clock with a non-weight-bearing toe to the floor.

The heel is raised.

To show walking, ⌀⌽ is used together with ⌒ if the walking is continual. When staved paper is not used, right foot may be filled in while leaving an outlined left.

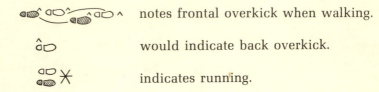 notes frontal overkick when walking.

would indicate back overkick.

indicates running.

LEFT LEG AND FOOT

Annotational system parallels that for the right leg and foot. For bimembral activity, ⌿⌊ is used. This same figure can be utilized to record the intrafemoral index. ⚠ indicates a standing figure, with legs akimbo at a 60-degree angle.

Macrokinesic Recording

Listed below are a series of recorded kinemes which have been selected as demonstration items. These have been tested as meaningful for middle majority Americans. While this is not an exhaustive list, the listing includes a sufficiently broad survey to demonstrate the logic of macrokinesic recording. Duration, repetition, and direction of movement, when kinemic, is recorded as it is for microkinesic recordings. Rhythm is indicated by / at beat points.

The following annotational system has been designed for reproduction by typewriter. The addition of four keys $>$, $\vee$, $<$, $\wedge$ for direction is all that is necessary for the adaptation of a business typewriter for kinemic recording. It should be remembered, however, that the intensive analysis of a protocol will require both kinic and kinemic recording to achieve control of both the conventional and the idiosyncratic elements of a scene.

Kinemorphs, in which there is a dependent relationship between kinemes or kines from more than one motion area, are noted by a fractional system.

Timing without a frame count presents the same problem for macrorecording as it does for microrecording. Without technical assistance timing remains a product of skilled impression. This may be indicated by utilizing the notational conventions for musical scores which indicate tempo without referring to the duration of the particular particle.

KINESIC MACRORECORDING KEY

Head and Face (with nose as pointer)*

Symbol		Interpretation
H		head in median sagittal plane
H	($>$1, 2, or 3)	head left one, two or three o'clock
	($<$1, 2, or 3)	head right one, two or three o'clock
	($\wedge$1, 2, or 3)	head up one, two or three o'clock
	($\vee$1, 2, or 3)	head down one, two or three o'clock
HN		full superior-inferior nod
H<u>N</u>		full inferior-superior nod
Hn		half superior-medial nod
H<u>n</u>		half inferior-medial nod
HS		full head shake left-right median
H<u>S</u>		full head shake right-left-median
Hs		half head shake left-median
H<u>s</u>		half head shake right-median
HQ		full head sweep left-right-median
H<u>Q</u>		full head sweep right-left-median

(with top of head as pointer)

Hq	($>$1, 2, or 3)	head cock left one, two or three
H<u>q</u>	($<$1, 2, or 3)	head cock right one, two or three

Face

OOOO		dead pan–
"expressionless" beyond zero

*Note: 1, 2, and 3, etc., refer to points on a clock either clockwise or inverted clockwise—thus 6 is directly opposite n (or normal) and is the highest number used. For movements less than 1 on clock 15', 30', and 45'' are used.

Forehead

Symbol	Interpretation
Hfo	forehead overlax bilateral
Hff	forehead furrowed bilateral
H<u>ff</u>	forehead deeply furrowed bilateral
Hfb-b	bilateral brow raised
Hf-b	right brow raised
Hfb-	left brow raised
Hfbb	brows knit

(Hf to be recorded only once when combination present)

Eyes

OO		eyes anterior at zero
<u>OO</u> object		eyes in focus on object
"OO"		staring (lids may be overwide)
oOOo		eyes overwide in focus
sOOs		eyes slit in focus
OO&		rolled eyes
OO	(1, 2, 3)	eyes left one, two or three
OO ::::		lid flutter
OOv		blink
OllO		lids closed
Ol<u>l</u>O		lids squeezed
=OO=		bilateral contraction
+OO+		bilateral crinkle (American humor)

Nose

M	nose
oMo	flared nostrils
~~M~~	wrinkled nose
-M-	nose pinched or contracted
"M"	bunny nose

Cheeks

Ch	cheeks
-Ch-	cheeks sucked in
oCho	cheeks puffed out
xChx	nonsmiling superior-inferior lined
sChs	smile-lined

Mouth

Symbol	Interpretation
LL	mouth
L/L	lips compressed
LoL	lips overlax
L-L	lips parted
-LL-	flat minimal smile
-L-L-	lip-parted smile
-tL-L-	smile, upper teeth showing
-L-Lt-	smile, lower teeth showing
LLL	open-mouthed laugh
xLLx	mouth drawn down
pL	protruding upper lip
Lp	protruding lower lip
pLp	pursed lips
oL	sucked in upper lip
Lo	sucked in lower lip
oLL:	both lips sucked in
8LL	tongue protrudes right
LL8	tongue protrudes left
L8L	tongue protrudes anterior
8LL8	tongue licks lips

Chin

Symbol	Interpretation
U	chin
xUx	thrust forward
xU	chin thrust right
Ux	chin thrust left
-U-	chin tight
oUo	chin drop

Neck

Symbol	Interpretation
nk	neck
onko	neck overlax
-nk-	neck tense
nk&	swallowing
&nk	Adam's apple jerk

Shoulders and Trunk

T	shoulders and trunk
"T	right shoulder involvement
T"	left shoulder involvement
Tn	short trunk nod—1 hour or less
TN	trunk nod or bow—more than 1 hour
T<1, 2, or 3	body right lean
T>1, 2, or 3	body left lean
xTx	body rigid
oTo	body slumped
pTp	chest thrust
bTb	belly thrust
-bTb-	belly slump
T∠	pelvic bend
T≠	thoracic bend
T7	upper trunk bend

Arms

The arm can be seen as a member forming three angles, which, taken together with their position(s) in space, determine the recording system outlined below. The term LAnnn describes the left arm hanging at the side. The initial n refers to the shoulder, the second n to the elbow and the final n to the wrist. The numerals represent clock points; the arrows following the numerals indicate the *direction* of the member immediately inferior to and forming the base line of the joint angle. Thus LAn3≥n indicates that the left arm, humerus roughly parallel to or touching the body (depending on Z) bends at the elbow, with the lower arm thrust forward at a 90-degree angle to the upper and with the wrist held at n. Minute marks (′) can be used to refine the recording when it is seen to be kinemically necessary. Since this is a macrorecording key, only already standardized positions will be described below. u plus arrow indicates ulnar pivot; r plus arrow indicates radial pivot.

AA	biarmed activity
RA	right arm
XAA	arms behind back
AXA	arms folded across chest
AxA	arms across body—hands touching below the chest

AxbA	arms across body—hands touching across belly
AxgA	arms across body—hands touching across genitals
ATA	arms hanging at sides
"ATA"	arms swinging (as in walking)
A,TA	right hand in pocket, left hanging
AoTA	right hand carrying object, left hanging
A-TA + hand record	right hand on hip, right hand recorded
A;TA	right hand thumb in belt
$\dfrac{\text{A-TA} + \text{R hand record}}{\text{Ln3n} + \text{hand record}}$	right hand on hip, left hand across chest upper-lower arm angle at 90 degrees
RAN	right hand nod involving lower and/or upper arm
Ra/N	right hand nod involving wrist and hand only
RAS	right hand shake or sweep-upper and/or lower arm involved
RAC	right half (or portion thereof) circle involving arm
AAC	biarmed circle involving arm
R/S	right hand shake or sweep, wrist and hand involved
R/C	right half (or portion thereof) circle involving wrist and hand only

HAND NOTATION

The logic of hand notation, because of the number of parts involved is necessarily complex. However, the fact that there is considerable conventionality in hand activity simplifies the task. Presented below are a series of tested kinemes. / indicates, when used initially that a hand // is bimanual.

//C	bimanual circle
./-/	clapping movement—right hand over

/-/	clapping movement—no superiority of right or left
R/M	right hand to nose
R/LL	right hand to mouth
R/OO	right hand to eyes
R/-OO	right hand over eyes
R/Y2	right hand to knee
R/E	right hand to ear
R/f	right hand to forehead
R/fS	right hand brow wipe
R/.H	right hand to occiput
R/H̄	right hand to frontal region above brow
R/.nk	right hand to back neck muscle
R/nk.	right hand to throat
R/Y3	right hand to ankle
R/:	right hand fly check

Hand

The palm in recording may be used as a separate kineme or as an aspect of a full hand kineme. The direction of the palm is often a discrete symbol apart from the variation in finger position. Thus, it seems desirable to refer in recording to the palm as (P+arrow for direction). Otherwise the wrist number and finger numbers are regarded as sufficient referral signals. If the palm is involved as in a palm caress or palm nail-dig this can be signaled by a -p convention. The fingers are numbered 1 to 5 and are unbracketed, brackets being reserved for special positions. The joints are recorded as *a* or *b* or *c* respectively from the terminal joint as a. Finger position is indicated in the four positions which have been tested as kinemic. These are hook, crook, curl, and close which are recorded following the / sign + finger number. n̲ indicates finger straight beyond zero.

R/2?	Right hand's forefinger in position backward beyond n. Right forefinger hook.
R/2c	Right forefinger bent at first and/or second joint forming angle with third joint of less than 90 degrees. Right forefinger crook.

R/2C   Right forefinger bent at first or second joint forming angle with third joint beyond 90 degrees but without touching palm. Right forefinger curl.

R/2p   Right forefinger bent to tight position. May or may not touch palm at portion proximal to third joint. Right forefinger close.

When number is underlined this signals coordinate activity with lateral occlusion between finger. Thus:

R/1?$\underline{3}$1   Right thumb hooked, fingers 2, 3, and 4 laterally occluded at Z, finger five separate at Z.

R/1?1n$\underline{3}$p   Right hand point. Thumb hooked, 3, 4, and 5 to palm.

R/1$\underline{4}$c   Right hand thumb at Z not touching remainder of fingers which are crooked.

R/1$\underline{4}$c(P∧)   Hand cup-14c + palm up

//1$\underline{4}$c(P∧)   Bimanual cup

R/1$\underline{4}$c(P>)   Hand shake position

R/1$\underline{4}$c(P∨)   Inverted cup

//5X5   Hands folded

//1$\underline{4}$X1$\underline{4}$ Hands clasped

//1-5$\underline{a}$ Hands steepled-apical finger joints contracting, palms separate.

R/$\underline{14}$-p   Male fist. Thumb superior and in occlusion with posterior aspect of 2b and 3b.

R/$\underline{1n4}$-p   Infantile fist. 1 at n and superiorly occluding with lateral aspect of 2.

R/$\overline{\ \underline{1c4}}$ Thumb circled fist.

Underlined small letters indicate contact with another body part or external object. The object is listed immediately below the hand record. If the object is held, that is, supported by hand, the participant hand parts are underlined and an o between the finger number-joint letter compounds signals the position of the object. Underlined P indicates palm involvement. Note the shorthand kineme below male and female cigarette examples.

R/12b̲o3b̲3c
cigarette, or
R/̲o
cigarette

Right hand holding cigarette with
2, 3, 4, 5 crooked and the cigarette
held between joint b of fingers 2
and 3. Middle majority male
American cigarette grasp.

R/1?2̲ao3b̲45
cigarette, or
R/ȯ̲o
cigarette

Right hand holding cigarette with
1 hooked, cigarette between 2a
and 3b and 4 and 5 in position
at n. Middle majority female
American cigarette grasp. The
shorthand kineme covers cigarette
placement varying allokinically
from 2a to 2b and from 3 ab to 3b.
3 is separate from 4. 4 and 5 are
usually separate and hook, curl,
crook and close in 4 and 5 are allokinic.

R/ȯ̲o.
cigarette

Middle majority female American
cigarette grasp with little finger
overcrook and hook.

R/1̲ao2̲a3c4c5cP≥ or
P≤ cigarette, or
R/1o2P≥ or P≤
cigarette

Right hand grasps cigarette
between 1a and 2a, palm out, 3, 4,
and 5 in crook (or curl).
European male cigarette grasp.
Or lighting hold American or
European. Palm direction may be
allokinic(?)

R/1̲ao2̲a4CP≥ or P≤
cigarette, or
R/1o4
cigarette

Cigarette hand cup. Cigarette
between 1a and 2a and held with
the lighted end between curled
fingers and palm. Palm direction
seems allokinic.

    In the above examples the underlined lower-case letter indicates
holding, e.g. (1̲ao2̲b). Two other activities seem sufficiently conventionalized in western European and American culture to record them
kinemically. *Feeling* is shown by ooo signal: e.g. (1̲4ooo) indicates
                                        object
that with the thumb at n, 2345a's are involved in touching an object
for a variedly extended period of time. *Grasping*, which involves

muscular contraction in fingers around object is recorded by ." following member record, e.g. (/1"4") records a thumb four-finger grasp. Addition of -p indicates palm involvement, e.g. (/1"4"-p) is a full hand grasp.

HIPS

Hips are recorded only when there is special involvement. Otherwise the T for trunk signifies hips at n.

x____	right hip tense
x____x	buttocks tense
_S_	hip swing
_I_	*inverted pelvis
_V_	*protruding buttocks
____	Male n which is not recorded is kinemic in the female and must be recorded.
xs____sx	buttocks shift
xx____xx	buttocks bounce

LEGS AND FEET

The leg can be seen as a member forming three angles, which, taken together with their position(s) in space, determine the recording system outlined below. The term LYnnn describes the left leg in normal weight carrying, standing position. The initial n refers to the hip joint, the second to the knee, and the third to the ankle. When numbers are substituted for any of the n's, these refer to clock positions; the arrows following the numerals indicate the *direction* of the member immediately inferior to and forming the base line of the joint angle. Eg: LY<3∨3n indicates that the left leg is held up at a 90-degree angle to the left and with the upper-lower leg angle at 90 degrees and the ankle at n. Minute marks (') can refine the recording when it is seen to be kinesically necessary. Since this is

*n for male and female middle majority American differs. n for female involves a degree of pelvis inversion which is kinemically significant when it appears in the male. Similarly with regard to buttock protrusion; n in the female, which is allokinic with pelvic inversion, becomes kinemic for the male.

a macrorecording key, only positions already standardized will be described below.

YY	Standing on both feet. (American n no more than 5 inches apart for the male or 3 inches for female.)
Y-Y	Standing feet apart. Legs separated by more than 5 inches for male; more than 3 inches for female
Y--Y	Legs overspread standing
Y$\underline{Y}$	Standing, left leg back
Y$\overline{Y}$	Standing, left leg forward
-YY-	Stooping, knees together
-Y-Y-	Stooping, knees apart
Y:	Step
Y::Y	Walking
"Y::Y"	Running
Y:S:Y	Walking: long stride
Y:s:Y	Walking: stride overshort
Y:$\underline{s}$:Y	Stride overshort and with one foot placed before the other: mincing
$\overline{Y}$: $\overline{Y}$	Swagger: legs curve laterally at each step
Y:Y:Y	Marching: feet in direct anterior-posterior line, equal time distance between steps
Y"Y	Dancing: repetitive pattern of nonequidistant steps
Y.:Y	Right foot stumble
.Y:.Y	Heel clicking or scraping while walking. Clicking usually accompanied by marching.
YskY	Skipping
Y̤:Y	Tiptoeing
Ɏɏ	Seated: body upright with Z or 90 degree angle at hips, 90 degrees at knee and feet flat on the floor. (Or zero for particular actor.)
4Ɏ	Seated, right leg crossed with ankle over left femur above knee. Middle majority American male young or informal.

¥4	Same as above, left leg over
¥4¥	Legs crossed, left over, at knee. American middle majority female . . . knee over knee. For male, left knee immediately posterior to knee. More formal than ¥4.
¥4K″	Knee over knee cross—male actor
¥4K=	Knee cross immediately behind knee, lower limbs parallel and touching. Standard upper or middle status British cross.
¥4a	Ankle cross, knees close
¥4-a	Ankle cross with knees spread
¥4a&	Legs intertwined
¥4k∠	Legs crossed at knees. Leg in short superior-inferior kick or dangle (depending on velocity).
¥4k⁄	Legs crossed at knees. Leg in median (5–8 inches) kick or dangle.
¥4k⁻	Legs crossed at knees. Leg in overkick (10 inches plus).
¥s4K	Lateral movement of crossed knee over knee. Often combined with kick or dangle.
¥¥s	Lateral leg movement seated.
¥¥S	Lateral movement, seated. Legs moved more than 1 hour.
¥¥n	Superior-inferior leg nod—less than 1 hour
¥¥N	Superior-inferior leg nod—1 hour or more
¥4ks	Legs crossed above knee. Short leg sweep. Less than 1 hour
¥4kS	Legs crossed above knee. Leg sweep. More than 1 hour

Intrafemoral index: When an individual is either seated or standing, the spread of the two legs may be seen as forming the superior planes of a triangle, the base of the triangle being formed by an invisible line connecting the two knees. The angle with its apex at the crotch is recorded. Underlined double numerals signify angle rather than position number.

Y45Y	Standing, legs apart, roughly one half the length of the upper leg between knees

Y<u>90</u>Y   Standing, legs apart, roughly the length of the upper leg apart

If legs are not equidistant from midline at knee, the weight-bearing leg is recorded as _Y. When the individual is sitting, leg nearest midline is recorded_¥. Arrows following recorded member indicate direction.

_Y<u>45</u>Y   Standing legs apart one half length of femur, right leg bearing weight.

_Y<u>45</u>Y._   With legs at 45′, weight is shifted from right to left leg.

THE FOOT

This recording system is being designed for a normally shod culture. When the naked foot is recorded, the system is comparable to that used for fingers.

Ry	foot
Ryp	right foot pat
RyN	right foot full nod
Ryn	right foot half nod
RyS	right foot full sweep
Rys	right foot half shake
Ry&	right foot circle or curve
R-y	right foot bent right
-Ly	left foot bent right
-y-	foot firm on base
—y	heel firm on base, remainder of foot up
y—	toe firm on base, remainder up
y?	toes hooked back
yC	toes curled or crooked
Ry1c4	Right big toe curled; toes 2, 3, 4, and 5, laterally touching and at n.

List of Examples of Body Motions

[Page numbers follow for all of Birdwhistell's examples, mostly motions that he describes or analyzes; they are in no particular order. The list will probably be most useful to people who have already read the book.—B.J.]

The message "I'm sick" in Border County, 208–211
Sniffing as Communication, 52–53
Smiling, 29–37
"Overwide focus" of babies and some older children, 10
American facial kinemes, 99–101
Head nods, 160–165
The Interrupting Therapist, 161–162
Kutenai speaking English, 28
Language-bound motions: La Guardia, 102–103
American English motions:
    Kinesic markers, 103, 119–127
    Kinesic stress, 103–107, 132–142, 240–245
    Kinesic junctures, 132–142, 237–239

Bibliography

ADAMS, J. K. 1955. "Expressive Behavior Aspects of Scientific Language." In *On Expressive Language,* ed. H. Werner. Papers presented at the Clark University Conference on Expressive Language Behavior. Worcester, Mass.: Clark University Press. Pp. 47–52.

ALDRICH, V. C. 1955. "Expression By Enactment." *Phil. Phenomenol. Res.* 16:188–200.

ALLPORT, G. W. 1961. *Pattern and Growth in Personality.* New York: Holt, Rinehart and Winston.

ALLPORT, G. W., and CANTRILL, H. 1934. "Judging Personality from Voice." *J. Soc. Psychol.* 5:37–55.

ALLPORT, G. W., and VERNON, P. E. 1933. *Studies in Expressive Movements.* New York: Macmillan.

AMBROSE, J. A. 1961. "The Development of the Smiling Response in Early Infancy." In *Determinants of Infant Behaviour,* ed. B. M. Foss. Proceedings of a Tavistock study group on mother-infant interaction held in the house of the CIBA Foundation, London, September, 1959. London: Methuen; New York: Wiley. Pp. 179–201.

AMES, L. B. 1944. "Early Individual Differences in Visual and Motor Behavior Patterns: A Comparative Study of Two Normal Infants by the Method of Cinemanalysis." *J. Gen. Psychol.* 65:219–226.

ANDERSON, J. D. 1920. "The Language of Gesture." *Folklore* 31:70ff.

ANDREW, R. J. 1963. "Evolution of Facial Expression." *Science* 142:1034–1041.

ARENSBERG, C. M., and KIMBALL, S. J. 1940. *Family and Community in Ireland.* Cambridge, Mass.: Harvard University Press.

ARKOFF, A., MEREDITH, G., and IWAHARA, S. 1962. "Dominance-Deference Patterning in Motherland Japanese, Japanese-American and Caucasian-American Students." *J. Soc. Psychol.* 58:61–66.

ARNHEIM, RUDOLF. 1949. "The Gestalt Theory of Expression." *Psychol. Rev.* 56:156–171.

AUSTIN, WILLIAM. 1965. "Some Social Aspects of Paralanguage." *CJL/RCL* 11(1):31–39.

AX, A. F. 1953. "The Physiological Differentiation between Fear and Anger in Humans." *Psychosom. Med.* 15:433–442.

AX, A. F., and GREENBLATT, MILTON. 1963. "Autonomic Response and Emotions: Further Discussion." In *Expression of the Emotions in Man,* ed. P. H. Knapp. New York: International Universities Press. Pp. 197ff.

AYER, A. J. 1950. *Language, Truth, and Logic.* New York: Dover.

BANDURA, A., ROSS, D., and ROSS, S. A. 1963. "Imitation of Film-mediated Aggressive Models." *J. Abnorm. Soc. Psychol.* 66:3–11.

BARBA, P. S. 1952. "Posture Changes in the Growing Child." *Med. Clin. N. Amer.* 36:1533–1540.

BARBARA, D. A. 1956. "The Value of Nonverbal Communication in Personality Understanding." *J. Nerv. Ment. Dis.* 123:286–291.

BAR-HILLEL, Y. 1955. "An Examination of Information Theory." *Phil. Sci.* 22(2):86–105.

BARKER, G. C. 1947. "Social Functions of Language in a Mexican-American Community." *Acta Americana* 5:185–202.

BARKER, R. G. 1963a. *The Stream of Behavior.* New York: Meredith.

———. ed. 1963b. *The Stream of Behavior: Explorations of Its Structure and Content.* New York: Appleton.

BASTIAN, J. 1965. "Primate Signaling Systems and Human Languages." In *Primate Behavior: Field Studies of Monkeys and Apes,* ed. I. DeVore. New York: Holt, Rinehart and Winston. Pp. 585–606.

BATESON, G., ed. 1949. Introduction to *Percival's Narrative.* London: Hogarth.

———. 1955. "The Message 'This Is Play.'" *Group Processes. Transactions of the Second Conference of the Josiah Macy, Jr. Foundation,* ed. Bert Shaffner. Princeton, October 9–12.

———. 1936. *Naven.* Cambridge, England. 2nd ed., Stanford, Calif.: Stanford University Press, 1958.

———. 1958. "Language and Psychotherapy—Frieda Fromm-Reichmann's Last Project." *Psychiatry* 21:96–100.

———. 1959. "Cultural Problems Posed by a Study of Schizophrenic Process." In *Schizophrenia: An Integrated Approach,* ed. A. Auerback. New York: Ronald Press. Pp. 125–146.

———. 1963. "A Social Scientist Views the Emotions." In *Expression of the Emotions in Man,* ed. P. H. Knapp. New York: International Universities Press.

BATESON, G., JACKSON, D. D., HALEY, J., and WEAKLAND, J. 1956. "Toward a Theory of Schizophrenia." *Behav. Sci.* 1:251–264.

BATESON, G., and JACKSON, D. D. 1964. "Social Factors and Disorders of Communication. Some Varieties of Pathogenic Organization." *Res. Publ. Assoc. Res. Nerv. Ment. Dis.* 42:270–290.

BATESON, G., and MEAD, M. 1942. *Balinese Character: A Photographic Analysis.* New York: Special Publications of the New York Academy of Sciences. Vol. II.

BATESON, M. C. 1963. "Kinesics and Paralanguage." *Science* 139:200.

BATTLE, L. D. 1963. "New Dimensions in Cultural Communication." *Publications of the Modern Language Association* 78(2):15–19.

BELL, SIR CHARLES. 1806. *Essays on the Anatomy of Expression in Painting.* London: Printed for Longman, Hurst, Rees, and Orme, Patterson–Row. 1st ed.

——. 1873. *Expression: Its Anatomy and Philosophy.* New York: Samuel Wells.

BENDER, L. 1934. "Psychoses Associated with Somatic Diseases that Distort the Body Structure." *Arch. Neurol. Psychiat.* 32:1000–1029.

BENEDEK, T. 1963. "An Investigation of the Sexual Cycle in Women." *Arch. Gen. Psychiat.* 8:311–322.

BENEDICT, R. 1934. *Patterns of Culture.* Boston and New York: Houghton Mifflin.

——. 1950. "The Study of Cultural Continuities." In *Towards World Understanding,* Vol. I., *The Influence of Home and Community on Children under Thirteen Years of Age.* Paris: UNESCO. Pp. 5–13.

BENESH, M., KRAMER, E., and LANE, H. 1963. "Recognition of Portrayed Emotion in a Foreign Language." in *Experimental Analysis of the Control of Speech Production and Perception: III.* Ann Arbor, Michigan: University of Michigan Office of Research Administration.

BENNEY, M., RIESMAN, D., and STAR, SHIRLEY A. 1956. "Age and Sex in the Interview." *Amer. J. Psychiat.* 62:143–152.

BENTON, A. L., HARTMAN, B. H., and SARASON, I. G. 1955. "Some Relations between Speech Behavior and Anxiety Level." *J. Abnorm. Soc. Psychol.* 51:295–297.

BERBLINGER, K., and GREENHILL, M. H. 1954. "Levels of Communication in Ulcerative Colitis: A Case Study." *Psychosom. Med.* 16:156–162.

BERELSON, B. 1952. *Content Analysis in Communication.* New York: Free Press.

BERES, D. 1957. "Communication in Psychoanalysis and in the Creative Process: A Parallel." *J. Amer. Psychoanalyt. Assoc.* 5:408–423.

BERGER, M. M. 1958. "Nonverbal Communications in Group Psychotherapy." *Internat. J. Group Psychoth.* 8:161–178.

BERKELEY SYMPOSIUM. 1954. "On Statistical Methods in Communication Engineering." *Transcript I.R.E. Prof. Group on Information Theory,* March 1954.

BERNE, E. 1953. "Concerning the Nature of Communication." *Psychiat. Quart.* 27:185–198.

BERNFELD, S. 1941. "The Facts of Observation in Psychoanalysis." *J. Psychol.* 12:289–305.

BIRDWHISTELL, R. L. 1952. *Introduction to Kinesics.* (Photo-offset) Foreign Service Institute. Louisville: University of Louisville Press, 1952. Now available in microfilm only, from University Microfilms Inc., 313 North First St., Ann Arbor, Mich.

——. 1954. "Frames in the Communication Process." Presented at the American Society of Clinical Hypnosis Annual Scientific Assembly, October 10, 1954.

——. 1955. "Background to Kinesics." *ETC. Rev. Gen. Seman.* 13:10–18.

——. 1958. "Implications of Recent Developments in Communication Research for Evolutionary Theory." In *Reports on the Ninth Annual*

Round Table Meeting on Linguistics and Language Studies, ed. W. M. Austin, No. II. Washington, D.C.: Georgetown University Press.

———. 1959a. "Contribution of Linguistic-Kinesic Studies to the Understanding of Schizophrenia." In *Schizophrenia,* ed. A. Auerback. New York: Ronald Press. Pp. 99–123.

———. 1959b. "Communicational Theory and Educational Television." *Proceedings of the Conference on Educational Television.* Ohio: Ohio State University.

———. 1960. "Kinesics and Communication." In *Explorations in Communication,* ed. E. Carpenter and M. McLuhan. Boston: Beacon Press. Pp. 54–64.

———. 1961a. "Paralanguage: Twenty-Five Years After Sapir." In *Lectures on Experimental Psychiatry,* ed. H. W. Brosin. Pittsburgh: University of Pittsburgh Press.

———. 1961b. "A Development in Communication Research and Evolutionary Theory." *Proceedings of the Georgetown Roundtable in Anthropology and Linguistics,* ed. William Austin.

———. 1962a. "An Approach to Communication." *Fam. Proc.* I(2):194–201.

———. 1962b. "Critical Moments in the Psychiatric Interview." In *Research Approaches to a Psychiatric Problem,* ed. T. T. Tourlentes. New York: Grune & Stratton, (Galesburg Symposium). Pp. 179–188.

———. 1963a. "The Use of Audio-Visual Aids." In *Resources for the Teaching of Anthropology,* ed. D. G. Mandelbaum, *et al.* Memoir: American Anthropological Association. Pp. 49–61.

———. 1963b. "Research in the Structure of Group Psychotherapy." *Internat. J. Group Psychoth.* 13:485–493.

———. 1963c. "The Kinesic Level in the Investigation of the Emotions." In *Expression of the Emotions in Man,* ed. P. H. Knapp. New York: International Universities Press. Pp. 123–139.

———. 1963d. "Some Relationships between American Kinesics and Spoken American English." Presented before Section H., AAAS. Cleveland. Pp. 27–28.

———. 1964a. In discussion in *Approaches to Semiotics* (a contribution), eds. T. A. Sebeok, Alfred S. Hayes and Mary Catherine Bateson. The Hague: Mouton.

———. 1964b. "Communicational Analysis in the Residency Setting." In *Teaching of Psychotherapy,* ed. F. H. Hoffman. Boston: Little, Brown 1(2):389–402.

———. 1965a. "Communication: Group Structure and Process." *Penn. Psychiat. Quart.* (Spring 1965,) Pp. 37–45.

———. 1965b. "Communicative Signals and Their Clinical Assessment." In *Voices: The Art and Science of Psychotherapy* I(2), 37–42.

———. 1965c. "The Search for the Nature of Communication." In *The American Family in Crisis.* . . Des Plaines: Forest Hospital Publications. Chapter 3, pp. 14–21.

———. 1966a. "Some Relationships between American Kinesics and Spoken

American English." In *Communication and Culture*, ed. A. G. Smith. New York: Holt, Rinehart and Winston. Pp. 182–189.

——. 1966b. "Human Communication and Human Potentialities." In Explorations in Human Potentialities, ed. H. A. Otto. Springfield, Ill.: Charles C Thomas. Chap. 22, pp. 309–322.

——. 1967. "Some Body Motion Elements Accompanying Spoken American English." In *Communication: Concepts and Perspectives*, ed. Lee Thayer. London: Macmillan; Washington, D.C.: Spartan Books, 1967. Chapter II, pp. 53–76.

——. 1968a. "Uncomfortable Room at the Top." In *Hospital and Community Psychiatry* (A Journal of the American Psychiatric Association, Washington, D.C.) 19(2):33–42.

——. 1968b. "Communication." In *International Encyclopedia of Social Sciences*. New York: Macmillan and The Free Press. Vol. 3, p. 24.

——. 1968c. "Kinesics." In *International Encyclopedia of Social Sciences*. David L. Sills, ed. New York: Macmillan and The Free Press. Vol. 8, p. 379.

——. 1968d. "Communication without Words." In *L'Aventure Humaine*, Encyclopedie des Sciences de l'Homme, Geneva: Kister S.A. Paris; De La Grange Batelière S.A., Vol. 5, pp. 157–166.

——. 1968e. "Certain Considerations in the Concepts of Culture and Communication." In *Perspectives on Communication*, eds. Carl E. Larson and Frank E. X. Dance. Milwaukee, Wisc., Speech Communication Center, The University of Wisconsin-Milwaukee, pp. 144–165.

——. 1968f. "Communication: A Continuous Multichannel Process." In *Conceptual Bases and Applications of the Communicational Sciences*. New York: John Wiley & Sons.

BLAUVELT, H. 1956. "Neonate-Mother Relationships in the Goat." In *Group Processes. Transactions of the Second Conference of the Josiah Macy, Jr., Foundation*. New York. Pp. 94–140.

BLOCH, B., and TRAGER, G. L. 1941. "The Syllabic Phonemes of English." *Language* 17:223–246.

——. 1942. *Outline of Linguistic Analysis*. Baltimore, Md.: Linguistic Society of America.

BLOOMFIELD, L. 1914. *An Introduction to the Study of Language*. New York: Holt.

——. 1926. "A Set of Postulates for the Science of Language." *Language*. 2:153–164.

——. 1933. *Language*. New York: Holt.

BLUMENTHAL, A. 1935. *The Place of the Term "Culture" in the Social Sciences*. Hanover, Minneapolis and Liverpool: The Sociological Press.

BOAS, F. 1938. *The Mind of Primitive Man*. Rev. ed., n.d. New York: Macmillan.

BOERNSTEIN, W. 1936. "On the Functional Relations of the Sense Organs to One Another and to the Organism as a Whole." *J. Gen. Psychol.* 15:117–131.

BONNER, M. R. 1943. "Changes in the Speech Pattern under Emotional Tension." *Amer. J. Psychol.* 56:262-273.

BOOMER, D. S. 1963. "Speech Disturbance and Body Movement in Interviews." *J. Nerv. Ment. Dis.* 136:263-266.

BOOMER, D. S., and DITTMANN, A. T. 1964. "Speech Rate, Filled Pause, and Body Movement in Interviews." *J. Nerv. Ment. Dis.* 139:324-327.

BOWEN, M. 1959. "Family Relationships in Schizophrenia." In *Schizophrenia: An Integrated Approach*, ed. A. Auerback. New York: Ronald Press. Pp. 147-178.

BRAATOEY, T. F. 1954. *Fundamentals of Psychoanalytic Technique*. New York: Wiley.

BRAIN, SIR RUSSELL. 1961. "The Neurology of Language." *Brain* 84:145-166.

BREWER, W. D. 1951. "Patterns of Gesture among the Levantine Arabs." *Amer. Anthrop.* 53:232-237.

BRILLIANT, R. 1963. *Gesture and Rank in Roman Art: The Use of Gestures to Denote Status in Roman Sculpture and Coinage*. New Haven: Memoirs of the Connecticut Academy of Arts and Sciences, Vol. 14.

BROADBENT, D. E. 1958. *Perception and Communication*. New York: Pergamon Press.

BRODY, M. W. 1943. "Neurotic Manifestations of the Voice." *Psychoanal. Quart.* 12:371-380.

BRONNER, A. F., KUBIE, L. S., HENDRICK, I., et al. 1949. "The Objective Evaluation of Psychotherapy." Round Table, 1948. *Amer. J. Orthopsych.* 19:463-491.

BROSIN, H. W. 1957. "The Primary Process and Psychoses." *Behav. Sci.* 2:62-67.

———. 1959. Discussion of R. L. Birdwhistell's paper: "Contribution of Linguistic-Kinesic Studies to the Understanding of Schizophrenia." In *Schizophrenia: An Integrated Approach*, ed. A. Auerback. New York: Ronald Press. Pp. 118-123.

———. 1964. "Studies in Human Communication in Clinical Settings Using Sound Film and Tape." *Wisc. Med. J.* 63:503-506.

BROWN, ROGER. 1958. *Words and Things*. Glencoe, Ill.: The Free Press.

BRUCH, HILDE. 1963. "Effectiveness in Psychotherapy, or the Constructive Use of Ignorance." *Psychiat. Quart.* 37:322-339.

———. 1961. "Some Comments on Talking and Listening in Psychotherapy." *Psychiat.* 24:269-272.

BRUNER, J. S. 1956. *A Study of Thinking*. New York: Wiley.

———. 1960. "The Functions of Perceiving: New Look Retrospect." In *Perspectives in Psychological Theory*, eds. B. Kaplan and S. Wapner. New York: International Universities Press. Pp. 61-77.

BRUNER, J. S., and TAGIURE, R. 1954. "The Perception of People." In *Handbook of Social Psychology*, ed. G. Lindsay. Cambridge: Addison-Wesley. Vol. 2, pp. 634-654.

BULLER, A. J., LIPPOLD, O. C. J., and TAYLOR, A. 1961. "Discussion on Normal and Abnormal Willed Movement." *Proc. Royal. Soc. Med.* 54:199-203.

BULLOWA, M., JONES, L. G., and BEVER, T. G. 1964. "The Development from Vocal to Verbal Behavior in Children." *Monogr. Soc. Res. Child Develop.* 29:101–107.

BURKE, K. 1945. *A Grammar of Motives*. New York: Prentice-Hall.

BURROW, T. 1958. *A Search for Man's Sanity*. New York: Oxford University Press. See also: *Science and Man's Behavior*, ed. W. Egalt. (Contains "The Neurosis of Man.") New York: Philosophical Library, 1953.

CALHOUN, J. B. 1963. The *Ecology and Sociology of the Norway Rat*. Washington, D.C.: U.S. Government Printing Office, Public Health Service 1008.

CAMPA, A. L. 1951. "Language Barriers in Intercultural Communication." *J. Comm.* 1(2):41–45.

CAMPBELL, H., BREWER, R. F., NEVILLE, H., HARRISON, C., CORDER, F., and HAWLEY, S. 1912. *Voice, Speech and Gesture: Elocutionary Art*. Edinburgh, England: John Grant.

CARMICHAEL, H. T. 1956. "Sound Film Recording of Psychoanalytic Therapy: A Therapist's Experiences and Reactions." *J. Iowa Med. Soc.* 46:590–595.

CARNAP, R. 1937. *Logical Syntax of Language*. New York: Harcourt, Brace.

———. 1943. *Formalization of Logic*. Cambridge: Harvard University Press.

CARPENTER, E. S., and McLUHAN, M., eds. 1960. *Explorations in Communication: An Anthology*. Boston: Beacon Press.

CARROLL, J. G. 1953. *The Study of Language: A Survey of Linguistics and Related Disciplines in America*. Cambridge: Harvard University Press.

———. 1958. "Process and Content in Psycholinguistics." In *Current Trends in the Description and Analysis of Behavior*. Pittsburgh: University of Pittsburgh Press. Pp. 175–200.

CARROLL, J. G., and CASAGRANDE, J. B. 1958. "The Function of Language Classifications in Behavior." In *Reading in Social Psychology*, eds. E. Macoby, T. H. Newcombe, and E. L. Hartley. 3rd ed., New York: Holt.

CASSIRER, E. 1946. *Language and Myth*. Translation by S. K. Langer. New York: Harper.

———. 1953. *The Philosophy of Symbolic Forms*. Vol. I *Language*. New Haven: Yale University Press.

CHAPPLE, E. D. 1939. "Quantitative Analysis of the Interaction of Individuals." *Proc. Nat. Acad. Sci.* 25:58–67.

———. 1949. "The Interaction Chronograph: Its Evolution and Present Application." *Personnel* 25:295–307.

———. 1953. "The Standard Experimental (Stress) Interview as Used in Interaction Chronograph Investigations." *Human Org.* 12:23–32.

———. 1956. *The Interaction Chronograph Manual*. Norton, Conn.: E. D. Chapple Co.

CHAPPLE, E. D., and ARENSBERG, C. M. 1940. "Measuring Human Relations: An Introduction to the Study of Interaction of Individuals." *Genet. Psychol. Monogr.* 22:3–147.

CHAPPLE, E. D., CHAPPLE, M. F., and REPP, JUDITH A. 1955. "Behavioral Definitions of Personality and Temperament Characteristics." *Human Org.* 13:34–39.

CHAPPLE, E. D., and LINDEMANN, E. 1942. "Clinical Implications of Measurements of Interaction Rates in Psychiatric Interviews." *Appl. Anthrop.* 1:1–11.

CHASE, S. 1938. *The Tyranny of Words.* New York: Harcourt, Brace.

——. 1954. *Power of Words.* New York: Harcourt, Brace.

CHERRY, C. 1957. *On Human Communication: A Review, A Survey, and A Criticism.* Cambridge: Technology Press of Massachusetts Institute of Technology; New York: Wiley, 1958.

CHOMSKY, N. 1955. "Logical Syntax and Semantics: Their Linguistic Relevance." *Language* 31:36–45.

——. 1957. *Syntactic Structures.* New York: Humanities Press.

——. 1958. "Finite State Languages." *Info. & Cont.* 1:91–112.

——. 1959. Review of Skinner's *Verbal Behavior. Language* 35(1):26–28.

CHRISTIANSEN, B. 1963. *Thus Speaks the Body. Attempts toward a Personology from the Point of View of Respiration and Postures.* Oslo: Institute for Social Research.

CLEMENS, T. L. 1957. "Autonomic Nervous System Responses Related to the Fuakenstein Test." I. To Epinephrine." *Psychosom. Med.* 19:267–274.

COCCHIARA, G. 1932. *11 Linguaggio del Besto.* Bocva: Terine.

COHEN, S. I., SILVERMAN, A. J., and BURCH, N. R. 1956. "A Technique for the Assessment of Affect Change." *J. Nerv. Ment. Dis.* 124:352–360.

COLBY, K. M. 1963. "A Psychoanalyst's View of Methods for Studying Emotions." In *Expression of the Emotions in Man,* ed. P. H. Knapp. New York: International Universities Press.

COLEMAN, H. O. 1914. "Intonation and Emphasis." *Misc. Phonet.* 1:6ff.

Communication and Interaction in Three Families. Film. 16 mm. b. & w. Sound. 75 min. 1953. Produced by Jurgen Ruesch. Available through Kinesis, Inc., 566 Commercial St., San Francisco, Calif.

Conference on Verbal Learning and Verbal Behavior. 1961. New York University, 1959. "Verbal Learning and Verbal Behavior: Proceedings," ed. C. N. Cofer with the assistance of Barbara S. Musgrave. Sponsored by the Office of Naval Research and New York University. New York: McGraw-Hill.

COOLEY, C. H. 1902. *Human Nature and the Social Order.* New York: Scribner's.

CORBIN, E. I. 1962. "Muscle Action as Nonverbal and Preverbal Communication." *Psychoanalyt. Quart.* 31:351–363.

CORNELISON, F. S., and ARSENIAN, J. 1960. "A Study of the Response of Psychotic Patients to Photographic Self-image Experience." *Psychiat. Quart.* 34:1–8.

CRAIG, W. 1956. "Replacement of Auxiliary Expressions." *Phil. Rev.* 65(1):38–55.

CRITCHLEY, M. 1939. *The Language of Gesture.* London: Arnold.

———. 1958. "A Critical Survey of Our Conceptions as to the Origins of Language." In *The History and Philosophy of Knowledge of the Brain and Its Functions,* ed. F. N. L. Poynter. Springfield, Ill.: Charles C Thomas. Pp. 45–72.

———. 1963. "Kinesics: Gestural and Mimic Language—An Aspect of Non-Verbal Communication." In *Problems of Dynamic Neurology: An International Volume,* ed. Lipman Halpern. Studies on the higher functions of the human nervous system. Jerusalem, Israel: Hebrew University. Pp. 181–200.

CURRY, E. T. 1940. "The Pitch Characteristics of the Adolescent Male Voice." *Monogr.* 7:48–62.

CUTNER, M. 1953. "On the Inclusion of Certain 'Body Experiments' in Analysis." *Brit. J. M. Psychol.* 26:263–277.

DAMON, A., STOUDTARD, H. W., and McFARLAND, R. A. 1966. *The Human Body in Equipment Design.* Cambridge, Mass.: Harvard University Press.

DANIEL, J. 1964. "Novšie Metŏdy Analýzy Pracovných Pohybov." (New method of motion analysis.) *Československá Psychologie* No. 3:256–264.

DARWIN, C. 1859. *The Origin of Species and the Descent of Man.* New York: Modern Library, n.d. P. 391.

———. 1873. *The Expression of the Emotions in Man and Animals.* New York: Appleton. New York: Philosophical Library, 1955.

DAVIS, A., and HAVIGHURST, R. J. 1946. "Social Class and Color Differences in Child Rearing." *Amer. Sociol. Rev.* 11:698–710.

DAVIS, R. C., BUCHWALD, A. M., and FRANKMAN, R. W. 1955. "Autonomic and Muscular Responses, and their Relation to Simple Stimuli." *Psychol. Monogr.* 69: No. 20 (Whole No. 405).

DAVIS, R. C., and BUCHWALD, A. M. 1957. "An Exploration of Somatic Response Patterns: Stimulus and Sex Differences." *J. Comp. Physiol. Psychol.* 50:44–52.

DAVITZ, J. R., and DAVITZ, L. J. 1959. "The Communication of Feelings by Content-Free Speech." *J. Comm.* 9:6–13.

———. 1959. "Correlates of Accuracy in the Communication of Feelings." *J. Comm.* 9:110–117.

DEUTSCH, F. 1947. "Analysis of Postural Behavior." ("Thus Speaks the Body," I.) *Psychoanalyt. Quart.* 16:195–213.

———. 1949. "Thus Speaks the Body—An Analysis of Postural Behavior." *Transactions, New York Academy of the Sciences,* Series II, 12(2):58–62.

———. 1950. "Thus Speaks the Body. II. A Psychosomatic Study of Vasomotor Behavior (Capillaroscopy and Plethysmography)." *Acta Med. Orient.* 9:199–215.

———. 1951a. "Thus Speaks the Body. IV. Some Psychosomatic Aspects of the Respiratory Disorder Asthma." *Acta Med. Orient.* 10:67–86.

———. 1951b. "Thus Speaks the Body. Analytic Posturology. Note of the N.Y. Psychoanalytic Society Meeting, Oct. 31, 1950, by Joseph Lander." *Psychoanalyt. Quart.* 20:338–339.

———. 1952. "Analytic Posturology." *Psychoanalyt. Quart.* 21:196–214.

———. 1954. "Analytic Synesthesiology: Analytic Interpretation of Intersensory Perception." *Internat. J. Psycho-Analysis* 35:293–301.

———. 1959a. "Correlations of Verbal and Nonverbal Communication in Interviews Elicited by the Associative Anamnesis." *Psychosom. Med.* 21:123–130.

———. ed. 1959b. *On the Mysterious Leap from the Mind to the Body.* New York: International Universities Press.

DEUTSCH, F., and MURPHY, W. F. 1955. *The Clinical Interview.* New York: International Universities Press. Vol. I, Diagnoses; Vol. 2, Therapy.

DEUTSCH, K. W. 1952a. "Communication Theory and Social Science." *Amer. J. Ortho. Psychiat.* 22:469–483.

———. 1952b. "On Communication Models in the Social Sciences." *Publ. Opin. Quart.* 16:356–380.

DEVEREUX, G. 1949a. "Mohave Voice and Speech Mannerisms." *Word* 6:268–272.

———. 1949b. "Some Mohave Gestures." *Amer. Anthropol.* n.s., LI.

———. 1951. "Mohave Indian Verbal and Motor Profanity." *Psychoanal. and the Soc. Sci.* 3:99–127.

DIEBOLD, A. R., JR. 1968. "Anthropological Perspectives: Anthropology and the Comparative Psychology of Communicative Behavior." In *Animal Communication: Techniques of Study and Results of Research,* ed. T. A. Sebeok. Bloomington and London: Indiana University Press. Chap. 19, pp. 525–560.

DIEHL, C. F., WHITE, R., and BURK, K. W. 1959. "Voice Quality and Anxiety," *J. Speech Hear. Res.* 2:282–285.

DITTMANN, A. T. 1962. "The Relationship between Body Movements and Moods in Interviews." *J. Consult. Psychol.* 26:480.

———. 1963. "Kinesic Research and Therapeutic Processes: Further Discussion." In *Expression of the Emotions in Man,* ed. P. H. Knapp. New York: International Universities Press. Pp. 140–147.

DITTMANN, A. T., and WYNNE, L. C. 1961. "Linguistic Techniques and the Analysis of Emotionality in Interviews." *J. Abnorm. Soc. Psychol.* 63:201–204.

DITTMANN, A. T., PARLOFF, M. B., and BOOMER, D. S. 1965. "Facial and Bodily Expression: A Study of Receptivity of Emotional Cues." *Psychiatry* 28:239–244.

DREXLER, A. B. 1959. "An Investigation of Pitch, Sound Pressure Level, and Rate in Institutionalized Mentally Retarded Adults." *Speech Monogr.* 26:134–135.

DUBOIS, CORA. 1944. *The Peoples of Alor.* Minneapolis: University of Minnesota Press.

DUFFY, R. J. 1958. "The Vocal Pitch Characteristics of Eleven-, Thirteen-, and Fifteen-year-old Female Speakers." *Diss. Abstr.* 18:599.

DUMAS, G. and O. 1930. *Andre Nouveau traite de psychologie.* Paris. 5 vols.

DUNBAR, F. 1954. *Emotions and Bodily Changes.* 4th ed. New York: Columbia University Press.

———. 1960. "Interpretation of Body Behavior During Psychotherapy." In *Science and Psychoanalysis,* Vol. 3, *Psychoanalysis and Human Values,* ed. J. H. Masserman. New York & London: Grune & Stratton. Pp. 223–230.

DUNLAP, K. 1927. "A Project for Investigating the Facial Signs of Personality." *J. Psychol.* 39:156–161.

———. 1927. "The Role of Eye Muscles and Mouth Muscles in the Expression of Emotions." *Genet. Psychol. Monogr.* 11:199–233.

DURKHEIM, E. 1926. *The Elementary Forms of the Religious Life.* Trans. by W. Swain. New York: Macmillan.

———. 1951. *Suicide.* Tr. by John A. Spaudling and George Simpson. Glencoe, Ill.: The Free Press.

DUVALL, E. N. 1959. *Kinesiology: The Anatomy of Motion.* Englewood Cliffs, N.J.: Prentice–Hall.

DYMOND, R. 1952. "Measurable Changes in Empathy with Age." *J. Consult. Psychol.* 16:202–206.

EFRON, D. 1942. *Gesture and Environment.* New York: Kings Crown Press.

EFRON, D., and FOLEY, J. P. 1947. "Gestural Behavior and Social Setting." In *Readings in Social Psychology,* eds. T. L. Newcombe and E. L. Hartley. New York: Ronald Press.

EINSTEIN, A., and INFELD, L. 1938. *The Evolution of Physics.* New York: Simon & Schuster.

EISENBERG, P. 1937. "Expressive Movements Related to Feeling of Dominance." *Arch. Psychol.* 30:5–72.

EISENBERG, P., and ZALOWITZ, E. 1938. "Judging Expressive Movement: III. Judgments of Dominance Feeling from Phonograph Records of Voice." *J. Appl. Psychol.* 22:620–631.

EISENSTADT, S. N. 1942. "Some Problems in Communication Research in Israel." *Internat. Soc. Sci. Bul.* 14:(2):337–348.

EKMAN, P. 1957. "A Methodological Discussion of Nonverbal Behavior." *J. Psychol.* 43:141–149.

———. 1964. "Body Position, Facial Expression and Verbal Behavior during Interview." *J. Abnorm. Soc. Psychol.,* 68:295–301.

———. 1965. "Communication through Nonverbal Behavior: A Source of Information about an Interpersonal Relationship." In *Affect, Cognition and Personality,* eds. S. S. Tomkins and C. E. Izard. New York: Springer Press. Pp. 390–442.

ELDRED, S. H., HAMBURG, D. A., INWOOD, EUGENE R., SALZMAN, LEON, MEYERSBURG, HERMAN A. and GOODRICH, GENEVA. 1954. "A Procedure for the Systematic Analysis of Psychotherapeutic Interviews." *Psychiatry* 17:337–345.

ELDRED, S. H., and PRICE, D. B. 1958. "A Linguistic Evaluation of Feeling States in Psychotherapy." *Psychiatry* 21:115–121.

ENGEN, T., and LEVY, N. 1956. "Constant-Sum Judgments of Facial Expressions." *J. Exp. Psychol.* 51:396–398.

ENGEN, T., LEVY, N., and SCHLOSBERG, HAROLD. 1957. "A New Series of Facial Expressions." *Amer. Psychol.*, 12:264–266.

ENGLISH, O. S., HAMPE, WARREN W. JR., BACON, CATHERINE L. and SETTLAGE, CALVIN F. 1961. *Direct Analysis and Schizophrenia: Clinical Observations and Evaluations.* New York: Grune & Stratton.

ESTES, S. G. 1938. "Judging Personality from Expressive Behavior." *J. Abnorm. Soc. Psychol.* 3:217–236.

FAIRBANKS, G. 1944. "Studies in Language Behavior. II. The Quantitative Differentiation of Samples of Spoken Language." *Psychol. Monogr.* 56:19–38.

FAIRBANKS, G. and PRONOVOST, W. 1939. "Pitch of Voice and Expression of Emotion." *Speech Monogr.* 6:87–104.

FELDMAN, S. S. 1959. *Mannerisms of Speech and Gestures in Everyday Life.* New York: International Universities Press.

FENICHEL, O. 1954. "On Acting." In *Collected Papers,* O. Fenichel, 2nd series. New York: Norton. Pp. 349–361.

FIELDS, S. J. 1950. "Discrimination of Facial Expression and Its Relation to Personal Adjustment." *Amer. Psychol.* 5:309.

FINE, L. J. 1959. "Nonverbal Aspects of Psychodrama." *Prog. Psychother.* 4:212–218.

FISHER, S., and Cleveland, S. E. 1958. *Body Image and Personality.* Princeton, N. J.: Van Nostrand.

FISHMAN, J. 1960. "A Systematization of the Whorfian Hypothesis." *Behav. Sci.* 5:323–339.

FLACK, M. J. 1966. "Communicable and Uncommunicable Aspects in Personal International Relationships." *J. Comm.* 16(4):283–290.

FLIESS, R. 1949. "Silence and Verbalization." *Internat. J. Psychoan.* 30:21–30.

FLUGEL, J. 1950. *The Psychology of Clothes.* London: Hogarth.

FRANK, L. K. 1957. "Tactile Communication." *Genet. Psychol. Monogr.* 56:209–255.

FREUD, S. 1960. *The Psychopathology of Everyday Life,* Vol. 6 (1901) of the Standard Edition of the Complete Psychological Works of Sigmund Freud. London: Hogarth.

FRIES, C. C. 1952. *The Structure of English.* New York: Harcourt.

FRIJDA, N. H. 1953. "The Understanding of Facial Expression of Emotion." *Acta. Psychol.* 9:294–362.

———. 1958. "Facial Expression and Situational Cues." *J. Abnorm. Soc. Psychol.*, 57:149–154.

FROMM, E. 1941. *Escape from Freedom.* New York: Farrar and Rinehart.

FROMM-REICHMANN, F. 1955. "Clinical Significance of Intuitive Processes of the Psychoanalyst." *J. Amer. Psychoanal. Assoc.* 3:5–6, 82–88.

GAGE, H. L. 1952. "Judging Interests from Expressive Behavior." *Psychol. Monogr.* 66, No. 350.

GESELL, A. 1939. "Reciprocal Interweaving in Neuro-Motor Development. A Principle of Spiral Organization Shown in the Patterning of Infant Behavior." *J. Comp. Neur.* 70:161–180.

———. 1946. *The Child from Five to Ten.* New York: Harper.

GILL, M., NEWMAN, R., and REDLICH, F. C. 1954. *The Initial Interview in Psychiatric Practice.* New York: International Universities Press.

GLAZER, N. and MOYNIHAN, D. P. 1963. *Beyond the Melting Pot: The Negroes, Puerto Ricans, Jews, Italians and the Irish.* New York and Cambridge, Mass.: MIT Press.

GLEASON, H. A. 1956. *An Introduction to Descriptive Linguistics.* New York: Holt.

GLENN, E. S. 1957–58. "Introduction to the Special Issue: Interpretation and Intercultural Communication." *ETC* 15:87–95.

———. 1966. "Meaning and Behavior: Communication and Culture." *J. Comm.* 16(4):248–272.

GOFFMAN, E. 1956. *The Presentation of Self in Everyday Life.* Edinburgh: University of Edinburgh, Social Science Research Centre; New York: Doubleday, 1959.

———. 1963. *Behavior in Public Places.* Glencoe, Ill.: The Free Press; London: Collier-Macmillan Ltd.

GOLDMAN-EISLER, F. 1952. "Individual Differences between Interviews and Their Effect on Interviewees: Conversational Behavior." *J. Ment. Sci.* 08:660–671.

———. 1954. "On the Variability of the Speed of Talking and Its Relation to the Length of Utterances in Conversations." *Brit. J. Psychol.* 45:94–107.

GOOLKER, P. 1961. "Affect Communication in Therapy." *J. Hillside Hospital,* 10:170–182.

GOSTYNSKI, E. 1951. "A Clinical Contribution to the Analysis of Gestures." *Internat. J. Psycho-Analy.* 32:310–318.

GOTTSCHALK, L. A., ed. 1961. *Comparative Psycholinguistic Analysis of Two Psychotherapeutic Interviews.* New York: International Universities Press.

———. 1964. "Measurement of Verbal and Vocal Behavior. Distinguishing Characteristics of the Verbal Communications of Schizophrenic Patients." *Res. Publ. Ass. Res. Nerv. Ment. Dis.* 42:400–413.

GOTTSCHALK, L. A., and Gleser, G. C. 1963. "Distinguishing Characteristics of the Verbal Communications of Schizophrenic Patients." In A.R.N.M.D. *Disorders of Communication.* Baltimore: Williams & Wilkins.

GOTTSCHALK, L. A., and HAMBIDGE, G. 1955. "Verbal Behavior Analysis: A Systematic Approach to the Problem of Quantifying Psychologic Processes." *J. Proj. Tech.* 19:387–409.

GREENACRE, P. 1952. "Pathological Weeping." In *Trauma, Growth, and Personality*. New York: Norton. Pp. 120–131.

GREENBERG, J. H. 1959. "Current Trends in Linguistics." *Science* 130:1165–1170.

GREENHILL, M. H. 1958. "The Focal Communication Concept." *Amer. J. Psychoth.* 12:30–41.

GRIMM, J. J. 1870. *Deutch Grammatik*. 2nd ed. Gottinger, 1822–1840. Reprinted: Berlin: W. Scherer.

GRINKER, R. R. 1964. "Reception of Communications by Patients in Depressive States." *Arch. Gen. Psychiat.* 10:576–580.

GRODDECK, G. 1950. *The Book of the It*. New York: Brunner. P. 72.

GROTJAHN, M. 1957. *Beyond Laughter*. New York: McGraw–Hill.

HALEY, J. 1959. "An Interactional Description of Schizophrenia." *Psychiatry* 22:321–332.

———. 1962. "Whither Family Therapy." *Fam. Proc.* 1(1):69–100.

———. 1962. "Our Silent Language." *Americas* 14(2):5–8.

HALL, E. T. 1959. *The Silent Language*. New York: Doubleday.

———. 1963. "A System for the Notation of Proxemic Behavior." *Amer. Anthropol.* 65(5):1003–1026.

———. 1964. "Adumbration as a Feature of Intercultural Communication." In special publication, *The Ethnography of Communication*, Part 2. *Amer. Anthrop.* 66(6):154–163.

———. 1966. *The Hidden Dimension*. New York: Doubleday.

HALL, E. T., and TRAGER, G. L. 1953. *The Analysis of Culture*. Washington, D.C.: American Council of Learned Societies.

HALL, E. T., and WHYTE, W. F. 1960. "Intercultural Communication." *Human Org.* 19:5–12.

HALLOWELL, A. 1955. *Culture and Experience*. Philadelphia: University of Pennsylvania Press.

HAMBIDGE, G., JR., and GOTTSCHALK, L. A. 1958. "Verbal Behavior Analysis—Psychodynamic, Structural, and Temporal Correlates of Specific Variables." In *Psychopathology of Communication*, eds. P. Hoch and J. Zubin. New York: Grune & Stratton. Pp. 84–97.

HAMBURG, D. A. 1963. "Emotions in the Perspective of Human Evolution." in *Expression of the Emotions in Man*, ed. P. H. Knapp. New York: International Universities Press.

HAMILTON, R. V. 1957. "A Psycholinguistic Analysis of Some Interpretive Processes of Three Basic Personality Types." *J. Soc. Psychol.* 46:153–177.

HARE, A. P., WAXLER, N., SASLOW, G., and MATARAZZO, J. D. 1960. "Simultaneous Recordings of Bales and Chapple Interaction Measures during Initial Psychiatric Interviews." *J. Consult. Psychol.* 24:193.

HARGREAVES, W. A. 1960. "A Model for Speech Unit Duration." *Lang. & Speech* 3:164–173.

HARING, D. 1941. "Aspects of Personal Character in Japan." *Far Eastern Quarterly* 1(1):12–22. Reprinted in *Personal Character and Cultural Milieu.* Rev. ed. Syracuse: Syracuse University Press. Pp. 396–407.

HARLOW, H. F. 1957. "Experimental Analysis of Behavior." *Amer. Psychol.* 12:485–490.

———. 1963. "An Experimentalist Views the Emotions." In *Expression of the Emotions in Man,* ed. P. H. Knapp. New York: International Universities Press.

HARRIS, MARVIN. 1964. *The Nature of Cultural Things.* New York: Random House.

HARRIS, Z. S. 1946. "From Morpheme to Utterance." *Language* 22:161–183.

———. 1951. *Methods in Structural Linguistics.* Chicago: University of Chicago Press.

———. 1952a. "Discourse Analysis." *Language* 28:1–30.

———. 1952b. "Discourse Analysis." (A Sample Test) *Language* 28:474–494.

HARRISON, R. 1964. "Pictic Analysis: Toward a Vocabulary and Syntax for the Pictorial Code—with Research on Facial Communication." A thesis submitted to Michigan State University, Department of Communication.

HAWTHORNE, J. W. 1934. "An Attempt to Measure Certain Phases of Speech." *J. Gen. Psychol.* 10:399–414.

HAYAKAWA, S. I. 1951. *Language in Action.* New York: Harcourt.

HAYES, A. S. 1962. "A Tentative Schemetization for Research in the Teaching of Cross-Cultural Communication." In *Materials and Techniques for the Language Laboratory,* ed. E. W. Najam. *Internat. J. Amer. Ling.* 23(1): Part 2.

———. 1962. "A Tentative Schematization for Research in the Teaching of Cross-Cultural Communication." *Amer. J. Ling.* 28(1):155–167.

HAYES, A. S., LANE, H., MUELLER, T., SWEET, W. E. 1962. "A New Look at Learning." In *Current Issues in Language Teaching,* ed. W. F. Bottiglia. Reports of the Working Committees, 1962 Northeast Conference on the Teaching of Foreign Languages. Manchester, New Hampshire: Lew H. Cummings Co.

HAYES, F. 1957. "Gestures: A Working Bibliography." *So. Folk. Quart.* 21:218–317.

HENDRIX, G. 1960a. "The Case for Basic Research on Theory of Instruction." *Amer. Math. Mo.* 67(5):466–467.

———. 1960b. "Non-verbal Awareness in the Learning of Mathematics." In *Research Problems in Mathematics Education.* Cooperative Research Monograph, No. 3. Washington, D.C.: U.S. Department of Health, Education and Welfare. Pp. 57–61.

———. 1961. "Learning by Discovery." *The Math. Teach.* 53(5):290–299.

HENRY, J. 1936. "The Linguistic Expression of Emotion." *Amer. Anthropol.* 38:250–256.

——. 1957. "Types of Institutional Structure." *Psychiatry* 20:47–60.

HESS, W. R. 1954. *Diencephalon, Autonomic and Extrapyramidal Functions.* New York: Grune & Stratton.

HEWES, G. W. 1955. "World Distribution of Certain Postural Habits." *Amer. Anthropol.* 57:231–244.

——. 1957. "The Anthropology of Posture." *Sci. Amer.* 196:123–132.

HILGARD, E. R. 1952. "Experimental Approaches to Psychoanalysis." In *Psychoanalysis as Science*, ed. E. Pumpian-Mindlin. Stanford: Stanford University Press. Pp. 3–45.

——. 1958. "Interviewing Variables, Hypothetical Constructs, Parameters, and Constants." *Amer. J. Psychol.* 71:238–246.

HILL, A. A. 1958. *Introduction to Linguistic Structures.* New York: Harcourt, Brace.

HINDE, R. A. 1959. "Some Recent Trends in Ethology." In *Psychology: A Study of a Science*, ed. S. Koch, Vol. 2. New York: McGraw-Hill. Pp. 561–610.

HOCH, P., and ZUBIN, J., eds. 1958. *Psychopathology of Communication.* New York: Grune & Stratton.

HOCKETT, C. F. 1958. "Ethnolinguistic Implications of Recent Studies in Linguistics and Psychiatry." Monograph Series. Georgetown: Georgetown University Institute of Language and Linguistics.

——. 1958. *A Course in Modern Linguistics.* New York: Macmillan. Pp. 15–32.

——. 1959. "Animal 'Languages' and Human Language." In *The Evolution of Man's Capacity for Culture*, arr. by J. N. Spuhler. Detroit: Wayne State University Press.

——. 1960a. "The Origins of Speech." *Sci. Amer.* 203(3):89–96.

——. 1960b. "Logical Consideration in the Study of Animal Communication." In *Animal Sounds and Communication*, eds. W. E. Lanyon and T. N. Tavolga. Washington, D.C.: Intelligencer. Pp. 392–420.

HOCKETT, C. F., and ASCHER, R. 1964. "The Human Revolution." *Cur. Anthropol.* 5:135–168.

HOIJER, H. 1953. "The Relation of Language to Culture." In *Anthropology Today: An Encyclopedic Inventory*, ed. A. L. Kroeber. Chicago: University of Chicago Press. Pp. 554–573.

HOIJER, H., MARTINET, A., *et al.* 1953. "Linguistics." (Discussion) In *An Appraisal of Anthropology Today*, ed. Sol Tax, *et al.* Chicago: University of Chicago Press. Pp. 273–298.

HOLLINGSHEAD, A. B. 1949. *Elmtown's Youth.* New York: Wiley.

HONHAVAARA, S. 1961. *The Psychology of Expression: Dimensions in Human Perception.* Cambridge, Eng.: Cambridge University Press.

HONIGMANN, J. J. 1954. *Culture and Personality.* New York: Harper.

HOWES, D., and GESCHWIND, N. 1964. "The Brain and Disorders of Communication. Quantitative Studies of Aphasic Language." *Res. Publ. Ass. Res. Nerv. Ment. Dis.* 42:229–244.

HUBER, E. 1931. *Evolution of Facial Musculature and Facial Expression.* Baltimore: Johns Hopkins Press.

HUGHES, E. C. and H. M. 1952. *Where Peoples Meet.* Glencoe, Ill.: Free Press.

HUGHES, R. M. 1941. (La Meri) *The Gesture Language of the Hindu Dance.* New York: Columbia University Press.

HULIN, W. S., and KATZ, D. 1935. "The Frois-Wittmann Pictures of Facial Expression." *J. Exp. Psychol.* 18:482–498.

HUNTLY, C. W. 1940. "Judgments of Self Based upon Records of Expressive Behavior." *J. Abnorm. Soc. Psychol.* 35:398–426.

HUTCHINSON, A. 1954. *Labanotation.* New York: New Directions.

HYMES, D. 1964. *Language in Culture and Society.* New York, Evanston and London: Harper & Row.

JACKSON, C. V. 1954. "The Influence of Previous Movement and Posture on Subsequent Posture." *Quart. J. Exp. Psychol.* 6:72–78.

JACKSON, D. D., and WEAKLAND, J. H. 1959. "Schizophrenic Symptoms and Family Interaction." *A.M.A. Arch. Gen. Psychiat.* 1:618–621.

———. 1961. "Conjoint Family Therapy." *Psychiatry* 24(2).

JACKSON, D. D., RISKIN, JULES, and SATIR, VIRGINIA. 1961. "A Method of Analysis of a Family Interview." *Arch. Gen. Psychiat.* 5:321–339.

JAFFE, J. 1957. "An Objective Study of Communication in Psychiatric Interviews." *J. Hillside Hospital* 6:207–215.

———. 1958a. "Language of the Dyad: A Method of Interaction Analysis in Psychiatric Interviews." *Psychiatry* 21:249–258.

———. 1958b. "Communication Networks in Freud's Interview Technique." *Psychiat. Quart.* 32:456–473.

———. 1960. "Social Factors in the Doctor-Patient Relationship. Part II. Psychoanalysis and Transactional Dynamics." *Sci. & Psychoanal.* 4:81–88.

———. 1961. "Dyadic Analysis of Two Psychotherapeutic Interviews." In *Comparative Psycholinguistic Analysis of Two Psychotherapeutic Interviews,* ed. L. A. Gottschalk. New York: International Universities Press. Pp. 73–90.

———. 1962. "Computer Analysis of Verbal Behavior in Psychiatric Interviews." In *Disorders of Communication,* ed. D. Rioch. Proceedings of the Association for Research in Nervous and Mental Disease. Vol. 42 Pp. 389–399.

JAKOBSON, R., FANT, G., GUNNAR, M., and HALLE, M. 1952. *Preliminaries to Speech Analysis: The Distinctive Features and Their Correlates.* Cambridge: Acoustic Laboratory, Massachusetts Institute of Technology, Technical Report No. 13.

JAKOBSON, R., and HALLE, M. 1956. *Fundamentals of Language.* The Hague: Mouton; New York: Humanities Press, 1956. (See also review in *Psychoanal. Quart.* 26:548–551, 1957.

JAMES, W. 1892. *Psychology.* New York: Holt. P. 375.

JAMES, W. T. 1932. "A Study of the Expression of Bodily Posture." *J. Genet. Psychol.* 7:405–437.

JELLIFFE, S. E. 1940. "The Parkinsonian Body Posture: Some Considerations in Unconscious Hostility." *Psychoanalyt. Rev.* 27:467–479.

JESPERSON, O. 1922. *Language: Its Nature, Development and Origin.* London: G. Allen and Unwin.

JOHANNESSON, A. 1944. "Gesture Origin of Indo-European Languages." *Nature (Lond.)* 153:171–172.

———. 1946. "Origin of Language." *Nature (Lond.)* 157:847–848.

JOHNSON, W. 1944. "Studies in Language Behavior. I. A. Program of Research." *Psychol. Monogr.* 56:1–15.

JONES, D. 1950. *The Pronunciation of English.* 3rd ed. London: Cambridge University Press. (See also review by H. L. Smith in *Language* 28:144–149, Jan.-Mar. 1952.)

JONES, F. P., GRAY, F. E., FLORENCE, E., HANSON, A., and O'CONNELL, D. N. 1959. "A Experimental Study of the Effect of Head Balance on Patterns of Posture and Movement in Man." *J. Psychol.* 47:247–258.

JONES, M. R. 1943. "Studies in 'Nervous Movements.' II. The Effect of Inhibition of Micturition on the Frequency and Patterning of Movements." *J. Gen. Psychol.* 29:303.

JOOS, M. 1950. "Description of Language Design." *J. Acous. Soc. Amer.* 22:701–708.

———. 1958. "Semology: A Linguistic Theory of Meaning." *Stud. Ling.* 13:53–70.

JOSIAH MACY, JR. FOUNDATION. 1950–1955. *Conference on Cybernetics. Transactions,* 6th–10th, 1949–1953. Ed. H. Von Foerster. New York. 5 vols.

———. 1950–1954. *Conference on Problems of Consciousness. Transactions,* 1st–5th. Ed. H. A. Abramson. New York.

KALIS, B. L., and BENNETT, L. F. 1957. "The Assessment of Communication: The Relation of Clinical Improvement to Measured Changes in Communicative Behavior." *J. Consult. Psychol.* 21:10–14.

KANZER, M. 1961. "Verbal and Nonverbal Aspects of Free Association." *Psychoanalyt. Quart.* 30(3):327–350.

KAPLAN, B. 1955. "Some Psychological Methods for the Investigation of Expressive Language." In *On Expressive Language,* ed. H. Werner. Worcester, Mass.: Clark University Press. Pp. 19–27.

KARDINER, A., and LINTON, R. 1939. *The Individual and His Society.* New York: Columbia University Press.

KARELTZ, S., FISKHELL, V. R., COSTA, J., KARELITA, R., and ROSENFIELD, L. 1964. "Relation of Crying Activity in Early Infancy to Speech and Intellectual Development at Age Three Years." *Child Develop.* 35:769–777.

KATAN, M. 1939. "A Contribution to the Understanding of Schizophrenic Speech." *Internat. J. Psycho-Analy.* 20:353–362.

KATZ, R. 1946. "Kann der Tastsinn Ausdruck erfassen? (Can Facial Expression be Perceived by Touch?) Schweiz. Z. *Psychol. Anwend.* 5:117–126.

KELMAN, H. C., ed. 1965. *International Behavior*. New York: Holt, Rinehart & Winston.

KERDMAN, L., and PECK, J. E. 1957. "Modes of Communication in the Psychotherapeutic Process." *Amer. J. Psychoth.* 11:599–617.

KHAN, M. M. R. 1963. "Silence as Communication." *Bull. Menninger Clinic* 27:300–313.

KIMBALL, S. T. 1963. "Communication Modalities as a Function of Social Relationships." *Trans. N.Y. Acad. Sci.* 25:459–468.

KIMBALL, S., and McCLELLAN, J. E., JR. 1966. *Education and the New America*. Paper ed. New York, Toronto: Vintage Books.

KING, H. V. 1964. "English Internal Juncture and Syllable Division." In *Studies in Language and Linguistics*, in honor of Charles C. Fries, ed. A. H. Marckwardt. Michigan: University of Michigan, English Language Institute.

KLINEBERG, O. 1927. "Racial Differences in Speed and Accuracy." *J. Abnorm. and Soc. Psychol.* 22:273–277.

———. 1964. *The Human Dimension in International Relations*. New York: Holt, Rinehart & Winston.

KLOPFER, P. 1962. *Behavioral Aspects of Ecology*. Englewood Cliffs, N.J.: Prentice-Hall. Pp. 136–137.

KLUCKHOHN, C. 1949. *Mirror for Man*. New York: Whittlesby House, McGraw-Hill.

KLUCKHOHN, C., and KLUCKHOHN, F. 1947. "American Culture: Generalized and Class Patterns." In *Conflicts of Power in Modern Culture*, Seventh Symposium. Conference on Science, Philosophy and Religion. Ed. by Lyman Bryson. New York, Cooper Square. Pp. 106–128.

KLUCKHOHN, C., and LÉVI-STRAUSS, C. 1953. "Pattern in Biology, Linguistics, and Culture." In *An Appraisal of Anthropology Today*, ed. S. Tax, et al. Chicago: University of Chicago Press. Pp. 299–321.

KNAPP, P. H. 1954. "The Ear, Listening and Hearing." *Yearbook of Psychoanal.* 10:177–192.

———. ed. 1963a. *Expression of Emotion in Man*. New York: International Universities Press.

———. 1963b. "Introduction: Emotional Expression—Past and Present." In *Expression of the Emotions in Man*. New York: International Universities Press. Pp. 3–15.

KOLB, L. C. 1959. "The Body Image in the Schizophrenic Reaction." In *Schizophrenia: An Integrated Approach*. New York: Ronald Press. Pp. 87–97.

KORZYBSKI, A. 1941. *Science and Sanity: An Introduction to Non-Aristotelian Systems and General Semantics*. New York: The Science Press.

KRAMER, E. 1963. "The Judgment of Personal Characteristics and Emotions from Nonverbal Properties of Speech." *Psychol. Bull.* 60:408–420.

KRAUS, W. M. 1926. "The Constant Relation between Postures of Motile and Rigid States." *Arch. Neurol. & Psychiat.* 15:597–606.

KRIM, A. 1953. "A Study in Non-Verbal Communications: Expressive Movements during Interviews." *Smith Col. Stud. Soc. Work.* 24:41–80.

KRIS, E. 1940. "Laughter as an Expressive Behavior: Contributions to the Psychoanalysis of Expressive Behavior." *Internat. J. Psycho-Anal.* 21:314–341.

KROEBER, A. L. 1939. *Cultural and Natural Areas of Native North America.* Berkeley: University of California Press. Pp. 3ff.

KROEBER, A. L., and KLUCKHOHN, C. 1952. "Culture: A Critical Review of Concepts and Definitions." *Papers of the Peabody Museum of American Archaeology and Ethnology.* Cambridge, Mass.: Harvard University, 47(1):1–223.

KROUT, M. H. 1931. "Symbolic Gestures in the Clinical Study of Personality." *Trans. Illinois State Acad. Sci.* 24:519–523.

———. 1935a. "Autistic Gestures, and Experimental Study in Symbolic Movements." *Psychol. Monogr.* 46:208.

———. 1935b. "The Social and Psychological Significance of Gestures (A Differential Analysis)." *J. Genet. Psychol.* 47:385–412.

KUBIE, L. 1934. "Body Symbolization and the Development of Languages." *Psychoanalyt. Quart.* 3:430–444.

———. 1947. "Problems in Clinical Research." *Amer. J. Orthopsych.* 17:196–203.

LABARRE, W. 1947. "The Cultural Basis of Emotions and Gestures." *J. Person.* 16:49–68.

———. 1948. "Columbia University Research in Contemporary Cultures." *Sci. Month.* LXVII(3):114–127.

———. 1954. *The Human Animal.* Chicago: University of Chicago Press.

LACEY, J. I. 1950. "Individual Differences in Somatic Response Patterns." *J. Comp. Physiol. Psychol.* 43:338–350.

———. KAGAN, J., LACEY, B. C., Moss, H. A. 1963. "The Visceral Level: Situational Determinants and Behavioral Correlates of Autonomic Response Patterns." In *Expression of the Emotions in Man,* ed. Peter H. Knapp. New York: International Universities Press.

LADO, R., and FRIES, C. C. 1958. *English Pattern Practices: Establishing the Patterns as Habits.* Rev. ed. Ann Arbor, Mich.: University of Michigan Press.

LAFFAL, JULIUS. 1965. *Pathological and Normal Language.* New York: Atherton.

LANGER, S. K. 1948. *Philosophy in a New Key.* New York: New American Library (Mentor, No. 25).

———. 1953. *An Introduction to Symbolic Logic.* 2nd ed. (rev.) New York: Dover.

———. 1955. " 'Expressive Language' and the Expressive Function of Poetry." In *On Expressive Language,* ed. H. Werner. Worcester, Mass.: Clark University Press. Pp. 3ff.

LASHLEY, K. S. 1951. "The Problem of Serial Order in Behavior." In *Cerebral Mechanisms in Behavior: The Hixon Symposium,* ed. L. A. Jeffress.

New York: Wiley, Pp. 112–146. (Also in *The Neuropsychology of Lashley: Selected Papers of K. S. Lashley*, ed. F. A. Beach, D. O. Hebb, et al.) New York: McGraw-Hill, 1960. Pp. 506–528.

LAVATER, J. C. (1741–1801) *Essays on Physiognomy*. Trans. by Thomas Holcroft. 18th ed. London and New York: Ward, Lock and Co., n. d.

LEARY, T. 1955. "The Theory and Measurement Methodology of Inter-Personal Communication." *Psychiatry* 18:147–161.

LEE, I. J. 1941. *Language Habits in Human Affairs*. New York: Harper.

LEIGHTON, A. D. 1949. *Human Relations in a Changing World*. New York: Dutton.

LEITES, N. 1948. "Psycho-cultural Hypotheses about Political Acts." *World Politics* 1(1):102–119.

LENNARD, H. L., and BERNSTEIN, A. 1960. *The Anatomy of Psychotherapy: Systems of Communication and Expectation*. New York: Columbia University Press.

LENNEBERG, E. H. 1953. "Cognition in Ethnolinguistics." *Language* 29:463–471.

———. 1957. "A Probabilistic Approach to Language Learning." *Behav. Sci.* 2:1–12.

———. 1967. *Biological Foundations of Language*. New York: Wiley.

———. 1969. "On Explaining Language." *Science* 164(3880):635–643.

LENNEBERG, E. H., and ROBERTS, J. M. 1956. "The Language of Experience." *Memoir Internat. J. Amer. Ling.* 22(13).

LEONHARDT, K. 1949. *Ausdrucksweise der Seele: Mimek, Gestik und Phonik der Menschen*. Württenberg, Haug, Saalgau.

LERNER, D., and SCHRAMM, W. 1957. *Communication and Change in Developing Countries*. Honolulu: East–West Center Press.

LERSCH, P. 1928. "Die Bedeutuag des Mimischen Ausdrucksersheinungen fur die Beurteilung der Personlichkeit." *Indus. Psychotech.* 5:178–183.

———. 1951. *Gesicht und Seele: Grundlinien einer mimischen Diagnostik*. Basel, Reinhardt.

LÉVI-STRAUSS, C. 1963. *Totemism*. Trans. by Rodney Needham. Boston: Beacon Press.

LEVY, D. M. 1928. "Finger Sucking and Accessory Movements in Early Infancy." *Amer. J. Psychiat.* 7:881–918.

———. 1954. "On the Problem of Movement Restraint: Tics, Stereotyped Movements, Hyperactivity." *Amer. J. Orthopsychiat.* 14:644–671.

———. 1962. "The Act as a Unit." *Psychiatry* 25:295–314.

LEVY, K. 1958. "Silence in the Analytic Session." *Internat. J. Psycho-Anal.* 39:50–58.

LEWIS, M. M. 1951. *Infant Speech: A Study of the Beginnings of Language*. New York: Humanities Press.

LHAMON, W. 1953. "Time and Rhythm in Psychosomatic Relationships." In *Current Problems in Psychiatric Diagnosis*, eds. P. Hoch and I. Zubin. New York: Grune & Stratton. Pp. 244–255.

LIDZ, T., CORNELISON, A. R., FLECK, S., and TERRY, D. 1957. "The Intrafamilial Environment of the Schizophrenic Patient. I. The Father." *Psychiatry* 20:329–342.

LIFER, S. 1940. *Annotation of Movement, Kinetography* (in Russian). Moscow: Art Publishing House.

LILLY, J. C. 1963. "Productive and Creative Research with Man and Dolphin." *Arch. Gen. Psychiat.* 8:111–116.

LLOYD, D. J., and WARFEL, H. R. 1956. *American English in its Cultural Setting.* New York: Knopf.

LOMAX, A. 1968. *Folk Song Style and Culture.* Washington, D.C.: American Association for Advancement of Science, Pub. No. 88.

LORENZ, K. 1952. *King Solomon's Ring.* New York: Crowell.

———. 1957. "The Role of Aggression in Group Formation." In *Group Processes,* ed. B. Schaffner. Transactions of the 4th Conference of the Josiah Macy, Jr., Foundation. Pp. 181ff.

LORENZ, M. 1953. "Language as Expressive Behavior." *A.M.A. Arch. Neurol. Psychiat.* 70:277–285.

———. 1957. "Expressive Form in Schizophrenic Language." *A.M.A. Arch. Neurol. Psychiat.* 78:643–652.

LORENZ, M., and COBB, S. 1954. "Language Patterns in Psychotic and Psychoneurotic Subjects." *Arch. Neurol. Psychiat.* 72:665–673.

LOTZ, J. 1954. "The Structure of Human Speech." *Trans. N.Y. Acad. Sci.* Series II, 16:373–384.

———. 1956. "Linguistics: Symbols Make Man." In *Frontiers of Knowledge,* ed. L. White. New York: Harper. Pp. 207–231.

LOUNSBURY, F. G. 1953. "Field Method and Techniques of Linguistics." In *Anthropology Today,* ed. A. L. Kroeber. Chicago: Chicago University Press.

———. 1954. "Pausal, Juncture, and Hesitation Phenomena." In *Psycholinguistics: A Survey of Theory and Research Problems,* eds. C. E. Osgood and T. A. Sebeok. *J. Abnorm. Soc. Psychol.* 49:98–101, Supplement.

LOWEN, A. 1958. *Physical Dynamics of Character Structure: Bodily Form and Movement in Analytic Therapy.* New York: Grune & Stratton.

LOWIE, R. H. 1937. *The History of Ethnological Theory.* New York: Farrar, Strauss & Rinehart. Pp. 256ff.

LURIA, A. R. 1961. *The Role of Speech in the Regulation of Behavior.* New York: Pergamon Press.

LYNN, J. G., and LYNN, D. R. 1943. "Smile and Hand Dominance in Relation to Basic Modes of Adaptation." *J. Abnorm. Soc. Psychol.* 38:250–276.

MARCKWARDT, A. H. 1958. *American English.* New York: Oxford University Press.

McCARTHY, D. 1954. "Language Development in Children." In *Manual of Child Psychology,* ed. L. Carmichael. New York: Wiley. Pp. 492–630.

MacKAY, D. M. 1952. "In Search of Basic Symbols." In *Cybernetics, Transactions of the 8th Conference.* New York.

———. 1962. "Theoretical Models of Space Perception." In *Aspects of the Theory of Artificial Intelligence.* Proceedings of the First International Symposium on Biosimulation. Locarno, June 29–July 5, 1960. New York: Plenum Press. Pp. 83–103.

MacLay, H., and Osgood, C. E. 1959. "Hesitation Phenomena in Spontaneous English Speech." *Word* 15:19–44.

McLuhan, M. 1962. *Gutenberg Galaxy.* Toronto: University of Toronto Press.

McQuown, N. A. 1954a. "Analysis of the Cultural Content of Language Materials." In *Language in Culture,* ed. H. Hoijer. Chicago: University of Chicago Press. Pp. 20–31.

———. 1954b. "Cultural Implications of Linguistic Science." In Georgetown University *Monograph Series on Languages and Linguistics,* No. 7, Sept. 1954, Pp. 57–61.

———. 1957. "Linguistic Transcription and Specification of Psychiatric Interview Material." *Psychiatry* 20:79–86.

Maginnis, M. 1958. "Gesture and Status." *Group Psychother.* 11:105–109.

Mahl, G. F. 1956. "Disturbances and Silences in the Patient's Speech in Psychotherapy." *J. Abnorm. Soc. Psychol.* 53:1–15.

———. 1958. "On the Use of 'ah' in Spontaneous Speech: Quantitative Developmental, Characterological, Situational, and Linguistic Aspects." *Amer. Psychol.* 13:349.

———. 1959. "Measuring the Patient's Anxiety during Interviews from 'Expressive' Aspects of His Speech." *Trans. N.Y. Acad. Sci.,* Ser. 2, 21:249–257.

———. 1963. "The Lexical and Linguistic Levels in the Expression of the Emotions." In *Expression of the Emotions in Man,* ed. P. H. Knapp. New York: International Universities Press.

Mahl, G. F., Dollard, J., Reddick, F. C. 1954. "Facilities for the Sound Recording and Observation of Interviews." *Science* 120:235–239.

Malmo, R. B., Shagass, C., and Davis, F. H. 1950. "Specificity of Bodily Reactions under Stress. A Physiological Study of Somatic Mechanisms in Psychiatric Patients." *Res. Publ. Ass. Nerv. Ment. Dis.* 29:231–261.

Malmo, R. B., Shagass, C., Belauger, D. J., and Smith, A. A. 1951. "Motor Control in Psychiatric Patients under Experimental Stress." *J. Abnorm. Soc. Psychol.* 46:539–547.

Malmo, R. B., Smith, A. A., and Kohlmeyer, W. A. 1956. "Motor Manifestation of Conflict in Interview: A Case Study." *J. Abnorm. Soc. Psychol.* 52:268–271.

Maranon, G. 1950. "The Psychology of Gesture." *J. Nerv. Ment. Dis.* 112:469–497.

Marler, Peter. 1965. "Communication in Monkeys and Apes." In *Primate Behavior: Field Studies of Monkeys and Apes,* ed. I. DeVore. New York: Holt, Rinehart and Winston. Pp. 544–584.

Matarazzo, J. D., Saslow, G. and Matarazzo, R. G. 1956. "The Interaction

Chronograph as an Instrument for Objective Measurement of Interaction Patterns during Interviews." *J. Psychol.* 41:347-367.

MEAD, G. H. 1934. *Mind, Self, and Society.* Chicago: University of Chicago Press.

MEAD, M. 1928. *Coming of Age in Samoa.* New York: Morrow.

——. 1930. *Growing up in New Guinea.* New York: Morrow.

——. 1935. *Sex and Temperament in Three Primitive Societies.* New York: Morrow.

——. 1942. *And Keep Your Powder Dry.* New York: Morrow.

——. 1948. "A Case History in Cross-National Communications." In *The Communication of Ideas,* ed. Lyman Bryson. New York: Harper. Chap. 13, pp. 209-229.

——. 1953a. *Male and Female,* 3rd ed. New York: Morrow.

——. 1953b. "National Character." In *Anthropology Today,* ed. A. L. Kroeber. Chicago: University of Chicago Press. Pp. 642-667.

MEAD, M. 1956. "On the Implications for Anthropology of the Gesell-Ilg Approach to Maturation." *Personal Character and the Cultural Millieu,* ed. D. G. Haring. 3rd ed. Syracuse: Syracuse University Press. Pp. 584-593.

——. 1964. *Continuities in Cultural Evolution.* The Terry Lectures, Vol. 34. New Haven: Yale University Press.

MEAD, M., and BYERS, P. 1968. *The Small Conference.* Paris, The Hague: Mouton.

MEAD, M., and MacGREGOR, F. 1951. *Growth and Culture.* New York: Putnam.

MEAD, M., and METRAUX, R. 1953. *The Study of Culture at a Distance.* Chicago and London: The University of Chicago Press.

MEERLOO, J. A. M. 1952. *Conversation and Communication: A Psychological Inquiry into Language and Human Relations.* New York: International Universities Press.

——. 1952. "Free Association, Silence and the Multiple Function of Speech." *Psychiat. Quart.* 26:21-32.

MENNINGER, K. A. 1952. *A Manual for Psychiatric Case Study.* New York: Grune & Stratton.

MERTON, R. K., FISKE, MARJORIE, and KENDALL, PATRICIA. 1952. *The Focussed Interview: A Manual.* 2nd ed. New York: Bureau of Applied Social Research, Columbia University.

MILLER, G. A. 1951a. *Language and Communication.* New York: McGraw-Hill.

——. 1951b. "Speech and Language." In *Handbook of Experimental Psychology,* ed. S. S. Stevens. New York: Wiley. Pp. 789-810.

MILLER, G. A., GALANTER, E., and PRIBRAM, K. H. 1960. *Plans and the Structure of Behavior.* New York: Holt. Pp. 155ff.

MIRSKY, I. A., MILLER, R. E., and MURPHY, J. V. 1958. "The Communication of Affect in Rhesus Monkeys: I. An Experimental Method." *J. Amer. Psychoanal. Assoc.* 6:433–441.

MITTELMANN, B. 1954. "Motility in Infants, Children and Adults: Patterning and Psychodynamics." *Psychoanal. Study Child.* 9:142–177.

——. 1957. "Motility in the Therapy of Children and Adults." *Psychoanal. Study Child.* 12:284–319.

——. 1958. "Psychodynamics of Motility." *Internat. J. Psycho-Anal.* 39: 196–199.

MOORE, F. J., CHERNELL, E., and WEST, J. M. 1965. "Television as a Therapeutic Tool." *Arch. Gen. Psychiat.* 12:217–220.

MORRIS, C. W. 1938. *Foundations of the Theory of Signs.* Chicago, Ill.: University of Chicago Press.

——. 1946. *Signs, Language, and Behavior.* New York: Prentice-Hall; New York: G. Braziller, 1955.

MORTON, D. J., and FULLER, D. D. 1952. *Human Locomotion and Body Form.* Baltimore: Williams & Wilkins.

MOSES, P. J. 1942. "The Study of Personality from Records of the Voice." *J. Consult. Psychol.* 6:257–261.

——. 1948. "Vocal Analysis." *Arch. Otolaryngol.* 48:171–186.

——. 1958. "Reorientation of Concepts and Facts in Phonetics." *Logos* 1:45–51.

——. 1959. "The Vocal Expression of Emotional Disturbances." *Kaiser Found. Med. Bull.* 7:107–111.

MOSHER, H. D. 1951. "The Expression of the Face and Man's Type of Body as Indicators of His Character." *Laryngo.* (St. Louis) 61:1–38.

MOWRER, O. H. 1953. *Psychotherapy: Theory and Research.* New York: Ronald Press. Pp. 463–545.

——, LIGHT, D. H., LURIA, ZELLA, and SELENY, MARJORIE P. 1953. "Tension Changes during Psychotherapy." In *Psychotherapy: Theory and Research,* ed. O. H. Mowrer. New York: Ronald Press. Pp. 546–640.

MURPHY, G. 1947. *Personality.* New York: Harpers.

MURRAY, H. A. 1938. *Explorations in Personality.* New York: Oxford University Press.

MYSAK, E. D. 1958. "Gerontological Processes in Speech: Pitch and Duration Characteristics." *Diss. Abstr.* 18:2259–2260.

NACHT, S. 1963. "The Non-Verbal Relationship in Psychoanalytic Treatment." *Intern. J. Psycho-Anal.* 44:328–333.

NASH, H. 1958. "Assignment of Gender to Body Regions." *J. Gen. Psychol.* 92:113–115.

——. 1959. "The Behavioral World." *J. Psychol.* 47:277–288.

NEEDLES, W. 1959. "Gesticulation and Speech." *Internat. J. Psycho-Anal.* 40:291–294.

NIELSEN, G. 1962a. *Studies in Self Confrontation.* Copenhagen: University of Copenhagen, The Psychological Laboratory.

———. 1962b. *Studies in Self Confrontation:* Viewing a Sound Motion Picture of Self and Another Person in a Stressful Dyadic Interaction. Copenhagen: Munksgarrd.

OGDEN, C. K., and RICHARDS, I. A. 1938. *The Meaning of Meaning.* 5th ed. New York: Harcourt, Brace. Reprints New York, 1949, 1959.

O'KELLEY, L. I. 1953. "Physiological Changes during Psychotherapy." In *Psychotherapy, Theory and Research,* ed. O. H. Mowrer. New York: Ronald Press. Pp. 641–655.

OLMSTED, D. L. 1950. "Ethnolinguistics So Far." *Studies in Linguistics, Occasional Papers,* No. 2.

OLSON, W. C., and KOETZLE, V. S. 1936. "Amount and Rate of Talking of Young Children." *J. Exp. Educ.* 5:175–179.

OSGOOD, C. E. 1953. *Method and Theory in Experimental Psychology.* New York: Oxford University Press.

OSGOOD, C. E., and HEYER, A. W., JR. 1950. "Objective Studies in Meaning. II. The Validity of Posed Facial Expressions as Gestural Signs in Interpersonal Communication." *Amer. Psychol.* 5:298.

OSGOOD, C. E., and SEBEOK, T. A., eds. 1954. *Psycholinguistics: A Survey of Theory and Research Problems.* Report of the 1953 Summer Seminar sponsored by the Committee on Linguistics and Psychology of the Social Science Research Council. Baltimore: Waverly Press.

OSGOOD, C. E., SUCI, GEORGE J., and TANNENBAUM, PERCY H. 1957. *The Measurement of Meaning.* Urbana, Ill.: University of Illinois Press.

OSTWALD, P. F. 1960. "Human Sounds." In *Psychological and Psychiatric Aspects of Speech and Hearing,* ed. D. Barbara. Springfield, Ill.: Charles C Thomas. Pp. 110–137.

———. 1962. "Acoustic Manifestations of Emotional Disturbance." (Presented at the 42nd Annual Meeting of the Association for Research in Nervous and Mental Disease.) New York City, Dec. 8, 1962. Unpublished manuscript.

———. 1963. *Soundmaking—The Acoustic Communication of Emotion.* Springfield, Ill.: Charles C Thomas.

———. 1964. "Measurement of Verbal and Vocal Behavior. Acoustic Manifestations of Emotional Disturbance." *Res. Publ. Ass. Res. Nerv. Ment. Dis.* 42:450–465.

PAGET, R. A. S. 1937. "Gesture Language." *Nature (Lond.)* 139:198.

PANDEYA, G. A. 1943. *The Art of Kathakali.* Kitabistan, Allabahabad.

PEAR, T. H. 1931. *Voice and Personality.* London: Chapmen & Hall.

PEI, M. A. 1949. *The Story of Language.* Philadelphia: Lippincott.

PENFIELD, W., and ROBERTS, L. 1959. *Speech and Brain Mechanisms.* Princeton, N.J.: Princeton University Press.

PENGNIEZ, P. 1927. "Cinématique de la main; la main du prestidigatateur." *Presse Medicale* 35:123–125.

PERCY, W. 1961. "The Symbols Structure of Interpersonal Process." *Psychiatry* 24:39–52.

PHILLIPS, J. S., MATARAZZO, J. D., MATARAZZO, R. G., SASLOW, G. 1957. "Observer Reliability of Interaction Patterns during Interviews." *J. Consult. Psychol.* 21:269–275.

PHILLIPS, J. S., MATARAZZO, R. G., MATARAZZO, J. D. and SASLOW, G. 1961. "Relationships between Descriptive Content and Interaction Behavior in Interviews." *J. Consult. Psychol.* 25:260–266.

PIAGET, J. 1926. *The Language and Thought of the Child.* New York: Harcourt.

PIKE, K. L. 1946. *The Intonation of American English.* Ann Arbor, Mich.: University of Michigan Press, IX, University of Michigan Publications Linguistics 1.

———. 1957. *Language in Relation to a Unified Theory of the Structure of Human Behavior.* Glendale, California: Summer Institute of Linguistics. Preliminary Edition. Part I: Chaps. 1–7, 1954; Part II: Chaps. 8–10, 1955. (Published in *Amer. Anthropol.* 59:189–192.)

PIMSLEUR, PAUL, and BONKOWSKI, R. J. 1961. "The Transfer of Verbal Material Across Sense Modalities." *J. Educ. Psychol.* 52(2):104–107.

PITTENGER, R. E. 1957. "Linguistic Analysis of Tone of Voice in Communication of Affect." *Psychiat. Res. Rep.* 8:41–54.

———, HOCKETT, C. F., and DANEHY, J. J. 1960. *The First Five Minutes: A Sample of Microscopic Interview Analysis.* Ithaca, N.Y.: Paul Martineau.

———, KNAPP, P. H., and ROMANO, J. 1957. "Symposium: Communication and Affects." Psychiatric Research Reports, No. 8, Pp. 41–87.

——— and SMITH, H. L., JR. 1957. "A Basis for Some Contributions of Linguistics to Psychiatry." *Psychiatry* 20:61–78.

POLLENZ, PHILLIPPA. 1949. "Methods for the Comparative Study of the Dance." *Amer. Anthropol.* 51:428–435.

POLYAK, S. 1957. *The Vertebrate Visual System.* Chicago: Chicago University Press.

POWDERMAKER, F. 1948. "Techniques of Initial Interview and Methods of Teaching Them." *Amer. J. Psychiat.* 104:642–646.

PRIBRAM, K. H. 1963. "A Neurophysiological Model: Some Observations on the Structure of Psychological Processes." In *Expression of the Emotions in Man,* ed. P. H. Knapp. New York: International Universities Press.

PYE, LUCIAN, ed. 1963. *Communication and Political Development.* Princeton, N.J.: Princeton University Press.

RADCLIFFE-BROWN, A. R. 1957. *A Natural Science of Society.* Glencoe, Ill.: Free Press. (Foreword by F. Eggan.)

RADIN, P. 1927. *Primitive Man as a Philosopher.* New York: Appleton-Century.

RANGELL, L. 1954. "The Psychology of Poise; With a Special Elaboration on the Psychic Significance of the Snout and Perioral Region." *Internat. J. Psycho-Anal.* 35:313–332.

RAPAPORT, A. 1957. "Comment: Language as Behavior." Review of *On*

Human Communication: A Review, A Survey, and a Criticism, by Colin Cherry and *Language as Choice and Chance*, by G. Herdan. In *Behav. Sci.* 2:308–316.

REICH, W. 1947. *The Function of the Orgasm-Muscular Attitude and Bodily Expressions.* New York: Orgone Institute Press.

——. 1949. *Character Analysis.* New York: Orgone Institute Press. 3rd ed.

REICHENBACH, H. 1951. *The Rise of Scientific Philosophy.* Berkeley: University of California Press.

REIK, T. 1954. *Listening with the Third Ear.* New York: Farrar-Strauss.

——. 1954. "Men and Women Speak Different Languages." *Psychoanal.* 2:13–15.

RENNEKER, R. E. 1960. "Microscopic Analysis of Sound Tape: A Method of Studying Preconscious Communication in the Therapeutic Process." *Psychiatry* 23(4):347–355.

RIESMAN, D. 1950. *The Lonely Crowd.* New Haven: Yale University Press.

RIESMAN, D., and BENNEY, M. 1955–56. "The Sociology of the Interview." *Midwest Sociol.* 1–15.

RIESS, B. F. 1957. "Communication in Psychotherapy." *Amer. J. Psychother.* 11:774–789.

RIOCH, D. McK. 1961. "Dimensions of Human Behavior." In *Lectures on Experimental Psychiatry*, ed. H. Brosin. Pittsburgh, Penn.: University of Pittsburgh Press. Pp. 341–361.

ROSA, L. A. 1929. *Expressioni e mimica.* Milan: Hoepli.

RUESCH, J. 1951. *Communication: The Social Matrix of Psychiatry.* New York: Norton.

——. 1955. "Nonverbal Language and Therapy." *Psychiatry* 18:323–330.

RUESCH, J., and BATESON, G. 1949. "Structure and Process of Social Relations." *Psychiatry* 12:105–124.

RUESCH, J., and KEES, W. 1956. *Nonverbal Communication: Notes on the Visual Perception of Human Relations.* Berkeley: University of California Press.

RUESCH, J., BLOCK, J., BENNETT, L. 1953. "The Assessment of Communication. I. A Method for the Analysis of Social Interaction." *J. Psychol.* 35:59–79.

RYAN, J. 1965. "Teaching and Consultation by Television. II. Teaching by Videotape." *Ment. Hosp.* 16:101–104.

SAINSBURY, P. 1954. "A Method of Measuring Spontaneous Movements by Time-Sampling Motion Pictures." *J. Ment. Sci.* 100:742–748.

——. 1955. "Gestural Movement during Psychiatric Interview." *Psychosom. Med.* 17:458–569.

SAITZ, R. L., and CERVENKA, E. J. 1962. *Columbian and North American Gestures on Experimental Study.* Bogota, Columbia: Centro Columbo Americano, Carerro 7, No. 23–49.

SAPIR, E. A. 1921. *Language: An Introduction to the Study of Speech.* New York: Harcourt, Brace.

———. 1927a. "The Unconscious Patterning of Behavior in Society." In *The Unconscious*, ed. E. S. Dummer. New York: Knopf.

———. 1927b. "Speech as a Personality Trait." *Amer. J. Sociol.* 32:892–905.

———. 1949. "Communication." in *Selected Writings of Edward Sapir in Language, Culture, and Personality*, ed. D. G. Mandelbaum. Berkeley: University of California Press. Pp. 104–109.

———. 1951. "Speech as a Personality Trait." In *Selected Writings of Edward Sapir in Language, Culture and Personality*, ed. D. G. Mandelbaum. Berkeley and Los Angeles: University of California Press. Pp. 533–543.

———. 1958. *Culture, Language and Personality*, ed. D. G. Mandelbaum. Berkeley: University of California Press.

SAPORTA, S., ed. 1961. *Psycholinguistics*. New York: Holt, Rinehart & Winston.

———, ed. 1962. *Readings in Psycholinguistics*. New York: Holt, Rinehart & Winston.

SASLOW, G., GOODRICH, D. W., and STEIN, MARVIN. 1956. "Study of Therapist Behavior in Diagnostic Interviews by Means of the Interaction Chronograph." *J. Clin. Psychol.* 12:133–139.

SASLOW, G., MATARAZZO, J. D., and GUZE, SAMUEL B. 1955. "The Stability of Interaction Chronograph Patterns in Psychiatric Interviews." *J. Consult. Psychol.* 19:417–430.

SASLOW, G., and MATARAZZO, J. D. 1959. "A Technique for Studying Changes in Interview Behavior." In *Research in Psychotherapy*, eds. E. A. Rubinstein and M. B. Parloff. Proceedings of a Conference, Washington, D.C., April 9–12, 1958. Washington, D.C.: American Psychological Association. Pp. 125–159; 221–234.

SAUSSURE, F. DE. 1959. *Course in General Linguistics*, ed. C. Bally, *et al.* Translated from the French by W. Baskin. 3rd ed. New York: Philosophical Library.

SCHAFFNER, B., ed. 1954–1958. *Group Processes*. (5 volumes: 1954–1958.) New York: Josiah Macy, Jr., Foundation.

SCHEFLEN, A. E. 1960. "Regressive One-to-One Relationships." *Psychiat. Quart.* 34:1.

———. 1961a. *Psychotherapy of Schizophrenia*. Springfield, Ill.: Charles C Thomas.

———. 1961b. "The Role of Introjection in the Psychotherapy of Schizophrenia." In *Symposium of Psychotherapy of Schizophrenia*, ed. N. Delles. Baton Rouge: Louisiana State University Press. Pp. 79–97.

———. 1961c. "The Extrapolation from Feeding Experience to Object Relationship." *Psychiatry* 24:143–152.

———. 1962. "Aims and Methods in Psychotherapy." In *Psychosomatic Medicine*, eds. J. H. Nodine and J. H. Moyer. Philadelphia: Lea & Febiger.

———. 1963. "Communication and Regulation in Psychotherapy." *Psychiatry* 26:126–136.

———. 1964. "The Significance of Posture in Communication Systems." *Psychiatry* 27:316–331.

——. 1965b. "Natural History Method in Psychotherapy. In *Methods of Research in Psychotherapy*, eds. L. A. Gottschalk and A. Auerback. New York: Appleton-Century-Crofts.

——. 1965c. *Stream and Structure of Communicational Behavior: Context Analysis of a Psychotherapy Session.* Commonwealth of Pennsylvania: EPPI, Behavioral Studies Monograph, No. 1.

——, SCHEFLEN, A. E., ENGLISH, D. S., HAMPE, W. W., and AUERBACK, A. 1965a. *Strategy and Structure: Three Research Approaches to Whitaker and Malone's Multiple Therapy.* Pennsylvania: Commonwealth of Pennsylvania Monograph Press, No. 2.

SCHILDER, P. 1950. *The Image and Appearance of the Human Body.* New York: International Universities Press.

SCHILDER, P., and HOFF, H. 1926. "Posture and Attitude Reflexes and Similar Phenomenon." *Deutsche Ztschr. f. Nervenh.* 89:67–72.

SCHLOSBERG, H. 1941. "A Scale for the Judgment of Facial Expressions." *J. Exp. Psychol.* 29:497–510.

——. 1952. "The Description of Facial Expressions in Terms of Two Dimensions." *J. Exp. Psychol.* 44:229–237.

——. 1954. "Three Dimensions of Emotion." *Psychol. Rev.* 61:81–88.

SCHOSSBERGER, J. A. 1963. "Deanimation. A Study of the Communication of Meaning by Transient Expressive Configuration." *PSA Quart.* 32:479–532.

SCHUHL, P. M. 1948. "Remarque sur le regard." *J. de Psychologie Normale et Pathologique* 41:184–193.

SCOTT, J. P. 1958. *Animal Behavior.* Chicago: University of Chicago Press.

SCOTT, W. C. 1958. "Noise, Speech and Technique." *Internat. J. Psycho-Anal.* 39:108–111.

SEARLES, H. F. 1960. *The Nonhuman Environment.* New York: International Universities Press.

——. 1961. "Schizophrenic Communication." *Psychoanalyt. Rev.* 43:3–50.

SEBEOK, T. A. 1962. "Coding in the Evolution of Signaling Behavior." *Behav. Sci.* 7:430–442.

SEBEOK, T. A., HAYES, A. S., and BATESON, M. C. 1964. *Approaches to Semiotics.* London-The Hague (Paris): Mouton.

SEELEY, JOHN R., JUNKER, B. H., JONES, R. W. JR., JENKINS, N. C., HAUGH, M. T., and MILLER, I. 1957. *Community Chest: A Study in Philanthropy.* Indianapolis: Community Surveys, Inc.: Toronto: University of Toronto Press.

SELTZER, C. C. 1946. "Body Disproportions and Dominant Personality Traits." *Psychosom. Med.* 8:75–97.

SHAGASS, C., and MALMO, R. M. 1954. "Psychodynamic Themes and Localized Muscular Tension during Psychotherapy." *Psychosom. Med.* 16:295–314.

SHAKOW, D. 1960. "The Recorded Psychoanalytic Interview as an Objective Approach to Research in Psychoanalysis." *Psychoanalyt. Quart.* 29:82–97.

SHANNON, C. E., and WEAVER, W. 1949. *The Mathematical Theory of Communication.* Urbana, Ill.: University of Illinois Press.

SILVER, A. A. 1952. "Postural and Righting Responses in Children." *J. Pediat.* 41:493–498.

SINGLETON, W. T. 1954. "The Change of Movement Timing with Age." *Brit. J. Psychol.* 45:166–172.

SKINNER, B. F. 1957. *Verbal Behavior.* New York: Appleton-Century-Crofts.

SLAVSON, S. R. 1955. "Group Psychotherapies." In *Six Approaches to Psychotherapy,* eds. J. L. McCary and D. E. Sheer. New York: Dryden Press. Pp. 127–178.

SMITH, A. A. ed. 1966. *Communication and Culture.* New York: Holt, Rinehart & Winston.

SMITH, H. L., JR. 1952. *An Outline of Metalinguistic Analysis.* Tentative draft. Washington, D.C.: U.S. Department of State, Foreign Service Institute. Mimeographed.

———. 1953. *The Communication Situation.* Washington, D. C.: U.S. Department of State, Foreign Service Institute.

Social Science Research Council. Committee on Linguistics and Psychology. 1954. *Psycholinguistics: A Survey of Theory and Research Problems.* Report of the 1953 Summer Seminar sponsored by the Committee on Linguistics and Psychology of the Social Science Research Council by J. B. Carroll, *et al.* Ed. C. E. Osgood; assoc. ed. T. H. Sebeok. Baltimore: Waverly Press.

SONNE, J. C., SPECK, R. V., and JUNGRIS, J. E. 1962. "The Absent-Member Maneuver as a Resistance in Family Therapy." *Fam. Proc.* 1(1):44–62.

SPERBER, H. 1955. "Expressive Aspects of Political Language." In *On Expressive Language,* ed. H. Werner. Worcester, Mass.: Clark University Press. Pp. 39–45.

SPIER, L., HALLOWELL, A. I., and NEWMAN, S. S., eds. 1941. *Language, Culture, and Personality.* Menasha, Wisc.: Sapir Memorial Publication Fund. P. 57.

SPITZ, R. A. 1945. "Hospitalism, An Inquiry into the Genesis of Psychiatric Conditions in Early Childhood." In *The Psychoanalytic Study of the Child.* New York: International Universities Press. Vol. 1, pp. 53–74.

———. "Hospitalism, A Follow Up." 1946. In *The Psychoanalytic Study of the Child.* New York: International Universities Press. Vol. 2, Pp. 113–117.

SPITZ, R. A., and WOLF, K. M. 1946. "The Smiling Response: A Contribution to the Ontogenesis of Social Relations." *Genet. Psychol. Monogr.* 34:57–125.

STARKWEATHER, J. A. 1956. "The Communication-Value of Content-Free Speech." *Amer. J. Psychol.* 69:121–123.

———. 1961. "Vocal Communication of Personality and Human Feelings." *J. of Comm.* 11:63–72.

STEINDLER, ARTHUR. 1955. *Kinesiology of the Human Body under Normal and Pathological Conditions.* Springfield, Ill.: Charles C Thomas.

STEINZOR, B. 1950. "The Spatial Factor in Face-to-Face Discussion Groups." J. Abnorm. Soc. Psychol. 45:552–555.

STERN, K. 1950. "The Semantics of 'Organ Language': A Comparative Study of English, French, and German." Amer. J. Psychiat. 106:851–860.

STREHLE, H. 1935. Analyse des gebardens. Erforschung der Ausdrucks der Korpesbewegung. Berlin: Bernard u. Graefe.

STRUPP, H. H. 1957a. "A Multidimensional Analysis of Technique in Brief Psychotherapy." Psychiatry 20:387–397.

———. 1957b. "A Multidimensional Comparison of Therapist Activity in Analytic and Client-Centered Therapy." J. Consult. Psychol. 21:301–308.

———. 1957c. "A Multidimensional System for Analyzing Psychotherapeutic Techniques." Psychiatry 20:293–306.

———. 1958. "The Performance of Psychiatrists and Psychologists in a Therapeutic Interview." J. Clin. Psychol. 14:219–226.

———. 1962. "Psychotherapy." An. Rev. Psychol. 13:445–478.

SULLIVAN, H. S. 1953. The Interpersonal Theory of Psychiatry, eds. H. S. Perry and M. L. Gawell. New York: Norton.

———. 1954. The Psychiatric Interview. New York: Norton.

TAX, S. ed. 1960. Evolution after Darwin: The University of Chicago Centennial. Vol. 2 The Evolution of Man: Vol. 3, Chicago: University of Chicago Press. Pp. 289–308.

TAYLOR, J. E., POTASH, R. R. and HEAD, D. 1959. "Body Language in the Treatment of the Psychotic." Prog. Psychoth. 4:227–231.

Texas Conference on Problems of Linguistic Analysis in English, ed. A. A. Hill. 1962. First, April 27–30, 1956; Second, April 26–29, 1957; Third, May 9–12, 1958. Austin, Texas: University of Texas.

THAYER, L. 1968. Communication and Communication Systems. Homewood, Ill.: Richard D. Erwin.

THORPE, W. H. 1956. Learning and Instinct in Animals. Cambridge: Harvard University Press.

———. 1957. "Some Implications of the Study of Human Behavior." Sci. Month. 84:309–320.

TINBERGEN, N. 1951. The Study of Instinct. Oxford: Clarendon Press.

———. 1953. Social Behavior in Animals. New York: Wiley.

TRAGER, G. L. 1958. "Paralanguage: A First Approximation." Stud. Ling. 13:1–12.

TRAGER, G. L., and HALL, E. T. 1954. "Culture and Communication: A Model and an Analysis." Explorations 3:137–149.

TRAGER, G. L., and SMITH, H. L., JR. 1951. An Outline of English Structure. Norman, Oklahoma: Battenburg, 1951, 2nd, 3rd printing, Washington, D.C.: ACLS, 1956–1957.

TYLOR, E. B. 1924. Primitive Culture. New York: Brentano's.

———. 1964. Researches into the Early History of Mankind and the Development of Civilization. Edited and abridged by P. Bohannan. Chicago and London: University of Chicago Press.

Vygotsky, L. S. 1962. *Thought and Language.* New York: Wiley.

Wallace, A. F. C. 1954. "A Science of Human Behaviour." *Explorations* 3:127–136.

Waltern, W. G. 1953. *The Living Brain.* New York: Norton.

Warkentin, John, Whitaker, Carl A., Malone, Thomas P. 1959. "Social Origins of Delusions." *So. Med. J.* 52:1418–1420.

Warner, W. L. 1962. *American Life, Dream and Reality.* Rev. ed. Phoenix Books. Chicago and London: University of Chicago Press.

Warner, W. L., and Lunt, P. S. 1941. *The Social Life of a Modern Community.* Yankee City Series, I. New Haven: Yale University Press.

Warner, W. L., and Srole, Leo. 1945. *The Social Systems of American Ethnic Groups.* Yankee City Series, III. New Haven: Yale University Press.

Weiner, M., and Mehrabian, A. 1968. *Language within Language: Immediacy a Channel in Verbal Communication.* New York: Appleton-Century-Crofts.

Weiss, P. 1943. "The Social Character of Gestures." *Phil. Rev.* 52:182–186.

Wells, R. S. 1945. "The Pitch Phonemes of English." *Language* 21:17–39.

Wendland, D. 1954. "Gesicht und Antlitz im Ausdrucksvorgang Personaler Geschlechtsliebe." (Face and Countenance in the Expressive Process of Love between the Sexes.) *Jb. Psychol. Psychother.* 2:371–394.

Wenger, M. A. 1943. "An Attempt to Appraise Individual Differences in Level of Muscular Tension." *J. Exper. Psychol.* 32:213–225.

Werner, H. 1955. "A Psychological Analysis of Expressive Language." In *On Expressive Language,* ed. H. Werner. Worcester, Mass.: Clark University Press. Pp. 11–18.

———, ed. 1955. *On Expressive Language.* Papers presented at the Clark University Conference on Expressive Language Behavior. Worcester, Mass.: Clark University Press.

Wescott, R. W. 1966. "Introducing Coenetics." *Amer. Scholar,* 35:342–356.

———. 1967. "Strepital Communication." *The Bulletin* 12:30–34.

West, J. 1947. *Plainsville, U.S.A.* New York: Columbia University Press.

Whitaker, E., ed. 1958. *Psychotherapy of Chronic Schizophrenic Patients.* Boston: Little, Brown.

Whitehall, H. 1956. *Structural Essentials of English.* New York: Harcourt, Brace.

Whitehead, A. N. 1958. *Symbolism: Its Meaning and Effect.* New York: Macmillan.

Whorf, B. L. 1952. *Collected Papers on Metalinguistics.* Washington, D.C.: U.S. Department of State, Foreign Service Institute.

———. 1956. *Language, Thought, and Reality: Selected Writings.* Edited with an introduction by J. B. Carroll. New York: Wiley. P. 252; Cambridge: M.I.T.

Winick, C., and Holt, H. 1961. "Seating Position as Nonverbal Communication in Group Analysis." *Psychiatry* 24:171–182.

———. 1962. "Eye and Face Movements as Nonverbal Communication in Group Psychotherapy." *J. Hillside Hospital* 9:67–79. (Also see these authors in *Amer. J. Psychoth.* 15:56–62, 1961; *Psychiatry* 24:171–182, 1961.)

WOLFF, C. 1945. *Psychology of Gesture.* Trans. from the French by A. Tennant. London: Methuen.

———. 1952. *The Hand in Psychological Diagnosis.* New York: Philosophical Library.

WOLFF, H. 1954. "Intelligibility and Inter-Ethnic Attitudes." In *Language, Culture and Society,* ed. D. Hymes. New York; Evanston and London: Harper & Row. Pp. 440ff.

WOLFF, P. H. 1963. "Observations on the Early Development of Smiling." In *Determinants of Infant Behavior. II.,* ed. B. M. Foss. Proceedings of the Second Tavistock Seminar on Mother-Infant Interaction held under the auspices of the CIBA Foundation at the House of the Royal Society of Medicine, London, September, 1961. London: Methuen; New York: Wiley. Pp. 113–138.

WOLFF, W. 1943. *The Expression of Personality: Experimental Depth Psychology.* New York: Harper.

WYNNE, L. C. 1961. "The Study of Intrafamilial Alignments and Splits in Exploratory Family Therapy." In *Exploring the Base for Family Therapy,* ed. N. W. Ackerman, *et al.* New York: Family Service Association of America. Pp. 95–115.

WYNNE, L. C., and SINGER, M. T. 1963. "Thought Disorder and Family Relations of Schizophrenics. I. A Research Strategy." *Arch. Gen. Psychiat.* 9:191–198.

YOUNG, F. M. 1947. "The Incidence of Nervous Habits observed in College Students." *J. Personal.* 15:309.

YOUNG, P. T. 1943. *Emotion in Man and Animal.* New York; Wiley. Chap. 6, pp. 233–269.

ZELIGS, M. A. 1957. "Acting In: A Contribution to the Meaning of Some Postural Attitudes Observed during Analysis." *J. Amer. Psychoanalyt. Assoc.* 5:685–706.

———. 1961. "The Psychology of Silence: Its Role in Transference, Counter-Transference and the Psychoanalytic Process." *J. Amer. Psychoanalyt. Assoc.* 9:7–43.